VMware View 5

VMware Press is the official publisher of VMware books and training materials, which provide guidance on the critical topics facing today's technology professionals and students. Enterprises, as well as small- and medium-sized organizations, adopt virtualization as a more agile way of scaling IT to meet business needs. VMware Press provides proven, technically accurate information that will help them meet their goals for customizing, building, and maintaining their virtual environment.

With books, certification, study guides, video training, and learning tools produced by world-class architects and IT experts, VMware Press helps IT professionals master a diverse range of topics on virtualization and cloud computing and is the official source of reference materials for preparing for the VMware Certified Professional Examination.

VMware Press is also pleased to have localization partners that can publish its products into more than 42 languages, including, but not limited to, Chinese (Simplified), Chinese (Traditional), French, German, Greek, Hindi, Japanese, Korean, Polish, Russian, and Spanish.

For more information about VMware Press, please visit
http://www.vmware.com/go/vmwarepress

VMware View 5

BUILDING A SUCCESSFUL VIRTUAL DESKTOP

Paul O'Doherty

vmware® PRESS

Upper Saddle River, NJ • Boston • Indianapolis • San Francisco
New York • Toronto • Montreal • London • Munich • Paris • Madrid
Capetown • Sydney • Tokyo • Singapore • Mexico City

VMWARE VIEW 5

Copyright © 2013 VMware, Inc.

Published by Pearson Education, Inc.

Publishing as VMware Press

Warning and Disclaimer

Corporate and Government Sales

VMware Press offers excellent discounts on this book when ordered in quantity for bulk purchases or special sales, which may include electronic versions and/or custom covers and content particular to your business, training goals, marketing focus, and branding interests. For more information, please contact U.S. Corporate and Government Sales, (800) 382-3419, corpsales@pearsontechgroup.com. For sales outside the United States, please contact International Sales, international@pearsoned.com.

Library of Congress Cataloging-in-Publication data is on file.

ISBN-13: 978-0-321-82234-5
ISBN-10:   0-321-82234-X

First printing November 2012

VMWARE PRESS PROGRAM MANAGER
Erik Ullanderson

ASSOCIATE PUBLISHER
David Dusthimer

ACQUISITIONS EDITOR
Joan Murray

DEVELOPMENT EDITOR
Ellie Bru

MANAGING EDITOR
Sandra Schroeder

COPY EDITOR
Chuck Hutchinson

PROOFREADER
Deborah Williams

INDEXER
Brad Herriman

EDITORIAL ASSISTANT
Vanessa Evans

BOOK DESIGNER
Gary Adair

COMPOSITOR
Mary Sudul

I would like to dedicate this book to my wonderful wife, Heather, for her patience and support. I also want to thank my two beautiful girls, Briar and Hannah, who have managed to give Daddy time to write.

Contents

Preface

The first edition of *VMware View 5: Building a Successful Virtual Desktop* is the first book from VMware Press to cover virtual desktop computing.

About This Book

VMware View 5 is a truly enterprise class virtual desktop product that has integrated all the necessary technology, such as View Persona and Local Mode desktops, to deliver a complete solution for delivering desktops. When we set out to write this book, there was very little available that provided a single source and reference for all the pieces. Although there is a wealth of information on all the individual components provided online by VMware and independent bloggers, it was difficult to find the information all in one place. Our approach was to take the most important topics and bring them together under one cover. As we go to publication, there are a number of items that we would like to have included, such as VMware's Project Horizon, which has been released as VMware's Horizon Application Manager.

Products like Horizon attempt to bridge between the PC and Post-PC era. With the aggressive trend toward Cloud, HTML5, and pure application delivery, opinions vary on any long-term trend toward desktop virtualization. The reality is, though, that the virtualization of the desktop is important for many reasons. As IT professionals, we are very familiar with the concept of a desktop PC. The technologies and lifecycle processes for desktop management have been around almost as long as the desktop itself. What we are less comfortable with is running IT as a Service. This is the transformation that is being driven by the promise of Cloud computing. In preparing for this paradigm shift, the virtualization of your desktops becomes a necessity. It allows IT departments to move closer to the IT as a Service model using a form factor that they are comfortable with: the desktop. This book is designed to get you moving down the path comfortably. We have taken a very operational viewpoint and looked at not just the deployment but also what is required to ensure success.

Some of the points we make are not necessarily about the VMware View software but the importance of your approach. From our experience, one of the most important considerations is the engagement of the end users in the process in a structured way. This comes back to thinking about the service of delivering desktops versus the mechanics. As you are designing a service to meet the requirements of your end users, it stands to reason that involving them in the process provides an opportunity to "market test" before opening up the service to everyone.

It is our hope in providing this book, we will have simplified some of the challenges and taken some of the mystery out of how the technology works.

In Chapter 5, "Building Your Virtual Desktop," we initially developed two versions of the chapter: the first based purely on what was capable using VMware tools, and a second based on using a more generic tool, the Microsoft Deployment Toolkit (MDT). Given the series and audience, we decided to include the one on VMware tools in the final print version. However, if you are interested in the MDT version, it is available via Safari Books Online. There is a coupon code in the back of the book that provides free limited access (45 days) to the book and the additional chapter.

On a more general note, in this book, we use the terms *View desktop*, *virtual desktop*, and *desktop instance* interchangeably. These terms refer to the deployment of a Windows desktop OS deployed in a virtual machine, running on VMware vSphere and managed by VMware View.

What This Book Covers

Here is a quick overview of all the topics covered in this book:

- Chapter 1, "Virtual Desktop Infrastructure Overview"

  In this chapter we cover the grassroots of desktop virtualization and how it evolved to become a key technology today. We delve into all the components of a virtual desktop environment in a general way so you understand their value and where they fit into your planning. We also review licensing and the underlying infrastructure at a high level.

- Chapter 2, "VMware View Architecture"

  From the more general topics in Chapter 1, we delve into the specific architecture of VMware View 5. In addition, we cover key aspects of the supporting vSphere virtual infrastructure and how they add value to a virtual desktop environment. We also look carefully at network and storage because problems in these layers can quickly translate to performance issues in your virtual desktop environment.

- Chapter 3, "VMware View 5 Implementation"

  In this chapter we go through the steps required to set up the virtual infrastructure and add VMware View software. This is the step-by-step guide to installing and configuring your VMware View environment properly. We also cover the integration of View Persona.

- Chapter 4, "Application Virtualization"

  In Chapter 4 we discuss the benefits of application virtualization and then the specifics of ThinApp. We discuss how to properly set up, package, and manage the process in your VMware View environment. Originally, I had considered changing the order of Chapters 4 and 5 because we are four chapters into the book and have not yet talked about building a virtual desktop or desktop template. In my experience, however, I find that ThinApp is often not considered carefully in many View environments. By ordering the chapters this way, I am hoping that you consider the capabilities and benefits at an earlier stage so that you can get the most out of this technology.

- Chapter 5, "Building Your Virtual Desktop"

In Chapter 5 we discuss the building of the virtual desktop and tuning it properly. We have incorporated a shared server desktop as a component of this chapter. This was actually debated by the technical team quite a bit because the integration of Windows 2008 R2 RDS is an underused feature of the View platform. It does provide a real opportunity for cost savings if you can meet the requirements of a user segment using this versus a full-featured desktop, so we considered it important to include. We review all the steps required to make this appear as seamless as possible.

- Chapter 6, "View Operations and Management"

Many books do a good job of explaining software installation. To add additional value, we thought it was important to talk about the long-term management of things like ThinApp packages. We also wanted to spend some time reviewing the features of pools and how pools are applied to user segments and translated to functional requirements, which can be a challenge in large environments.

- Chapter 7, "VMware vShield EndPoint"

Antivirus software can be a challenge in a virtual desktop environment if you take a traditional approach involving distributing agents to all endpoints. The solution is integrated in VMware View as vShield EndPoint but often not well understood to enable you to take advantage of it. In Chapter 7 we step through how it works and then use a sample installation so that you are comfortable with the implementation and configuration.

- Chapter 8, "A Rich End-User Experience"

How do you ensure that the end-user experience is good, and more importantly, how do you qualify and quantify it in a controlled manner before you deploy the solution in production? We review the many improvements in PCoIP and additional parameters you can tune in Chapter 8. We then look at a number of tools to enable you to simulate different conditions and quantify the effect it has on the PCoIP protocol.

- Chapter 9, "Offline Desktops"

Offline desktops allow you to deliver View desktops in a variety of different situations. To do so, you must understand the requirements and how to control them through policy. In Chapter 9 we review the benefits, go through the configuration, and discuss the policies required to manage offline desktops.

- Chapter 10, "Migrating from Older Versions of View"

In Chapter 10 we look at a scenario that allows us to go through the migration process from start to finish. We provide detailed steps on how to ensure the components are properly backed up before the migration and the steps required finish it properly.

- Chapter 11, "High Availability Considerations"

To provide a production VMware View environment, you must make sure that you have considered all the single points of failure. In Chapter 11 we start looking at multipathing from the ESXi hosts all the way up to clustering and site-to-site replication using native technologies. We examine a real-world scenario and go through the step-by-step process to configuring the environment to provide HA within a site and to extend that to a second site.

- Chapter 12, "Performance and Monitoring"

In Chapter 12 we review the importance of monitoring the VMware View environment. We go through all the steps to integrate vCenter Operations Manager with the recently released VMware View Adapter. We review all the information that is provided by integrating vCenter Operations. We also discuss how you can turn up the Alerting feature of vCenter Operations Manager to ensure that the environment is being actively managed.

Author Disclaimer

All steps in this book have been reviewed to ensure they are accurate; however, because we are dealing with software, they may change from release to release. Although every precaution has been taken in the preparation of this book, the contributors and author assume no responsibility for errors or omissions. Neither is any liability assumed for damages resulting from the use of the information contained herein.

I appreciate your buying this book and hope this helps ensure that your VMware View environments can scale to meet the needs of your users.

Featured in Safari Edition

In the version of Chapter 5 only available in the Safari Online version, the integration of Windows 2008 R2 RDS is covered as a component of the complete build process. If you don't have a subscriptions to Safari, you can access this version free for 45 days. See the ad in the back of the book for more details.

Acknowledgments

Anyone who undertakes the writing of a book knows that your ability to deliver is largely determined by the quality of your supporting team. I consider myself extremely lucky to have had the privilege of working with my team. From the initial acceptance of the project by Joan Murray, the Editor/Program Manager with Pearson, and her support throughout the process, and the tireless efforts of Eleanor "Ellie" Bru, my primary technical editor, I am deeply grateful.

I also had great support from my two technical content reviewers: Stephane Asselin and Shawn Tooley. Stephane was a direct contributor to Chapter 5 and offered his expertise in all matters related to VMware View. Stephane is a leading expert in VMware View working with VMware. Shawn Tooley is a published author himself, and his suggestions greatly contributed to the polish of this book. I also want to thank Seth Kerney, who worked hard to put this book together.

About the Author

Paul O'Doherty is a Cloud Solution Manager at Onx.com, specializing in the architecture and delivery of cloud-based services. Prior to that, Paul spent 10 years as the Managing Principal Consultant at Gibraltar Solutions architecting and delivering end-user computer and virtualization environments in Fortune 500 companies involving VMware, VMware View, Citrix XenApp, and XenDesktop technologies. Paul has a broad range of infrastructure experience and has achieved numerous industry certifications such as VCP, CCEA, MCITP, RCSP, and is recognized as a VMware vExpert. In addition, Paul maintains a blog at http://virtualguru.org and has contributed to sites such as http://virtualization.info and is reoccurring speaker at VMUG sessions and other technical conferences.

About the Technical Reviewers

Stephane Asselin, with his 20 years of experience in IT, is a Senior Consultant for the Global Center of Excellence (CoE) for the End-User Computing business unit at VMware. In his recent role, he had national responsibility for Canada for EUC planning, designing, and implementing virtual infrastructure solutions, and all processes involved. At VMware, Stephane has worked on EUC pre-sales activities, internal IP, product development, and as technical specialist lead on BETA programs. He has also done work as a Subject Matter Expert for projects Octopus, Horizon, View, vCOPs and ThinApp. Previously, he was with CA as Senior Systems Engineer, where he has worked on Enterprise Monitoring pre-sales activities and as technical specialist. As a Senior Consultant at Microsoft, he was responsible for the planning, design, and implementation of Microsoft solutions within major provincial and federal governments, financial, education, and telco. In his current role in the CoE at VMware, he's one of the resources developing presentation materials and technical documentation for training and knowledge transfer to customers and peer systems engineers. Stephane also contributed content to this book.

Shawn Tooley is a Senior Virtualization/Cloud Architect and VMware, Citrix, and Microsoft Virtualization Subject Matter Expert at IBM, with more than 20 years of experience in information technology. As a Senior Architect with IBM, he takes pride and enjoyment in bringing solutions to real-world problems by first understanding the customer's problem and then designing an effective solution. Shawn is also an author and blogs at http://www.shawntooley.com. Shawn's certifications include Microsoft Certified Trainer—Information Systems, Microsoft Certified Systems Engineer, MCITP, VMware Sales Professional, VMware Technical Sales Professional, Citrix Certified Enterprise Administrator, Citrix Certified Sales Professional, HP ASE, IBM XSeries Server Specialist, CompTIA A+, and CompTIA Certified Trainer, among many others. In his free time, he enjoys spending time with his family and playing golf. Shawn dedicates his work on this book to his wife Heather, for supporting and understanding the long hours being away from home to do what I love—and also, to their newborn son Gavin Tooley.

We Want to Hear from You!

As the reader of this book, *you* are our most important critic and commentator. We value your opinion and want to know what we're doing right, what we could do better, what areas you'd like to see us publish in, and any other words of wisdom you're willing to pass our way.

As an associate publisher for Pearson, I welcome your comments. You can email or write me directly to let me know what you did or didn't like about this book—as well as what we can do to make our books better.

Please note that I cannot help you with technical problems related to the topic of this book. We do have a User Services group, however, where I will forward specific technical questions related to the book.

When you write, please be sure to include this book's title and author as well as your name, email address, and phone number. I will carefully review your comments and share them with the author and editors who worked on the book.

Email: VMwarePress@vmware.com

Mail: David Dusthimer
Associate Publisher
Pearson
800 East 96th Street
Indianapolis, IN 46240 USA

Reader Services

Visit our website at www.informit.com/title/9780321822345 and register this book for convenient access to any updates, downloads, or errata that might be available for this book.

Chapter 1

Virtual Desktop Infrastructure Overview

The Evolution of the Virtual Desktop

The notion of x86 virtualization actually started with the idea of consolidating underutilized server infrastructure. As VMware evolved the product line, it was quickly realized that virtualization could not only add value to underutilized server hardware, but also could deliver desktop operating systems. Of course, virtualizing a desktop creates operational challenges that the virtual infrastructure itself cannot solve. Just as in server-based computing environments or terminal services, the ability to manage sessions became a necessity. From the early beginnings of simple session management, the concept of virtual desktops has evolved into a suite of products designed to deal with many challenges apparent with end-user computing. In this book we start from the early beginning and work our way to the development and current release of VMware View.

Where Did It All Start?

The concept of Virtual Desktop Infrastructure (VDI) began not with a software solution, but with an idea from VMware's user community. Although people had been virtualizing servers for years on ESX servers, customers were also deploying a limited number of desktop OSes. The notion of deploying a desktop operating system on the same infrastructure evolved to deal with a very specific set of use cases, such as centralizing developer desktops or delivering an isolated remote access environment. VDI has grown from a technology applicable to certain scenarios to become a strategy for delivering end-user computing requirements and supplanting physical desktops. From the early concept of deploying a desktop on ESX, the solution has matured considerably.

VMware recognized an opportunity in virtual desktop infrastructure and developed a Professional Service offering that included 10 days of professional services and a web-based connection broker. Other independent software companies realized an opportunity as well and began realigning their products for desktop virtualization. One of these independent companies was a software company in the UK called Propero. Propero had traditionally competed with Citrix in the server-based computing arena. As Citrix Solutions continued to scale and incorporate new features and services in server-based computing, Propero decided to specialize in desktop virtualization to capitalize on the emerging market. Propero had an integrated Java-based RDP client that allowed you to connect to both desktops and terminal servers. In addition, it had a feature that allowed you to blend access to applications, virtual desktops, and servers on a single web page that was similar to Citrix's Web Interface. Ironically, the traditional "desktop replacement solution" from Citrix was late to catch on to the value of virtualizing the desktop.

VMware decided to jumpstart its VDI solution by acquiring Propero in April 2007, and the first VMware version was released as Virtual Desktop Manager, or VDM. The solution was criticized by former Propero customers and new VMware VDI customers because much of the functionality had been removed. It was rumored that a lot of code required rewriting from the ground up, so VMware had been forced to drop many features to meet the release date. These early solutions primarily focused around the introduction of a management role more commonly called a connection broker. Because VDM was closely tied to ESX (now ESXi) and Virtual Center (now vCenter), it was able to make use of the templates and auto deployment to quickly scale up additional virtual desktops.

Figure 1.1 depicts a simple overview of the technology involved in VDI, including both end clients, which can consist of thin clients, physical desktops, or laptops.

A connection broker provided a new management point by brokering user requests for virtual desktops and end-user connections. Doing so allowed administrators to see the status of the connections and whether they were connected or disconnected. In addition, it allowed some administrator functionality, such as the ability to reset the connection or reboot the virtual desktop. One of the main use cases for VDI was similar to the value of Terminal Services: you could deliver a higher-powered virtual desktop (more CPU and memory) to an underpowered physical one.

Although you could deploy virtual desktops without connection broker technology, they did not scale because the more users you deployed, the less manageability and visibility you had. It is important to be able to see the number of users with active sessions and the number of virtual desktops in use and to have some ability to manage these connections. In addition to visibility, the broker gave the administrator the ability to "entitle" or enable the users to access a virtual desktop.

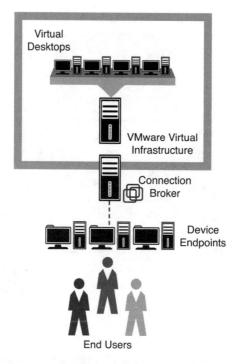

Figure 1.1 Early virtual desktop infrastructure.

Although these early connection brokers generally enabled the deployment of virtual desktops, they were a long way from enabling customers to replace a true physical desktop experience. In addition, these connection brokers did nothing to address the cost of deploying virtual desktops against traditional storage area network (SAN) –attached VMware virtual infrastructure.

One of the big challenges in these early virtual desktop environments was the cost of storage. Deploying virtual desktop OSes could be costly because most early VDI environments used the same underlying hardware and storage assets found in their server virtualization environment. Scalable virtual infrastructure consisted of several VMware ESX hosts attached to SAN storage.

Figure 1.2 shows a logical layout of all the components involved, excluding the virtual desktop management infrastructure. This layout includes the VMware ESX hosts attached to switches that, in turn, attach to SAN storage. The virtual desktops run on the ESX hosts, with the storage shared between all hosts, thus creating a cluster.

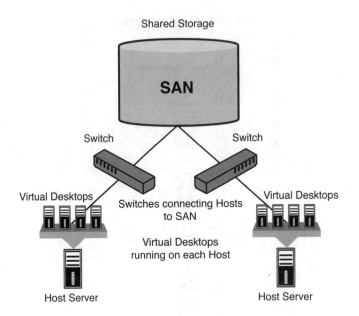

Figure 1.2 Logical layout.

Most customers at the time tended to extend their virtual server environment to allow for virtual desktops. Making the use case for storage was easy in a server virtualization environment because servers store critical data and are backed up. The nature of a desktop image makes the business case difficult because organizations treat their desktop images as disposable. In a distributed physical desktop environment, much work is done to redirect user data to file repositories so that in the event a desktop fails, no user information is lost. It is extremely uncommon for desktops to be backed up in a distributed desktop environment. To illustrate this scenario, let's look at an example in Figure 1.3.

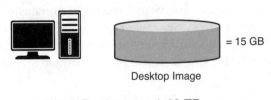

X 100 Desktops = 1.46 TB

Figure 1.3 Storage requirements for 100 Desktops.

For example, let's say my desktop image is 15 GB, and I want to provide virtual desktops to 100 users. My storage requirement is approximately 1.46 TB.

Convincing an organization to commit a large amount of expensive storage space in which only a small portion of the data is actually critical to the organization is a difficult sale. This is not to say that companies did not deploy this technology for certain use cases, but it was not common for an organization to look at scaling the solution because the cost was prohibitive. Clearly, more engineering would be required to increase the scalability of the solution and lower the price point.

Virtual infrastructure is enabled through the use of shared storage. Host clustering, hot migrations, and distributed resource leveling are not possible without the use of some form of shared storage. Many options available today provide great performance, such as NAS, NFS, and iSCSI. Historically, however, the choices were limited. Many organizations would tier storage to rationalize the cost of virtual desktop infrastructure, but it was still relatively expensive when contrasted with the price of local storage. Clearly, for the technology to have practical applications, a simpler approach was required to manage the images and reduce storage costs. Today modern VDI products such as VMware View allow you to incorporate both local and shared storage to deliver the best cost advantage. In earlier releases, this issue was addressed using advanced image management solutions to deliver storage savings on traditional shared storage technology.

The latest generation of virtual desktop infrastructure comes bundled with image management software that allows a single image to be served out to many virtual desktops. VMware added the linked clone technology that was available on VMware Workstation and VMware Lab Manager into its VDI product line. The technology was integrated and called VMware View Composer. It allowed a single image to be represented to many different users without requiring a full clone of the parent image for each virtual desktop. The impact this development had to SAN storage was dramatic. Now a single 15 GB desktop image could be shared by multiple virtual machines (VMs) while appearing to be an independent desktop OS to each user. This technology lowered costs and dramatically simplified the management of images. When the master could be patched and upgraded once and have these changes propagated to all users at the next reboot or login, operational costs were also lowered when compared to a distributed desktop environment. The integration of VMware View Composer allowed customers to consume less storage space to deliver a higher number of desktops, making VDI a more cost-effective technology.

Virtual Desktop Manager evolved to become VMware View. VMware View introduced a technology to address the storage cost of VDI. The product integrated a method of using linked clones to mitigate the cost of storage. The feature was called View Composer, and it enabled a larger number of virtual desktops to be deployed while reducing the storage requirement to lower overall costs. As with any feature, sometimes it should be used and sometimes it may not be the ideal approach. The "usability" of View Composer depends on how much work is done to redirect user data and whether the desktop will be persistent or nonpersistent (floating).

With the introduction of VMware View 5, companies now have an enterprise solution that lowers the cost of delivering virtual desktops so that they are a competitive alternative to a distributed desktop environment. In some organizations, this still means that they maintain a certain percentage of physical desktops, but virtual desktops are becoming an integral part of the desktop environment. In other organizations, virtual desktops are replacing physical desktops entirely. As the technology has improved, the return on investment (ROI), or the amount of money returned in relation to the amount of investment, has increased so that the cost of deploying a virtual desktop can be cheaper than the cost of deploying a physical desktop. This situation is especially true if you look at the operational cost of managing virtual desktops that incorporate technology such as application virtualization and View Composer. The overall cost, or total cost of ownership (TCO), on a properly designed virtual desktop infrastructure can allow a smaller number of administrators to manage a larger number of desktops. As with any technology change, to take advantage of it, you need to thoroughly understand and master it.

We go through the architecture of VMware View 5 in detail later in this book. This book examines each of the features of VMware View so that you fully understand how the technology works and when it should or should not be applied. More than that, however, the book leads you through the process of introducing virtual desktops in a way that ensures the technology can be used both tactically and, more importantly, strategically across the organization.

The Importance of Application Virtualization

One of the early realizations with virtual desktops is that just moving a desktop OS to the datacenter did not enable you to take full advantage of the technology. Some of the challenges in decentralized desktop management do not change when you virtualize desktops. What VMware realized is that it could make the VDI story even more compelling by addressing some of the support problems that are common in desktop environments.

One of the problems in distributed desktop environments is application lifecycle management. Lifecycle management is the testing, deploying, upgrading, and removing of applications that are no longer needed. In addition, installing applications into desktop images increases the number of images that need to be maintained. With every unique application workload, a separate image is developed so that different users or business groups have the appropriate applications. This development led to desktops being segregated based on the types of applications; for example, the finance department used a finance image, and the marketing department used a marketing image, and so on. As application incompatibilities were discovered, desktop images became locked to a specific build with static application and operating system versions.

In a terminal server environment, this situation caused servers to be siloed based on application compatibility. Application streaming or application virtualization was originally developed to solve this problem on shared server environments; however, it was ported to the desktop space to deal with the same operational set of problems. VMware provides ThinApp as a part of the VMware View Suite. ThinApp can be integrated into your virtual desktop environment to handle most application incompatibilities. Dealing with application incompatibilities reduces the number of images you need to maintain and further reduces the TCO.

Application virtualization is a form of packaging that isolates the application in a separate set of files that have read access to the underlying operating system but only limited or redirected writes, and in some cases, no writes to the underlying operating system. Packaged applications and sequenced applications like VMware ThinApp can be configured to write no files to the underlying operating system. When the application is abstracted from the desktop image, the number of images that need to be maintained is reduced. In addition, depending on the software, the applications can be delivered to users based on file or Active Directory (AD) permissions. The big benefit to implementing application virtualization is that applications can be tied to users versus the more traditional approach of installing them into a desktop image. It is common for organizations that manage large distributed desktop environments to over-license software by installing it on every desktop instead of just to the required users because this approach simplifies management. Application virtualization allows the desktop image to be truly universal because a single image can be applied to all users.

Unless you have the same application workload for every business unit, you should consider "application virtualization" to reduce the operational overhead of managing applications in a VDI environment. Virtualization eliminates application interoperability problems and reduces the management of deploying new applications. Because the applications are prepackaged, the application configurations are centrally managed, lowering application support. Although these technologies are available without desktop virtualization, they are more problematic to implement because it is difficult to maintain a consistent desktop OS baseline in a physical environment even if user changes to the desktop are restricted. Because of the consistent representation of physical hardware within a virtual machine, a consistent desktop baseline is much easier to enforce in a VDI environment, also making application virtualization easier to implement.

To add application virtualization to the VMware View platform, VMware acquired ThinStall in January 2008, and it became VMware ThinApp. At the time, there were three main players in the application virtualization space: Citrix XenApp, Microsoft App-V (formerly Softricity), and ThinApp. They were not the only organizations in the market, but they were the three most commonly found deployed in customers' environments. One of the competitive advantages that ThinApp had over the other two was that it did not require additional back-end infrastructure to integrate the technology. It is essentially agentless. To be fair, Microsoft also developed the capability to deploy application virtualization as a standalone MSI, but this was an option, not a core design feature. ThinApp was truly a method of packaging the application in a manner that isolated it from other applications without supporting infrastructure or agent integration.

Application virtualization is similar to application packaging in the sense that you go through the installation routine of an application to customize the install package. If you have ever attempted to automate application installations, you know it can be a painstaking and laborious process. In addition, after you have packaged it, the testing and remediation process is typically quite lengthy because everything must happen unattended.

Application virtualization is similar but can be much more straightforward. In standard application packaging, we typically take a packaging desktop, run a baseline analyzer, install the application, and then rerun the analyzer so that the application can be packaged into a standard executable. There are differences in the way that each vendor approaches this; for example, Citrix uses a streaming client to build a streaming package not an MSI or EXE like ThinApp or App-V. In addition, App-V refers to the process as *sequencing* versus *packaging*, or in Citrix, *case profiling*. The application is then tested to ensure the desired result is achieved and the application installs.

With application virtualization, an additional step is added: the execution of the application. This additional step is required because the secret sauce of the application virtualization process is that the installer looks for the portions of the operating system that the application writes to during runtime. The portions of the registry, DLLs, and files that are written to are incorporated into the final package. This becomes the application *bubble*, or the *sandbox* in VMware terminology. This sandbox is a separate application-specific location that ensures one application cannot interfere with another by isolating the code. This virtual application can be executed from the local desktop or "streamed" down from a centralized file repository or website. I use *streaming* loosely here, as in the case of ThinApp, the package can be stored on a file share and executed in memory versus using a streaming protocol, as in Citrix XenApp or as an option in App-V. When you purchase the ThinApp Suite, you receive a copy of VMware workstation that you can use in combination with the snapshot feature to capture different OS states before, during, and after the application packaging process. These snapshots can speed up the packaging process by enabling the possibility of rollbacks when needed. We go through this subject in detail in Chapter 4, "Application Virtualization."

When VMware acquired ThinStall, the company rebranded it ThinApp. The version of ThinApp shipped with VMware View 5 is 4.6 although your license is carried forward to ThinApp 4.7. ThinApp 4.6 supports linking virtual applications to each other to avoid having to layer multiple codependent applications together into a single application virtualization package. This capability reduces the complexity of deploying applications that are codependent on each other. For example, say you have an application that uses a feature in Microsoft Office. Prior to the capability to link virtual applications, you had to include a full version of Microsoft Office in each application package. Now you can package both applications separately and simply link them.

Now, in addition to virtualizing desktops, you can solve operational problems that make desktop support difficult with ThinApp. We review application virtualization in depth in Chapter 4.

The Importance of User Data Management

Another challenge that has been overcome is user data management, or *persona management* as it is called in VMware View 5. To take full advantage of the advanced image management capabilities in a virtual desktop environment, you have to homogenize the image by ensuring user data is redirected, not written to the desktop image. Within a Windows environment, user configuration information is typically stored in local or roaming profiles. To ensure this information is maintained across multiple sessions on different desktops, the profile is typically stored centrally and cached locally at login (roaming). When the user logs off, any changes are synchronized to the centrally stored profile.

This technology has been around for many years and has been used in both desktop and terminal server environments. Profiles can be configured as read-only (mandatory), read-write (normal), or a mixture of both (flex) profiles. Flex profiles are based on a mandatory profile, but user changes are written to a separate location, such as a user directory. The flex profile merges both the read-only profile and user customizations to provide the speed of a mandatory profile while still allowing user customizations.

A number of things must work in harmony to ensure a user profile loads and unloads properly: the profile directory must be available, the user must have the appropriate permissions, adequate space must be available on the login device, and all this must happen within a reasonable window of time so that the user is not affected. The same mixture of technology must also work when the user logs off to ensure that any changes are properly captured and the profile unloads cleanly. If a user is logged in to two separate environments, the profile that is unloaded last overwrites any prior updates. Given the number of components that must interoperate, it is quite common to experience many operational challenges when introducing Windows roaming profiles.

In a traditional server-based computing model, this situation is typically addressed using Windows profiles. The problem with Windows profiles is that they do not perform well when you are attempting to manage thousands of users. To resolve this problem, VMware acquired a profile or user data management company called RTO Software. RTO software can be used in place of Windows profiles or complementary to them. With the release of VMware View 5, the integration of the acquisition is complete and is now called Persona Manager.

The Importance of Multimedia

To replace a feature-rich, multimedia-capable desktop device with virtual desktop technology, companies are putting a lot of development work into display protocols. Much of that development is increasing the bandwidth utilization of the display protocols. In some cases LAN speeds may be required, and throughput will have to be more carefully considered on consolidated desktop infrastructure. The concept of simply extending an existing server virtual infrastructure to incorporate virtual desktops may be overly simplistic because virtual desktop infrastructure may require more engineering than a virtual server environment.

Originally, when VMware acquired Propero, the display protocol was based on the Remote Desktop Protocol, or RDP. Microsoft developed RDP and introduced it in Microsoft Terminal Server 4. RDP was designed to deal with high-latency low-bandwidth links. The problem with using RDP as the primary display protocol in delivering virtual desktops is that today's desktops are driven by high-definition multimedia because most of the content we now view over the Internet is visual versus textual. Microsoft has evolved RDP to a new set of features and capabilities designed to deliver a high-fidelity desktop experience called RemoteFX. In a similar manner, Citrix has evolved the ICA protocol for multimedia delivery and rebranded all the capabilities as HDX.

Historically, one of the early attempts to provide a more robust protocol came when VMware integrated HP Remote Graphics Software (HP RGS). HP RGS was designed to provide 2D and 3D graphics support when connecting to PC Blade servers. Support for the protocol appeared in VMware View 3.X but has been dropped as of VMware View 4.6.

VMware looked at all the options and finally made an arrangement with the company that developed the chipset used in most digital television sets, Teradici. What better way to deliver high definition than to look into some of the technology embedded in HDTVs? An agreement was signed, and the technology was moved from microchip to a software kit designed to run over IP. The display protocol was aptly named PC over IP (PCoIP). It is different from RDP, which is based on bitmaps and bitmap caching. PCoIP is based on compressing and sending pixels in a similar manner to HDTV. PCoIP is a lossless protocol by default, which means it builds the display without losing any of the definition or quality.

When we are looking at an HD picture on a television screen, only the pixels that are changing in the screen are compressed and sent, not the entire screen. PCoIP is designed to work in the same way. This has also been a bit of a drawback because scaling the protocol across longer distances requires a trade-off in the quality of display. The capability to tweak PCoIP to perform better across wider distances and a 75% increase in bandwidth efficiency over prior releases are some of the many enhancements in VMware View 5. We review how to tweak the display protocol in Chapter 8, "A Rich End-User Experience."

VoIP

The capability to do VoIP often comes up in discussions when deploying virtual desktops because computers are largely converging into an all-in-one appliance that is our phone, television, and primary business device. VoIP does not perform well as you tend to impose longer routes in traffic by sending it to and from a virtual desktop. Consider the example of two thin clients located in the same branch office. If a user wants to call from one thin client to another, the traffic would typically need to pass all the way down to the private branch exchange (PBX) and back even if the thin client is located on the other side of the local office. This scenario is referred to a *hairpinning* and leads to unnecessary penalties on VoIP traffic. Essentially, the communication takes place over a much longer path than the shortest possible circuit between the two endpoints. With VMware View 5, it is now possible to integrate VoIP into your virtual desktop environments. Many traditional VoIP vendors have integrated platforms that allow a unified delivery of both virtual desktops and softphone technology. These integrated solutions allow the virtual desktop display and VoIP traffic to be dealt with as separate streams but integrated from the thin client device to provide a seamless experience for the end user.

Through the support of thin client PCs, it is possible to integrate VoIP and a VMware View experience. You need to check which vendors actually support this feature, but essentially it integrates a VoIP phone into the thin client on which you access the VMware View environment. Although it appears as though the environment is completely integrated, the remote and local software are married so that they appear as one to the end user. These solutions not only can provide two-way voice audio but also enhance video conferencing through the support of the H.264 channel for video encoding. The integration of these features does have hardware requirements, such as local hard drives to manage the compression and decompression of the video encoding.

Considerations for Deploying VDI

To deliver a successful VDI environment, you need to understand various related technologies—from storage to network and the software layers in between. This book guides you through how to properly plan out all the aspects of the deployment. We look at designing the underlying software to deploying the VMware View components to supporting the adoption of the technology within your organization.

There are several ways to approach deploying virtual desktops, such as identifying the ideal use case or as a strategic replacement of a decentralized desktop environment. The general term for this process is a *desktop rationalization study*. A desktop rationalization study finds a business requirement that is ideal for VMware View, such as providing desktops to contractors while they are working onsite. Strategically, the approach may be similar to a virtual server project in which all desktops from a certain point are virtual versus physical unless there is adequate justification for them not to be.

You must also factor in a certain part of your strategy if it is to replace a distributed desktop environment to deal with the migration phase of your project. Often in this phase the overhead is quite high because the user may operate with two desktops for a short period of time while transitioning to a virtual desktop. With VMware View 5.1, the transition is made easier because you can deploy Persona Manager for both physical and virtual desktops, ensuring the user data is consistent during the transition phase.

One of the key drivers of costs in scaling a VDI solution is the percentage of persistent versus nonpersistent desktops in your design. Persistent desktops are those desktops associated with the same user unless a problem occurs; nonpersistent desktops or floating desktops are assigned based on the availability of the virtual desktop with no association with the user. From experience, I can tell you that the higher the proportion of nonpersistent desktops the better the return on investment. ROI is one of the metrics used to assess whether a technology will provide value to an organization. When you are deploying virtual desktops, if the company invests in the infrastructure, it is important to understand how long will it take to recoup the value of the investment. The return on virtual desktop technology is a combination of capital and operational costs.

To help calculate your ROI, VMware has an online tool available at http://roitco .vmware.com/vmv/. In general, the ROI calculations are based on taking the loaded costs of buying, supporting, and maintaining physical desktops. These costs typically include user administration, hardware and software deployment, application management and support, and IT administration. They are measured against the cost savings of virtual desktops, which can provide efficiencies in reducing hardware replacement, simplified management, higher security, and PC power savings when including thin clients. These savings are factored over the desktop lifecycle, which is typically three to five years, to provide your overall ROI.

Nonpersistent desktops can further reduce the overall costs of deploying virtual desktops. It is often the percentage of persistent versus nonpersistent that influences the ROI that you are likely to see. Nonpersistent desktops are more difficult to engineer because the profile of a nonpersistent desktop has a static application load unless application virtualization is applied. I often come across environments where the desktop management team allows the users to self-provision applications that are advertised but not installed to the users. This approach can be a problem if users hit a new desktop every time because they are forced to reprovision all over again. An improperly designed nonpersistent or floating desktop would penalize the users and create a terrible user experience. With View 5, VMware offers Persona Manager to help deal with profile management to allow users to leverage floating desktops while ensuring their user data roams with them. ThinApp also prevents the problem by enabling you to put the common applications into an image and stream or host applications that not all users are entitled to.

Image management has always been a challenge in physical desktop environments due to the number of desktop hardware profiles that need to be maintained in large organizations. Although virtualizing eliminates the problem of hardware profiles, it adds the requirement for centralizing the storage of desktop images. If we look at "typical" desktop policies, it is common for desktop images to be categorized as disposable. User data, which may consist of desktop and application customizations and files, is redirected from the desktop to a file server that is backed up on a regular basis. Often this practice is reinforced with a company policy that requires users to utilize centralized file storage through mapped user and group directories. This problem was compounded in early virtual desktop environments because you often had a mixed mode of a physical desktop and a virtual desktop image to manage for each user. Even in current environments, customers rarely consider the support overhead of running in mixed mode for a period of time while physical desktops are replaced by thin client (desktop appliance) devices. When VDI was first introduced, the overhead of doubling the number of desktops per user during the rollout phase and the high cost of storing the virtual desktop centrally made it difficult to support and costly when compared to a physical desktop approach. With VMware View 5.1, it is possible to integrate Persona Manager for use in a physical desktop environment to simplify migration of users to a View desktop, making it easier to transition to a thin client.

How you approach a virtual desktop deployment is as important as your design and architecture. You must keep in mind that you are taking something that is locally available to the users and delivering it over-the-wire. In so doing, you are introducing dependencies that are more critical to a virtual desktop than they are to a physical desktop. These concerns have been mitigated over the years as networks have proliferated, ensuring much more accessibility and reliability than before. One of the keys to being successful is to be able to change everything about how the desktop is constructed and delivered in a way that is transparent to the users. If you can do that, you will have a successful implementation.

To create this implementation, you must focus on performance and functionality of the virtual desktop. It is very important to profile users to fully understand how they consume a desktop. End user profiling is to virtual desktop projects what capacity planning is to server virtualization environments. End user profiling involves surveying how users use the virtual desktop at a fairly early stage in the virtual desktop project. The purpose is to understand the expectations each user has from the desktop and what features the user deems critical. This early feedback can be invaluable to you in helping you be successful. It also is important for other aspects because often, as IT people, we believe we understand the business requirements but may not fully understand how the user interprets and uses them in practice.

In addition to surveying users, you should use tools that collect empirical data over a period of time (30–60 days). You should inventory software so that a complete understanding of the desktop environment is available for planning. Some tools that are highly recommended are LakeSide Software's SysTrack tool or Microsoft SysTrack Virtual Machine Planner.

Profiling of users and desktops also ensures adequate physical resources are available in the VDI environment. A successful virtual desktop implementation changes the desktop infrastructure without changing the end-user experience. The only way to map that end-user experience is to carefully profile the way the users leverage their existing desktop by using auditing tools. This task is similar to the requirement to profile physical workloads before P2Ving or migrating them to a virtual server environment. Profiling provides a benchmark to ensure the new technology meets all the resource and feature requirements that are delivered by the existing desktop. The risk to not understanding or not properly matching the user requirements to the virtual desktop solution is the failure of the users to adopt the new technology. Once the end user has rejected the technology, it is exceedingly difficult to restart the deployment. Some of the key areas that should be understood are the requirement for multimedia, printing, synchronization to any peripherals, or unified communications such as VoIP and messaging, in addition to physical resources (CPU, memory, disk I/O, network bandwidth).

For anyone familiar with server-based computing, profiling was an integral component to designing a server-based computing environment. Typically, a single user session was monitored to provide metrics on CPU, memory, disk I/O, and network bandwidth. This raw data was averaged with the usage type of profiled user (for example, power user, task-based, or intermittent). These numbers were adjusted based on items such as region or time zone and whether shift work was involved to understand the concurrency rate (number of connected users) at different times of the day, week, or month.

If you want to deliver successful VDI, your design specifications should include not only the VMware View components, but also your network requirements, storage requirements, and end-user client and device considerations. You should also review your support processes, technical expertise on the helpdesk, and possible training considerations.

From a networking perspective, you need to understand the distance that you are moving the desktop to and from. Distance translates to latency in networking terms, but it is also influenced by the type of connection, such as T1, OC3, or broadband. Specifically, the concern is based around taking a locally available resource to the user (a physical desktop) and then moving it so that it is subject to latency (a virtual desktop). Latency is the round-trip time it takes for a network packet to go from the user to the datacenter. The round-trip latency is the return distance. Virtual desktop technology is generally designed to be optimal at 150 ms of latency and less.

Although this technology can be tweaked to perform at latencies longer than 100 ms, this is typically the point at which you are introducing some concessions to the end-user experience. For example, you may degrade the end-user experience by restricting Flash to ensure Office applications perform better. PCoIP has been tested up to 250 ms latency with good performance, but your job, from an IT perspective, is to make sure that this performance is consistent for everyone.

As with server-based computing, latency and bandwidth may dramatically impact the overall user experience. It is important to thoroughly test the user experience under various network conditions to understand how users experience a hosted virtual desktop. Emulating different bandwidth and latency settings can be very helpful during the testing phase of any virtual desktop rollout. In addition, you should conduct a thorough review of the network topology to uncover any existing problems and determine how traffic is prioritized to ensure the environment is ready for large-scale VDI deployment.

By moving from a physical desktop to a virtual desktop, you are moving from a locally available resource to a wired service. As with any service delivered over the wire, it is subject to more environmental elements that will impact the end-user experience that you need to consider. In many cases, the deployment of virtual desktops actually reduces the bandwidth requirement to the user network because virtual desktops are typically deployed in the datacenter, so only screen display and keystroke information is transferred over the wire. This is not always the case, however, if the virtual desktop is being bundled with additional user services. In any case, the environment will likely consist of both physical desktops and virtual desktops during the migration period.

From a storage perspective, you have burst I/O and operational I/O to contend with. Burst I/O is a demand for large amounts of storage I/O typically caused by a mass deployment of virtual machines or a boot storm. Operational I/O is the storage I/O demanded by virtual desktops that are up and running.

Thin Clients

Another often under-considered component in a VDI environment is the thin client device or "desktop appliance." Reducing the total cost of ownership with a virtual desktop environment often depends on removing the thick client device and replacing it with a desktop appliance. Although the operational requirements are reduced on a desktop appliance, you still need to consider and plan for them as part of the deployment strategy.

Desktop appliances come with an integrated operating system that may be Windows or Linux based. In addition, they may have image management solutions that need to be deployed, although for proof of concept or a limited-scale environment, imaging can usually be done by unlocking and shuttling the image through a USB device.

One of the common problems with desktop appliances is the integrated version of the desktop agent that is shipped is typically not current enough to provide all the features of the VDI solution. Other vendors use their own version of the View Client, so updates may not be readily available when VMware has a new release. In addition, the desktop agent may have additional requirements such as Windows compatibility that need to be considered before selecting a specific embedded OS for the desktop appliance. Desktop agents may not have feature parity between Linux or Windows agents or may limit support to Windows derivatives only. Enough time should be allowed in the deployment plan to understand how to manage the desktop appliance and also how to apply upgrades to the embedded image. It is useful to have surplus units available for ongoing operational support, such as image testing or agent upgrades.

An interesting alternative developed for VDI is the no-software desktop appliance or Zero-client. These devices reduce the management overhead by running only firmware on the desktop appliance and moving the management to a centralized administration console. While reducing operational overhead, these devices currently are very vendor biased and restrict the customer to certain vendor platforms only. The other potential drawback is the possible physical replacement of the device for any major revisions to the product line or feature set. These devices are designed for VDI only, so if the environment requires a blend of server-based computing and VDI, a standard desktop appliance may be better suited. In addition, Zero-clients come with integrated management consoles providing simplified management. For example, the PCoIP Management Console from Teradici is free and supports all compatible Zero-clients.

Test Failure Scenarios

Session management is an integral part of any virtual desktop environment. Any environment larger than a few dozen users needs a way to intelligently associate users to virtual desktops. The technology that makes these associations is the session manager or connection broker. Connection brokers can tunnel connections between the users and virtual desktops to provide additional security such as SSL encryption or simply hand off the connection. The connection broker becomes a proxy to the user and the View desktop and therefore is a critical component and needs to be available at all times. Most connection brokers work in an active-passive mode with a designated primary broker. VMware View allows the Connection Server to be used in an active-active configuration. Both the View Connection Server and View Security servers are in fact both brokers but the View Security Server proxies connections to the Connection Server.

It is important to thoroughly understand what happens in the event a connection broker is unavailable. Often the testing of a broker failure uncovers another single point of failure such as where the virtual desktop environment stores its configuration information. It may also uncover the requirement for additional front end services such as hardware based load balancing to ensure failover occurs without administrator intervention. As with any technology, failures can occur; it is important to fully understand what happens when each component fails so that you can either reduce or understand the associated risks.

Engage the Users

Whenever you embark on any major changes to the end-user environment, it is important to engage the users in the review and verification of the environment at various stages in the deployment process. Involving a user representative in the early stages of the testing and development of the virtual desktop environment is a great way of building acceptance and buy in for any major rollout. Generally speaking, this step is called user acceptance testing (UAT) and is one of the most important pieces of a virtual desktop deployment and very often overlooked. When you design the verification process, you should ensure that the tests that the users run are detailed but allow an appropriate amount of space for additional comments and feedback. Detailing the tests ensures that any problems can be resolved and rechecked for consistency. Additional comments allow any requirements that may not have been identified to be documented and integrated or deferred for a follow-up phase. Often it is a good idea to start with a department such as desktop support or the IT department because these departments are more forgiving when problems arise and often are very helpful in resolving issues.

Planning for VMware View

One of the main areas that people tend to neglect in the design and scoping of their VMware View environment is the impact on the network, as shown in Figure 1.4. When you virtualize the desktop, the monitor cable essentially becomes your network path because the display is dependent on the underlying network environment. If the network is poorly managed or close to saturation, it is likely that adding another service may create more problems than it solves. This result is not always true because moving the desktops into the datacenter can actually reduce the overall load on the networks. The point, however, is that it is not something that you can leave to chance. You must clearly understand what load you will add and what load you are likely to remove by introducing virtual desktop technology. We go through this topic in depth in Chapter 10.

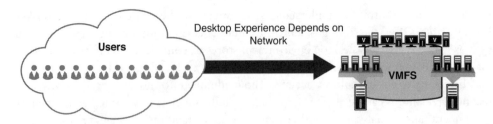

Figure 1.4 The display protocol is dependent on the network.

Although it is possible to deploy VMware View out of the box running the default configurations, the environment is not properly tuned for performance. You can tune performance at many different points in the VMware View architecture—from the VMware View Administrator or View Connection Server through to the optimization of the desktop images themselves and the configuration and layout of the storage. This book is designed to guide you through all the configurations and explain how adjusting them will benefit your virtual infrastructure.

Much has been incorporated into VMware View 5, and many of the options and configurations are largely intuitive. To ensure this book provides value, we go beyond the default configurations and drill in depth into the optimizations and settings that will ensure your VDI environment is tuned properly.

Where your project begins depends on what your drivers are for the VDI environment and who is doing the driving. If you are driving the introduction of the technology, you may have to start with the business case to ensure that the project can be funded. If you are being directed to implement VMware View, maybe starting with the architecture and design is more appropriate.

The business case for virtual desktops is a little different from the business case that drove the consolidation of physical server workloads. The point at which they overlap is perhaps the general underutilization of computing resources, both in our datacenters and end-user environments. Much has been done over the past few years to drive down the cost of the virtual desktop, but as with all technologies, there is a price of admission. The price of admission often requires that we buy additional host servers and ensure that we have a storage strategy in place to enable us to virtualize our desktops. Many of the advancements in shared storage, such as deduplication and thin provisioning, have made this more cost effective. As most organizations do not typically start with wholesale replacement of physical desktops, the rate of return on your virtual desktop investment might be longer than your server virtualization investment. In addition, desktop virtualization adds a layer of complexity that, although dramatically simplifying the operation and support, may introduce a new requirement for skills in your desktop support environment.

There is, of course, another driving reason for virtualizing your desktops, and that is the demand for mobility that has never been more prevalent than today with the introduction of the tablet computer. To deliver your business applications without redeveloping them, you may need a virtual desktop. This virtual desktop essentially allows your end users the flexibility to work from anywhere in a way that allows you to maintain your security and data integrity.

If you are starting with architecture, then in addition to the VMware View components, you need to understand what sorts of technologies need to be addressed in your design that View depends on. They include storage, networking, user data management, and also intelligent load balancing in front of the VMware View environment.

The other thing that should be part of your planning exercise is how to ensure the people you have supporting your physical desktops will be comfortable supporting your virtual desktops. This task may involve both retraining and the introduction of the new process. For example, say that your desktop strategy is to hold the line going forward on physical desktop replacements with virtual ones. So any new desktops purchased will be virtual unless there is some mitigating factor that requires otherwise. You should introduce the notification and creation of a virtual desktop for a user into your desktop request process. In the early stages of virtual desktop adoption, we also recommend that you maintain a user profiling process.

For example, when you receive a new request for a desktop, this starts a creation phase in which you author the combination of technologies that meet the user requirement. For example, do the users need the desktop to persist between reboots, or should it always roll back to a clean, pristine state? After the desktop is configured, the users should verify it does meet their requirements before the View desktop is released into production. This process is highlighted in Figure 1.5.

Figure 1.5 The process of creating a virtual desktop instance.

A slightly different strategy may involve doing all the pre-vetting upfront so that new users are not really aware whether the desktop is physical or virtual. Each approach is valid and can be appropriate depending on how you introduce virtual desktops. If you introduce them properly, the users should not notice anything different except for better performance if the desktops are designed properly.

Your virtual desktop should always be designed for virtualization. For example, many of the default settings on a Windows 7 desktop are designed with physical hardware in mind. For instance, it makes sense to ensure good power savings when you are running a physical desktop; however, in a virtualization platform, you are not looking for power savings of the individual desktop instance. You want the resources to be retuned back to the pool when a user logs off to make them available to another desktop instance. VMware provides a VMware View Optimization Guide, which we discuss at length later in the book. You can find it at http://www.vmware.com/files/pdf/VMware-View-OptimizationGuide-Windows7-EN.pdf.

VMware View can deploy three types of desktops: virtual, physical, or shared server desktops. To be frank, it is rare that shared server desktops are incorporated into most VMware View environments, but the integration is still included and enables the View Connection Servers to become a single point of access for both environments. Most information typically focuses on virtual desktops, but in some situations the other two make sense. This is especially the case now that all can essentially give that individualized desktop feel. For example, in Windows 2008 an option called Desktop Experience installs some features of the Windows 7 desktop. After they are installed, you can selectively enable certain aspects to make the shared server desktop appear as if it is a Windows 7 desktop. This feature includes

- Windows Media Player
- Desktop themes
- Video for Windows (AVI support)
- Windows SideShow
- Windows Defender
- Disk Cleanup
- Sync Center
- Sound Recorder
- Character Map
- Snipping Tool

We go into this topic more in Chapter 5, "Building Your Virtual Desktop," so that you can offer up a shared server desktop from within your VMware View environment that appears as if it is an individual virtual machine.

VMware View provides a great platform on which you can virtualize your desktop instances, but it requires that you understand PCoIP, Persona Management, ThinApp, View composer, Orchestrator, vShield, and many other features that all need to be designed and architected properly. We briefly introduce these components in this chapter and review the architecture in Chapter 2, "VMware View Architecture."

VMware View Versions

VMware View comes in two versions: VMware View Enterprise and VMware View Premier. VMware View Enterprise comes with everything that is required to deliver a VDI environment, but many of the advanced features such as ViewComposer are not included. VMware View Premier comes with all the features. Although pricing varies by vendor, in general Premier is about 60 percent more expensive than Enterprise. The actual component list for both products is shown in Table 1.1.

Table 1.1 VMware View Version Overview

Component	VMware View Enterprise	VMware View Premier
VMware vSphere Desktop	✔	✔
VMware vCenter Server	✔	✔
VMware View Manager	✔	✔
VMware View Composer		✔
View Persona Management		✔
VMware View Client with Local Mode		✔
vShield Endpoint		✔
VMware ThinApp		✔
VMware Workstation		✔

The source for version information is http://www.vmware.com/products/view/howtobuy.html.

In addition to the product being available in the two bundles, there are also upgrade options available for customers who are using older versions. When you buy VMware View, you get VMware vSphere Desktop edition, which we discuss in the following section. VMware vSphere Desktop edition is essentially vSphere and vCenter but deployed under different licensing conditions.

Licensing Considerations

One of the new announcements with vSphere 5 was a change in licensing by vRAM. Prior to vSphere 5, vSphere was licensed based on the number of CPUs and cores on the server. Recently VMware has announced the retirement of the vRAM licensing program; however, the vSphere Desktop Edition licensing is still in place. A review of vRAM licensing is included here, but you should check for the latest information from VMware.

To break the relationships between licensing physical CPUs, VMware introduced vRAM licensing in vSphere 5. The principle behind vRAM licensing is to start to license based on usage versus the number of physical cores on a CPU. Now you can have as many cores or as much physical memory as you like on the server. vRAM is used as a soft limit to the amount of RAM applied to a powered-on VM. For example, if you configure a VM to use 4 GB of memory, this is equivalent to using 4 GB of vRAM. In vSphere 5, each edition of vSphere has an allowance for vRAM:

VMware vSphere Standard Edition has an allowance of 32 GB of vRAM.

VMware vSphere Enterprise Edition has an allowance of 64 GB of vRAM.

VMware vSphere Enterprise Plus Editions has an allowance of 96 GB of vRAM.

You still license based on the number of CPUs, but now the limit is based on the amount of configured RAM on powered-on VMs. The licenses can be pooled within editions. For example, if you have two dual-core servers licensed at Enterprise Plus, you need four vSphere Enterprise Plus Edition licenses to cover the four CPUs, for a total allowance of 384 GB of vRAM.

A new edition of vSphere called VMware vSphere Desktop edition was introduced to enable VDI deployments. VMware vSphere Desktop edition is equivalent to vSphere Enterprise Plus but is licensed by the total number of powered-on virtual desktop machines and is sold in bundles of 100 license packs. Because the licensing is applied per powered-on virtual desktop, there is an unlimited vRAM allowance on vSphere Desktop edition.

Using vSphere Desktop edition, you can also run server VMs that are dedicated to managing the desktop environment. For example, your View Connection Server, View Composer, and related SQL databases can all be licensed under this model. The license can even be applied to VMware Operations for VMware View, which we discuss in Chapter 12, "Performance and Monitoring." The specific SKUs for vSphere Desktop edition, broken out by industry, are

- VS5-DT100VM-C (Commercial)

- VS5-DT100VM-A (Academic)

- VS5-DT100VM-F (Government)

For customers buying VMware View, vSphere Desktop and vCenter Standard licenses are included in either edition: Enterprise and Premier. Customers running other VDI products have the option of using vSphere Desktop edition or any one of the other editions of vSphere. The desktop consolidation ratio largely determines which is more cost effective. For example, say you are deploying an environment based on 1000 virtual desktops and are looking at a consolidation ratio of 42 virtual desktops per CPU. In this case, if you were to license using the vSphere Enterprise Plus licensing, it would cost you $83,880.00. If you licensed under vSphere Desktop edition, the same 1000-desktop deployment would cost you $65,000, as shown in the Table 1.2. In addition, with vSphere Desktop edition, you need to be less concerned about hitting a target consolidation ratio.

Table 1.2 Licensing Example

Total number of virtual desktops	1000	
Consolidation ratio	42	Virtual desktop/CPU
Number of CPUs	24	(1000/42) = Number of CPUs
Cost of vSphere Enterprise Plus	$3,495.00	USD
Total cost of license environment	$83,880.00	(24 * $3,495.00)
Cost of vSphere Desktop	$65.00	/Powered on desktop
Total cost to license environment	$65,000.00	(1000 * $65)

vSphere Desktop edition provides all the features of vSphere Enterprise +, which is the full-featured edition of vSphere. vSphere 5 includes some specific optimizations for virtual desktops; we discuss them later in Chapter 3, "VMware View 5 Implementation."

The bundling of vSphere Desktop Edition as part of VMware View allows you to deploy the underlying vSphere 5 environment at no additional cost. The introduction of the vSphere Desktop Edition SKU allows you to license using the most cost-effective method for you.

The Main Components of VMware View

The main components of VMware View are described next.

VMware ESXi 5

VMware ESXi is a bare-metal hypervisor. Bare-metal hypervisors run directly on physical hardware without any underlying operating system. ESXi is essentially its own micro operating system. ESXi runs the vmkernel, which handles access to the underlying CPU and memory resources on the physical server. When the guest operating systems request access to resources, the vmkernel controls access and execution either natively to CPU and memory or through additional modules for networking and storage, for example. Prior to VMware vSphere 5, ESX was available in a native and ESXi version. vSphere 5 has standardized on ESXi. ESXi has a lightweight footprint because the console operating system, or COS, has been removed so that the entire installation takes only 32 MB of space. The COS was replaced by a bare-bones console called the direct console user interface (DCUI). You can still run an encrypted console or SSH session to the ESXi host, but it is disabled by default. It is still possible to reactivate SSH access to ESXi either from the console or DCUI for troubleshooting purposes, but with vSphere 5, most commands can be done through the PowerCLI.

To perform these steps through the vSphere Client, do the following:

1. Connect to ESXi through the vSphere Client.

2. Select the ESXi host in the inventory and click the Configuration tab.

3. From the Software section, select **Security Profile.**

4. Click **Properties**, select **SSH**, and then click **Options**.

5. Click **Start** and click **OK** to return.

To reactivate SSH through the DCUI, complete the following steps:

1. Open console access.

2. Press **F2** to log in to the DCUI. When prompted, supply the username and password.

3. Navigate to the troubleshooting options and press **Enter**.

4. Select **Enable SSH** and press **Esc** until you return to the main DCUI screen.

For complete details on using the PowerCLI, see VMware's PowerCLI reference site: http://www.vmware.com/support/developer/PowerCLI/index.html.

ESXi supports its own proprietary file system format called the Virtual Machine File System, or VMFS. VMFS version 5 (VMFS-5) increases performance by increasing the size of the VMFS so that customers can reduce the number of VMFS partitions in their virtual infrastructure. A VMFS-5 volume supports a maximum size of 60 TB without the use of extents. In addition, the number of files supported on a VMFS has grown from 30,000 to 100,000.[1] If you want to ensure that all the features and scalability are available, it is better to create clean VMFS-5 partitions versus upgrading from VMFS-3 partitions.

---

[1]Information based on VMware's storage teams post (http://blogs.vmware.com/vsphere/2011/07 /new-vsphere-50-storage-features-part-1-vmfs-5.html).

VMware vCenter Server

vCenter server allows you to manage multiple ESXi hosts and enables key features of the platform. vCenter server also provides centralized configuration of all resources integrated into your virtual infrastructure platform, including networking, storage, and time synchronization, or NTP. vCenter provides a top-down view of all the components of virtual infrastructure, including the virtual datacenter, clusters, hosts, resource pools, and virtual machines. The virtual datacenter is the top-level logical grouping of clusters, hosts, and VMs. You can create multiple virtual datacenters within vCenter server.

Resource pools allow you to define a relationship between a group of virtual machines and their access to CPU and memory. Resource pools are built on the concept of reservations, limits, and shares. A reservation reserves a portion of CPU and memory for use by a pool, and a limit creates a ceiling for this use. Shares come into effect only when there is resource contention in the environment. Care must be taken when configuring shares because the generic settings are Normal, *Medium, and High. What is a little counterintuitive is that you would assume that you could set the shares using the defaults and that you would get the expected results. For example, say you have configured two resource pools, one with 10 virtual desktops and the other with one. Call the one with 10 virtual desktops Production and call the other with one virtual desktop Development. If you set the shares on Production to high and Development to low, you would expect everything to run smoothly. Resources, however, are divided at the pool level, not at the virtual machine level. It is possible that, at the pool level, after the resources are split, even if Production receives 75 percent of the resources, each individual machine would receive less than the Development resource pool.

If you want to avoid this problem, it is recommended that in setting shares, you start from the perspective of the virtual machines and define each with a value and then calculate and assign custom values. For example, if you assign 100 shares to each virtual machine, the custom value of the Production pool is 1000 (10 VMs in the Production Pool × 100 shares), whereas Development should have a value of 100 (1 VM in the Development Pool × 100 shares). This ensures that if there is contention in the environment, you get the expected results.

In a virtual desktop environment, you could, for example, create several groups of virtual desktop resource pools designed for certain types of users, such as high-end or task-level workers. Using resource pools and shares (calculated as mentioned), you could ensure that more demanding users have greater access to resources if resources are in short supply. Resource pools allow you to do this on a collection of virtual machines running on a number of ESXi hosts.

Figure 1.6 shows the default configuration for shares that we should customize to ensure we get consistent results.

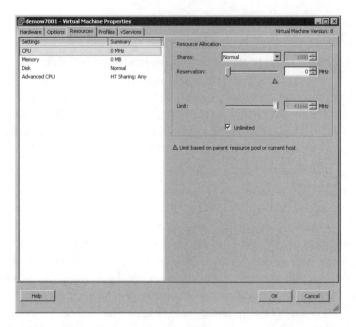

Figure 1.6 Make sure you customize the Shares value.

vCenter also allows you to manage and run migrations of virtual machines from one ESXi server to another. In a *hot migration*, the VM is powered on. A *cold migration* is performed when the VM is powered off. Hot migrations are called VMotions or storage VMotion. A VMotion migrates a running virtual machine without moving the virtual machine's files, whereas a storage VMotion also allows you to move the files.

Clusters allow you to group ESXi host servers and enable advanced features such as Distributed Resource Scheduling (DRS) and vSphere high availability (HA). Distributed Resource Scheduling is an enhancement on VMotion; it automates the migrations based on the collection of performance data. Should performance on an ESXi host be affected, DRS can move a virtual machine to a host with more available resources. DRS can be set to Automatic, Partially Automatic, or Manual. The difference is that Automatic both determines the best host during the initial placement of the VM and automates migrations; Partially Automatic provides automated initial placements but just recommended migrations; and in Manual, placement and migrations are recommended only.

In vSphere 5, this capability was extended to incorporate performance on storage partitions. If throughput performance comes into question, storage DRS will VMotion a VM to a partition with more I/O capacity.

vSphere HA enables the hosts to monitor each other for host failures. In vSphere 5, the underlying technology has changed so that every ESXi server runs an agent of Fault

Domain Manager (FDM).[2] One ESXi server assumes the role of master, and all others operate as slaves. The architecture improves on prior releases of HA because the master is elected, ensuring that any failure within the cluster can quickly be resolved to restore monitoring of both the ESXi servers and VMs. HA can be applied at both the ESXi host level or at the virtual machine level to restart individual VMs. In a VMware View environment, we want to ensure that HA is turned on for all ESXi hosts and that some of the core VMware View management pieces are protected by VM HA.

VMware View Components

The View Connection Server

The View Connection Server fills the role of the connection broker, enabling you to authenticate users to a Windows Active Directory, associating users or groups of users to certain desktops (Physical, Virtual, or Shared server desktops). The View Connection Server also associates ThinApp applications to an individual desktop or groups of desktops. In VMware's architecture, the process of associating desktops or virtual applications is referred to as *entitling*. For consistency, we also use the term *entitling*. This distinction is important when we look at ThinApp in Chapter 4. You will realize that entitlement is more of an association process than a delivery mechanism for application virtualization packages. The Connection Server manages user sessions and enables single sign-on between the Connection Server and the desktop sessions. The View Connection Server also allows you to configure policies to control the display protocol, multimedia features, and offline mode.

The View Connection Server can also be used to proxy secure connections for remote access. When used for this purpose, the Connection Server is installed as a View Security Server. When installed as a View Security Server, it is typically installed in the DMZ between the internal and external company firewalls. Because it is typically being deployed in the DMZ, a View Security Server should not be part of the Active Directory. We review the architecture in Chapter 3; for now, you need to know that a View Security Server tunnels the users' sessions to reduce the number of ports that need to be opened in the firewall. The Server Role is selected as part of the View Connection Server installation process (see Figure 1.7).

---

[2]Based on the VMware presentation "vSphere 5 High Availability (HA)."

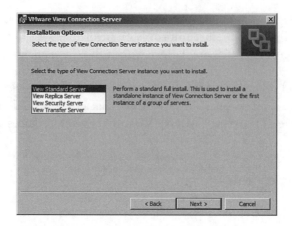

Figure 1.7 The Server Role is selected as part of the installation.

The View Administrator

The View Administrator console is the management interface to the View Connection Server. It allows you to control all aspects of the VMware View environment.

The VMware View Administrator dashboard is based on Adobe Flex technology and therefore requires the installation of Adobe Flash. The dashboard provides visibility on all the components within the VMware View environment (see Figure 1.8).

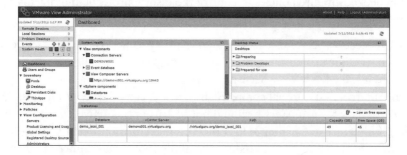

Figure 1.8 VMware View Administrator console.

The dashboard allows you to quickly determine the health of your VMware View environment. It is the place where you do the configuration for the environment. When you install the View Connection Server, the Web console is also installed. You can access it through the shortcut on the desktop or through a web browser by using **http://[View Connection Server]/admin** (note the *admin* in this case is case sensitive and needs to be lowercase).

The View Client

To access the VMware View environment, you can install the VMware View Client or access the VMware View Portal. The VMware View Portal is installed when you install the Connection Servers; you can access it by pointing a web browser to the Connection Server http://[VMware Connection Server]. When you hit the web page, it detects whether you are running the View Client, and if not, you are prompted to download and install it.

You are given a choice between a View Client or a View Client with local mode if you are accessing the Connection Server from a Windows desktop. The Native View Client allows you to connect to a VMware View environment and adjust some of the parameters, such as the display protocol and whether or not you operate in full-screen mode. In addition, a View Client with local mode allows you to check out your virtual desktop and run it locally on a Windows Client. Because VMware Player is included in this client download, the View Client with local mode has a larger installation source. VMware Player is software that installs on a Windows OS and allows you to run a VM. The flexibility to adjust the Client settings can be controlled through the enforcement of policies on the VMware View Connection Server. If you do not want the users to be able to change settings, you can enforce this policy. The View Client provides the necessary software for you to run PC over IP (PCoIP). PCoIP is the display protocol developed by VMware and Teradici to enable a multimedia experience for VMware View users. RDP is also supported with the View Client. The View Client is available for Windows, Apple OS X (including iPads), Android tablets, and Linux clients.

Because many of VMware's partners provide Linux-based thin clients, VMware View Clients are available for Linux. In addition, VMware has made a major effort to support and make a variety of clients available. Now all VMware View Clients can be downloaded from http://www.vmware.com/go/viewclients.

The VMware View Client with local support enables users to check out a virtual desktop for offline use. It requires that the users be running a Windows OS on the desktop from which they will be accessing the environment. We talk more about local mode in Chapter 3.

The View Client can be run from any number of client devices, including thin clients, tablets, and PCs. Although there is a lot of flexibility in the client device, VMware View supports only Windows virtual desktops.

View Transfer Server

The View Transfer server is a dedicated Windows server that offloads the overhead of transferring virtual desktops in and out of the VMware View environment when using local mode. When integrated into the VMware View environment, the Virtual Machine Disks (VMDKs) are first copied to a transfer server and then copied to the VMware Client making the checkout request using local mode.

VMware View Agent

The VMware View Agent is installed on the virtual desktop within the VMware View environment. It can also be installed on a physical desktop or terminal servers. The list of supported operating systems is shown in Table 1.3.

Table 1.3 View Agent Support

Guest Operating System	Version Edition	Service Pack
Windows 7 64-bit and 32-bit	Enterprise and Professional	None and SP1
Windows Vista 32-bit	Business and Enterprise	SP1 and SP2
Windows XP 32-bit	Professional	SP3
Windows 2008 R2 Terminal Server	64-bit Standard	None and SP1
Windows 2008 Terminal Server	64-bit Standard	SP2
Windows 2003 R2 Terminal Server	32-bit Standard	SP2
Windows 2003 Terminal Server	32-bit Standard	SP2

Unlike with the release of Windows 7, VMware View 5.1 provides support for Windows 8 from day one.

The VMware View Agent ensures that a desktop or terminal server can be managed by the View Connection Server. On a desktop OS, it also enables advanced features such as Persona Management access to USB devices and printing. As of VMware View 5.1, Persona Management is supported on virtual and physical desktops. If you are installing it on a terminal server, Persona Management is not supported.

View Composer

View Composer is a service that is installed on a vCenter server that has been integrated into the VMware View environment. It requires its own database to store the metadata required. It enables you to deploy linked clones to reduce the overall cost of storage. A linked clone is a copy of a virtual machine that continues to share the virtual disk of its parent VM but runs as a snapshot or differencing disk. Because it is a snapshot or differencing disk, it requires access to the parent so it is referred to as a "linked" clone.

View Composer has changed a lot in View 5.1. Composer can be installed on a separate machine, and it allows throttling to reduce the load when building out automated pools. One of the things that we will look at carefully is that although this technology reduces the storage requirements, it must be carefully implemented to ensure that it does not drive storage I/O.

ThinApp

ThinApp is the application virtualization product included in VMware View. It is integrated so that you can now entitle applications to pools of desktops simply by dragging and dropping them onto a pool. To integrate ThinApp into the VMware View platform, you define a file share, copy the ThinApp packages to the share, and then scan the directory to discover all the ThinApp application packages. After you have done so, they are available for entitlement.

Summary

Advanced image management, user data redirection, and application virtualization should be integrated into virtual desktop infrastructure to ease management and ensure the best possible end-user experience. These technologies introduce management points to the key elements that make up a desktop: the operating system, the user data, and the application workload. When management points are added into these key areas, tighter control is possible when delivering the desktop environment, delivering a better user experience. The introduction of these technologies must be carefully planned for and tested to ensure they are properly architected and integrated. They may require additional components such as storage, repackaging, and new policies. If these components are not already present in the environment, they can add additional deployment time and training requirements.

Virtual desktops provide the same opportunity for IT organizations that server virtualization architecture provides: the ability to re-create desktop architecture with a common set of high availability components and simplify many of the operational challenges. Because host clustering and shared storage can be layered with virtualization software, the environment can be leveraged by all virtual desktop operating systems. Careful planning and adequate time allowance to build out the required back-end environment ensure the success of a VDI project. It is important to be wary of some of the marketing messages that oversimplify the deployment and delivery of virtual desktops. Although there are compelling reasons to deploy virtual desktops, it is prudent to approach such a shift in the delivery of the user environment with careful and detailed planning and consideration to ensure successful user adoption of the technology.

With VMware View 5, you can deliver an enterprise service that is reliable, scalable, and robust. To do so, you need to understand all the aspects of the platform and how to take advantage of its many features. We start with an understanding of the components, how to deploy them, and optimize your virtual desktop. We then review the operational best practices and advanced features of the platform in the upcoming chapters.

Chapter 2

VMware View Architecture

Virtual

My approach to best practices is that they are useful guides to getting to where you want to go (as are books). You should always know the technology well enough to consider whether the best practice still applies or if you need to make adjustments. As an example, consider the concept of running vCenter as a virtual machine. In the history of VMware virtual infrastructure, the notion of running Virtual Center/vCenter as a virtual machine was a hotly contested topic (it may still be). VMware does consider it a best practice to run vCenter as a VM but not on hosts it is managing. I have worked with a few customers who insist that the management function be deployed on a physical machine. Rather than rely on a best practice, perhaps you need to understand the benefits versus risks from taking one approach over the other and adjust your design accordingly. This chapter provides an overview of all the components required to install VMware View on vSphere 5 and what benefits they provide to a virtual desktop platform.

As consultants, we are often asked to put forth a design that meets the business requirements and provides the level of performance, availability, and scale required. The ideal approach to developing a design is to perform a capacity planning exercise to ensure that the hardware and software can be properly estimated to run the virtual desktop workload. Capacity planning is quite common in server virtualization environments but not as common in virtual desktop planning, although it is recommended. A number of tools are specifically designed for virtual desktop analysis, such as Lakeside Software's SysTrack VP tool. SysTrack VP is a tool that is designed to provide information to help in planning your virtual desktop environment, such as inventorying the software in your desktop environment. It is agent based and allows you to take the collected data and model the configuration of the hosts by adjusting CPU and memory values and determining how many virtual desktop images you are likely to need. You can find additional information on the product at http://www.lakesidesoftware.com.

Understanding the configuration of the hosts and the number of images allows you to calculate the cost of the solution and is a key input in developing the ROI and TCO. To calculate ROI, you simply take the gain of an investment, subtract the cost of the investment, and divide the total by the cost of the investment. Or

$$ROI = (Gains - Cost)/Cost$$

Because it is important to understand the ROI when presenting the business case for virtual desktops, it is a good idea to calculate the ROI even if you need to estimate the gains. Keep in mind that gains can include hard cost savings such as the difference between thin clients and physical desktops and soft cost savings such as reducing the cost of desktop support.

Infrastructure Introduction

When you are considering a large deployment of VMware View, it is best to follow all the steps in developing valid hardware estimates. These steps are as follows:

1. Develop a baseline of current utilization in the desktop environment. The physical desktop baseline should be viewed as a starting point because the inclusion of many additional technologies such as View Composer often provides higher consolidation of features such as images in the virtual desktop environment versus the physical one.

   Initially, you used the same set of tools to perform virtual desktop assessments that you used in server consolidation exercises. Over time better tools were developed that now provide not just capacity planning information, but application inventory and license compliance. These tools can also assess whether or not an application is a candidate to be virtualized by ThinApp. It's ironic that with the exception of the application virtualization piece this is exactly the information you would need if you were planning a physical desktop migration in a large environment.

2. Estimate the hardware required to build a limited scale or proof of concept (PoC) to validate what features you will make use of in the VMware View platform and your hardware specifications (this should include not just servers but also storage space and throughput information). The PoC should also consider user segmentation or the types of users in an organization, such as knowledge and administrative users. To provide a viable reference for the production deployment, the PoC should include a proper variety of user segments.

3. Develop a production architecture and migration plan.

Although this approach is ideal, it is not the only one. Often virtual desktop engagements begin with limited-scale proof of concept environments versus a capacity planning exercise. A PoC, if properly designed, can be a great way of gathering information on what the "real" or representative workload will be for your production virtual desktop environment. By looking at the performance utilization within the PoC, you are able to extrapolate what is required to build out the production environment. You should baseline the information related to CPU, memory, and storage, including I/O.

The storage I/O information is very important and can be difficult to get a handle on. If you are dealing with a storage vendor and that vender makes a distinction between virtual desktop environments and server virtualization environments, it often has general sizing numbers to develop throughput specifications for Virtual Desktop Infrastructure (VDI) environments. What is unusual about virtual desktop environments is that two very different disk I/O conditions exist: burst and operational I/O. Burst I/O is more common in VDI environments because operational requirements necessitate large reboots of desktop operating systems not typical in virtual server environments. Operational I/O can also be problematic if factors such as virus scanning activities are synchronized based on time versus randomized to reduce the performance hit on the VMs. Even if you are careful in randomizing the activity, often AV scans follow very specific patterns. In a physical desktop world, this is minimal; in a virtualized environment, it can have a substantial impact.

Some storage vendors have a very utilitarian view of storage services; they do not view virtual desktop workloads as any more unique than other virtual workloads. The limitation with SAN vendors who do not differentiate between server and desktop virtualization environments is that to guarantee good throughput, you may have to consider their enterprise class storage systems for good performance.

Other storage vendors provide midtier solutions and solid state drives to deal with burst I/O. Although this approach is better, it still requires you to adjust your design so that high I/O requirements are segregated onto volumes made up of solid-state drives (SSDs). This leads to a very static design in which you may or may not make good use of high-performance drives. A growing number of options are available for I/O offload, such as cache cards (for example, Fusion IO; http://www.fusionio.com) or memory-based virtual appliance proxies for consolidating and dealing with I/O (such as Atlantis Computing's ILIO product; http://www.atlantiscomputing.com). In addition, storage vendors have designed solutions for virtualization consolidation and more specifically around the high I/O of virtual desktop workloads.

Most recently, storage vendors have started to build midtier storage systems that have some of the features of enterprise class systems such as *dynamic tiering*. Dynamic tiering is the capability to move hot data, or data that is in demand, to high-performance drives so that the SAN delivers great performance. This activity can typically be done on the fly or scheduled to happen periodically during the day. These solutions are ideal for virtual desktop environments because they do not require the premium of enterprise class storage systems but still deliver the features. EMC has clearly targeted the VNX line to provide features that make them ideally suited for virtual workloads. Of course, companies such as NetApp have been using programmable acceleration module (PAM) cards for years to deal with burst I/O.

Whichever solution you select, here are a few general considerations for putting together your design.

The difference between SAN solutions designed specifically for virtualization consolidation and some of the I/O offload products is in their application although they can be used to complement each other. If you are building a large virtual desktop environment and you have the option of architecting a dedicated SAN, you can plan for high I/O conditions. If you are integrating into a SAN framework shared across the entire organization, you know you may have to offload or boost the I/O provided.

Each SAN vendor has very different numbers when estimating I/Os for virtual/virtual desktop workloads. It is best to have your own reference numbers based on internal testing. Use these numbers to make sure the estimates provided meet your requirements.

Burst I/O and operational I/O are treated distinctly by most storage vendors. For example, if your numbers estimate that your environment may generate 15,000 burst I/Os and require 4 TB of storage, the vendor may suggest 6 X SSD drives (6 × 2500 IOs each = 15K burst, excluding RAID considerations) and approximately 12 of the 450 GB SAS drives to meet your operational I/O and total storage capacity. In this way, I/O and storage capacity are treated distinctly by the configuration.

Ensure that your virtual desktop design incorporates the SAN environment. A good design should provide consistent performance over the lifetime of the solution (typically three years). Achieving this result is not possible if you build a great VDI design that does not set specific requirements for storage. Although your VDI environment may run great during the first year, you may see high SAN utilization lead to problems over time.

Separate your expected read and write I/Os. Take the number of writes and ensure you factor the number by 4 to allow for an I/O penalty on writes. For example, if you expect 2000 reads and 2000 writes, multiply the writes by 4 for a total of 10,000 expected I/Os (2000 read I/O + 8000 write I/O).

One of the unique features of ESXi is the capability to use local SSDs. If you combine this capability to use local SSDs and incorporate it in your design, you can heavily subsidize your I/O requirement for storage. Doing so requires a little more consideration because local SSD drive partitions are not shared between ESXi hosts as SAN storage is. Because these virtual desktops would be localized, you would have to ensure that any data is nonpersistent in nature.

The design of VMware View can change dramatically because of the support of SSD drives in vSphere. Where before you spent a lot of time ensuring that the storage provided adequate throughput, now you have the option of also designing nonpersistent or floating VMs on localized SSD drives.

By factoring in both local and SAN options, you can reduce the overall price per desktop. This amount can be considerable depending on the percentage of persistent versus nonpersistent or floating desktops. SSDs change the framework considerably because they can provide incredible read I/O performance and impressive write performance. Although different benchmarking produces a variety of different results, it is not uncommon for SSD drives to deliver 25,000–30,000 read I/Os and 4,000–5,000 write I/Os. The only drawback with SSD drives is that they are still relatively expensive and still have a limited amount of storage space although this situation gets better and better every year. As of the time of this writing, an SSD with 600 GB of space is available.

VMware provides reference architecture for stateless virtual desktops in which they use SSD drives. It is not possible to apply this reference architecture as is to production, however, because most environments consist of both stateful and stateless virtual desktops. Using local SSDs is an option in vSphere 5 but does require some additional planning in your View architecture because you will have components of the virtual desktop environments configured on local SSDs, as shown in Figure 2.1.

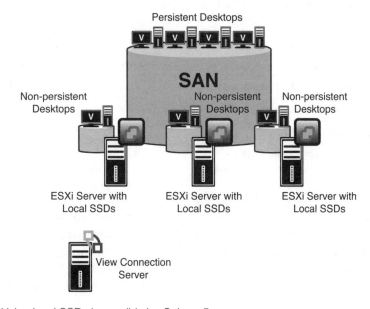

Figure 2.1 Using local SSDs is possible in vSphere 5.

You would use local SSD drives for stateless or nonpersistent desktops and fan out the number of desktops to reduce the overall risk in a production deployment. Persistent desktops (stateful) and any critical components would reside on the SAN, and the local SSDs would be used for low-storage high-I/O desktops like those provided through View Composer. This design, while possible, is not all that common because most SAN solutions now incorporate SSDs. The trade-off, however, is that at a certain scale one is likely to be more cost effective than the other.

Even with the best underlying measurements, you should always factor in the usage type of users consuming the virtual desktop environment. Generally speaking, usage type falls into three broad categories: low-, medium-, and high-end users. The point in planning for these broad categories of users is to make allowances in the hardware specifications. For example, say that from your PoC environment, you identify that most virtual desktop sessions are using about 2 GB of memory and a single vCPU with a 30 GB OS image. Rather than plan on the average, you should adjust the average with the usage types mentioned.

Taking an example, say that the production environment will service 500 desktops. As the IT architect for the company, you know that a large percentage of these desktops will go to engineers and designers, so out of the 500 seats you expect that 40% of those will be high-end users. The next largest portion of users has an average usage requirement and makes up another 40% of the population. The remaining 20% are extremely light users of the system. Your expected high-end desktop requirement is 2 vCPUs and 6 GB of memory, and your low-end user requirement is 1 GB and 1 vCPU. If you break this out, the planning starts to look like Table 2.1.

Table 2.1 User Segmentation

User Type	Seats	Percentage
High-end users (engineers and designers)	200	40%
Average users (day-to-day usage)	200	40%
Light users (light clerical work)	100	20%
Total number of seats on VMware view	500	

You can use the usage types to further refine your design to ensure your hardware estimates are accurate. You can then take the information gathered through either the capacity planning analysis or PoC and adjust it to factor in these usage types. This step is necessary because both capacity planning and PoC environments tend to provide a snapshot of usage versus actual. It is very difficult to ensure that you have captured data that represents exactly what you will see in production. There is really no single tool to do this, so you must combine what you know about the environment and your metrics to develop your hardware requirements. You can automate a good portion of this process by using tools such as the ones available from www.liquidwarelabs.com and www.lakesidesoftware.com.

If you are engaging a desktop replacement strategy where you must be able to justify the costs versus risks versus benefits, you might need to oversubscribe resources in your design. Justifying your design based on the cost per desktop and return on investment is a typical activity when you build a business case for VDI. With the focus on austerity and general move to reduce overall costs, it is important that you be able to speak to the cost per desktop. To get a better price point, you may run the environment at a higher rate of utilization to get a better price/VM or View desktop. For example, if you develop a conservative specification of 50% utilization, the hardware required to scale the environment may be cost prohibitive. You might need to oversubscribe the underlying physical resources to ensure the solution is both scalable and cost effective.

When you build scaled-out VDI environments, it is important to develop your specifications in blocks or logical groupings of servers, storage, and software. For example, you should know if you are scaling your solution to 10,000 desktops that a block of 5000 desktops requires 50 servers (an average of 100 desktops per server), 14 TB of storage (more on driving down storage requirements in Chapter 5, "Building Your Virtual Desktop"), and 100 licenses of vSphere Enterprise. The reason for this is it makes your solution much easier to grow if you design your solution to scale in building blocks that equal a certain number of virtual desktops with a fixed amount of resources. In this way, your capital costs can remain consistent during your desktop replacement strategy.

VMware vSphere 5 Architecture

In this chapter we discuss some fundamental design considerations, and then go through the setup of the VMware vSphere 5 environment in Chapter 3, "VMware View 5 Implementation." Because the architecting and deploying VMware vSphere 5 can be and are the subject of entire books, this discussion is not meant to be a comprehensive approach to the subject. It is designed to give you enough information to set up the environment properly and to consider which features of the VMware vSphere platform you should take advantage of in your VMware View design.

VMware View 5 is supported on virtual infrastructure 4 SP 2 and up. vSphere 5 has been designed to enhance the VMware View platform by adding additional capabilities tuned for Virtual Desktop Infrastructure. For example, VMware vSphere 5 supports solid-state drives, which enables you to offload storage I/O as part of your VMware View design. Indeed, one of the keys to a successful and scalable virtual desktop design is to understand the benefits of caching certain components of the architecture and what technology is available to do so. Using SSD drives in ESXi is a good example of taking advantage of the capability to cache to deliver good performance. If you are looking to integrate local SSD drives, you should check the compatibility matrix to ensure the hardware is supported (http://www.vmware.com/resources/compatibility/search.php?deviceCategory=vdm).

In addition, vSphere 5 introduced support for 3D graphics provided through the CPU or a supported 3D graphics cards installed in the vSphere 5 host. In this book we review how to set up a vSphere 5 environment. If you want to deploy it on an older version of VMware vSphere, refer to the installation documentation provided by VMware.

VMware vSphere 5

To deploy View, you first need to deploy your vSphere infrastructure. When you are planning the deployment, you should consider the technology that has been designed into the platform to aid in installation and configuration. As an example, say you are deploying a large VDI environment that will consist of 30–40 ESXi hosts. Your strategy may be to deploy vCenter, deploy one ESXi host as a configuration template, and then use a combination of Auto Deploy and host profiles to ensure the environment is built to proper specification. We review this technology and the installation in Chapter 3.

Planning a vSphere infrastructure starts with understanding the basic building blocks and key considerations. Virtual infrastructure involves the components described in the following sections.

VMware ESXi

With vSphere 5, VMware has moved completely to ESXi. ESXi has replaced the ESX native installation and comes in two installation options: embedded or installable mode. ESXi is a stripped-down version that removes many of the components included in the Console OS to provide a more purpose-driven and secure hypervisor platform. The original Console OS has been replaced with the direct console user interface (DCUI) , which reduces the configuration required at the console to eliminate much of the software that was provided with ESX native. You would think that this would reduce the number of features available on ESXi versus ESX native. ESXi and ESX native have feature parity, and as of vSphere 5, there is no longer an ESX native option.

ESXi is an operating system, and like all operating systems, it has a hardware compatibility list. Although the number of devices has increased dramatically as virtualization has become mainstream, it still is a good idea to verify that any hardware you will purchase for the environment is supported by VMware.

In deploying vSphere, you need to consider SAN, networking, and physical server requirements. It is a best practice to separate out the different layers of traffic that make up a virtual environment. At a base level, you have management, VMotion, and virtual machine traffic. In addition to these common traffic types, you also have VMware FT and storage VMotion, or sVMotion as it is sometimes called. In addition to segregation requirements, you also need to ensure that every network path is fully redundant within your vSphere platform.

You should follow some general guidelines for sizing virtual desktops on today's enterprise servers. For a truly redundant and low-risk environment, you could load all the ESXi servers at 50% utilization of CPU and memory. This is a judgment call, however, because architecting at 50% utilization is expensive and, it could be argued, somewhat overkill. To use a simple example, if you have a two-node cluster and you expect to run 100 virtual desktops, you would run 50 desktops on each in an active–active configuration. If you lose a host, you could run with no performance impact while replacing the failed server. This capability makes the architecture both resilient and low risk.

You also need to consider the level of VMware high availability (HA) that is required in your virtual desktop environment. As you consolidate the desktops onto a virtual environment, the underlying virtual infrastructure should be more fault tolerant. This does not necessarily mean that you need to consider the desktop highly available. For example, in a physical world you often treat desktops as disposable, so you essentially redirect critical data to file servers and don't typically back them up. In a virtual environment, you can apply the same concept using a better set of tools, such as Persona Manager. The supporting infrastructure or vSphere environment should be highly available and more fault tolerant because as the environment scales, the criticality of the service increases.

vCenter Server

vCenter Server is the management server for vSphere 5. It is the one-stop shop for managing everything in your virtual infrastructure. It runs on a Windows Server and requires a database for storing critical data. With vSphere 5, the vCenter Server is now a 64-bit application requiring Windows 2008 R2. You do have an option of deploying a vCenter Linux-based appliance as an option, but that appliance is generally considered ideal for smaller environments. As vCenter Server becomes increasingly more important as you start to scale out your Virtual Desktop Infrastructure, it is important to plan for this service to be highly available.

The deployment of vCenter Server enables some key features such as vMotion and storage vMotion. vMotion does not require you to move the files associated with the virtual machine, whereas sVMotion does. These files include the configuration, logs, swap, snapshots, and the virtual machine disks, which are commonly referred to as the virtual machine's home files. Logically, vMotion moves the running state of the VM, but not the associated virtual hard drive, as shown in Figure 2.2.

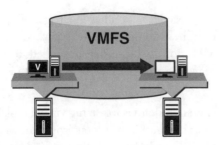

Figure 2.2 vMotion copies the running state.

VMotion copies the running state of the virtual machine from one ESXi host to another but does not copy the home files. VMotion has a start and a ending to the migration, or copy activity. This is in contrast to VMware FT, which uses the same mechanisms but keeps the copy running continuously to provide a mirrored copy that can be available in the event that the original source becomes unavailable.

Storage VMotion can "hot migrate" a running virtual machine between two different ESXi hosts and across different datastores. This capability is different from that of vMotion because vMotion enables a virtual machine to hot migrate from one ESXi host to another within the same VMFS, as shown logically in Figure 2.3.

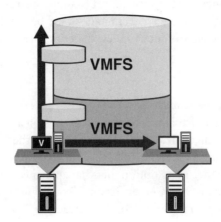

Figure 2.3 Storage vMotion.

Storage VMotion copies both the running state and the virtual machine's home files from one VMFS to another.

It is important that you understand these fundamental technologies within vSphere 5 so that you can use them to build a better VMware View design. VMotion and sVMotion have enhancements that enable you to automate and take advantage of both. VMotion can be automated through Distributed Resource Scheduler (DRS). DRS allows you to throttle the level of automatic VMotion within a virtual cluster from manual to full automation.

In a virtual desktop environment, DRS allows you to level the load across all the hosts so that utilization is evenly distributed. Consider the uneven workload distribution shown in Figure 2.4.

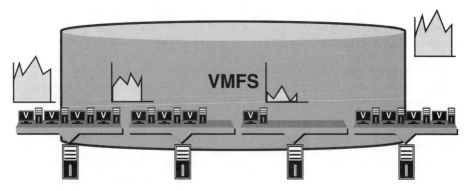

Figure 2.4 Uneven workload distribution.

In this figure, four ESXi virtual servers are running VMware View. Without DRS, however, the virtual desktops are not evenly distributed across the host servers, leading to very uneven utilization of resources across the virtual cluster. One host may be running at 70%–80% utilization, whereas another may be running at 10%–20%. This difference translates to very inconsistent performance across the virtual desktop environment. When you design the vSphere platform with DRS, you get an environment with even distribution. Look at the effect in the logical picture shown in Figure 2.5.

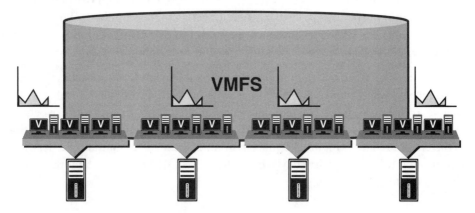

Figure 2.5 DRS ensures even distribution.

sVMotion enables you to do the same with storage utilization. vSphere 5 provides a feature called storage DRS that looks at disk reads and writes or storage input and output and will copy running virtual desktops to the appropriate storage tier by making use of sVMotion. In addition to storage DRS from VMware, your storage vendor might include dynamic tiering capabilities. Dynamic tiering is the capability of the storage system to move in demand data from slower disks to faster disks. Each storage vendor has a slightly different acronym to describe the feature, but in general, you should find out the level of automation, how quickly data is moved, how granular the blocks are in which the data is moved, and whether other storage systems are supported.

These technologies are designed to reduce storage hotspots. Storage hotspots are parts of the storage system characterized by high activity, causing long wait times for I/O requests and leading to long waits for data. These hotspots can lead to latency for storage requests that would slow down the performance of your virtual desktops.

One of the technical challenges for scaling VDI has been the demand on storage I/O. Storage DRS allows you to take advantage of storage tiering. Storage tiering allows you to put the most needed data on the fastest (most expensive) storage disks and data that is not in demand on the slower (cheaper) storage disks. Storage tiering is key in a virtual desktop environment because of the many types of data used to build out a desktop environment. For example, you have user profile information, Windows OS data, application data, and also different types of end users with different usage patterns.

Within one organization, you may have developers who are quite demanding of desktop resources and others who are not. Storage DRS is built on the Storage I/O Controller (SIOC), which monitors for latency at the datastore level. The Storage I/O Controller "controls" access to I/O on the datastore using a series of I/O queues and the number of assigned shares to a virtual machine. If latency is detected, the controller assigns a smaller number of I/O queue slots to virtual machines with a lower number of shares and a higher number of queue slots to virtual machines with a higher number of shares. This assignment is done at a volume level versus a host level so that prioritization is done across all hosts and virtual machines versus within a host and its running virtual machines.

Storage DRS has the capability to move running virtual machines to datastores that are experiencing lower or no latency to ensure consistent I/O is provided. From a VDI perspective, this feature allows you to combine faster storage drives (and more expensive) and slower storage drives (and less expensive) and have storage DRS level I/O utilization across the environment. In Figure 2.6, the environment is made up of multiple tiers with sVMotion and DRS moving Virtual Machine Disks (VMDKs) to ensure a more even distribution of utilization.

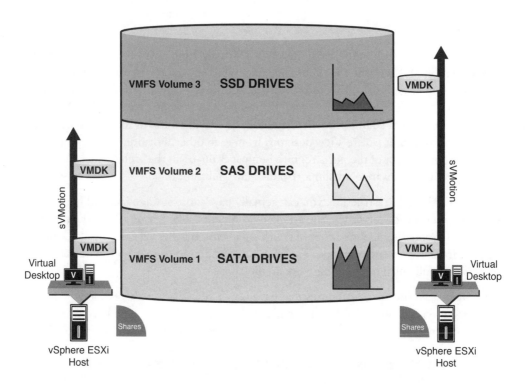

Figure 2.6 Storage DRS.

Host profiles are designed to ensure the configuration of ESXi hosts is consistent across a collection of ESXi hosts or a group of ESXi hosts in a virtual cluster. The availability of this technology in vCenter should influence how you deploy the environment. Perhaps your strategy may be to use host profiles and Auto Deploy and to run your vCenter as a virtual machine. vCenter should be running on a different cluster than the one it is managing to ensure availability if you are considering Auto Deploy.

To ensure availability, you should deploy two ESXi servers for redundancy, then deploy the vCenter VM, and finally deploy the remaining physical host servers using Auto Deploy with host profiles in a separate cluster. Auto Deploy allows you to customize the ESXi installable image and then deploy it consistently across all ESXi hosts. It is important that you configure your design and architecture and understand what features you will use and why. It is also important to consider a method of deployment that reduces the time and complexity it takes to get things up and running. Depending on how big the environment is, getting things running could take a considerable amount of time and effort.

Network

Various types of network traffic are required in a virtualization environment. The nature and segregation of this traffic should be fundamental to any good virtualization design. You can aggregate and logically separate network traffic in many different ways. Here, we delve into a few options and the reasoning behind each to provide guidance. In addition, you have the option of adding vShield technology as a layer on top of the virtual desktop environment to further isolate View desktops from each other. For firewall planning, you can find a complete list of the ports required on pages 66–67 in the architecture planning guide (http://www.vmware.com/support/pubs/view_pubs.html).

In Virtual Desktop Infrastructure, you can actually have more storage I/O and network I/O requirements than server virtualization environments. The reason is that the number of read/write requests and amount of network data being transferred can be greater than that of a virtual server environment. Therefore, in addition to storage considerations, you also must carefully plan out your network architecture.

Before we discuss the new capabilities that have been added with vSphere 5, let's go through a typical network setup. In configuring your ESXi server, you have two connection types, virtual machine and VMKernel connections, as shown in Figure 2.7.

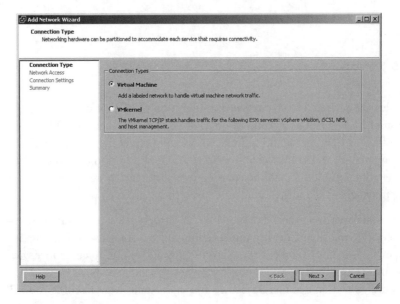

Figure 2.7 Connection Type.

Virtual machine connections facilitate traffic to and from the virtual machines on the ESXi host. VMkernel handles traffic to and from the host hypervisor or ESXi host. VMkernel traffic may include vMotion, storage (iSCSI and NFS), and connections to the DCUI. All ports are connected to a logical switch or vSwitch. A vSwitch is a piece of software that runs on the ESXi hosts that allows you to aggregate virtual machines to map them to a physical network interface. You can configure the number of ports and the maximum transfer units (MTUs), as shown in Figure 2.8. MTUs are adjusted for support of, for example, jumbo frames in iSCSI networks.

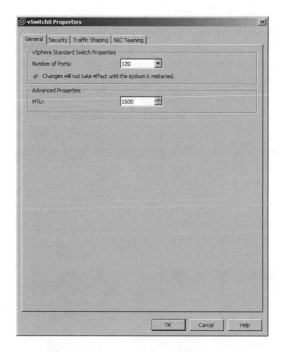

Figure 2.8 vSwitch Properties.

The 1500 MTUs in Figure 2.8 refer to the size of the payload in bytes carried by the Ethernet frame or Ethernet packet. Generally, a setting of 1500 bytes is appropriate for most traffic except if your network infrastructure supports jumbo frames. A jumbo frame increases the size of the payload. A jumbo frame is a packet that carries a greater number of bytes, increasing the payload of the packet. Because vSwitches are typically mapped to physical network cards, you need dedicated vSwitches mapped to physical network cards to be able to change the MTU to support jumbo frames. The recommended MTU for jumbo frames is 9000 bytes or MTUs.

To properly configure support for jumbo frames, you must ensure the max Ethernet frame size is consistent across everything the packet will traverse. If it is not, the packet is broken into fragments and sent piece by piece. This means to take advantage of jumbo frames, every device along the path must have the MTU adjusted.

The MTU must be configurable on the storage device's network card, the physical switch, and either the NIC card within the ESXi host or the iSCSI software initiator on the ESXi host. When you are planning to use iSCSI with your VDI environment, it is best practice to isolate all traffic on a separate VLAN segment. Often this segment is a flat layer two network, which is restricted to just iSCSI initiators and targets.

It is possible to segregate traffic physically or logically. Let's look at a real-world example to better illustrate this scenario. You have four types of traffic that you are going to ensure have adequate throughput and are fully redundant. They include the management console or DCUI, vMotion traffic, iSCSI storage area traffic, and virtual desktop traffic. In this case, you need eight physical network cards and four virtual switches. You can configure the DCUI for active-passive for redundancy and the vMotion, storage, and virtual desktop traffic to make use of both network cards. You need to review whether the storage vendor supports jumbo frames because you may need to customize the MTU or payload size on the VMkernel port to 9000 bytes and also the virtual switch. The benefit to this design is you have dedicated physical paths or NICs to separate out the traffic. The drawback to this design is you have a requirement for eight physical network adapters. This configuration may be problematic if you were looking to use small form factor, older blade servers. Newer blades tend to use converged network adapters (CNAs) and software to enable additional network paths and throughput. It is a standard to segment traffic by vSwitch and physical NICs, as depicted in Figure 2.9.

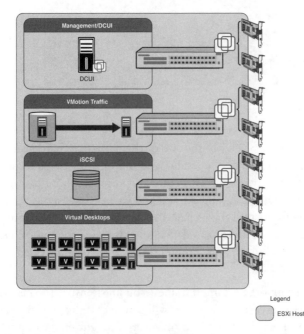

Figure 2.9 A typical vSwitch to physical NIC topology.

This method is not the only one, however, because you can do it logically with port groups to reduce the number of physical NICs required. Another way of achieving the same design principle of segregating the network traffic is through logical segregation of the traffic types using layer 2 technology or VLAN tagging. ESXi fully supports the capability to tag packets to enable the underlying network software to create different LAN segments or virtual LAN (VLAN) segments across the same physical path. VLAN tagging requires configuration on both the network hardware and the ESXi servers.

Let's look at how this configuration differs logically. In this case, you aggregate all the physical NICs so that they are connected to the same vSwitch. You then use VLAN IDs to create four virtual LAN segments to segregate all the traffic. In addition, you could add additional levels of redundancy by using port groups. Port groups are similar to VLANs, but you can assign specific NICs to the logical group and set active–active or active–passive network card configurations. Although aggregation is less common on GB networks, it is becoming increasingly prevalent on 10 GB networks. Be aware that 10 GB also further reduces the number of physical NICs required. Logically separated, the configuration looks like the one shown in Figure 2.10.

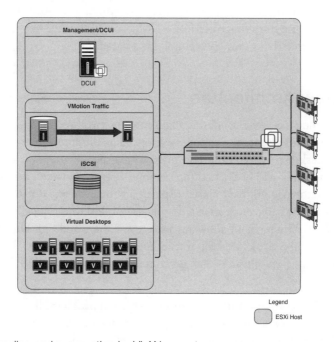

Figure 2.10 Bonding and segregating by VLAN or port group.

The benefit to using both VLANs and port groups is that you can use a smaller number of NICs but still have the same logical segregation of network traffic. The only risk is that one type of network traffic uses more bandwidth than it should, but you can use traffic shaping and network I/O control to prioritize traffic so that the virtual desktop traffic always receives priority, for example. We go through a sample configuration after the installation of ESXi.

It is therefore more important to estimate the network requirements properly and configure the number of physical network cards to provide adequate throughput.

Storage

Although it is possible to build a virtual environment based on local storage, doing so is highly inefficient because many of the high availability features require shared storage. Local storage also does not scale well because it becomes increasingly difficult to move things around. This is not to say that you may not make use of local storage for floating or nonpersistent desktops. We discussed some interesting scenarios making use of local storage and SSD drives in the introduction.

VMware supports Fiber Channel, iSCSI, and NAS storage solutions. Although there used to be recommendations based around performance for running one over the other, this is less of a concern because the storage platforms have evolved to drive better performance no matter what the underlying storage technology is based on.

VMware View Architecture

In general terms, the type of virtual desktop falls into the two broad categories of persistent versus nonpersistent, or floating, desktops. The difference between the two is that persistent desktops are typically associated with a specific user and also allow the data or writes committed within the desktop session to persist between desktop reboots. Nonpersistent desktops do not have a user associated with a specific desktop and do not allow the data to persist between reboots. Nonpersistent desktops typically provide a greater return on investment; they allow any user to use them and typically ensure good performance because the virtual desktop is reset to a clean, pristine state. This refreshing of the image cleans up a lot of things that get cluttered in a Windows OS that generally slow it down over time.

Nonpersistent desktops are not without their own share of problems because they can consolidate storage I/O on a SAN, impacting performance in general, if not properly designed. In addition, nonpersistent desktops require all data that is unique to the user consuming the desktop to be redirected elsewhere to ensure that the nonpersistence does not impose hardship to the user. For example, if you log in to your desktop and configure your Office suite software with particular settings and then log off, you probably don't want to go through the same effort every time you log in.

In VMware View, the Connection broker is referred to as the Connection Server. To ensure that the number of virtual desktops deployed can be increased, VMware View supports multiple Connection Servers.

When you introduce a second or third Connection Server, it is important that the configuration information is visible to all. This means that the metadata has to go into either a database or meta store that is inherently scalable. Unlike most VDI products, VMware View stores information in a lightweight mirror of the Windows Active Directory: Lightweight Directory Service (LDS). It was originally introduced by Microsoft as Active Directory Application Mode (ADAM) but is currently referred to as AD LDS. Rather than extend the Active Directory to incorporate application information, AD LDS can store application-specific information that does not need to be replicated to every domain controller in the Active Directory tree. VMware View uses AD LDS to ensure that multiple connection brokers have access to the same metadata. This capability is unique because many other vendors have chosen traditional databases to store this information.

Load Balancing

In addition to ensuring that the Connection Servers have access to the metadata, you also need to ensure that the Connection Servers are highly available. Assuming they are VMs, you can do this a number of ways using the capabilities of the vSphere platform. Let's look at each of these items and then discuss why you need load balancing.

Within vSphere, you have built-in capabilities to ensure a VM is highly available. The first is turning on vSphere HA. vSphere HA is supported in all versions of vSphere (Standard, Enterprise, and Enterprise Plus; http://www.vmware.com/products/vsphere/buy/editions_comparison.html). HA protects against host failure. When a host fails, the VM is restarted on another host, as shown in Figure 2.11.

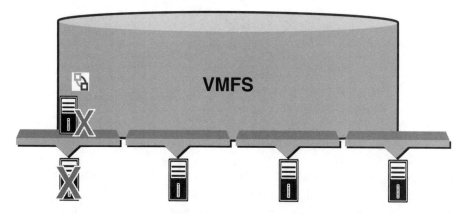

Figure 2.11 vSphere HA.

vSphere HA is typically enabled at the ESXi level and can be enabled at the VM level. In the event that either the ESXi host or the VM fails, it restarts on another host. This causes a service interruption, which may be fine for smaller environments but is problematic in large environments. The other option is to run VMware FT. VMware FT is available in Enterprise and Enterprise Plus license editions (http://www.vmware.com/products/vsphere/buy/editions_comparison.html). VMware FT essentially runs a constant VMotion between a source and target VM so that in the event of a problem, the service is immediately recovered on the target VM. Although this takes care of the service interruption, the limitation of VMware FT (single vCPU) prevents the solution from scaling. Future releases will support four vCPUs, but load balancing of your View Connection Servers is important for two reasons: availability and maintenance.

A load balancer essentially creates a single virtual IP masking the two Connection Servers' IP addresses. It is the virtual IP that is registered in the DNS to represent the service to the client devices. Most load balancers also monitor the availability of the IP address and service it is masking. With load balancing, you can not only provide availability but can also manage maintenance. Logically, there is one Virtual IP (VIP) that represents any number of View Connection Servers, as shown in Figure 2.12.

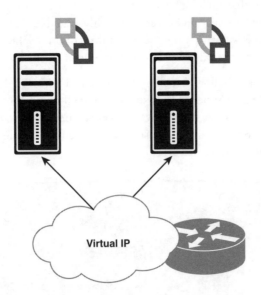

Figure 2.12 Load balancing and View Connection Servers.

For example, if you need to patch the underlying Windows operating system, you could use the load balancer to redirect all the sessions to a single Connection Server while you patch the server. You could then fail sessions over to the patched server to allow a maintenance or rolling maintenance window. Having a true load-balancing solution allows the architecture to scale as you can bring additional Connection Servers into the environment with little impact to the availability of the service. If you have also designed your architecture across sites and your load-balancing solution provides global load balancing, you can also bring in multiple sites. Logically, load balancers would be deployed in each site to allow even distribution of sessions within a site or across sites, as depicted in Figure 2.13.

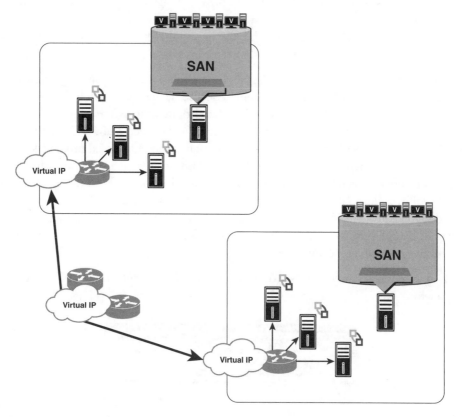

Figure 2.13 Load balancing across sites.

Active Directory

VMware View is a solution designed for Windows desktops; therefore, it is important to consider the layout of your Active Directory organizational units (OUs) before installing the pieces. Typically, you create an Active Directory OU for either administration or delegation. Administration includes policy control. One of the unique characteristics of a virtual desktop environment is that you want to do as much performance tuning as possible.

The performance tuning for virtual desktops is different from the tuning you do to a physical desktop, so you need to break out the virtual desktops in their own OU. In addition, you may have desktops that allow user interaction and others designed for kiosk use, so you may have a requirement to have an OU for typical virtual desktop configuration and ones that have hardened security policies designed to limit the interaction allowed on the desktop. The other requirement for OUs is based on bandwidth requirements. This requirement allows you to provide finer tuning to allow you to push the virtual desktop session further while still providing a good experience, such as when dealing with certain WAN conditions. The tuning or policies applied in this scenario differ from the ones applied to virtual desktops for internal use.

You need Active Directory groups for the administration of the environment and for users who will use the VMware View environment. You also need a dedicated user account or "service" account to connect the VMware View environment to vCenter. A service account is a regular AD account used to facilitate the interaction between View and vCenter. If the vCenter also runs View Composer, the service account needs additional privileges within the vCenter environment and needs to be a local administrator on a server on which vCenter is running. If you also intend to deploy virtual desktops in local mode, the service account requires additional levels of permission. You would think that VMware would have a designated role in vCenter to make it easy to create a service account and add it to a role with the right permissions. You can, however, use the following process to create the role with the appropriate permissions:

1. Log in to the vCenter, browse to Administration Roles, and clone the Virtual Machine Power User, as shown in Figure 2.14.

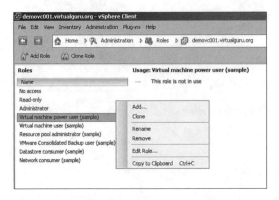

Figure 2.14 Creating a customized role.

2. Create a Group called VMware View Service User (see Figure 2.15).

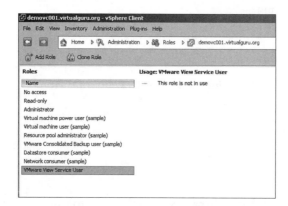

Figure 2.15 Role-based access.

3. Under Datastore, select the following, as shown in Figure 2.16:
  - Allocate Space
  - Browse Datastore
  - Low Level File Operations

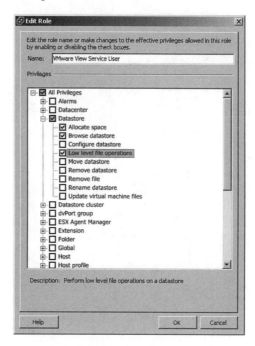

Figure 2.16 Edit Role.

4. Under Virtual Machine, select the following (see Figure 2.17):

- Configuration
- Inventory
- State

Under Virtual Machine\Interaction, select the following:

- Power Off
- Power On
- Reset
- Suspend

Under Virtual Machine\Provisioning, select the following:

- Allow Disk Access
- Clone Virtual Machine
- Customize
- Deploy Template
- Read Customization Specifications

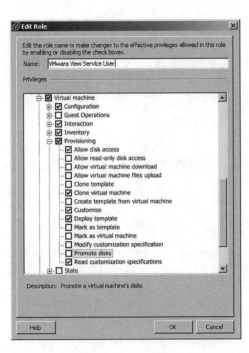

Figure 2.17 Selections under Virtual Machine.

5. Under Resource, select Assign Virtual Machine to Resource Pool, as shown in Figure 2.18.

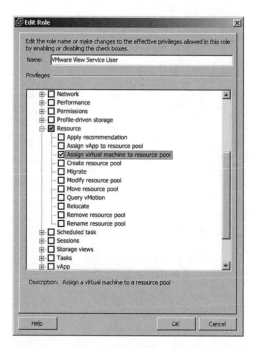

Figure 2.18 Assign Virtual Machine to Resource Pool.

6. Under Folder, select the following (see Figure 2.19):
   - Create Folder
   - Delete Folder

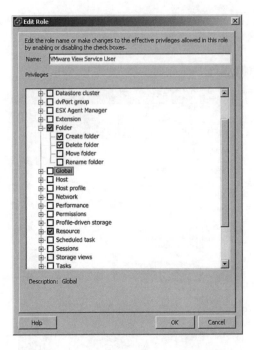

Figure 2.19 Selections under Folder.

7. Under Global, select the following (see Figure 2.20):

    ■ Cancel Task

    ■ Disable Methods

    ■ Enable Methods

    ■ Set Custom Attribute

    ■ System Tag

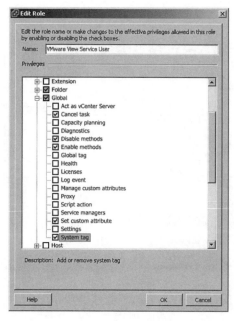

Figure 2.20 Selections under Global.

8. Under Host\Configuration, select System Management, as shown in Figure 2.21.

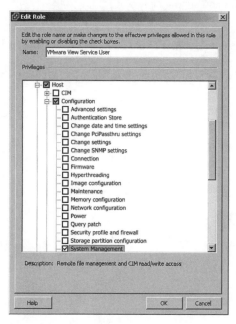

Figure 2.21 System Management.

9. Select all the options under Network, as shown in Figure 2.22.

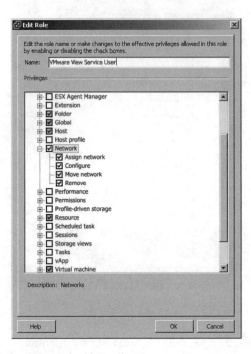

Figure 2.22 Select all the options under Network.

10. Under Resource, select Assign Virtual Machine to Resource Pool (see Figure 2.23).

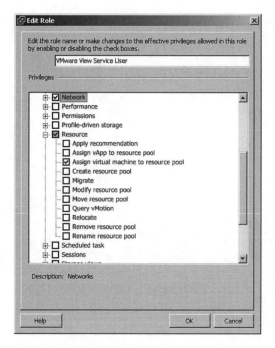

Figure 2.23 Assign Virtual Machine to Resource Pool.

After you have created the role, simply add your service account to the role by completing the following steps:

1. Within vCenter under Inventory and Hosts and Cluster, select the datacenter you want to use for your virtual desktop deployment.

2. Select the Permission tab on the right. Right-click on the pane and select Add Permission.

3. On the left, add the service users, and on the right, select the drop-down to add the user to the VMware View Service User role you just created.

4. Add the user to the newly created role at the datacenter or virtual cluster level.

   Your new role should appear under Users and Groups in the left pane, as depicted in Figure 2.24.

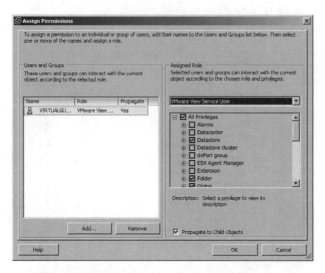

Figure 2.24 Add your newly created role.

PCoIP

PC over IP (PCoIP) is the principal display protocol for VMware View environments. The traffic is made up of TCP control plane traffic and User Datagram Protocol (UDP)–based data or user traffic. As of VMware View 4.6, PCoIP uses port 4172 for TCP and UDP traffic. PCoIP has reserved port numbers with the Internet Assigned Numbers Authority (IANA). A complete list of port requirements can be found on VMware's site at http://kb.vmware.com/selfservice/microsites/search.do?language=en_US&cmd=displayKC &externalId=1027217.

PCoIP continually checks the network for available bandwidth and to determine roundtrip latency. In a LAN environment, the default settings are configured to provide the best end-user experience. If you are going to be providing virtual desktops for remote access, you should create a testing environment where you can simulate latency and bandwidth scenarios to ensure you can properly tweak PCoIP and the virtual machines, as we discuss in Chapter 8, "A Rich End-User Experience."

Much work has been done in VMware View 5 to allow you to optimize the traffic. In addition, many new capabilities were added. You can now proxy PCoIP through a View Security Server. Figure 2.25 depicts the traffic flows when deploying the View Security Server.

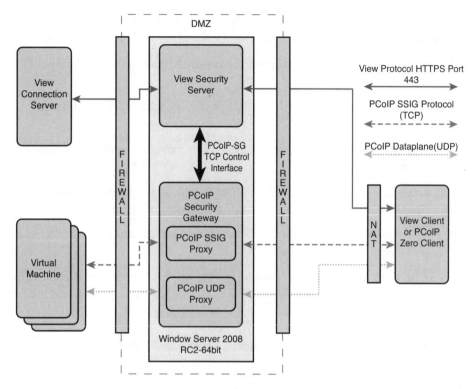

Figure 2.25 Traffic flow of the View Security Server.

Source: Myths, Truths, and Optimizations for the PCoIP Protocol, Teradici

You can add a PCoIP offload card or APEX 2800 to the ESXi host. By doing so, you can push some of the resource requirements to an accelerator card. The offload cards are designed to run up to 64 high-resolution screen sessions and allow you to increase the virtual desktop density by 30%–40%. Additional information on the APEX 2800 can be found at http://www.teradici.com/pcoip/pcoip-products/teradici-apex-2800.php.

According to Teradici's internal testing, PCoIP has been designed to run up to 250 ms of latency although the company has tested it beyond but generally finds the user experience degrades over this limit. Teradici offers a VDI university on its support site (http://techsupport.teradici.com/ics/support/default.asp?deptID=15164) that is a great reference. It goes through each possible tuning parameter in depth, but you need to sign up for a support account.

Prior to View 5, you could tweak a number of settings to adjust the protocol for WAN and latency. These settings are adjusted on the virtual desktop within the registry or using a GPO template on the OU of the virtual desktops.

- **Maximum Bandwidth**—This setting allows you to set the peak available bandwidth (BW) for each VM. The average bandwidth should fall well below this setting.

- **Bandwidth Floor**—When constrained, the bandwidth floor sets the minimum bandwidth PCoIP can drop to.

- **Maximum Initial Image Quality**—This option sets the initial BW when the PCoIP is rendering an image.

- **Minimum Image Quality**—This setting controls the minimum quality for video performance.

- **MTU size**—If you adjust the MTU, you also should adjust everything else along the path. See the Network section for additional information on jumbo frames.

- **PCoIP Encryption Setting**—This setting enables you to adjust the type of encryption to improve performance of the session.

- **Frame Rate Limit**—This setting is the most important adjustment that you can make. PCoIP is set to 30 frames per second (fps) out of the box. You can adjust this down to 10–15 fps and still get reasonable video performance.

Teradici provides the general reference guidelines shown in Table 2.2 to help you adjust these settings.

Table 2.2 PCoIP Adjustments

Maximum Frames per Second	Desktop Workload (Estimate)	Notes
60	PCoIP Host Card Default 3D CAD 3D video games	Extreme graphic
30	VMware View PCoIP Default HD video	
24	Film frame rate	
16	Better video	
10 to 12	Video	
8	Basic office desktop; no video required	Most users don't notice performance issues at 8 fps
4 to 6	Office administration, data entry	
2	Basic data entry	

As of VMware View 5, you can control a few additional settings; they are designed to improve the performance of PCoIP in certain scenarios. You can disable the build-to-lossless (BTL) capability of PCoIP. *Lossless* describes a class of data compression which essentially ensures that the exact original image is reconstructed. *Lossy* is a separate class that allows for some but not all the data to be reconstructed. As it relates to PCoIP, you can halt the rendering of the graphics at the lossy stage. Typically, when PCoIP renders an image, it goes from lossy to lossless as the graphic is constructed. Setting the display protocol to stop at lossy can save up to 30% of the total bandwidth consumption (see http://blogs.vmware.com/performance/2011/09/vmware-view-pcoip-build-to-lossless-.html).

You can configure these optimizations by importing the Group policy administrator template, which is installed when you install VMware View on the server. You can find it in the following location:

> <install_directory>\VMware\VMware View\Server\extras\GroupPolicyFiles\
> pcoip.adm

This template can be imported in the OU where the virtual desktops are installed or into the local policy of the virtual desktop. We look at the configuration in Chapter 3.

To avoid LAN congestion, you should implement quality of service (QoS) for your PCoIP traffic. Although QoS deals with prioritization when traffic is constrained, PCoIP should be prioritized on your network. Most organizations have only two classes of traffic on their network: VoIP and everything else. When designing your VMware View environment, you should treat PCoIP in a similar fashion to VoIP and prioritize it. You should prioritize both the TCP and UDP traffic on 4172.

QoS and PCoIP

One common problem is the default configuration for dealing with congestion when QoS is configured on Cisco routers. QoS allows you to configure a series of queues so that you can prioritize traffic. When congestion occurs, a router uses whatever congestion avoidance mechanism is configured. By default, an interface drops newly arrived packets when the queue is full, leading to data loss. This congestion avoidance mechanism is known as *tail drop* because essentially the tail end of the data stream is dropped to deal with congestion. UDP cannot tolerate a high degree of packet loss, and the default behavior may cause problems that are attributed to poor performance of the PCoIP protocol. The real problem is not PCoIP, but the default congestion avoidance mechanism and its effect on UDP traffic. The default should be changed to Cisco's Weighted Random Early Detection (WRED). WRED uses the IP precedence, which determines the importance or priority of the packet and randomly drops packets before the queue is full to maintain consistency. This allows WRED to differentiate between streams to be able to apply the random drops. To ensure good performance of UDP and in turn PCoIP, you should update the default congestion avoidance mechanism to WRED.

Desktop Pools

Within VMware View, virtual desktops are configured in *pools*. Pools are logical groups of virtual desktops that are configured in the VMware View Administrator Console and have certain configurations and settings applied to them. For example, you could have a pool of desktops configured to use the PCoIP protocol, to be autoprovisioned, or to be deployed in a certain OU in the active directory.

When planning a VMware View environment, you should predetermine what pools you need and what configurations are required within those pools. The critical component is whether the desktop is floating or persistent. Floating desktops tend to be stateless in nature and can take advantage of a View Composer to reduce the storage requirement to deploy them. Persistent desktops require the user to preserve data between desktop reboots.

You should also consider pool size if using View Composer. View Composer allows you to take advantage of linked clones. Because linked clones are essentially differential or snapshot files linked to a master or parent VM, you can make changes to the parent and propagate the files. If you update the parent VM with patches, for example, and want to push them to the associated linked clones, you can perform a *recompose*. This essentially re-creates the snapshot or differential disk to reflect the changes in the Parent VM. If you have created pools of more than 500 virtual desktops, recomposing can take substantially more time than if you had used pools of 50 virtual desktops, so be cautious when sizing your View desktop per pool.

Local Mode VMs

Local mode VMs are enabled through policy on the VMware View Server and are supported by Transfer Servers and View Clients running the local mode plug-in. Essentially, the local mode plug-in is similar to VMware Player, which allows you to run the virtual machine on the local client using desktop resources. View Client with local mode only works for Windows. The Transfer Server is essentially a large storage repository for the virtual desktop images so that the overhead of copying the VM does not have to run on the Connection Server and can run on a specific server. The Transfer Server runs on Windows Server 2003 or 2008. When the pieces are installed, users can check out a VM provided they have permissions to do so. You can halt transfers by putting the Transfer Server in maintenance mode.

Keep in mind that when using local mode you are running the virtual machine locally. This means that the local desktop should meet the Microsoft hardware specifications of the OS you have checked out. For example, you cannot check out a Windows 7 VM through local mode on a Pentium 233 MHz machine.

You also need to ensure that the local client has enough space to run the virtual desktop. Only the used space within the virtual desktop is transferred. For example, say your virtual desktop is 20 GB, but only 15 GB is being used. In this case, when you check out the desktop, only 15 GB are downloaded to the local client. It is important when planning space for local mode that you allow for the requirements of the local OS, the used space in the virtual machine, and any snapshots required for synchronizing or capturing any deltas in local mode.

Summary

A well-architected virtual desktop environment offers management, energy savings, and a higher level of security, and it delivers a good user experience. To ensure you can implement the solution properly, you need to understand what your bandwidth and storage requirements are going to be. You should also ensure that user profile information is properly delivered and centrally stored using View Persona. In addition, you should understand how to use application virtualization in your View environment. Because application virtualization is a big piece of View, we have dedicated Chapter 4 entirely to this topic.

Because a virtual desktop environment involves a multitude of technology, you should ensure you have a well-documented architecture and design document. Taking the time to complete this step will assist you greatly when you start talking to your storage and networking teams. The time spent in calculating your IO requirements from a network and storage perspective will ensure that each team understands what you need to deliver a View desktop to your end users and avoid problems down the road. Be cautious and ensure you have a complete picture and that anything you are unsure of is properly vetted so that you know how the deployment of VMware View will look in your environment.

Now that you understand the basic architecture of a VMware View environment, you are ready to look at implementation. In the next chapter, you look at what steps are required to install and configure the VMware View environment. When moving from architecture to implementation, ensure that you have also noted any additional training and transitioning that will be required to move from delivery to operations. The best technology solutions work because support and operation have been integral parts of the rollout of the solution. The same holds true when you are moving a large number of users from physical to virtual desktops. Although it is still desktop support, a number of capabilities will be new to the desktop support team and may change the way they provide support in some cases. Take, for example, the ability to refresh a desktop or application in a matter of minutes from View's Administrator Console. To take advantage of these capabilities, the desktop support team must also understand them.

Chapter 3

VMware View 5 Implementation

This chapter describes how to get the components of vSphere up and running. First, however, you need to install vCenter. Let's run through the installation of vCenter, starting from the configuration of the database.

Preparing a vCenter Installation

vCenter supports several different types of databases. The supported databases and versions are

- IBM DB2 Express, Workgroup, and Enterprise (versions 9.5–9.7.2, both 32- and 64-bit editions)

- Microsoft SQL Server 2008 Standard, Express, Enterprise, and Datacenter Editions (versions R2, SP1 and SP2, both 32- and 64-bit editions)

- Microsoft SQL Server 2005 Standard, Enterprise, and Datacenter Editions (versions running SP4, both 32- and 64-bit editions).

- Oracle 10g Standard, Standard ONE, and Enterprise Editions (versions 10.2.0.4, both 32- and 64-bit editions)

- Oracle 11g Standard, Enterprise Edition (Release 1 and 2, and versions 11.1.0.7.0 and 11.2.0.1)

VMware generally recommends that you use Microsoft SQL 2008 Express for smaller environments because it has a fixed limit on how large the database can grow. Although this limit used to be fixed at 4 GB, it is now fixed at 10 GB. VMware recommends that SQL Express be used in environments of no more than 5 hosts with 50 virtual machines.

The following steps assume you are deploying Microsoft SQL 2008 R2. vCenter 5 is a 64-bit operating system and so requires Windows 2008 R2. This section is by no means comprehensive, so you should check the content against your own internal SQL best practices. You can deploy vCenter as a VM or as a physical server or Linux virtual appliance.

Deploying vCenter as a VM used to be a heated topic, but doing so has now become common practice and is also a VMware best practice. What can be problematic is having vCenter as part of the environment it is managing or in the virtual cluster. This is why VMware recommends a separate management cluster in large environments. These problems can be mitigated by ensuring you have built redundancy into the vCenter Server configuration. VMware's best practice is to run Fault Tolerance (FT), which provides a constant mirrored copy of the virtual machine so that if the primary fails, the secondary takes over with no interruption. VMware refers to this technology as *virtual lockstep* or *vLockstep*. VMware FT does have some scaling limitations, however, which may not make it ideally suited for large environments. For example, VMware FT is limited to a single vCPU, so it does not support symmetric multiprocessing (SMP). Future releases will support up to four vCPUs. If you require a multiprocessor server or intend to deploy vCenter as a physical machine, vCenter Heartbeat is the recommended solution; it is discussed in Chapter 11, "High Availability Considerations." vCenter Heartbeat keeps two vCenter Servers in sync but provides more flexibility on the physical or virtual configuration of the server, such as the number of processors. If you mirror or cluster the SQL database, you do have a few other options for protecting the vCenter server:

- You can schedule physical-to-virtual (P2V) migrations of the vCenter server. You can schedule a P2V to create a virtual hot spare in the event you have a problem with the physical vCenter server.

- You can schedule a one-time P2V which is similar to the previous method only is not reoccurring. You can convert the vCenter after it is configured and leave it as a powered-off cold standby VM.

- You can run SQL database locally within the vCenter VM and use VM FT as mentioned.

VMware actually recommends using a standalone Microsoft SQL Server 2008 R2 cluster with redundant SAN and LAN connections in large scalable environments. The SQL cluster should have dedicated logical unit numbers (LUNs) based storage volumes on the SAN to offload the IO from the VMware cluster versus using datastore-based VMDKs. This option also ensures that the metadata is available outside the VMware cluster if you have a failure.

Although this chapter is not an extensive guide to vSphere 5 deployment, it is important that you configure your underlying installation properly. It also is important to ensure you have a production-grade deployment, which means proper configuration and backup.

To install vCenter, you need database services. In most cases, a separate database is recommended. For smaller environments, however, it is possible to use a copy of Microsoft SQL Server 2008 R2 Express. vCenter Server supports IBM DB2, Oracle, and Microsoft SQL Server databases. Be aware that Update Manager supports only Oracle and Microsoft SQL Server databases.

The minimum hardware requirements are as defined in Table 3.1.

Table 3.1 Minimum Hardware Requirements for Installing vCenter

Hardware	Requirement
Processor	Intel or AMD x86 processor with two or more logical cores, each with a speed of at least 2 GHz. The Intel Itanium (IA64) processor is not supported. Processor requirements might be higher if the database runs on the same machine.
Memory	4 GB RAM. RAM requirements may be higher if your database runs on the same machine. VMware VirtualCenter Management WebServices requires 512 Mb to 4.4 GB of additional memory. The maximum WebServices JVM memory can be specified during the installation depending on the inventory size.
Disk storage	4 GB. Disk requirements may be higher if the vCenter Server database runs on the same machine. In vCenter Server 5.0, the default size for vCenter Server logs is 450 MB, which is larger than in vCenter Server 4.x. Make sure the disk space allotted to the log folder is sufficient for this increase.
Microsoft SQL Server 2008 R2 Express disk requirements	Up to 2 GB free disk space to decompress the installation archive. Approximately 1.5 GB of these files are deleted after the installation is complete.
Networking	1 Gbit connection recommended.[1]

[1]Information based on VMware's vCenter best practice Knowledge Base article at http://kb.vmware.com/selfservice/microsites/search.do?language=en_US&cmd=displayKC&externalId=2003790

vCenter Server 5.0 is a 64-bit application, so it requires a 64-bit Windows operating system. The following platforms are supported for vCenter Server 5.0:

1. Microsoft Windows Server 2003 Standard, Enterprise, or Datacenter SP2 (required) 64-bit

2. Microsoft Windows Server 2003 Standard, Enterprise, or Datacenter R2 SP2 (required) 64-bit[2]

3. Microsoft Windows Server 2008 Standard, Enterprise, or Datacenter SP2 64-bit

4. Microsoft Windows Server 2008 Standard, Enterprise, or Datacenter R2 64-bit

Because Microsoft SQL Server is the most common platform selected, the following sample installation is based on vCenter Server 5.0 running on SQL Server. Before deploying your vCenter Server database instances, you should follow a few Microsoft SQL best practices. Microsoft recommends that you use separate accounts for all the SQL services. By default, the installer creates a virtual account, which is a local account on the server that a Windows user cannot use to log in to a Windows server. The default installation creates all services with a virtual account except for the SQL Server Browser, which is a local service account, and the SQL Server VSS Writer, which is a local system account. Unlike in prior releases of SQL in which you needed to assign permissions, now the setup takes care of assigning the appropriate permissions for you. However, you can still create the accounts manually, as shown in Figure 3.1. In most cases, the default accounts suffice; however, if you are deploying a cluster, the following need to be domain accounts:

- Database Engine Account

- SQL Server Agent

- The SQL Server Analysis Service account

Figure 3.1 shows the manual creation of specific service accounts.

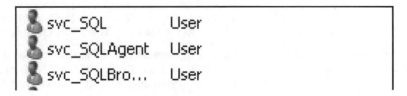

Figure 3.1 Manually creating SQL service accounts.

Although it is dated, Microsoft provides a guide called "Services and Service Accounts Security Planning Guide." This guide provides general best practices about securing

---

[2]To understand the impact of SP2, see http://technet.microsoft.com/en-us/windowserver/ bb286758.

service accounts and can be downloaded from http://technet.microsoft.com/en-us/library/cc170953.aspx.

In addition, you need to install the Microsoft .NET Framework. The installation detects if you have not done so and enables the feature for you. If you are installing VMware Update Manager and vCenter Server on the same 64-bit host, keep in mind that vCenter is a true 64-bit application and requires a 64-bit Data Source Name (DSN) file, and Update Manager is a 32-bit application that requires a 32-bit DSN. To create a 32-bit data source, you need to run the 32-bit version of the tool, which you can find at C:\Windows\SysWOW64\odbcad32.exe. To locate the 64-bit data source tool, go to the **Start** menu, **Administrative Tools**, and then click **Data Sources**.

Installing Microsoft SQL Server

Follow these steps to install Microsoft SQL Server:

1. Launch the installation. Click **OK** to have the SQL Server 2008 R2 setup enable the Microsoft .NET Framework, as shown in Figure 3.2.

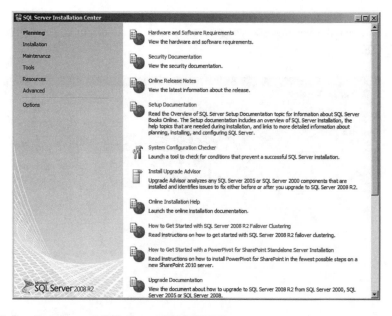

Figure 3.2 Run the Microsoft SQL Server 2008 R2 Setup.

2. Select **New Installation or Add Features to an Existing Installation,** as shown in Figure 3.3.

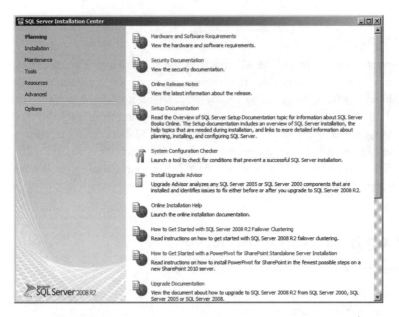

Figure 3.3 Select New Installation.

3. After the installer verifies that your server meets the requirements (see Figure 3.4), click **OK**.

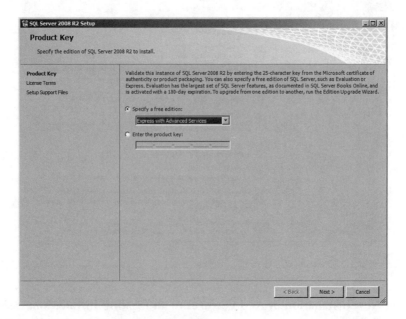

Figure 3.4 The Installer verifies the prerequisites.

4. Accept the licensing terms, as shown in Figure 3.5, and click **Next.** Click the check box if you want to help Microsoft further develop SQL by sending usage data. In most production environments, this option is not selected.

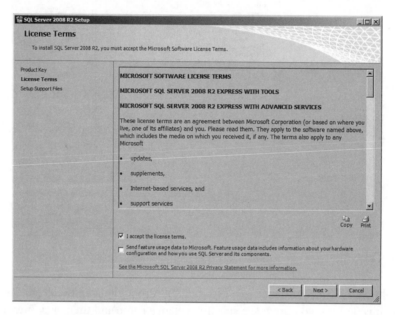

Figure 3.5 License terms.

5. Select the SQL features. The only features you need are the Database Engine Services and the Management Tools, as shown in Figure 3.6. After selecting the features, click **Next.**

   It is quite common to run into a deployment in which the SQL Server instance is already up and running, but the management tool has not been installed. Because the 2008 Management Tools are no longer available as a separate download, it is possible to use SQL Express Management Studio 2005. An even better solution is to have a ThinApp version of SQL Express Management Studio 2005 as part of your toolkit.

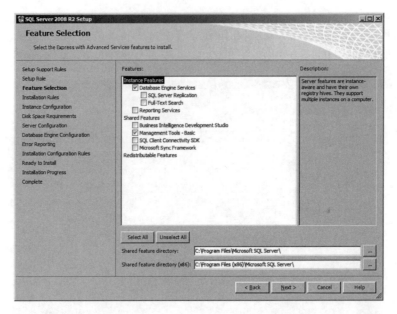

Figure 3.6 Select Database Engine Services and Management Tools.

6. Set the SQL named instance (see Figure 3.7). Although using the default instance is fine, it is better if you provide a specific instance name and then click **Next**.

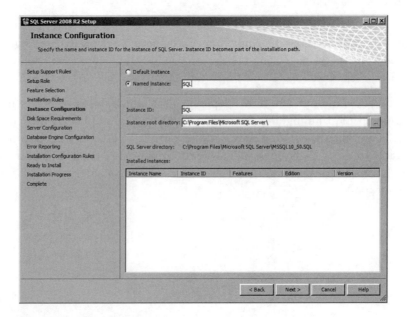

Figure 3.7 Name the SQL Instance.

7. Specify the SQL administrators (see Figure 3.8). After adding the appropriate SQL administrators, select **Data Directories**. Select **Mixed Mode** (SQL Server authentication and Windows authentication) if you intend to run all databases from one location. Although the vCenter database uses Windows authentication, the Event Database does not.

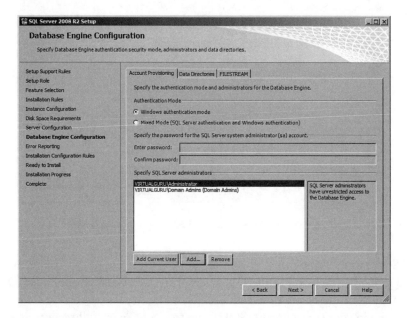

Figure 3.8 Select Mixed Mode.

8. Update the default locations for the databases and logs, as shown in Figure 3.9. Even if you are running the Windows Database Server as a VM, it is a good idea to separate the database and the logs on separate partitions. Separating the database and logs on separate partitions ensures that you can still manage the SQL Server in the event you run out of capacity on the volumes. If the SQL Server is virtual, you can separate different Virtual Machine Disks (VMDKs) on different storage tiers to more finely control IO.

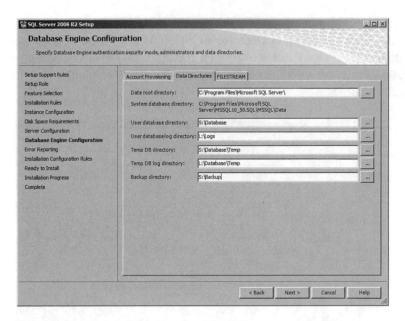

Figure 3.9 Separate the database logs from the OS partition.

After the SQL instance is installed, it is important to ensure your SQL databases are backed up properly. Microsoft SQL 2008 makes this process easy to configure. Of course, there are other third-party solutions that back up not only your database instances but also everything else in your environment. SQL supports a Simple or Full recovery model. A Simple recovery model does not back up the logs, so recovery is limited to the last backup. A Full recovery model includes the logs, so it allows you to recover the database to a certain point in time, assuming the log is not damaged.

For a VMware vCenter environment, you have a vCenter database, an Update Manager database (which is optional but highly recommended), and also with VMware View, a View Composer and Events database. We discuss View Composer more in Chapter 6, "View Operations and Management." Make sure that you create the database and also provide the permissions necessary for connecting to the SQL database. The account requires db_owner permissions to the vCenter and Update Manager database for the installation. In addition, the account requires temporary db_owner permissions to the MSDB System database for both vCenter and Update Manager. The purpose is to ensure the installation can create SQL Agent jobs for the vCenter statistic rollups, for example. The vCenter statistic rollup jobs allow vCenter to purge data it is collecting to populate the performance data within vCenter. The tables used to store this data are as follows:

- VPX_HIST_STAT1—Stores integral values at the lowest level of granularity (daily level)

- VPX_HIST_STAT2—Weekly Stats Rollup Job, which repeats every 30 minutes, performing rollups at a weekly level.

- VPX_HIST_STAT3—Monthly Stats Rollup Job, which repeats once every two hours, performing rollups at a monthly level

- VPX_HIST_STAT4—Yearly Stats Rollup Job, which repeats twice a day, performing rollups at a yearly level.

It is best to install vCenter and configure the VMware Update Manager before revoking the db_owner access to the System databases.

The default installation of SQL assigns a Simple recovery model. A Simple recovery model means that a point-in-time backup is the only one supported. Data added or changed between backups may be lost with a Simple recovery model. Changing the type to Full recovery allows you to restore data up to the point of recovery.

You can change the recovery model by selecting the properties of the database and, on the Options, changing the recovery model from Simple to Full, as shown in Figure 3.10.

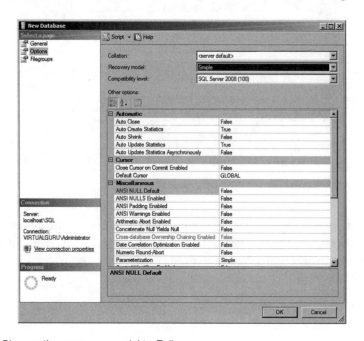

Figure 3.10 Change the recovery model to Full.

Let's step through the process required to create the database and assign the appropriate permissions; then we will review how to ensure the database is properly backed up.

Create each database by opening the Microsoft SQL Management Studio and taking the following steps:

1. Connect to the SQL database instance on the SQL Server.

2. Right-click the Database Module and select a new database.

   Ensure your database names are indicative of what they will be used for—that is, vCenter, VMware Update Manager (VUM), vComposer, and vEvents.

3. Expand the Security Module and add a new login.

The account should be the one that you created so that you can connect and perform the installation. In this case, we created a svc_SQL Account, as shown in Figure 3.11.

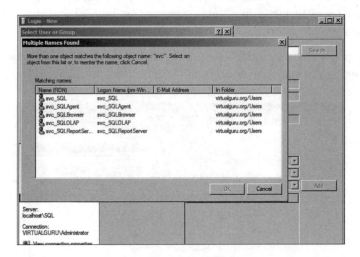

Figure 3.11 Choose the account that will be the db_owner.

Ensure the account is mapped to the appropriate database and has the db_owner permission. To ensure the SQL Agent jobs are created properly, db_owner permission is also required for the MSDB database. After the installation is complete, this permission should be revoked.

Figure 3.12 shows the three databases mapped to the db_owner role.

Figure 3.12 User mapping.

After you create the databases and have the appropriate permissions, you should schedule the database backups if an enterprise backup solution is not in place. Although most server virtualization environments do have enterprise backup solutions in place, due to the requirement of needing a second virtual server, this is not always the case in virtual desktop environments. It is recommended that you have a specific backup solution in place, but at a minimum, you should set up backups. In most cases, a dedicated SQL support team exists and has a defined backup process. The steps provided in this book are not meant to supersede established backup practices and policies, but instead serve as a reference in case an option is needed or if additional understanding is required on SQL backups.

When you are looking at a backup strategy for your vCenter and your virtual desktops, you should consider how valuable the data is, how much the data is changing, the overall size of the database, and how much the data is used. With vCenter, the database is a configuration database to store metadata. As your environment grows, however, the availability of the data and overall service becomes increasingly critical.

When using SQL Server 2008, you have three primary backup types: full, differential, and log backups.

Full Backup

A full backup copies all the information in the database. Full backups also include the transaction logs and any data that has not been written to the database. In a small virtualization environment, it is possible to run full backups for the vCenter database. When the environment grows beyond 20 ESXi hosts, the database can grow to 10–15 GB. In this case, a combination of full or differential backups might be necessary.

1. Open the SQL Server Management Studio and connect to the SQL Server instance.

2. Navigate to the Server\Databases folder.

3. Right-click the database you want to back up.

4. From the shortcut menu, select **Tasks, Backup**.

5. In the Database Backup dialog box, select the type of backup you want the server to perform, the backup destination path, and the backup options.

6. Click **OK** to back up the database or click the **Script** button if you want to generate a script to run the backup with the selected options.

You can also run backups from the SQL command line by performing the following:

1. Browse to c:\Program Files\Microsoft SQL Server\100\Tools\Binn.

2. Run SQLCMD. The 1> prompt tells you that you are connected to SQL Server instance 1.

3. Enter the backup command, as shown in Figure 3.13.

   The command to do a full backup is BACKUP DATABASE [Name of database] TO DISK = N'[PATH]'. In this example, we typed

```
BACKUP DATABASE vCenter TO DISK = N'S:\Backup\vCenter_12282011.bak'
```

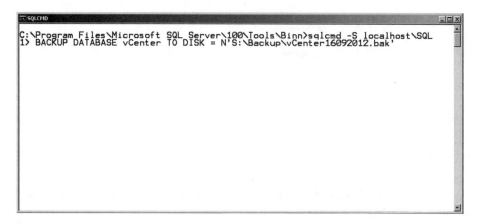

Figure 3.13 The BACKUP DATABASE command.

4. To execute the command, type **go** and press **Enter**. The backup should process successfully, as indicated in Figure 3.14.

```
SQLCMD                                                                    _ □ ×
C:\Program Files\Microsoft SQL Server\100\Tools\Binn>sqlcmd -S localhost\SQL
1> BACKUP DATABASE vCenter TO DISK = N'S:\Backup\vCenter16092012.bak'
2> go
Processed 184 pages for database 'vCenter', file 'vCenter' on file 1.
Processed 3 pages for database 'vCenter', file 'vCenter_log' on file 1.
BACKUP DATABASE successfully processed 187 pages in 0.310 seconds (4.711 MB/sec)
1>
```

Figure 3.14 A successful backup.

To set up reoccurring backups, you need to set up a maintenance plan under SQL and ensure that SQL Agent is started. If you are running a SQL Express Edition, you need to look at scheduling a SQLCMD command because maintenance plans are not available in the Express Edition.

After the SQL Agent starts, you can set the backups to happen according to a schedule. If you are not using a SQL Express Edition, you should see the Maintenance Plans module under Management, as shown in Figure 3.15.

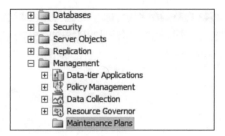

Figure 3.15 Maintenance Plans module.

Create a Back Up Database task and set it up according to a reoccurring schedule, as shown in Figure 3.16.

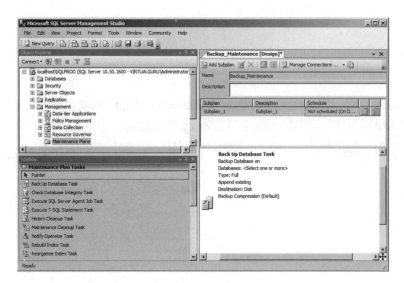

Figure 3.16 Set a reoccurring schedule.

If you are using SQL Express, you can use the following process to automate the SQLCMD Backup command. First, you need to create a SQL script using the command you ran from the command line:

```
BACKUP DATABASE vCenter TO DISK = N'S:\Backup\vCenter.bak'
```

The file extension does not matter, but in this case save the database with a .bak extension so that it is easy to identify. Now you need to create a scheduled task to initiate the SQLCMD command and execute the SQL script. You also need to create a local ID under which the scheduled task can run with suitable privileges including the logon as batch job privilege. You can add a policy through the Active Directory (AD) by separating out your vCenter Server in a separate OU. You should do this through Active Directory policy, but you can configure this locally by doing the following:

1. Navigate to Administrative Tools\Local Security Policy.

2. Expand the Security Settings\Local Policies\User Rights Assignment.

3. Add the account that will run the scheduled job to the Logon as Batch Job Properties and click **OK.**

When you are done, you can open the scheduler to create a basic task.

1. Open the scheduler on the SQL Express Server and create a basic task. Provide a descriptive name such as **vCenter Backup job** and a description of when the job occurs, as shown in Figure 3.17. Then click **Next.**

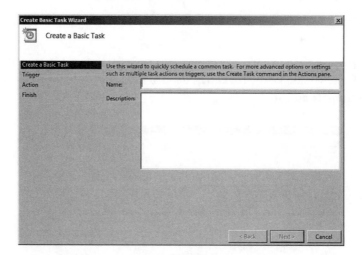

Figure 3.17 Create a Task.

2. Configure the trigger; in this case, set up the backup job to be triggered weekly (see Figure 3.18). Then click **Next.**

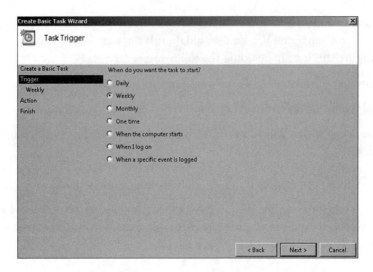

Figure 3.18 Configure a trigger (weekly).

3. Set the frequency you would like the backup to occur at (see Figure 3.19) and click **Next**. If you would like the backup to happen every two weeks, you can adjust the Recur setting from 1 to 2.

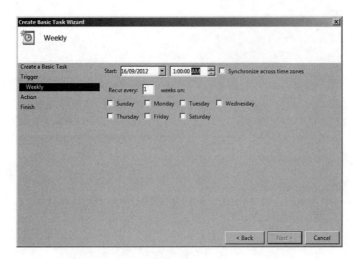

Figure 3.19 Determine the schedule and reoccurrence.

4. Set it to start the SQLCMD command with arguments. To do so, select **Start a Program** (see Figure 3.20). Then click **Next**.

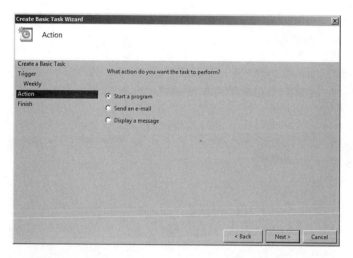

Figure 3.20 Select Start a Program.

5. Select the SQLCMD program and the argument as –i [*Path to your SQL script*], as shown in Figure 3.21.

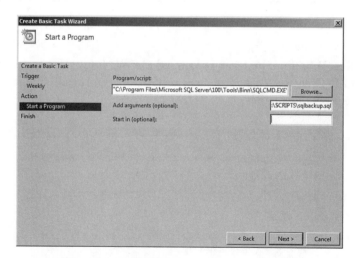

Figure 3.21 Select SQLCMD as the program and your script as the arguments.

After you complete these steps, you need to adjust the properties a little for the job:

1. Browse to the Task Scheduler Library and verify the reoccurring vCenter Database job appears in the right pane.

2. Select the task, right-click, and select the properties of the newly created batch job, as shown in Figure 3.22.

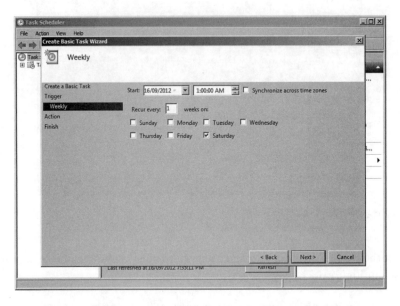

Figure 3.22 Right-click properties.

3. Ensure **Run Whether the User Is Logged On or Not** is selected, as shown in Figure 3.23. Then select **Change User or Group...** and ensure the job is running under the proper credentials.

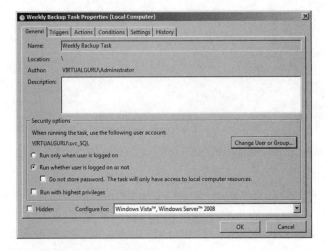

Figure 3.23 Select the user under which to run the task.

The preceding description is just a sample of how you can ensure you have regular full backups running if you have opted to run SQL Express. You might want to fine-tune your settings to keep several weeks' worth of full backups and also to move them to a separate location.

Differential

If your database is getting too big for a full backup, you can perform a differential backup. A differential backup copies any changes made since the last full backup job. It is designed to reduce the time needed to perform a full backup. You can make your backup job a differential job by adding the WITH DIFFERENTIAL statement, as shown in Figure 3.24. In this case, your final backup strategy adds a combination of full and differential backups, so you must ensure you have access to all the backup files.

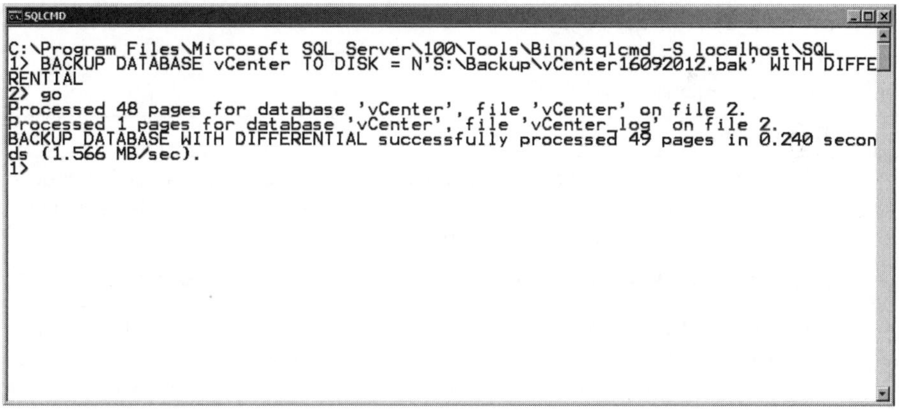

```
C:\Program Files\Microsoft SQL Server\100\Tools\Binn>sqlcmd -S localhost\SQL
1> BACKUP DATABASE vCenter TO DISK = N'S:\Backup\vCenter16092012.bak' WITH DIFFE
RENTIAL
2> go
Processed 48 pages for database 'vCenter', file 'vCenter' on file 2.
Processed 1 pages for database 'vCenter', file 'vCenter_log' on file 2.
BACKUP DATABASE WITH DIFFERENTIAL successfully processed 49 pages in 0.240 secon
ds (1.566 MB/sec).
1>
```

Figure 3.24 WITH DIFFERENTIAL command.

Log Backups

The third type of backup does not copy the changes; it copies only the transactional logs of the database. After the logs are copied, the portions of the log files not needed for active transactions are truncated. For regular maintenance, it is a good practice to back up your log files daily.

When you are happy with your scheduled job, you can quickly apply it to the remaining databases because the jobs are exportable to XML files from the Task Scheduler console. Simply export the job as an XML file, make some edits so that it can be applied to the other databases, and reimport it. In general, the VMware Update Manager View Composer or Event databases do not require the same frequency of backups as the vCenter database.

Installing vCenter

After checking to ensure the database is up and running and your backup rotations and recovery plans are properly configured, you are almost ready to begin the vCenter installation. Installing vCenter requires a domain account with local administrator privileges. If you are installing vCenter on a Windows 2008 R2 host, you have some decisions to make: Should you keep the firewall enabled, and what ports do you need to have open if you do? It is a best practice to keep the firewall active although it increases the complexity of the deployment. By keeping it on, however, you are dramatically reducing the attack vector or vulnerability of the service. This, of course, is both a judgment call and consideration of your internal security policy toward native Windows firewalls. In some organizations, the default is to turn off the firewalls. If you do want to keep the firewall on, you should be aware of which ports are opened during the installation of the vCenter Server. You can open these ports in advance, or during the installation, they are opened by default.

Table 3.2 provides a list of the ports.

Table 3.2 Port Descriptions

Port	Description
80	vCenter Server requires port 80 for direct HTTP connections. Port 80 redirects requests to HTTPS port 443. This redirection is useful if you accidentally use http://server instead of https://server/.
	Note: Microsoft Internet Information Services (IIS) also use port 80.
389	This port must be open on the local and all remote instances of vCenter Server. This is the LDAP port number for the Directory Services for the vCenter Server group. The vCenter Server system needs to bind to port 389, even if you are not joining this vCenter Server instance to a Linked Mode group. If another service is running on this port, it might be preferable to remove that service or change its port to a different port. You can run the LDAP service on any port from 1025 through 65535.
	If this instance is serving as the Microsoft Windows Active Directory, change the port number from 389 to an available port from 1025 through 65535.
443	This is the default port that the vCenter Server system uses to listen for connections from the vSphere Client. To enable the vCenter Server system to receive data from the vSphere Client, open port 443 in the firewall.
	The vCenter Server system also uses port 443 to monitor data transfer from SDK clients.
	If you use another port number for HTTPS, you must use ip-address:port when you log in to the vCenter Server system.

Port	Description
636	For vCenter Server Linked Mode, this is the SSL port of the local instance. If another service is running on this port, it might be preferable to remove that service or change its port to a different port. You can run the SSL service on any port from 1025 through 65535.
902	This is the default port that the vCenter Server system uses to send data to managed hosts. Managed hosts also send a regular heartbeat over UDP port 902 to the vCenter Server system. This port must not be blocked by firewalls between the server and the hosts or between hosts. Port 902 must not be blocked between the vSphere Client and the hosts. The vSphere Client uses this port to display virtual machine consoles.
8080	Web Services HTTP. This port is used for the VMware VirtualCenter Management Web Services.
8443	Web Services HTTPS. This port is used for the VMware VirtualCenter Management Web Services.
60099	Web Service change service notification port.
10443	vCenter Inventory Service HTTPS.
10109	vCenter Inventory Service Service Management.
10111	vCenter Inventory Service Linked Mode Communication.[3]

After reviewing the port requirements, you are ready to begin installing vCenter. Ensure you have the latest version of the vCenter 5 software downloaded and follow these steps:

1. Launch the installer. You will notice that several services and features can be installed from the Installation Utility, which we discuss later. To install vCenter, select the vCenter Server option and click **Install**.

2. Select the language from the drop-down; vCenter ships with language support.

3. When the installation wizard appears, click **Next**.

4. After reviewing the end-user patent agreement, click **Next**.

5. Agree to the license terms and click **Next**.

6. Enter your user name, organization, and license key in the fields provided and click **Next**.

---

[3]This information was referenced from the VMware Knowledge Base at http://kb.vmware.com/selfservice/microsites/search.do?cmd=displayKC&docType=kc&docTypeID=DT_KB_1_1&externalId=2005105.

7. You have the option of installing a Microsoft SQL Server 2008 Express instance or using a supporting database. Because vCenter is a true 64-bit operating system, it requires a 64-bit DSN. If you have not created one, you are prompted to do so. Click **Next** to start the creation of the DSN or select it from the drop-down list and proceed to step 15. Figure 3.25 assumes you need to create the DSN.

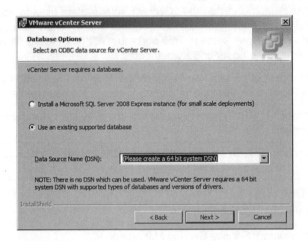

Figure 3.25 Select the database.

8. Provide a name for the vCenter DSN, provide a description, and then select the SQL instance you are connecting to (see Figure 3.26).

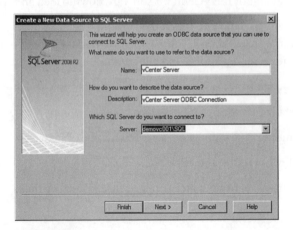

Figure 3.26 Specify SQL Server information.

9. Click **With Integrated Windows Authentication**, as shown in Figure 3.27. Integrated Windows security is more secure than SQL Server authentication, so you should use it. Click **Next**.

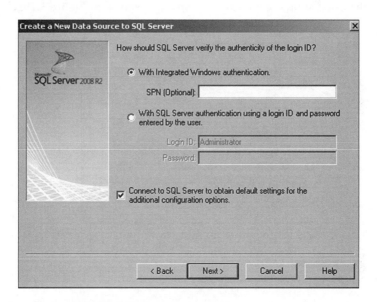

Figure 3.27 Select With Integrated Windows Authentication.

10. Ensure you are connecting to the vCenter Server, as shown in Figure 3.28, and click **Next**.

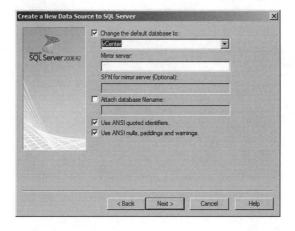

Figure 3.28 Change the default database.

11. Click **Finish**.

12. Click **Test the Data Source…**

13. When the installation completes successfully, as shown in Figure 3.29, click **OK**.

Figure 3.29 Check your database connectivity.

14. When you see your DSN in the highlighted area, as shown in Figure 3.30, select it and click **Next**.

Figure 3.30 Select your DSN.

15. Click **Next**.

16. Accept the default location and click **Next**.

17. You have the option of installing vCenter in linked mode so that you can view all vCenter information from a single management tool. It is common for the vCenter Server being deployed for the VDI environment to be the second vCenter Server deployed. If you install it in standalone mode and then want to update it to linked mode, you can be rerunning the installer. If this is the case, install the server in linked mode; otherwise, select **Create a Standalone VMware vCenter Server Instance**, as shown in Figure 3.31, and click **Next**.

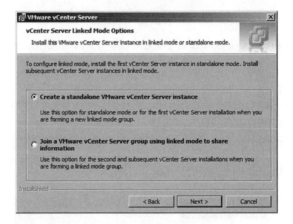

Figure 3.31 Select the standalone option unless this is the second vCenter Server.

18. vCenter Server Web services is provided by Tomcat. In this screen, shown in Figure 3.32, you are asked to tune the maximum memory pools for Java based on the expected size of the environment. Although this screen was introduced in vCenter 4.1, the capability to tune Tomcat has been available for a while through the Configure Tomcat utility that is provided. Select the maximum memory configuration based on the expected size and click **Next**.

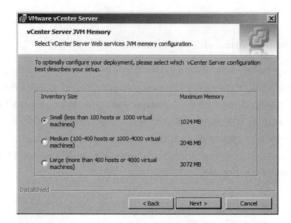

Figure 3.32 Select the appropriate inventory size to configure the Tomcat memory setting.

19. You have the option of increasing the number of ephemeral ports, as shown in Figure 3.33. An ephemeral port is a short-lived endpoint created by the Windows Server when a program makes a user port connection. Because virtual desktop environments can scale into the thousands of virtual desktop instances, it is typical that you adjust the ephemeral ports on both VMware View Servers and vCenter Servers. Click **Install** to begin the installation.

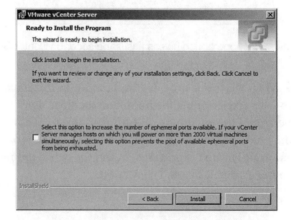

Figure 3.33 Increase the ephemeral ports for large View environments (thousands of instances) if needed and install vCenter.

20. Ensure the installation completes properly (see Figure 3.34) and click **Finish**.

Figure 3.34 Finalize the installation.

When the installation is complete, you need to install the vSphere client to connect to the environment. The vSphere client is a Windows-based client that allows you to connect to vCenter and the ESXi hosts in your environment. The difference in connecting to ESXi versus vCenter is that ESXi uses the local root login credentials, whereas the vCenter Server uses Windows login credentials. To get access to the vCenter Server you just installed, complete the following steps:

1. Launch the vCenter installer.

2. Select the vSphere Client and click **Install**.

3. Select the language for the installation and click **OK**.

4. Click **Next** on the welcome screen.

5. Click **Next** on the user patent agreement.

6. Agree to the license terms and click **Next**.

7. Click **Install** on the ready to install screen.

8. Click **Finish** when the installation completes.

9. Open the vSphere client in Programs\VMware\vSphere Client.

10. Enter the name of the vCenter Server and the Windows username and password and click **Login**.

To summarize the process, the high-level installation steps shown in Figure 3.35 are necessary to complete the installation.

Figure 3.35 Installation steps.

Installing vSphere

Installing VMware View starts with the installation of vSphere and related components. With vSphere 5, there are two options for vSphere: installable and embedded. Installable is an installation of vSphere ESXi because vSphere 5 no longer supports ESX native or the version that had the console operating system (COS) for management purposes. You can download the ESXi binaries from VMware at https://my.vmware.com/web/vmware/try-vmware or order the server with the embedded version.

If you download the binaries, it is possible to create a manual embedded version by installing to a USB drive in an internal or external port on the server. The embedded version is supplied by the hardware vendors and incorporates their specific tools to enable greater visibility on the hardware and software layer. For example, you can download an ESXi version from HP, Dell, IBM, and CISCO. One of the drawbacks of the embedded option is that the build from the vendor may not have the latest and greatest utilities or tools. With vSphere 5, this issue is addressed by providing an automated build option that allows you to add OEM packs to the installation. Let's review the installation:

To install ESXi installable, follow these steps:

1. Boot from the ISO file. After it boots, the splash screen comes up, and the necessary files to start the installer are loaded, as shown in Figure 3.36.

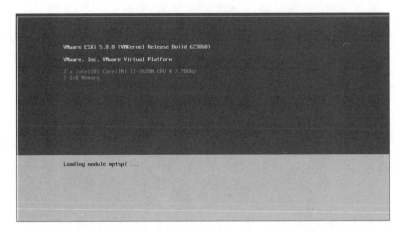

Figure 3.36 ESXi splash screen.

2. You can maneuver around the installer by using the Tab key. To continue the installation, press the **Tab** key and press **Enter** on the keyboard, as shown in Figure 3.37.

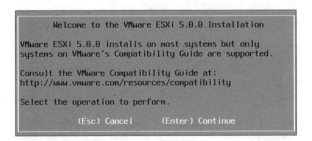

Figure 3.37 Select Enter to continue.

3. Press **F11** to accept the license agreement shown in Figure 3.38 and continue.

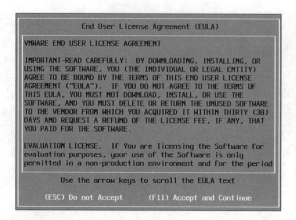

Figure 3.38 Press F11 to accept the license agreement.

4. Select a disk to install or upgrade, as shown in Figure 3.39. It is considered a best practice to install vSphere ESXi first before presenting storage so that you can be assured that you are installing ESXi on the right drive unless you intend to boot from SAN. Once you have selected the drive press **Enter**.

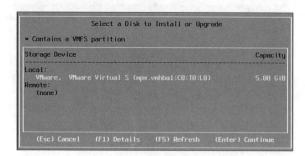

Figure 3.39 Select the storage device where you would like to install ESXi.

5. Select the correct keyboard layout (US Default), as shown in Figure 3.40, and press **Enter** to continue.

Figure 3.40 Select the keyboard layout.

6. Specify a password for the root account, as shown in Figure 3.41, and press **Enter**.

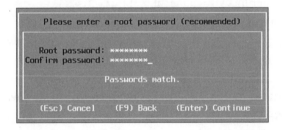

Figure 3.41 Specify the password.

7. Confirm the parameters, as shown in Figure 3.42, and press **F11** to begin the installation.

Figure 3.42 Press F11 to install.

If you are installing ESXi to a USB stick, you need to verify that your server is on the supported Hardware Compatibility List (HCL) and that the USB device is supported by the server vendor. If both conditions are met, the USB device shows up as an installable location. Rather than select a local drive, you can select the USB location to install ESXi.

For detailed instructions, refer to VMware's Knowledge Base article located at http://
kb.vmware.com/selfservice/documentLinkInt.do?micrositeID=&popup=true&languageId=
&externalID=2004784.

Auto Deploy

One of the other options you have is to use the new Auto Deploy feature, which essentially allows you to provision a vSphere 5 ESXi Server and apply the configurations in an
unattended manner through the Configuration Manager to create a truly stateless host.
Why would you use Auto Deploy in a VDI environment? VDI is a technology that scales
quite quickly. To reduce the time it takes to provision additional capacity, Auto Deploy
may be a good option. In addition, it allows you to design the ESXi configuration once
and have it consistently applied across the board. It does require extra consideration if you
are going to run vCenter in a virtual machine, however.

When you use Auto Deploy, you are creating a major dependency on the service for all
hosts that are set up to use it. You therefore need to run two ESXi hosts that are not
dependent on Auto Deploy in a cluster. A separate cluster ensures that your vCenter and
Auto Deploy Server can reside on a set of hosts that are running vSphere HA with the
boot priority properly set on the VMs so that the service is readily available all the time.
Before we get too far ahead ourselves, though, let's look at the requirements and process.

To deploy the Auto Deploy feature, you need a few additional components:

- PowerShell installed on the vCenter Server
- The PowerCLI from VMware
- A TFTP Server for downloading the files
- The ESXi downloadable files (The files can be downloaded from the VMware
  website.)

Using the vCenter that you have installed and running, you can add these additional
components to take advantage of rapid provisioning of stateless ESXi hosts in the VDI
environment.

The architecture of Auto Deploy is made up of the following components, also shown in
Figure 3.43:

- A TFTP Server to store the boot loader files
- Attributes in the DHCP scope to identify the TFTP Server and boot loader files
- Rules in the vCenter Server Auto Deploy feature to associate a physical ESXi Server
  to an image file
- A software depo where the ESXi installable files are located

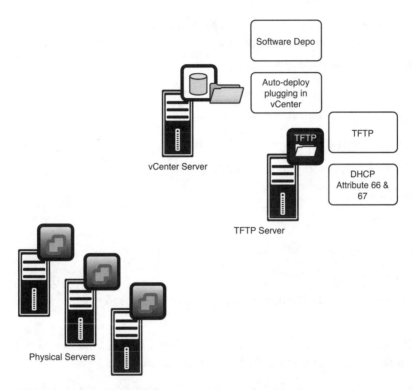

Figure 3.43 Auto Deploy components.

Let's enable and step through each of the components.

PowerShell is included in Windows 2008 R2, but you do have to add it as a feature. PowerShell should be installed on the vCenter Server along with the VMware PowerCLI. To install PowerShell, follow these steps:

1. To add PowerShell, open Server Manager.

2. Browse to the Add Features module and right-click **Add Feature**.

3. Select the **Windows PowerShell Integrated Scripting Environment**.

4. Click **Install**.

5. Open a PowerShell script window, browsing to Start\Programs\Administrative tools and opening a Windows PowerShell Module.

6. Enable the PowerCLI by changing the remote execution policy for scripts by typing **Set-ExecutionPolicy RemoteSigned**. This allows scripts that are not signed by a vendor to run on the vCenter Server.

You can download the VMware PowerCLI directly from VMware. After downloading it, simply follow these steps to install it properly:

1. Run the VMware Power CLI executable.

2. Click **Next** on the Installer screen.

3. Click **Next** on the Patent information screen.

4. Accept the license agreement and click **Next**.

5. Accept the default location and click **Next**.

6. Click **Install**.

7. Click **Finish**.

> **NOTE**
>
> You may be prompted to install the VMware VIX files; VMware VIX is an API that allows you to automate VM and guest operations. You should install VIX when prompted.

To get the boot loader files, you need to install the plug-in in vCenter for Auto Deploy. You can install the plug-in using the VMware vCenter Installer:

1. Click the **VMware Auto Deploy**, as shown in Figure 3.44, and click **Install.**

Figure 3.44 Select VMware Auto Deploy.

2. Choose the setup Language and click **OK**.

3. Click **Next** on the Auto Deploy Installation Wizard.

4. Click **Next** on the patent information screen.

5. Accept the license agreement and click **Next**.

6. Accept the default location and set the Auto Deploy Repository location and size. The default repository size is 5 GB. Because Auto Deploy is being used to provide ESXi images, the default size is sufficient.

7. Enter the IP address or hostname of the server, leave the default HTTP port, and enter the username and password. Then click **Next**.

NOTE

For network-based services, I prefer to go with IP addresses so that name resolution is not a requirement for the service. If you are likely to change IP addresses, it is best to put in a hostname.

8. The default Auto Deploy Server Port is 6501. Leave this setting and click **Next**.

9. Specify how vSphere Auto Deploy should be identified on the network and click **Next**.

   My recommendation is to use the IP address so that name resolution is not required for the deployment server to run.

10. Click **Install**.

11. Click **Finish**.

When you reconnect to vCenter, you see a new administration plug-in called Auto Deploy. Launch the Auto Deploy plug-in, which should look similar to the one in Figure 3.45.

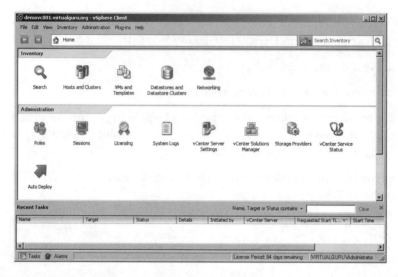

Figure 3.45 Auto Deploy appears under Administration.

The plug-in displays the boot loader filename, which in this case is undionly.kpxe. vmw-hardwired. The boot loader files can be downloaded from here, as shown in Figure 3.46.

Configuration	
BIOS DHCP File Name:	undionly.kpxe.vmw-hardwired
EFI DHCP File Name:	snponly64.efi.vmw-hardwired
gPXE Boot URL:	https://192.168.10.11:6501/vmw/rbd/tramp
Cache Size:	2.00 GiB
Cache Space In-Use:	<1 MiB

Actions
Download TFTP Boot Zip
Download AutoDeploy Log Files

Figure 3.46 Download bootloader files.

Now that you have the name of the boot loader file and the zip files containing those files, you can set the attributes for your DHCP scope and unzip the files on your TFTP Server. The files are downloaded as deploy-tftp.zip. When you unzip them, by default, they are placed in a subdirectory of your root folder (deploy-tftp) on your TFTP Server. To ensure you can find the files, unzip them in the root directory of your TFTP Server without the default subdirectory.

It is recommended that you restrict your Auto Deploy process to a service network. This means that your builds should happen on an isolated network segment separate from your production network. By doing so, you ensure that even though the building of an ESXi host involves a very small image file, the downloading and installing do not interfere with production traffic. In addition, DHCP is required for this process to work. From a security perspective, DHCP traffic should not be run on the same network as your ESXi management traffic. If you do not have the flexibility of separating your management and Auto Deploy service network, use nonroutable IP addresses to build the hosts and then apply production IPs afterward. A separate Auto Deploy network may require a dedicated port group on your vSphere ESXi vSwitches, so make sure that you build this into your planning.

When the boot loader files are in place, update options 66 and 67. In a Windows-based DHCP Server, follow these steps:

1. From the DHCP Management Utility, browse to the scope that you will be using to enable the Auto Deploy process.

2. Expand the scope and select **Options**. Then right-click and select **Configure Options**.

3. Under Available Options on the General tab, select **066** and add the IP address of your TFTP host under the string value.

4. Select **067**, and under the string value, add the name of the boot loader file, which in this case, is **undionly.kpxe.vmw-hardwired**.

5. Click **OK**.

At this point, you should have the boot loader process running. If you boot a physical server, it gets a DHCP address, contacts the TFTP Server, and downloads the boot loader file. It connects to the Auto Deploy service on the vCenter Server and halts because no rules have been configured to tell the server which image profile is assigned to the host. After downloading the boot loader file, the server contacts the vCenter Server but stops because the image profile has not been assigned to the host yet, as shown in Figure 3.47.

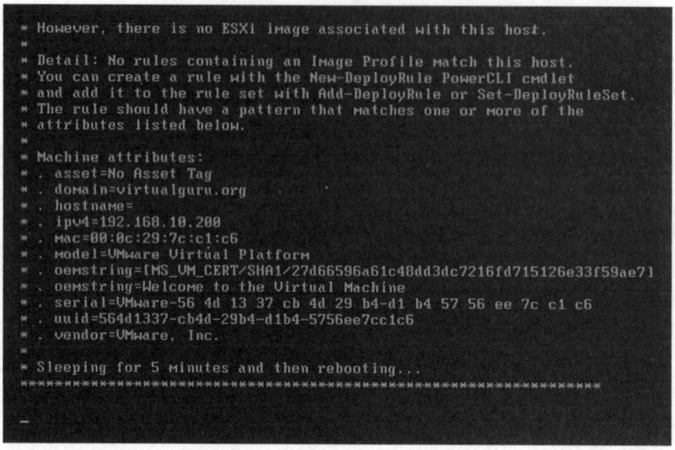

```
* However, there is no ESXi image associated with this host.
*
* Detail: No rules containing an Image Profile match this host.
* You can create a rule with the New-DeployRule PowerCLI cmdlet
* and add it to the rule set with Add-DeployRule or Set-DeployRuleSet.
* The rule should have a pattern that matches one or more of the
* attributes listed below.
*
* Machine attributes:
* . asset=No Asset Tag
* . domain=virtualguru.org
* . hostname=
* . ipv4=192.168.10.200
* . mac=00:0c:29:7c:c1:c6
* . model=VMware Virtual Platform
* . oemstring=[MS_VM_CERT/SHA1/27d66596a61c48dd3dc7216fd715126e33f59ae7]
* . oemstring=Welcome to the Virtual Machine
* . serial=VMware-56 4d 13 37 cb 4d 29 b4-d1 b4 57 56 ee 7c c1 c6
* . uuid=564d1337-cb4d-29b4-d1b4-5756ee7cc1c6
* . vendor=VMware, Inc.
*
* Sleeping for 5 minutes and then rebooting...
**********************************************************************
```

Figure 3.47 The server contacts vCenter.

To complete the Auto Deploy configuration, you must run some PowerCLI scripts from the vCenter Server to specify a software depo. Extract the ESXi downloadable images into the software depo and create a rule to associate the image with an image profile. The final step is to make this the default image profile.

Log in to your vCenter Server and start the PowerCLI interface. If you get an error message, it is likely that you have not set the execution policy properly in PowerShell. In this instance, run PowerShell and set the execution policy, as shown in Figure 3.48:

```
"Set-ExecutionPolicy RemoteSigned"
```

This command allows code that has not been signed by a trusted publisher such as Microsoft to run.

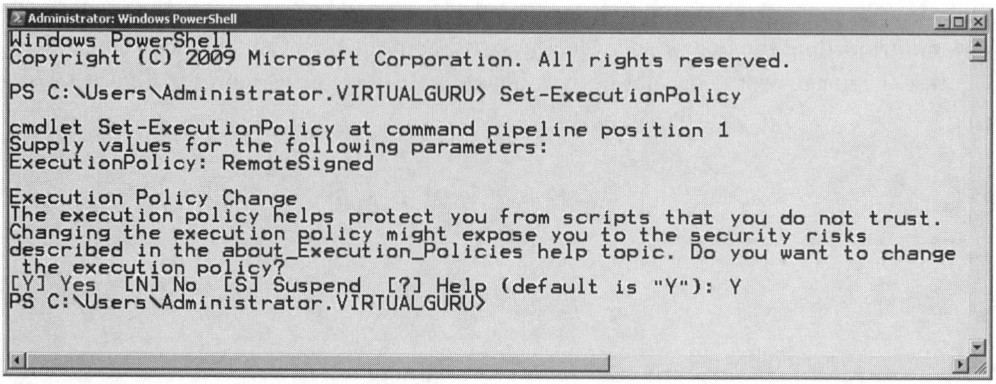

```
Administrator: Windows PowerShell
Windows PowerShell
Copyright (C) 2009 Microsoft Corporation. All rights reserved.

PS C:\Users\Administrator.VIRTUALGURU> Set-ExecutionPolicy

cmdlet Set-ExecutionPolicy at command pipeline position 1
Supply values for the following parameters:
ExecutionPolicy: RemoteSigned

Execution Policy Change
The execution policy helps protect you from scripts that you do not trust.
Changing the execution policy might expose you to the security risks
described in the about_Execution_Policies help topic. Do you want to change
the execution policy?
[Y] Yes  [N] No  [S] Suspend  [?] Help (default is "Y"): Y
PS C:\Users\Administrator.VIRTUALGURU>
```

Figure 3.48 Set the execution policy to unsigned.

Run vSphere PowerCLI and connect to your vCenter Server by typing **Connect-VIServer [servername]**, which results in the output shown in Figure 3.49.

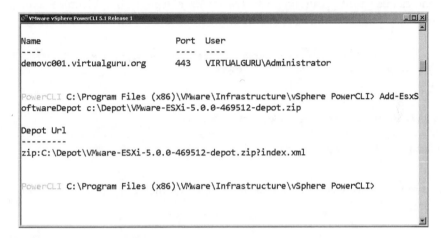

Figure 3.49 Connect to your vCenter Server.

After you are connected, you need to create a software or repository. You do this by running the Add-EsxSoftwareDepot command along with the path to your ESXi downloadable files. For example:

```
Add-EsxSoftwareDepot S:\Depo\VMware-ESXi-5.0.0-469512-depot.zip
```

After creating the software depo, you should verify it is set up properly by running the Get-EsxImageProfile command. The command should return information on the image profiles available in the software depository, like those shown in Figure 3.50.

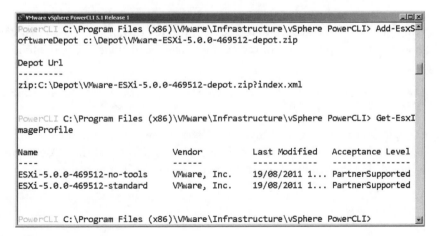

Figure 3.50 Image profiles.

Although the initial images are fine for a proof of concept, you need the vSphere HA modules for production deployment. These modules are part of the Auto Deploy software depot and can be added by running Add-EsxSoftwareDepot http://vCenter Server/ vSphere-HA-depot. The output is shown in Figure 3.51.

```
PowerCLI C:\Program Files (x86)\VMware\Infrastructure\vSphere PowerCLI> Add-EsxS
oftwareDepot http://192.168.10.11/vSphere-HA-depot

Depot Url
---------
http://192.168.10.11/vSphere-HA-depot/index.xml
```

Figure 3.51 Add the software depository URL.

To add the HA options, add the HA software depot on the vCenter Server, as shown in Figure 3.52.

```
PowerCLI C:\Program Files (x86)\VMware\Infrastructure\vSphere PowerCLI> New-EsxI
mageProfile -CloneProfile ESXi-5.0.0-469512-standard -Name "ESXi-5.0.0-469512-HA
"

cmdlet New-EsxImageProfile at command pipeline position 1
Supply values for the following parameters:
(Type !? for Help.)
Vendor: VMware

Name                        Vendor        Last Modified   Acceptance Level
----                        ------        -------------   ----------------
ESXi-5.0.0-469512-HA        VMware        19/08/2011 1... PartnerSupported
```

Figure 3.52 Add HA to your ESXi image.

After adding the HA files, you need to create a copy of the existing images so that you can add the new files to it. To take one of the existing images and clone it, run the following command:

```
PowerCLI> New-EsxImageProfile -CloneProfile ESXi-5.0.0-469512-standard
-Name "ESXi-5.0.0-469512-HA"
```

In this example, you are taking the ESXi-5.0.0-469512-standard image and copying it to one called ESXi-5.0.0-469512-HA, shown in Figure 3.53 (Note that the HA components were not included in the original ESX software depo zip files, but now they are).

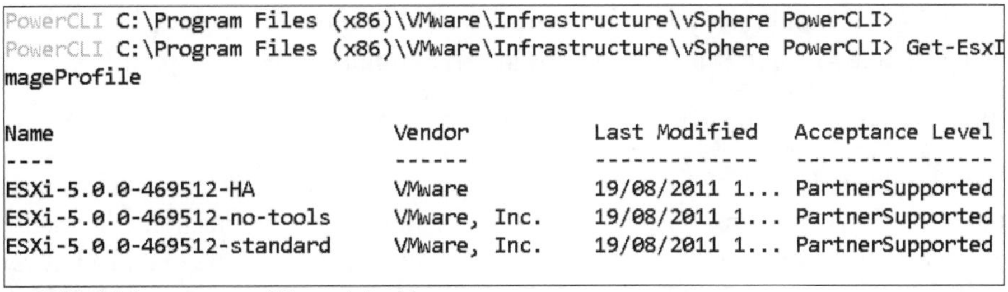

```
PowerCLI C:\Program Files (x86)\VMware\Infrastructure\vSphere PowerCLI>
PowerCLI C:\Program Files (x86)\VMware\Infrastructure\vSphere PowerCLI> Get-EsxI
mageProfile

Name                             Vendor            Last Modified     Acceptance Level
----                             ------            -------------     ----------------
ESXi-5.0.0-469512-HA             VMware            19/08/2011 1...   PartnerSupported
ESXi-5.0.0-469512-no-tools       VMware, Inc.      19/08/2011 1...   PartnerSupported
ESXi-5.0.0-469512-standard       VMware, Inc.      19/08/2011 1...   PartnerSupported
```

Figure 3.53 Make a copy of the original image.

If you rerun the Get-EsxImageProfile command, you see an additional image profile. You still need to add the vmware-fdm or HA package to the image. You do this by running the following command:

```
PowerCLI> Add-EsxSoftwarePackage -ImageProfile "ESXi-5.0.0-469512-HA"
-SoftwarePackage vmware-fdm
```

After verifying that the software depository is working and that you have images available, you can create a deployment rule. The syntax for creating a deployment rule is

```
New-Deployment—Name "Name of Rule"—Item "Image Name"
```

You have the option of pattern matching or making this image file available as the default by adding switches. The –Allhosts switch applies the rule to any server, and the –pattern switch allows you to specify specific attributes to match, such as vendor=VMware, Inc. You can concatenate multiple patterns by separating each with a comma. Perhaps the most useful of the patterns is specifying an IP range. If you have separated your build network and use a set range of IP addresses, you can restrict the build process to that range.

The syntax used in this example is as follows (see Figure 3.54):

```
PowerCLI> New-DeployRule -Name "ESXi Default Build v.01" -Item "ESXi-5.0.0-
469512-HA" -Pattern "ipv4=192.169.9.0-192.169.9.255"
```

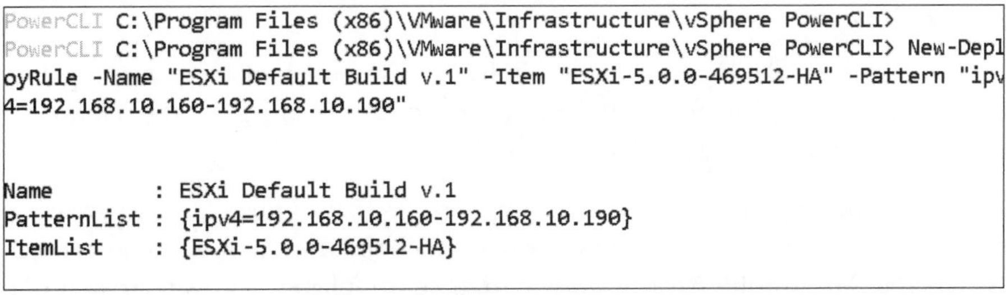

```
PowerCLI C:\Program Files (x86)\VMware\Infrastructure\vSphere PowerCLI>
PowerCLI C:\Program Files (x86)\VMware\Infrastructure\vSphere PowerCLI> New-Depl
oyRule -Name "ESXi Default Build v.1" -Item "ESXi-5.0.0-469512-HA" -Pattern "ipv
4=192.168.10.160-192.168.10.190"


Name        : ESXi Default Build v.1
PatternList : {ipv4=192.168.10.160-192.168.10.190}
ItemList    : {ESXi-5.0.0-469512-HA}
```

Figure 3.54 Associate the image to an IP pattern.

After creating the build rule, you must activate it. The command to activate it is Add-DeployRule –DeployRule "Name", as in this example:

```
Add-DeployRule -DeployRule "ESXi Default Build v.01"
```

One point to keep in mind with Auto Deploy is that the deployment can generate a significant load on the Auto Deploy service. Because the location of the image file is essentially a web server, it is possible to use reverse proxies to offload some of the overhead. A reverse proxy can also store the image file. It is possible to redistribute the load to the reverse proxy by editing one of the boot loader files. If you go into the TFTP root directory and edit a file called tramp, you can specify alternate locations. If you open the tramp file, you can easily specify alternate locations, as shown in Figure 3.55.

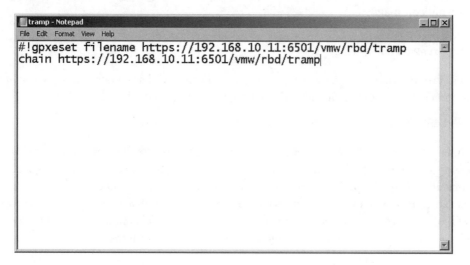

Figure 3.55 Edit the tramp file.

Host Profiles

After you set up Auto Deploy, essentially you have ESXi Servers that are running, but they do not yet have a production configuration applied to them. The other component to vCenter that you need to integrate is host profiles.

Host profiles allow you to create a set of configurations that can be consistently applied across the environment. They eliminate the manual configuration of ESXi hosts on an individual basis. Host profiles also allow you to force compliancy across your environment because after a host profile is associated, any changes made are identified and remediated. Because Auto Deploy essentially creates an installed ESXi, you need to use host profiles to apply a consistent production configuration. There are two ways to configure a host profile: You can import an existing profile through the vCenter console or create one from an existing ESXi host. Unless you have a company standard (and this should be adjusted for a VMware View environment), the easiest way is to just configure an ESXi host as you would like and create one from the host. A host profile assumes that the EXi hosts are configured the same way, so it is important to have everything configured properly on your reference ESXi Server.

Using host profiles is a four-step process:

1. Create a reference profile from an ESXi host.

2. Attach the profile to an existing host or cluster.

3. Run a comparison against the hosts assigned to the profile and the profile itself.

4. Apply the profile to fix any differences between the assigned hosts and the profile.

The actual process is as follows:

1. From vCenter, navigate to Home, Management and Host Profiles.

2. Click the **Create Profile** button and provide a name and description for the profile, as shown in Figure 3.56. Then click **Next**.

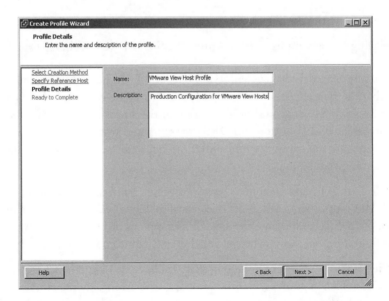

Figure 3.56 Create a host profile.

3. You can edit the profile to make any additional changes. Simply open the profile and expand the profile policies to update the settings, as shown in Figure 3.57.

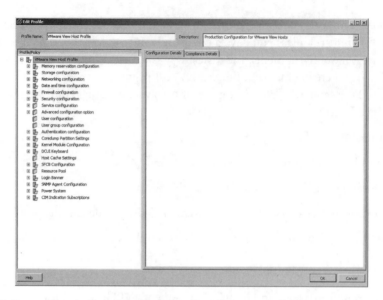

Figure 3.57 Expand the profile policies to edit settings.

4. You can select to attach the profile to an ESXi host or cluster.

5. After attaching the profile, click **Check Compliance**.

6. If anything is noncompliant, click **Apply Profile** to have the changes made.

At this point, you have deployed vCenter and have the ESXi hosts coming online. Now make sure that the reference server is properly configured before you build your host profile. For an ESXi Server, you should ensure that the storage is properly attached and that key features such as VMotion and DRS are set up and working. Let's review each of the technologies and the configuration so that the reference server is representative of what you want in production.

VMotion allows the virtual machine to be hot migrated from one ESXi host to another. To set up VMotion properly, you must make sure that any ESXi host you are migrating to and from has access to the same storage. ESXi supports just about every type of shared storage configuration out there, whether it is Fiber Channel (FC), iSCSI, or NFS.

VMware View environments are unique in that you have two kinds of I/O to contend with: operational I/O and burst I/O. Operational I/O is essentially the storage throughput requirement while the virtual desktop is on, whereas burst I/O, or "boot storms," is typically experienced when multiple virtual machines are being created. We look at the design principles in Chapter 12, "Performance and Monitoring," when we review performance, but for now let's talk mechanics. Rather than go into every aspect regarding storage considerations and configurations, let's stick to a few important considerations in setting up storage.

No matter which storage solution you select for your VMware View installation, you should understand and have calculated your throughput requirement. In addition, your storage connections from the ESXi host to the storage solution should use multipathing. Multipathing allows you to segregate the storage paths on isolated networks and ensure there are redundant paths to the same storage pool.

Storage Connectivity

vSphere 5 has simplified the setting up of multipathing using the iSCSI software initiator. In vSphere 5, a new graphical interface allows you to set up multipathing. You therefore can set up multiple VMkernel ports quickly and easily. You can now bind multiple VMkernel ports to the iSCSI software initiator. After you do so, however, the iSCSI traffic must be restricted to layer 2 traffic or nonroutable. If you use a single VMkernel port, you can route iSCSI traffic. In addition, if you have both VMkernel ports on the same vSwitch with two uplinks, one must be active and the other passive. Let's look at the configuration to understand how this works.

If you want two active paths to your iSCSI storage device, you need to create two separate vSwitches with two separate VMkernel ports with one active uplink each. This configuration has a separate management network and two separate paths to the iSCSI appliance, as you can see in Figure 3.58.

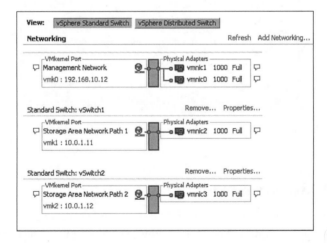

Figure 3.58 Two separate paths to the iSCSI appliance.

When you have the networking configuration in place, you can bind the second VMkernel port to the software initiator using the following process:

1. Log in to the vCenter.

2. Select the Configuration tab from the ESXi host.

3. Select **Storage Adapters** and the properties of the software iSCSI initiator.

4. Under the Network Configuration tab, add the second VMkernel port.

After the second VMkernel port is added, check the paths to ensure you have the appropriate number of paths, as shown in Figure 3.59:

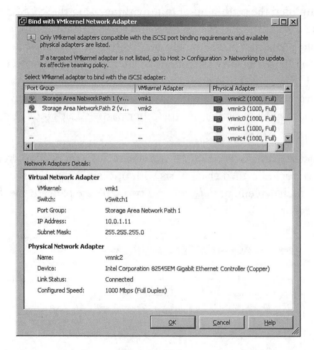

Figure 3.59 Check to ensure you have multiple paths.

Installing VMware View

If you are running VMware View as a virtual machine on Windows 2008 R2, much of the performance tuning is complete. You should, however, make the following changes to your VM.

Manually set the pagefile for the system based on 1.5 times the memory assigned to the VM. You can complete this process using the following steps:

1. Open Server Manager on the VM.

2. Select **Change System Properties**.

3. Select the **Advanced** tab and settings.

4. Select the **Advanced** tab, and under Virtual Memory, select **Change**.

5. Select **Custom Size** and set the minimum and maximum value to 1.5 times the memory allocated.

6. Click **Set** and click **OK** and **OK** again.

7. When prompted, reboot the VM.

The first server you should install is a standard Connection Server. As mentioned, there are actually four kinds of Connection Servers you can install: View Standard (or the first Connection Server in the environment), View Replica (or all servers after the initial Connection Server is installed), Security Server, and Transfer Server for local mode VMs.

To install the first Connection Server, follow these steps:

1. Launch the VMware View Installer and click **Next** on the welcome screen.

2. Click **Next** on the end user patent agreement.

3. Accept the license agreement and click **Next**.

4. Accept the default location and click **Next**.

5. Because this is the first server, select **View Standard Server,** as shown in Figure 3.60, and click **Next**.

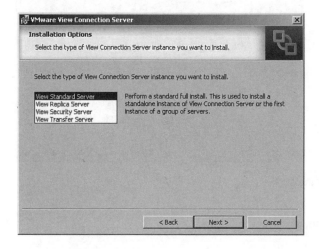

Figure 3.60 Choose View Standard Server.

6. Have the installer automatically configure the Windows Firewall and click **Next**. Note: The installer does not check the firewall state during the installation; it simply prompts you to configure it automatically or not to (see Figure 3.61).

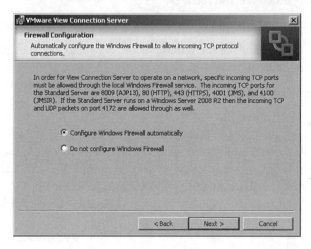

Figure 3.61 Adjust the Windows Firewall.

7. Click **Install,** as shown in Figure 3.62.

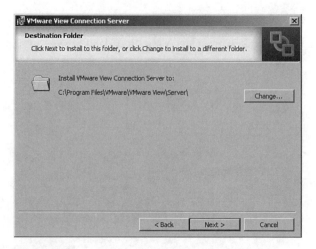

Figure 3.62 Click Install.

8. Click **Finish,** as shown in Figure 3.63.

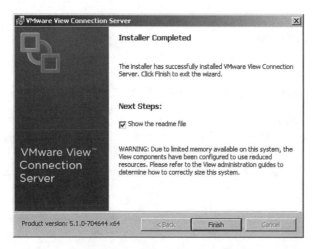

Figure 3.63 Click Finish.

The installer installs eight services on the Windows Server:

- VMwareVDMDS—Provides the View LDAP directory services.

- VMware View Web Component—Provides View Web Services.

- VMware View Security Gateway Component—Provides secure tunneling services for View.

- VMware View Script Host—Disabled by default but provides support for third-party scripts.

- VMware View PCoIP Secure Gateway—Provides secure tunneling for the PC over IP (PCoIP) protocol.

- VMware View Message Bus Component—Provides messaging services between View components.

- VMware View Framework Services—Provides event logging, security, and COM+ framework services for View Manager.

- VMware View Connection Server—Provides connection broker services.

After VMware View is installed, you can connect to it by launching the shortcut on the desktop or by opening a web browser and going to http://[Connection Server]/admin. Be aware that the *admin* is case sensitive, and the IP address can be used in place of the server name, which is not case sensitive. If you omit the /admin, you are redirected to the client installation page. When you connect to the console for the first time, you are prompted to install Adobe Flash Player. The Administrator Console requires Adobe Flash version

10 or higher. After you have logged in, you will need to configure the environment so that everything is running properly.

Configuring the View Connection Server

As mentioned in Chapter 1, "Virtual Desktop Infrastructure Overview," there are two versions of VMware View: Enterprise and Premier. Premier includes local mode and View Composer. If you apply a Premier license, you see View Composer and local mode VMs as options. After logging in, you need to add the license. Click **Edit License**, as shown in Figure 3.64.

Figure 3.64 Add the license.

Enter the VMware View Serial Number in the provided field (see Figure 3.65).

Figure 3.65 Enter the license key.

Premier licenses enable View Composer and local mode, as shown in Figure 3.66.

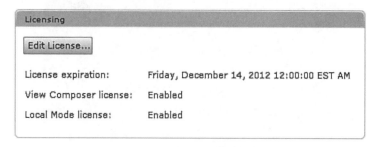

Figure 3.66 Premier enables View Composer and local mode.

You now have to add vCenter Server, but you should ensure the View Composer service is running first. View Composer supports both 32-bit and 64-bit versions of SQL and Oracle. In addition, VMware View 5.1 can be installed on a separate server, or with vCenter. In View 5.1, View Composer creates a self-signed certificate during installation, so a certificate exchange is done when configuring View to communicate with View Composer. It is also a good idea to ensure you can resolve the vCenter hostname from the Connection Server. You should do a forward-and-reverse lookup using the hostname and then IP. This can easily be done by running nslookup from the command prompt.

To install View Composer on vCenter, follow these steps:

1. Click **Next** on the installation wizard screen.

2. Click **Next** on the end user patent agreement.

3. Accept the license agreement and click **Next.**

4. Accept the default path for the installation and click **Next.**

5. Type in the name of the ODBC connection you created, as shown in Figure 3.67. You have the option of specifying a username and password. By default, the connection uses Windows NT integrated security. You should avoid hard-coding a password and ID because doing so creates a major security weakness.

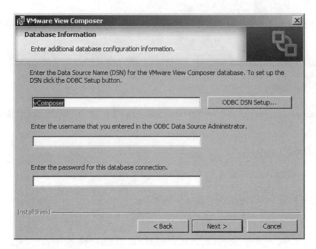

Figure 3.67 Specify the DSN connection.

6. Accept the default port and have the installer create an SSL certificate, as shown in Figure 3.68.

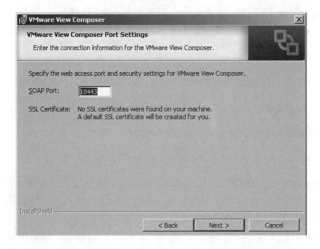

Figure 3.68 SOAP port.

7. Click **Install** to install the View Composer service, as shown in Figure 3.69, and click **Finish** when it is complete.

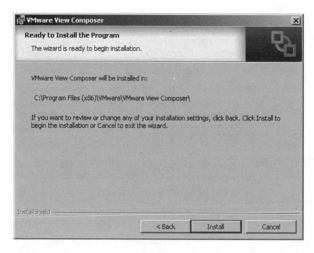

Figure 3.69 Click Install.

Adding vCenter Server

You are now ready to add vCenter Server to the View Connection Server. Under View Configuration and Servers in the right pane, click the **Add** button to configure your vCenter Server connection, as shown in Figure 3.70.

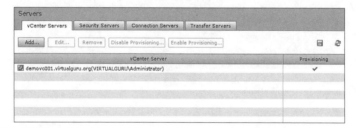

Figure 3.70 Add vCenter Server.

Specify the Fully Qualified Domain Name (FQDN) of your vCenter Server and the VMware View Service Account name created in Chapter 2, "VMware View Architecture." Enable View Composer because you have verified that the Composer service is running on the vCenter Server, as shown in Figure 3.71. It is important for View Composer connectivity that you use the format [Domain\User Name], but the vCenter connectivity accepts User Name only. For consistency, it is best to use the same format in both.

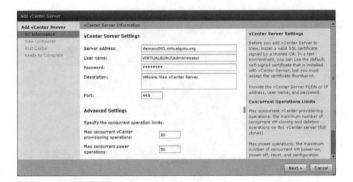

Figure 3.71 Add vCenter Server.

Click **Add** under Domains in the View Composer Settings, as shown in Figure 3.71. Then add the domain information in the Add Domain box, as shown in Figure 3.72. This enables the management of computer accounts in the Active Directory. Click **OK** and **OK** again to save the configuration.

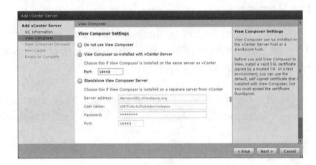

Figure 3.72 Enter domain information.

You should now see the vCenter Server and your first Connection Server as part of the configuration, as shown in Figure 3.73.

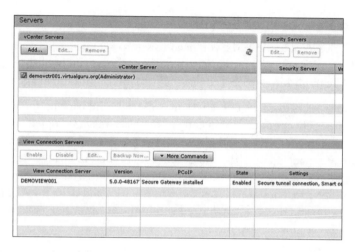

Figure 3.73 vCenter Server is added.

To ensure reliability, you should install a second View Server. For a PoC, you could use any one of the methods discussed to ensure a single connection broker such as VMware FT or vSphere VM HA is highly available. Keep in mind that VMware FT is limited to a single vCPU at this point in time. VMware recommends that two vCPUs be used for a View Connection Server, so it would not be suitable for a production deployment. For production, you want at least two View Servers that use an appliance-based load balancer such as F5. The process to install the second View Server is identical to the first, except that the second server is a Replica Server. The second Replica Server points to the first View Connection Server, as you can see in Figure 3.74.

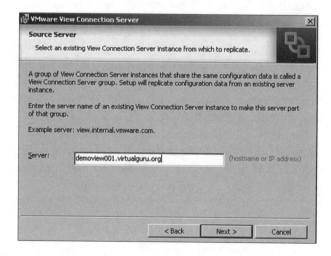

Figure 3.74 Adding a second View Connection Server.

Configuring the Transfer Server

If you intend to use local mode VMs, you need to set up a Transfer Server and image repository. After setting up a Transfer Server and repository, you publish a desktop for offline mode. The publishing process copies the base image into the image repository.

Local mode allows users to check in, check in, roll back, and back up the local mode VM. When the user checks out a VM, a copy of the base image is copied out of the image repository on the Transfer Server and placed on the user's local desktop hard drive. The virtual desktops are made up of a base image and a delta file. All changes are recorded in the delta file, and it is this file that is used to facilitate the functionality of the other three options. When the virtual desktop is checked out, the base and delta files are downloaded to the user's desktop and disk files are locked within the vCenter Server so that no changes can be made to the original source files.

Local mode can be a good option for roaming users who need to get work done both online and offline. It also is ideal if you have a remote branch with slow access to the datacenter. Local mode does enable you to copy any changes back the centralized VMware View environment to ensure that the local VM and locked VM stay in sync.

Checking in synchronizes the delta files stored locally to the one located in the VMware View environment and then deletes the base image on the local desktop and unlocks the files within the virtualization environment for use.

Rolling back does not synchronize; it simply deletes both files on the local user drive and unlocks the files within the virtualization environment for use.

Backing up synchronizes the delta files stored locally and the ones located in the View environment; however, it does not unlock the centrally stored files because a backup allows the local mode VM to keep running or remain primary for the user.

The process for setting up the Transfer Server is similar to the installation of the Connection Server. There are a few things to keep in mind if you are planning on using a virtual machine as the Transfer Server. Each Transfer Server can handle a maximum of 20 check-in or check-out requests according to VMware (http://pubs.vmware.com/view-50/ index.jsp?topic=/com.vmware.view.installation.doc/GUID-1A3719FC-C75A-4ED9- B5D3-70334150BD39.html). After they are added to the View Configuration, they are disabled from DRS. In addition, the servers are configured with an additional three SCSI LSI Logic Parallel controllers to allow them to handle more user requests, as shown in Figure 3.75.

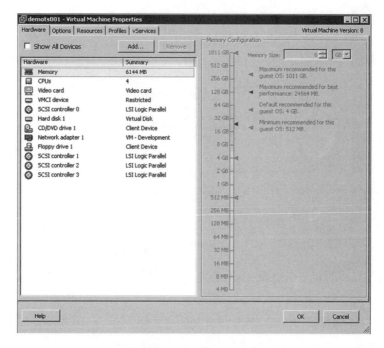

Figure 3.75 Three additional LSI Logic SCSI controllers are added for a total of four.

WARNING

Although Transfer Servers have to be virtual machines, you cannot use the LSI SAS adapter, which is the default for Windows Server 2008 R2, because it is unsupported.

If you are deploying the Transfer Server as a new VM, select the LSI Logic adapter, as shown in Figure 3.76.

Figure 3.76 You must use the LSI Logic adapter.

To install the Transfer Server, follow these instructions

1. Launch the Connection Server Installer and click **Next**.

2. Click **Next** on the patent agreement screen.

3. Accept the license agreement and click **Next**.

4. Accept the default location and click **Next**.

5. Select **View Transfer Server** and click **Next**.

6. On the Transfer Server Configuration screen, provide the name of the domain, server, and email address of the administrator.

7. If the firewall is enabled, select **Configure Firewall Automatically**; otherwise, skip this step.

8. Click **Install** and then **Finish**.

Adding the Transfer Server

To add a Transfer Server, you must first add the Transfer Server and then add the virtual machine storage repository as follows:

1. Log in to the View Connection Server using the View Administrator Console.

2. Under View Configuration, select **Server** and select **Add Transfer Server**.

3. Ensure your vCenter Server is listed as the source for the Transfer Server and click Next.

4. The utility queries the inventory of VMs, or you can manually enter the name.

5. Select your Transfer Server and click **Finish**.

Adding the Image Repository

After adding the Transfer Server, you need to add an image repository. The image repository is the place where VMDKs are copied and stored so that they are available for check-out.

To add a storage repository, complete the following steps:

1. Log in to the View Connection Server using the View Administrator Console.

2. Under Transfer Server Repository, click **Edit** to add the image repository information. You can specify a repository stored locally on a Transfer Server or on a centralized file share.

Publishing Virtual Machine for Offline Mode

To publish a VM for offline mode, you need to create a desktop virtual machine and take a snapshot to create the delta disk. After creating the snapshot, you can publish this virtual desktop for use as a local mode VM as follows:

1. Log in to the View Connection Server using the View Administrator Console.

2. Under Transfer Server Repository and under Content, select **Publish**.

3. Select **Snapshot Created Off Your Base Image.**

The Event Database

The Event Database was introduced in VMware View 4.5 to allow you to store any event that occurs in the View environment to an external database. Adding an Event Database is optional but highly recommended. It is difficult to manage the Connection Server without the Event Database, which can be a key source of information when you are troubleshooting issues. The database is supported on Microsoft SQL Server or the Oracle database. You can create an Event Database by first creating the database in SQL and then configuring the connection within VMware View. With the Event Database, unlike other database configurations, you don't need to create an ODBC connection. You simply add the connection information to View. The Event Database requires local SQL authentication, so the first step is to create a local SQL account and ensure it has the appropriate access to the Event Database. You can create a local SQL account using the following procedure:

1. Open SQL Management Studio and connect to your database instance.

2. Open the Security and then the Logins modules.

3. Right-click **Login** and select **New Login**.

4. Under the General Settings, ensure SQL Server authentication.

5. Provide a login name such as **svc_Events** and provide a password. Note: SQL 2008 requires this to be a complex password, so stay away from any dictionary words.

6. Retype the password to confirm it.

7. Because this is a service account, deselect the following:

   - Enforce Password Policy

   - Enforce Password Expiration

   - User Must Change Password at the Next Login

8. Under the default database, select your Event Database, such as vEvents.

9. Select the **User Mapping** page.

10. Select **db_owner** in addition to the default public access and click **OK.**

After creating the local SQL account, you can then add the Event Database from the View Administrator Console. Under View Configuration select **Event Configuration**.

Provide the name of your database server, the type, and a user ID in the fields shown in Figure 3.77 to connect. The table prefix ensures that the Event Database can be unique to this collection of VMware View Servers. If you have another site, both can use the same database service because the table prefix is unique. You have to provide a prefix, however, if you have only a single site for VMware View Servers.

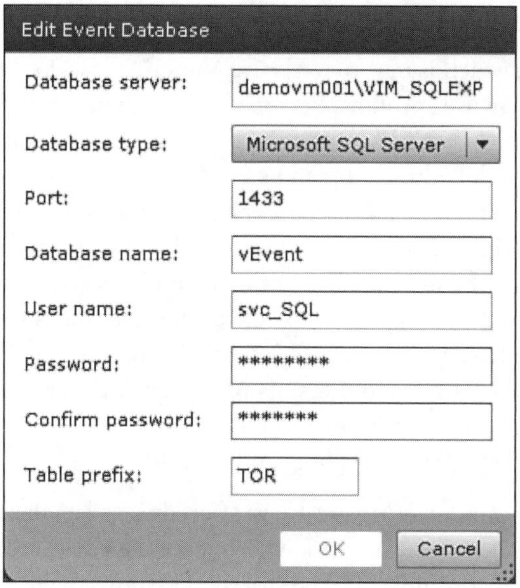

Figure 3.77 Add an Event Database.

After you connect the Event Database, you can set the period in which events appear in the console and the duration in which events are considered new, as shown in Figure 3.78. After you have the settings configured, click **OK**.

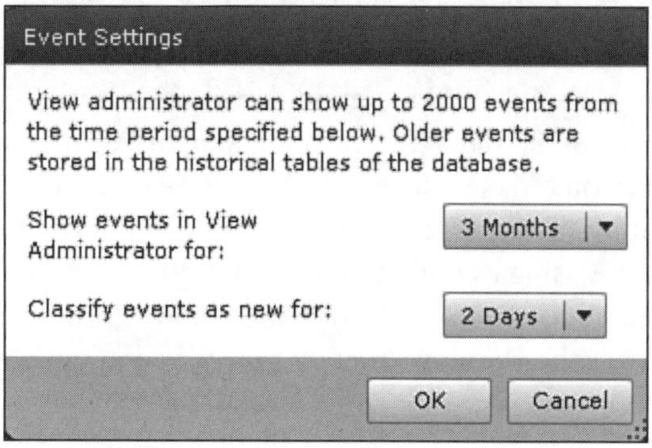

Figure 3.78 Set the event display options.

Persona Management

Persona Management, which is new to VMware View 5, allows you to deliver, synchronize, and manage user profiles. Persona Management came from a licensing and co-development agreement with RTO Software (http://www.vmware.com/company/news/releases/rto-vmworld09.html). It can be used as a replacement or an enhancement to Windows profiles. The difference between Persona Management and Windows profiles is that only the registry information that is required for the user to log in is downloaded, not the entire profile. As the user opens additional applications, the remaining files are downloaded. The minimalistic approach to data at the start keeps the user logon process quick and streamlined. Like Windows profiles, this feature uses a file server or CIFS share to ensure the user data is centralized. Persona Management also gives you finer control of the synchronization of data between the local user session and the storage repository. By default, this happens every 10 minutes but can be adjusted.

Prior to Persona Management, VMware View offered user data disks, which have now become persistent attached disks. A persistent attached disk is a second VMDK where any user writes (including the profile) could be stored. The only challenge with a secondary drive approach is that the information is local and associated with a virtual desktop versus centrally available. You can now use both of these technologies to essentially provide a local user cache. You can use the user persistent disk to provide a local user repository for linked clones or Composer-created View desktops and Persona to make sure the changes are synced centrally so that they are preserved in case the virtual machine drives are lost. You should ensure the local Persona persists between logoffs, so do not enable the Remove Local Persona at Log Off setting in this case. We review this topic more in Chapter 6.

The nice thing about Persona Management is that it applies to both physical and virtual desktops as of VMware View 5.1. Keep in mind that if you are using shared server-based desktops (TS Servers), Persona Management is not supported. If you have users accessing View desktops using Persona Management and Windows roaming profiles on regular desktops, the best solution prior to 5.1 was to separate them. Now you can use a single Persona profile. If you are using a combination of Windows and View profiles, the View desktops can be configured to override an existing Windows profile in the configuration settings. This ensures that the Windows roaming profiles don't overwrite Persona profile settings when the user logs out.

Outside the file server requirement, Persona Management does not require any additional infrastructure because it can be installed with the View Agent on the virtual or physical desktop. The configuration of Persona Management is managed through an Active Directory Administrative template, which can be imported into the OU that you are deploying the virtual machines to or the local policy settings of the virtual desktop. The Administrative template is located on the View Connection Server:

<install_directory>\VMware\VMwareView\Server\extras\GroupPolicyFiles\
ViewPM.adm

To import these policies into the AD, follow these steps:

1. Open your Group Policy Management Console.

2. Right-click your View Desktop OU and create or link a GPO policy.

3. Enter a name such as **View Persona Management Policy**.

4. Right-click the new policy and select **Edit**.

5. Browse to Administrative Templates and select **Add/Remove Templates**.

6. Click **Add** again, browse to the location on the View Server, and select the **ViewPM. adm** template.

7. Expand Administrative Templates and VMware View Agent Configuration and Persona Management.

To import these policies into the local user policy, follow these steps:

1. Open Local Security Policy.

2. Right-click Administrative Templates and click **Add\Remove Templates**.

3. Click **Add** again, browse to the location on the View Server, and select the **ViewPM. adm** template.

4. Expand Administrative Templates and VMware View Agent Configuration and Persona Management.

Security Servers

Security Servers are another type of View Server but designed to be deployed to simplify remote access. Because they are usually deployed in a DMZ situation, they are not required to be part of the Active Directory. They reduce the number of connections that are required to be open on the forward-facing firewall of a DMZ (demilitarized zone) and corporate or internal firewall. Each Security Server is paired with a specific Connection Server, so if you are load balancing two Security Servers in the DMZ, you require two View Servers deployed internally.

New in VMware View 5 is the capability to proxy PCoIP. Prior to version 5, only the Remote Desktop Protocol (RDP) was available through a Security Server. To work, the connections must be tunneled through the Security Servers. Typically, the Security Servers are deployed in a DMZ and should be load balanced behind an appliance-based firewall such as F5, as shown in Figure 3.79. If you are load balancing the Security Servers, you should not load balance the connectivity from the Security Servers to the Connection Servers because there is a one-to-one relationship between Security Servers and Connection Servers.

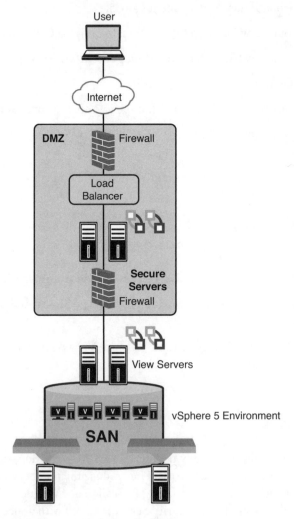

Figure 3.79 Security Servers are deployed in the DMZ.

Firewall Rules

To allow the traffic to pass through the external firewall to your Security Server, you should translate the external IP to the internal IP and ensure the required ports are open using NAT. You can find a detailed network flow diagram in the View 5 Architecture planning guide starting on page 61; it is downloadable from http://pubs.vmware.com/view-50/topic/com.vmware.ICbase/PDF/view-50-architecture-planning.pdf. The following ports need to be open:

1. PCoIP traffic between the View Client and Security Server (External)

    a. TCP 443 for the website

    b. TCP 4172 from Client to Security Server

    c. UDP 4172 between client and security server in both directions

    To allow the traffic to pass, you must set the following rules on the internal firewall.

2. PCoIP traffic between the View Security Server and Virtual Desktop (Internal)

    a. TCP 4172 from Security Server to virtual desktop

    b. UDP 4172 from Security Server to virtual desktop in both directions

You must set up several things for the Security Server to work properly. The first consideration is the external URL. If you are going to provide access to a View environment remotely, you must register a public-facing IP address and register it in DNS. Let's use the example of access.virtualguru.org. The DNS name is important because during the configuration of the Security Server, you configure it to respond to this external URL versus its own hostname. Although we discuss straight installation in this chapter, it is not typical that remote access is offered with single-factor authentication. It should always be combined with a two-factor authentication method such as RSA.

Adding the Security Servers

The first thing you should do is define a pairing password, which you do from the View Connection Server, not the Security Server.

First, log in to the View Connection Server. Then, under View Connection Servers, select the **More Commands** button, as shown in Figure 3.80.

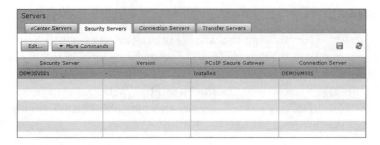

Figure 3.80 Add the Security Server.

Specify the Security Server pairing password, confirm the password and set the password timeout. You should specify a short amount of time for security reasons and also ensure that the Security Server pairing is done before the expiry.

Now you can install your Security Server using the following steps:

1. Launch the Connection Server Installer and click **Next**.

2. Click **Next** on the patent agreement screen.

3. Accept the license agreement and click **Next**.

4. Accept the default location and click **Next**.

5. Select **View Security Server** and click **Next**.

6. Provide the IP or hostname of the Connection Server to which this Security Server will be associated and click **Next**.

7. Provide the pairing password you configured in the View Server and click **Next**.

8. Specify the external URL that this Security Server should respond to—for example, access.virtualguru.org—and also the IP address that this DNS name is registered to for PCoIP connections. Then click **Next**.

9. Allow the installer to automatically configure the firewall. I recommend that you definitely leave the firewall intact when deploying the Security Server Security Server in the DMZ and click **Next**.

10. Click **Install** and then **Finish**.

If you are going to tunnel PCoIP, you must tell the View Server paired with the Security Server to use PCoIP Secure Gateway for PCoIP to desktop. Under the View Server, select **Edit** and ensure **User PCoIP Secure Gateway for PCoIP Connections to Desktop** is selected. The **Use Secure Tunnel Connection to Desktop** setting is the default and should be left as is, as shown in Figure 3.81. The External URL and PCoIP External URL point to themselves for the internal View Server, which is fine. Only the Security Server needs to respond to the external IP addresses.

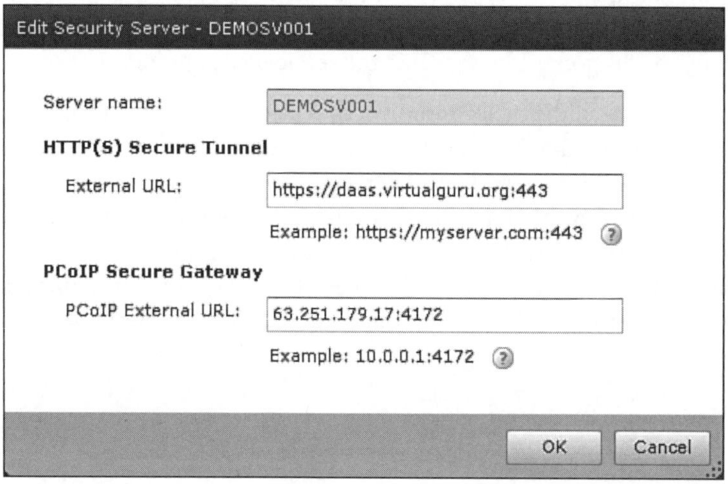

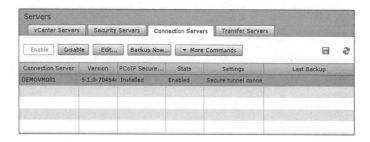

Figure 3.81 Enable the PCoIP Secure Gateway.

After the gateway is properly installed, if you refresh the View Administrator Console under Security Servers, you should see your server there, as shown in Figure 3.82.

Figure 3.82 View your Security Servers.

If you need to change the External URL or IP for tunneling PCoIP, you can click **Edit** on the Security Server.

Summary

It is important to ensure each component of the VMware View environment is functioning properly. Check the Event Viewer on the Windows Server for error messages related to the installation. In addition, make sure that the services start properly.

At this point, you have all the major infrastructure pieces of the VMware View environment up and running. You need to create virtual machines and tune them for optimal performance. Before you do, though, you should look at one other important piece of the VMware View platform: application virtualization. When you understand the benefit of application virtualization, you can integrate it into your View desktops. We discuss application virtualization next in Chapter 4, "Application Virtualization," and then put all the pieces together in Chapter 5, "Building Your Virtual Desktop."

Chapter 4

Application Virtualization

Why Virtualize Applications?

Application virtualization as a technology has been around for some time. It was originally developed to enhance Server-Based Computing (SBC) environments. In SBC environments, it was quite common to run into application incompatibility issues. For example, if you have two terminal servers that both run Applications A, B, and C, and you have 50 user sessions running on each, you have a pretty even distribution and resource utilization. What happens, however, if you get a request to load Application D also, and Application D is incompatible with one of the applications? You then have to introduce a third server to run Application D. Adding this server leads to an unequal distribution of sessions and the inefficiency of resource utilization across the servers.

What became apparent is that although designed for SBC environments, application incompatibility is a bigger issue on desktops. Application virtualization evolved as a solution to both SBC and desktop environments.

One of the earliest pioneers in application virtualization was a company called Softricity, which was acquired by Microsoft and evolved into App-V. Citrix, a leading provider of SBC solutions, also developed an application virtualization solution generally referred to as Citrix application streaming. These solutions allowed applications that were incompatible to run under a single server or desktop by isolating applications from each other.

One of the early problems with application virtualization was that applications were often interdependent of one another. Think of an application that makes use of some components of Microsoft Office such as Microsoft Word or Microsoft Excel.

Early versions of application virtualization required you to layer all the applications that were codependent into a single application virtualization package. Layering these applications caused management and licensing issues because when applications were isolated, they had no visibility into other applications that had also been isolated or virtualized. Imagine having to install a full version of Microsoft Office with every application that required it. Or having to deal with other dependencies such as .NET Framework, Silverlight, Adobe Reader, and Flash. Also imagine the additional overhead in managing additional licensing because of this limitation. The latest versions of Citrix application streaming, Microsoft App-V and VMware ThinApp, allow visibility into other packages and association to file types to allow a more seamless integration.

Fundamentally, the technology is similar to packaging applications for automated installation and follows many similar best practices. Application packaging essentially requires you to run a baseline, install an EXE file, configure it, and then rerun the baseline so that all deltas can be wrapped up in a neatly packaged MSI or EXE. Streamed applications are typically EXEs versus MSIs. Application virtualization adds one additional step: the execution of the application. The application is run so that the packager can track what portions of the operating system are being written to, and they can be pulled into the package also; this includes the registry, DLLs, and files that may be changed. These components all become part of the package to facilitate the application interoperation. If two application virtualization packages write to the same DLL, this file is included in its own bubble or sandbox, ensuring both can run happily side by side.

VMware acquired ThinStall in 2008, and it became ThinApp. One of the unique features of ThinApp is that it does not require any supported back-end infrastructure of the other platforms and is essentially agentless. Unlike other solutions that require a client installation to support the application streaming, a ThinApp package is a self-contained application virtualization file and does not require a preinstalled client or agent. There are a few different options for delivering ThinApp applications within a VMware View environment, such as from a file share or Distributed File Share (DFS) to support replication, on a user persistent disk, or "installed" on the virtual machine, which we discuss.

Figure 4.1 shows a logical view of a ThinApp package. Inside the application is a sandbox or virtual container that stores the redirected writes to the registry and file system.

ThinApp packages run as the user, and no special user privileges are required to run the application. You can maintain Active Directory (AD) group permissions by storing ThinApp packages on a central file share that allows access to the appropriate Active Directory groups. You can then create shortcuts to the Start menu and desktop and add file associations to the centrally located applications using ThinReg.

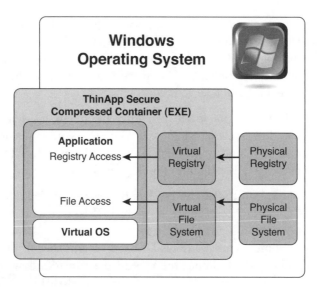

Figure 4.1 ThinApp package.

ThinReg is a utility included with ThinApp. It you include the ThinReg utility in a logon script, it can query the file directory and automatically register any applications in the folder when you use the following syntax:

```
THINREG.EXE <UNC or Drive\Path>\*.EXE> /Q
```

As part of the packaging process, you can also specify groups with permissions to launch the application. The point to keep in mind if you specify an Active Directory group during the packaging stage is that the ThinApp package uses the Security ID (SID) of the group. The SID is the way the AD references the group object. This allows the group name to change, but if the group is deleted, the application needs to be repackaged to update the SID information.

Setting Up the ThinApp Packaging Environment

Let's discuss how to set up the ThinApp packaging environment. Because it is a process, you must set up a workflow to virtualizing applications. The components that you need to consider are the packaging environment, the storage repository, and the production delivery method.

The packaging environment is the desktop on which you prepare your ThinApp applications. What is unusual about ThinApp is that the best practices for most application virtualization platforms require you to create the package on the environment you will be deploying to; that is, packaging a Windows XP application for deployment on Windows

XP. ThinApp is unique because it supports application portability. You can create the package once and deploy it to all versions of Windows, with the exception of x86 and 64-bit. You cannot package a 64-bit application to run on an x86 operating system. Although this is true today, 32-bit and 64-bit interoperability are on the roadmap and may be released by the time this book goes to press.

ThinApp packages allow you to move between different operating systems by fully supporting Windows side-by-side technology, or WinSxS. Note this is not to be confused with side-by-side application updating, which is an operational feature of ThinApp that uses a versioning number to allow ThinApp package updates in a seamless manner.

Prior to WinSxS support, most DLLs and system files were installed into the c:\windows\system32 directory. Conflicts occurred when you had DLLs overwrite one another on application installations and essentially create problems between DLLs, causing applications to blow up at runtime. WinSxS installs DLLs in version-specific directories under %SystemRoot%\WinSxS. For example, the WordPad.exe on Windows 7 64-bit is stored in winsxs\wow64_microsoft-windows-wordpad_31bf3856ad364e35_6.1.7600.16624_none_9443fa1cbac783db.

Every operating system installs DLLs in a separate path. The master file that controls which DLLs the application uses and versions of the DLLs to load is called the *manifest*. ThinApp has native support for WinSxS and examines the manifest file to determine what DLLs are used and which version to run. WinSxS was actually introduced in Windows XP, but because ThinApp has its own WinSxS processing, virtual applications can be ported easily between Windows operating systems.[1]

To create the packaging environment, you need to deploy a packaging machine. This VM should be representative of the environment you will be deploying on (x86 or 64-bit) and should be a clean desktop but also the oldest version of the target desktop virtual machines you will be deploying to that supports WinSxS. For example, if you are deploying on Windows XP, Windows 7 x86, and Windows 7 64-bit, you should package on Windows XP. One point to note if you do have a legacy Windows environment is that VMware supports ThinApp applications only on current Windows operating systems that are still supported by Microsoft.

The packaging desktop should include only the OS and the ThinApp packager to ensure the package does not include anything unattended such as OS patches. The packaging machines should be virtual machines because the capability to snapshot is an invaluable timesaver in application virtualization packaging. For example, say you are packaging an application and you forget to execute a specific feature. With a VM, you are able to set a bookmark at the execution stage of the packaging process to allow you to easily "roll back time" to this point. If you intend to use Active Directory groups to assign permissions

---

[1]Based on information researched on VMware's ThinApp blog.

to the ThinApp packages, your VM should be joined to the Active Directory. Ensure, however, that the packaging environment is set up as a dedicated OU that ensures that general desktop operational processes such as application installations are not pushed to the environment.

To install the packaging machine, follow these steps:

1. Launch the ThinApp 4.7 Enterprise Installer.

2. Enter the license key and license display name and click **Install**.

3. Click the **Finish** button.

In the ThinApp Capture utility, creation of a ThinApp package involves five stages, the first of which is Prescan. In the Prescan stage, a scan is done from a baseline before the application is installed. In stage two, the application is installed. Stage three scans to identify the application changes that were made. In stage four, you can customize the application by identifying the application shortcuts and entry points. In the final stage, you build the ThinApp package, as depicted in Figure 4.2.

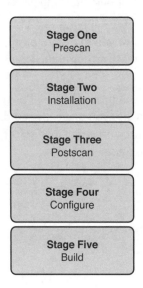

Figure 4.2 ThinApp creation stages.

In Prescan, the utility takes a baseline of the packaging system. As mentioned, this should be a clean virtual machine with no packages installed to ensure that any registry key changes or added files are captured as part of the packaging process. You have the option of adjusting the prescanning locations on the prescan page. By default, the entire C:\ directory and the following registry keys are scanned:

- HKEY_LOCAL_MACHINE

- HKEY_CURRENT_USER

- HKEY_USERS

Under Advanced, you can add additional locations, such as network drives or additional registry keys. The prescan process invokes the snapshot.exe file, which is controlled by snapshot.ini. The snapshot.ini file adds granular control on what is excluded and can be manually edited to either add things or remove registry or file locations from the list, although editing is not typically necessary. You must edit the file before the prescan process to ensure the changes go into effect.

You can alternately run the entire process from the command line by using snapshot.exe. For example, to build a sample baseline, you could run the Snapshot utility as follows:

```
Snapshot.exe [name of baseline].snapshot.
```

This alternative can be beneficial in maintaining packages against separate baseline images because you can logically name them when you run the process manually. We go through an example when we discuss maintaining ThinApp packages.

The next stage is the installation of the application. This part of the ThinApp Capture utility is just a splash screen to allow you to install the application. Keep in mind that you should run your application and make any customizations that you want or need during this part of the process.

After stage two is complete, you can proceed to the Postscan stage, which essentially reruns the snapshot.exe executable. If you manually run this tool, you see the utility checking the Windows\winsxs directories and manifests for the specific DLLs and their respective versions, as shown in Figure 4.3.

```
c:\Program Files\VMware\VMware ThinApp>snapshot.exe post_install_notepad++.snapshot
VMware ThinApp Snapshot Tool Version 4.7.0-519532, Built Nov  2 2011
Copyright 2006-2011, VMware, Inc. All rights reserved
Scanning system, this may take a few minutes...
> c:\Users\sysadmin\Favorites\Links for United States
> c:\Windows\Media\Delta
> c:\Windows\System32\DriverStore\FileRepository\averfx2hbtv.inf_x86_neutral_30c25b3574f8b
> c:\Windows\System32\DriverStore\FileRepository\prnhp002.inf_x86_neutral_e6daa9c39ac001a3
> c:\Windows\System32\DriverStore\FileRepository\wstorflt.inf_x86_neutral_f91032fad599ad3e
> c:\Windows\winsxs
> c:\Windows\winsxs
> c:\Windows\winsxs
> c:\Windows\winsxs\Backup
```

Figure 4.3 The Postscan stage.

Figure 4.4 shows the Build stage, which allows you to select the shortcuts for the application. Most applications have several standard shortcuts and executables, such as the readme and uninstall.exe. On the entry points, you can ensure that only the correct executable is presented to the user.

Figure 4.4 Build stage.

ThinApp packages can be integrated into the VMware Horizon Application Manager, which is a forward-looking technology that brings the idea of the "Appstore" to the VMware product portfolio. Horizon Application Manager is unique in that it provides single sign-on capability to both internally deployed applications as well as third-party Software as a Service (SaaS) applications such as Salesforce and Google Apps. It is configured through the integration of a virtual appliance. You can allow your ThinApp applications to be managed by your Horizon Application Manager appliance, which is shown in Figure 4.5.

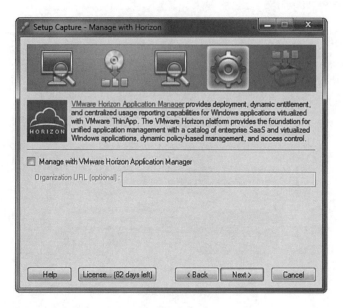

Figure 4.5 VMware Horizon Application Manager.

As you can see in Figure 4.6, you can integrate the permission to execute your ThinApp application with your Windows Active Directory. At build time, ThinApp converts the group name to SID values. The Security ID is the way Windows references the group to allow you to change the name without changing the unique numeric value associated with it. This means that your packaging desktop should be joined to the Active Directory. If you accidentally delete the group, you have to rebuild the package. It is a best practice to create Active Directory groups for your ThinApp applications. Start with a general-purpose AD group for applications used by everyone and then add specific groups for applications used by specific users.

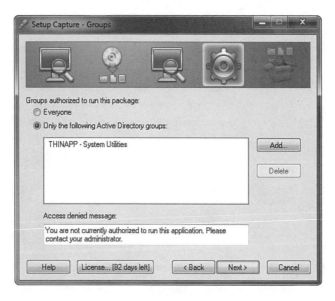

Figure 4.6 You have the option of integrating Active Directory groups.

The next screen, shown in Figure 4.7, allows you to control where the writes are allowed: either outside the application sandbox or restricted to the sandbox only. It is recommended that common certified applications such as Microsoft Office be allowed to write outside the sandbox and less common applications be restricted to writing only within the sandbox. Although the default is Full write, you should actually follow a policy that restricts write access to most applications to enforce a higher level of security.

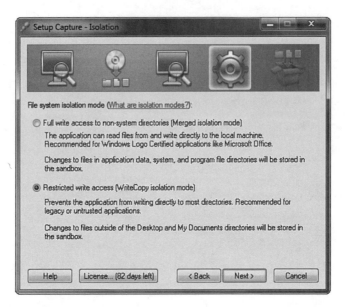

Figure 4.7 Restricted write access.

Figure 4.8 shows where you control the storage location of user configurations. With Windows Vista and later versions, the application configuration information is stored in AppData. This file is hidden by default and is equivalent to the Documents and Settings folder in Windows XP. If the ThinApp application is being deployed in a VMware View virtual desktop environment, the default option of the user profile in %AppData%\ ThinApp ensures the configurations are written to the profile directory. If you are deploying this as a portable app (USB and portable media), you have the option of redirecting it to the same directory as the application. The last option is to redirect it to a custom network share. The %AppData%\Thinstall location is appropriate for most VMware View environments. AppData is a folder that can be redirected by Persona Management under the Folder redirection settings.

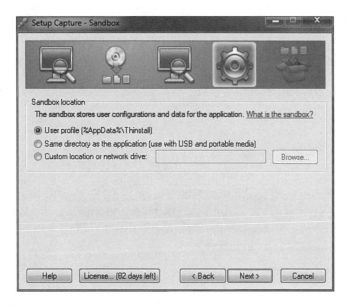

Figure 4.8 Location of the user configurations.

If you are feeling generous, you can opt to send metric and monitoring information to VMware to help in its development of ThinApp, as shown in Figure 4.9. This is anonymous data, so no private data is sent.

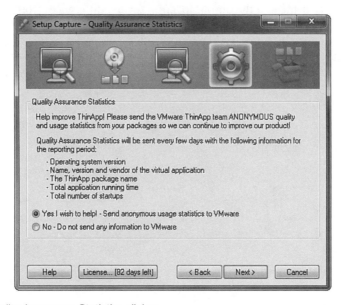

Figure 4.9 Quality Assurance Statistics dialog.

The Inventory name is used to help track the ThinApp package. A software development kit (SDK) is available from VMware at http://vmware.com/go/thinappsdk. It is a COM object that can be used in most programming languages. A COM object is a binary interface that allows communication between the object and a programming language. For example, to query the inventory name, you can use the following Windows script host command[2]:

```
Set Management = WScript.CreateObject("ThinApp.Management")
Set Package = Management.OpenPackage(WScript.Arguments(0))
WScript.Echo "Inventory name: " & Package.InventoryName
```

To use this script, you need to download the ThinApp SDK from VMware. After it is downloaded, you need to extract ThinAppSDK.DLL and copy it to the desktop you want to query. Then you need to register the ThinAppSDK.DLL using REGSVR32.EXE. Simply open a command prompt and type

REGSVR32.EXE ThinAppSDK.DLL

After the SDK is registered, you can use it to query the ThinApp.Management Object. To execute the sample script shown previously, copy it to a text file and save it with a .vbs extension, such as queryThinApp.vbs. You can double-click this file from Windows or run cscript queryThinApp.vbs from the command line. Additional information can be found at VMware's ThinApp blog at http://blogs.vmware.com/thinapp/2012/03/configuring-the-thinapp-sdk-in-place-of-thinreg.html.

Type the Inventory name and the output location for the differences from the pre- and postscans. The compiled "ThinApp'd" files are stored in the bin subdirectory of this location, which you can change on the Project Settings screen, as shown in Figure 4.10.

---

[2]http://blogs.vmware.com/thinapp/2010/08/vmware-thinapp-46-whats-new.html

Figure 4.10 Project settings.

If you also plan to deploy this file as a portable application, you have the option of compiling it as an MSI and an EXE or DAT file. Plus, you have the option of enabling compression. Compression has an extremely fast decompression algorithm, so it has little impact on the ThinApp package unless the package is extremely large. On an extremely large package (2.5–3 GB), compression can make the application slower. It is similar to a file zip and has low memory consumption and very little impact at application launch. Compressing applications is generally recommended, as shown in Figure 4.11.

Figure 4.11 Package settings.

The next steps identify the differences between the pre-snapshot and post-snapshot jobs and dump the deltas in the project directory. In addition, they create a package.ini file that controls many features of the ThinApp process, such as compression and isolation functionality (see Figure 4.12).

Figure 4.12 Save the project.

You can edit the project files to add additional switches and files. You also have the option to edit the package.ini file directly because many additional switches are not exposed through the VMware Capture utility (see Figure 4.13). When this is done, click **Build** and the package is built and stored in a subdirectory of the project directory bin. If you selected MSI and an EXE or DAT file, you find them both there.

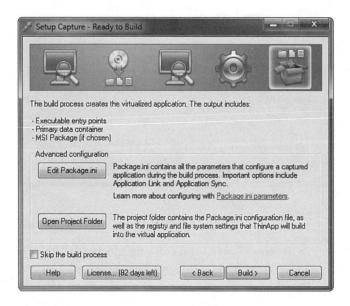

Figure 4.13 Ready to build.

At this point, the packaging process is finished, and your screen should look like the one in Figure 4.14.

Figure 4.14 Building a project.

A storage repository or file share is needed for storing source files and ThinApp applications. It is worth putting some thought into your file structure. You need source installation files or a library of installation packages, a preverified ThinApp directory, a production ThinApp directory, a revision and update directory preverified, and a backup directory. Follow your company's own internal naming standards, but they should follow the same logical workflow.

FOR EXAMPLE:

\\Source_Application_installations

\\Pre-verified ThinApp Packages

\\Production ThinApp Packages

\\Production ThinApp Backup

\\Updated ThinApp Packages

\\Preverified Updated ThinApp Packages

The reason you break out the production and update directories (both preverified and production) is to ensure that multiple rollback points are available. For example, as part of the update process, you upgrade the production ThinApp package and copy it to the

Preverified Updated ThinApp Packages folder. After it is tested, it goes to the Updated ThinApp Packages and essentially is suitable to integrate into the View desktops. If, after deploying the package to a number of View desktops, you find an issue that was not uncovered in the initial testing, you can fall back to the Production folder, which contains the original production ThinApp package. After user testing, you then take the Updated ThinApp Packages and move them to production, allowing the process to repeat with the next request. The directory structure is more about process management than ThinApp technology, but a consistent and understood process helps you avoid issues and aids in problem resolution.

You can integrate ThinApp packages in a View environment in a number of ways. VMware refers to this as the *execution mode*.[3] The execution simply refers to the place where the ThinApp package is executed from. VMware calls running the ThinApp package from a file share *streaming execution* while running it from local storage devices such as a USB key or off the virtual or physical desktops hard drive is *deployed execution*. With streaming execution, you should ensure that the file service has great performance and is highly available because you are introducing a dependency to the network share.

Streaming execution provides more flexibility with less administration and faster provisioning; however, you are dependent on the network for performance. Deployed execution provides arguably higher availability and guaranteed performance but comes with more administration and less flexibility because the packages are deployed to the individual View desktops. We discuss different methods of ensuring availability in Chapter 11, "High Availability Considerations."

When you are looking at which method to use with VMware View, the most straight-forward is through the "App Factory," which, according to VMware's definition, is streaming execution. (Note that this should not be confused with VMware ThinApp Factory from VMware labs, which is designed to automate the conversion of software packages to ThinApp packages.) The App Factory involves updating your View Connection server configuration so that it knows were the Production ThinApp Packages folder is. After you do that, you can scan the directory for ThinApp packages. And after these packages are identified in the inventory, you can entitle them to your virtual desktops. The process to do this is as follows:

1. Open the View Administrator website.

2. Browse to **View Configuration, ThinApp Configuration**.

3. Click **Add Repository**.

4. For the repository, provide a display name, the Fully Qualified Domain Name (FQDN) to the server, share where the ThinApp packages will be stored, a description, and click **Save**.

---

[3]VMware ThinApp reference architecture.

When this process is complete, you can scan for available packages under **Inventory and ThinApp** from the View Administrator Console and select **Scan New ThinApps**.

ThinApp Packages and Microsoft Activation

Application licensing bears consideration when you are looking into application virtualization. Although each vendor has its own method of licensing, in general, these methods are similar to at least one of the methods Microsoft employs to license its products. Let's review some general background on Microsoft licensing.

Licenses for Microsoft applications can be obtained through one of three basic channels: retail, original equipment manufacturer (OEM), or volume licensing. Retail applications come with a unique key that is used to complete the activation after installation either by phone or over the Internet. OEM activation is usually done prior to the product being shipped to the customer but is valid only as long as the OEM version is used on the hardware shipped. These licenses cannot be transferred for use in virtual desktop environments. Volume license agreements are tailored agreements that are customized based on the size of the organization and Microsoft products used. A volume license agreement is the most complementary license arrangement when you are looking at virtual applications and desktops. For a comprehensive list of the types of volume license agreements, refer to Microsoft's volume licensing information at http://www.microsoft.com/licensing/.

If you are under a volume license agreement, you can use either the Key Management Service (KMS) or Multiple Activation Key (MAK) or a combination of the two. For enterprise environments, KMS is recommended. The fundamental difference is that KMS allows you to activate products within your network, whereas MAK activates products on a one-time basis using Microsoft's hosted activation service.

KMS is a client/server architecture with Microsoft KMS clients contacting KMS hosts using DNS or static settings. KMS requires a minimum number of client connections to begin activating clients. This number is referred to as the *KMS threshold*. Windows 7, for example, requires a minimum of ≥ 25 activation requests. KMS activations are good for 180 days and require the clients to renew their activation once within that 180-day period. To deploy KMS, you install the services on a host and then complete the activation of the host with Microsoft. Microsoft recommends that a minimum of two KMS hosts be deployed for redundancy and failover.

To help you manage all these options, Microsoft introduced the Volume Activation Management Tool (VAMT). The VAMT helps you inventory, track, and manage the retail MAK and KMS requests across your environment. You can use the VAMT to collect all the Installation IDs (IIDs) from each client request. This information is sent from the VAMT, and then the activations are done by the VAMT through Microsoft. After the service is activated, the corresponding ID (CID) is returned to the client by the VAMT, completing the activation process.[4]

If you are deploying virtual desktops in secure zones, you can choose from four options available to deal with activation of Microsoft products:

1. You can use KMS and open TCP outbound port 1688 in the firewall and RPC inbound. This assumes the virtual desktops are allowed access to the core network and the KMS hosts can communicate with the isolated VMs.

2. If the number of isolated virtual desktops exceeds 25, you can deploy an internal KMS server and activate it over the phone.

3. If the number of desktops does not exceed 25 and changes to the firewall are not allowed, you can activate each MAK license over the phone.

4. You can deploy a VAMT in the isolated network, collect all IIDs from the clients, and copy this information to portable media. You import this information to a VAMT that has access to the Internet. Then you retrieve the CIDs and re-import them into the isolated VAMT to activate the Microsoft products.

KMS is fine for centrally stored and operated virtual desktops. If you are using local mode and allowing both the ThinApp packages and the virtual machine to be checked out, enforcing the reregistration may be both confusing to the end users and difficult to manage. Specifically for Office and ThinApp, the one-time registration process, or MAK, is ideal. In these examples we assume that you are using the MAK process.

Creating a Package

To provide a guide for ThinApp packaging, let's consider the example of packing Office 2010 on Windows XP and testing it on Windows 7 x86 and Windows 7 64-bit, running on WOW 64 (WOW 64 is the Windows on Windows emulator designed to run 32-bit applications on Windows 64-bit operating systems). For ThinApp Office 2010, a minimum version of the packager should be used; it is 4.7.0 Build 556613. In addition, it is a good idea to review the KnowledgeBase (KB) article at http://kb.vmware.com/kb/1022287 because it reviews the activation process for Office 2010. The Office ThinApp process is available online from VMware at http://blogs.vmware.com/thinapp/2011/02/quick-start-guide-for-deploying-office-2010-using-thinapp-461.html. VMware has a very active ThinApp user community; for other tips on ThinApp, it is recommended that you join the user community, especially if you will be involved in packaging on a reoccurring basis.

---

[4]http://technet.microsoft.com/en-us/library/ff686876.aspx

To ensure you have everything you need to package Office 2010, you need to have the following components:

- Microsoft .NET 3.5

- Office 2010 x86

- Access to the Internet to facilitate the installation of Microsoft .NET 3.5

- A virtual desktop running Windows XP SP3 with the VMware ThinApp Capture utility installed

- A virtual desktop running Windows 7 x86 for verifying the package

- A virtual desktop running Windows 7 64-bit for verifying the package

After verifying you have the prerequisites, you are ready to begin the installation.

First, take a snapshot of the virtual machine in its pristine state to allow you to roll back to this point after this exercise. Then launch the Setup Capture utility, as shown in Figure 4.15.

Figure 4.15 Launch the Setup Capture utility.

Start the prescan process by clicking **Prescan**, shown in Figure 4.16.

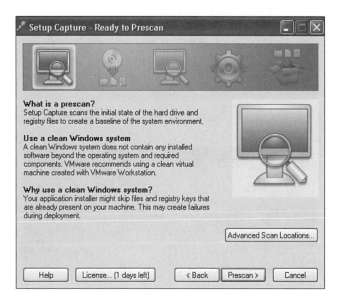

Figure 4.16 Start the prescan process.

Minimize the screen (as mentioned in Figure 4.17) to start the installation of Office and its related components.

Figure 4.17 Minimize for Office installation and related components.

When Microsoft .NET finishes the installation, as shown in Figure 4.18, it launches a background process to compile .NET assemblies in the background. Because this process can take some time and you want to ensure it completes prior to installing Office, you can hurry things along by running the following command line from the root of the .NET folder to force the compile to happen:

```
C:\windows\Microsoft.NET\Framework\v2.0.50727\ngen.exe executequeueditems
```

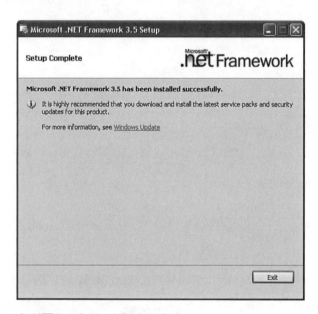

Figure 4.18 Microsoft .NET has finished the installation.

In the installation directory for Office under ProPlus.WW, you find the config.xml. You must put your MAK key inside the config.xml file using

```
<PIDKEY value"[LICENSE]"/>
```

Launch the setup and specify the config.xml using

```
setup /config [Path to config.xml]
```

See Figure 4.19.

```
1   □<Configuration Product="ProPlus">
2
3       <!-- <Display Level="full" CompletionNotice="yes" SuppressModal="no"
    AcceptEula="no" /> -->
4
5       <!-- <Logging Type="standard" Path="%temp%" Template="Microsoft Office
    Professional Plus Setup(*).txt" /> -->
6
7       <!-- <USERNAME Value="Virtualguru Default User" /> -->
8
9       <!-- <COMPANYNAME Value="virtualguru.org" /> -->
10
11      <!-- <INSTALLLOCATION Value="%programfiles%\Microsoft Office" /> -->
12
13      <!-- <LIS CACHEACTION="CacheOnly" /> -->
14
15      <!-- <LIS SOURCELIST="\\server1\share\Office;\\server2\share\Office"
    /> -->
16
17      <!-- <DistributionPoint Location="\\server\share\Office" /> -->
18
19      <!-- <OptionState Id="OptionID" State="absent" Children="force" /> -->
20
```

Figure 4.19 Edit config.xml.

After updating config.xml, you are ready to install Microsoft Office 2010. To install Office 2010, complete the following steps:

1. Launch the installer and accept the terms of agreement.

2. On the **Choose the Installation You Want** dialog box, click the **Customize** button.

3. Select **Microsoft Office, Run All from My Computer**.

4. Click **Install Now** to install Microsoft Office 2010.

5. Run the Postscan process by clicking **Postscan**, as shown in Figure 4.20.

Figure 4.20 Run Postscan.

After you finish running the Postscan, review the entry points. Remember, entry points are the executables that the user will use to launch the applications. Office has many, so you only need the common ones such as Word and Excel. Click **Next**, as shown in Figure 4.21.

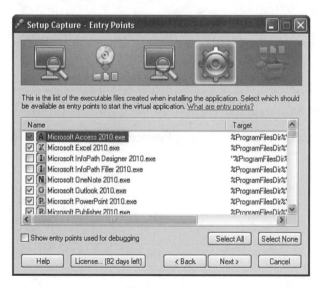

Figure 4.21 Entry points.

For now, bypass Horizon integration, so click Next, as shown in Figure 4.22.

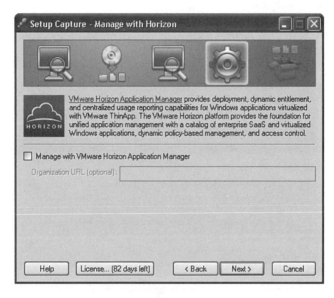

Figure 4.22 Click Next to bypass Horizon integration.

For this example, select **Everyone**, as shown in Figure 4.23. However, in practice, it is more secure to specify groups. As mentioned before, if the group is deleted, you have to rebuild the project.

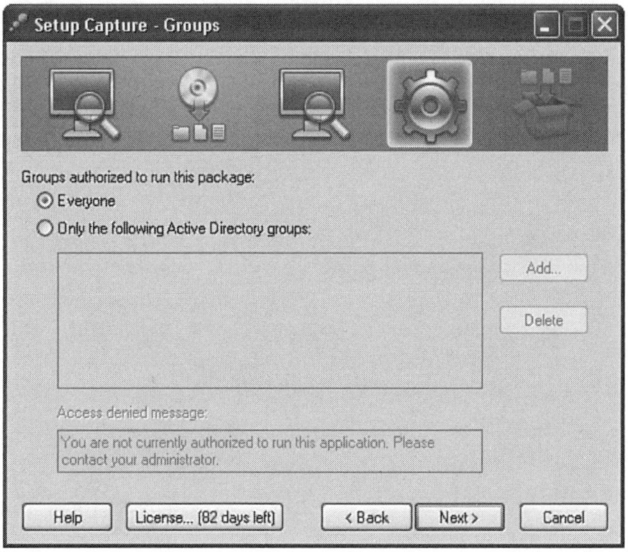

Figure 4.23 Groups.

Because this is Microsoft Office, full write access is acceptable, so click the **Full Write Access to Non-System Directories (Merged Isolation Mode)** radio button, as shown in Figure 4.24. Then click **Next.**

Figure 4.24 Click the radio button indicating Full Write Access and click Next.

Because you are creating this application for View virtual desktops, select **User Profile** (shown in Figure 4.25) and click **Next.**

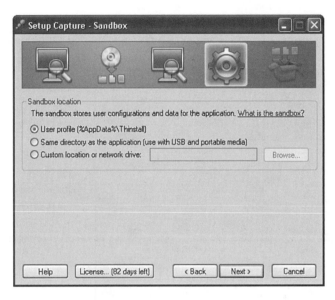

Figure 4.25 Select User Profile and click Next.

Change the Inventory name to **Office 2010 v1.01** (see Figure 4.26), leave the default Project Location, and click **Next**.

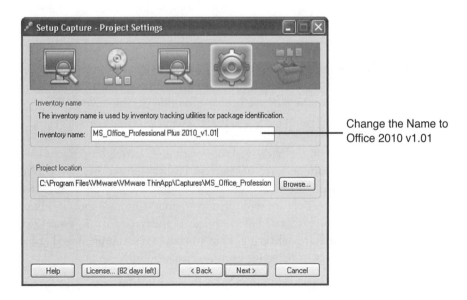

Change the Name to Office 2010 v1.01

Figure 4.26 Project setting.

Because versioning is important to the update process, append **_v1** to the default names and do the same with the .msi file. Then click **Save**, as shown in Figure 4.27.

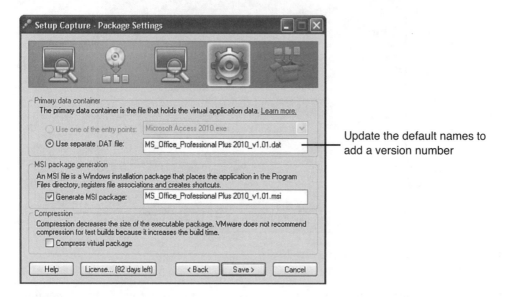

Update the default names to add a version number

Figure 4.27 Package settings.

The project files are saved. Now you need to make some changes before you build the application.

For testing this application on Windows 7, you need to determine how to handle User Access Control (UAC). To force the application to ask for elevated permissions when run, add the following parameter to the package.ini file and build the application:

```
UACRequestedPrivilegesLevel=requireAdministrator
```

You can disable UAC locally on the View desktops or though Active Directory Group Policy Objects (GPOs). You can set UAC at different levels to either disallow, prompt, or enable an application to run and access areas of the Windows 7 operating system that are normally restricted from users. Because typically most applications are thoroughly tested, it is normally turned off in an enterprise environment. If you have a Bring Your Own Computer (BYOC) policy and are delivering ThinApp packages to unmanaged end client devices, you may want to affect its behavior using the package.ini.

Now open the Project folder by clicking the **Open Project Folder** button, as shown in Figure 4.28.

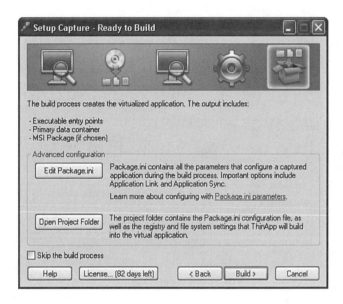

Figure 4.28 Open the Project folder.

Move the OfficeSoftwareProtectionPlatform folder from %drive_C%\Documents and Settings\All Users\Microsoft to %Common AppData%\Microsoft.

Put the following in HKEY_CURRENT_USER.txt:

```
isolation_writecopy HKEY_CURRENT_USER\Environment
  Value=ALLUSERSPROFILE
  REG_SZ~%Common AppData%
```

Put the following in HKEY_LOCAL_MACHINE.txt:

```
isolation_full HKEY_LOCAL_MACHINE\Software\Microsoft\Windows\Windows
Search\Preferences
  Value=PreventIndexingOutlook
  REG_DWORD=#01#00#00#00
```

Run the build process and ensure it completes successfully. Then click **Finish**, as shown in Figure 4.29.

Figure 4.29 Click Finish.

You should now see your ThinApp versions of Office 2010, as shown in Figure 4.30.

Figure 4.30 ThinAPP versions of Office 2010.

Now add the ThinApp version of Office 2010 to your ThinApp repository—\\
Pre-verified ThinApp Packages—so that you can test it before copying it to production.

Deploying a Package Through View

We already reviewed how to set up a ThinApp repository. When you have packages that you have tested, you are ready to deploy them within View. The packages are available from the VMware View Administrator Console under ThinApp. If they do not appear, simply do a rescan of your ThinApp repository by clicking the **Scan New ThinApps** button shown in Figure 4.31.

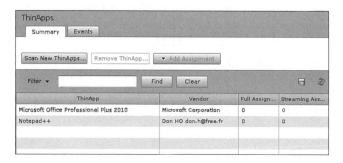

Figure 4.31 Rescan.

Entitling packages to desktops requires assigning them to an individual desktop or pool, which is a collection of desktops. To do this, select a ThinApp package and then click the **Add Assignment** button. From this drop-down, you can select **Pools**, a group of virtual desktops, as shown in Figure 4.32. You also can assign applications to individual desktops.

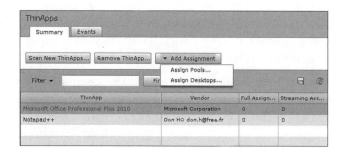

Figure 4.32 Entitle desktops.

If you choose **Pools**, you can choose any one of your virtual desktop pools. We discuss pools further in Chapter 5, "Building Your Virtual Desktop." You also have the option of selecting the installation type. *Installation type* is somewhat of a misnomer here because it really means whether the shortcut on the desktop will map to a ThinApp package on a file share or a locally copied ThinApp package.

If you select a Full installation type, a shortcut gets created on the desktop, and the ThinApp package is copied locally to the virtual desktop. The files can be found in the C:\Program Files location with the label VMware ThinApp in the name. If you want to integrate ThinApp packages with user persistent disks, which are essentially a second

VMDK associated with the virtual desktop, you have to prepopulate the drive with the ThinApp packages and create the shortcuts within the desktop image.

If you want to do this, the process is similar to deploying ThinApp Packages in Execution mode but involves a few more manual steps. When you enable user persistent disks, you are essentially enabling an additional VMDK associated with the View desktop that persists between reboots. From a Windows perspective, this second VMDK appears as another partition and is assigned a drive letter and formatted with a file system. After creating it, you can copy your ThinApp package to a local directory on this Windows volume. To link the packages to the View desktop, you use the ThinReg utility:

```
THINREG.EXE < Drive\Path>\*.EXE> /Q
```

This utility creates shortcuts and file associations within the View desktop that are linked to the local directory on the user persistent disk. This method ensures good performance. The user persistent disks are created during deployment, so although the ThinReg links can be built into a template, you need to copy the ThinApp packages after the deployment of the virtual desktop. Of course, it would not be difficult to automate this task by using a Run Once option in a vSphere Client Windows Guest Customization profile. This would run the copy on the first user login without any manual intervention. Windows Guest Customizations are required to fully automate the deployment of Windows servers and desktops in a vSphere environment and are similar to the sysprep process. Because this method is a little more complex, it is more common to use the streaming method or link to ThinApp packages on centralized file shares.

You likely will have specific applications for certain virtual desktop pools or perhaps a common set of applications across many virtual machines. View provides you a mechanism to group many ThinApp packages by creating templates. Rather than assign individual applications to virtual desktops or pools, you can assign whole templates, as shown in Figure 4.33.

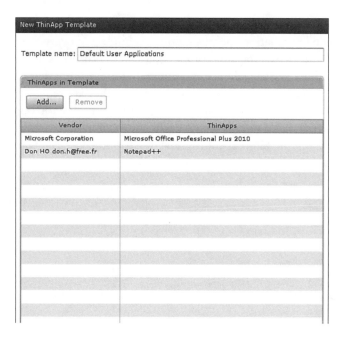

Figure 4.33 You can use templates to group many ThinApp packages.

Summary

In this chapter, we looked at the mechanics of creating a ThinApp package and the methods of deploying it. Applications, whether virtualized or not, also require upgrading. Because there are a number of operational and management considerations, I centralized this information in Chapter 6, "View Operations and Management," where we look at updating and maintaining ThinApp packages.

ThinApp provides a great solution to solving some of the problems that are common to both physical and virtual environments. It does require a repackaging process to virtualize the applications. Because large enterprise organizations typically already have a commitment and investment to an existing set of application lifecycle tools, it is more common that application virtualization is phased in. What is great about ThinApp—because it is not agent based and requires no back-end supporting infrastructure—is that it is easy to do. You can simply use your existing set of tools to deliver the ThinApp EXE or MSI package.

Due to the requirement to repackage and learn a new tool, it is common for the migration to VMware View and ThinApp to be broken into two distinct phases. Once provided an overview, however, application analysts often find it easier to use the ThinApp packager versus an unattended installation package method. ThinApp is a very flexible tool that can be integrated into an existing application deployment process or added as a feature of VMware View to simplify management. To integrate it, make sure that you have a defined process for packaging and certifying new applications as they are requested. Although it is a little unusual to discuss the application before building your desktop (in Chapter 5), I did so intentionally. I find that if you are aware of the integration requirements for ThinApp, you can better plan out the build of your virtual desktop to take advantage of it.

Chapter 5

Building Your Virtual Desktop

P2V or Clean Build?

You can create your original virtual desktop image in a number of ways, but essentially they break down into either performing a physical-to-virtual (P2V) migration on a target physical desktop or starting with a clean build. In most cases, a clean build is preferred, but there are always a few exceptions to this rule. For example, it may make sense to do a P2V migration to create a virtual desktop for a small proof of concept (PoC) environment. If you are considering this method, there are several issues to keep in mind, such as ensuring that after everything is converted, any services or configurations that are not applicable or detrimental to a virtual environment are updated. One of the common services is the power policy. On a physical desktop, it makes sense to have certain features power off if they are idle, such as dimming the display or putting the computer to sleep.

Often, cleaning an image that has been migrated from physical to virtual can be more problematic than building one from scratch. For any production implementation, using a clean imaging process is necessary. There are also a number of tweaks that you will want in place as part of the image. As mentioned in Chapter 3, "VMware View 5 Implementation," you may also want to customize the local computer policy to ensure any configurations are incorporated into the image.

One point to keep in mind when you are optimizing a virtual desktop is that there are lots of recommendations to drive the ultimate performance. There is a fine line between great performance and the end-user experience, because the more you optimize, the more you impact the end-user experience. You do not want to drive performance at the risk of disabling useful end-user features. This is again the point at which user profiling adds value, but also knowing what effect you are having is key. Even when the optimization seems benign, you have to be careful because it may lead to problems or issues down the road. My rule of thumb is to optimize and test and be wary of turning off useful features to drive every bit of performance out of the desktop.

One other issue that comes up quite often is whether you should standardize on the x86 or x64 version if you are deploying Windows 7. In general, if your virtual desktop is going to be deployed with less than 4 GB of memory, running Windows 7 x32-bit is ideal. If you plan to deploy desktops with memory requirements larger than 4 GB, 64-bit versions are better.

When we talk about imaging, we generally refer to source desktops and target desktops. *Source* generally refers to the image source desktop or VMDK or OVF file, and *target* describes the desktop on which the image or process is being applied.

If you are going to build the image from scratch, you can choose from three available methods: manually installing and configuring, using a desktop build process such as the Microsoft Deployment Toolkit (MDT),[1] or using a VM through vCenter to create an image build. VMware provides a straightforward process to perform an image build directly in vSphere/vCenter to ensure that the recommended optimizations for Windows 7 are incorporated into the automated build process.

We go through both the manual and automated build process. In the automated build process, we show how to extend the process to include ThinApp packages and also to manage the integration of Terminal Services, or Windows 2008 Remote Desktop Services as it is now called. The automated process starts with the OS installation files, necessary VMware drivers and tools, and View agents. The manual process requires installing the OS files, VMware drivers, and View agents; tuning; and then cloning the image, as shown in Figure 5.1.

---

[1]These procedures are based on the VMware View Optimization Guide for Windows 7 white paper from VMware.

Figure 5.1 Building the desktop image.

Using MDT, you can create a Windows image file that can be applied to any desktop (virtual or physical), and you can build on the OS deployment with applications and custom tasks. Is the flexibility worth the additional time and effort? You have to look at the overall situation to make that determination.

If you are creating a master image that will be applied to a percentage of physical and virtual machines that may have many different application loads based on business unit, the additional effort spent on MDT makes sense. If you are running only virtual machines, you should use vSphere. If you have only one or two images with a fairly generic application load, the cloning and sysprep available within the virtualization tools are probably sufficient. In this book we go through the vSphere method of creating the Windows 7 image and some of the optimizations that should be applied to the image.

Manually Installing Windows 7

When manually installing Windows 7, you should understand the following:

- System Requirements: The recommended minimum specs for Windows 7 are
  - 1 GHz 32-bit or 64-bit processor
  - 1 GB of system memory
  - 16 GB of available disk space

- Support for DirectX 9 graphics with 128 MB memory (to enable the Aero theme)

- DVD-R/W drive

- Internet access (to activate and get updates)

- The size of the virtual hard drive needed

You need to decide whether to install the 32-bit or 64-bit version of Windows 7. The Windows 7 installation media includes both 32-bit and 64-bit versions of Windows 7. If you plan on using Windows 7 on a virtual machine with more than 3 GB of RAM, you should use the 64-bit version; otherwise, use 32-bit. Most programs designed for the 32-bit version of Windows work on the 64-bit version of Windows, so application compatibility is not typically a problem.

In creating the master image, you do a custom, or clean, installation. This installation formats the hard drive and installs a new copy of the operating system.

When installing on a virtual machine, simply map the virtual CD/DVD to the source ISO file and reboot the VM.

Like in Windows Server 2008, Windows 7 boots directly into the graphical user interface (GUI) mode.

1. After a few moments, you see the first prompt. Set whatever regional options are appropriate and click **Next**.

2. Click the **Install Now** button.

3. Accept the license terms and click **Next**.

4. Click the **Custom (Advanced)** installation type button, as shown in Figure 5.2.

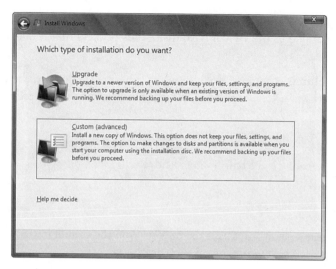

Figure 5.2 Select the custom installation.

Because this computer has a new virtual hard disk that hasn't been formatted previously, you have only the option to create a new partition on it. Click **Next** to begin the installation (see Figure 5.3).

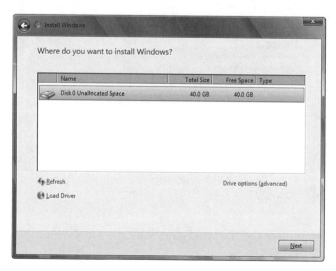

Figure 5.3 Format the unallocated space.

The setup process now begins to copy files from the installation DVD media virtually mapped to the virtual hard disk. This process might take awhile to complete.

After the setup is complete, the computer reboots. By default, the computer's name is *username*-PC, where *username* is the username you entered.

NOTE

The user you're creating is the only user currently available on the system.

5. Click **Next**.

6. Enter the user's password; this is the only user on the system initially. You must also enter a password hint (see Figure 5.4). Click **Next**.

Figure 5.4 Provide a password.

7. Type in your product key. To avoid any problems, you should use the Multiple Activation Key (MAK).

8. Choose the type of protection for the computer: Use Recommended Settings, Install Important Updates Only, or Ask Me Later. In most cases, Use Recommended is fine. Make the selection.

9. Set the time zone, date, and time and click Next.

10. Select your computer's current location: Home Network, Work Network, or Public Network. On an internal corporate network, Work Network is the typical choice.

11. When the welcome screen opens, log in and check your installation.

Manually Installing the VMware View Agent

You are able to manually install the VMware View Agent. It is required on any desktop OSes or Windows Terminal Servers that you plan to offer through the View Connection Server. Separate install packages are available for the x86 and x64 operating systems, but the same package is used for both desktop and server operating systems. The components that get installed on a desktop versus a Terminal Server are different, however, as shown in Table 5.1. Features such as PCoIP and Persona Management are not supported on a Terminal Server. The platform is dedicated during the installation, and the unsupported components are not available for installation based on the OS.

Table 5.1 Components Supported on a Desktop Versus Terminal Server

Guest Operating System	Version	Edition	Service Pack
Windows 7	64-bit and 32-bit	Enterprise and Professional	None and SP1
Windows Vista	32-bit	Business and Enterprise	SP1 and SP2
Windows XP	32-bit	Professional	SP3
Windows 2008 R2 Terminal Server	64-bit	Standard	None and SP1
Windows Terminal Server	64-bit	Standard	SP2
Windows 2003 R2 Terminal Server	32-bit	Standard	SP2
Windows 2003 Terminal Server	32-bit	Standard	SP2

To install the VMware View Agent manually, follow these steps:

1. Ensure you use the appropriate installer depending on whether you are installing on the x86 or x64 platform. Launch the installer and click **Next**.

2. Click **Next** on the patent agreements.

3. Accept the license agreement and click **Next**.

4. If this is a Windows 7 virtual desktop, all the components are eligible for installation. Accept the defaults (see Figure 5.5) and click **Next**.

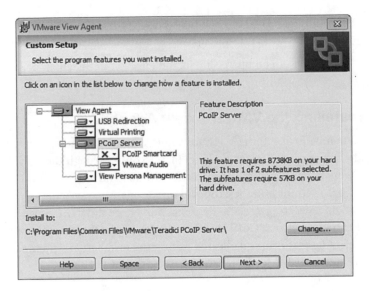

Figure 5.5 Installing the View Agent.

Figure 5.6 shows what the same screen looks like when installed on a Windows 2008 R2 RDS server. Note that many of the features are available for installation on the server platform.

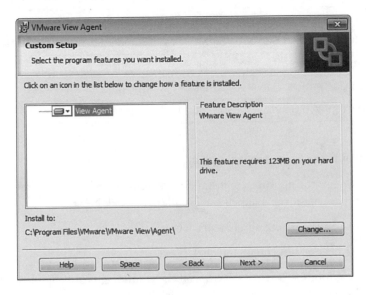

Figure 5.6 View Agent installation on a Terminal Server.

5. Specify your View Connection Server information and an account that can authenticate to the server. If you are the administrator on the View Server, you can select **Authenticate as the Currently Logged On User.** Click **Next** (see Figure 5.7).

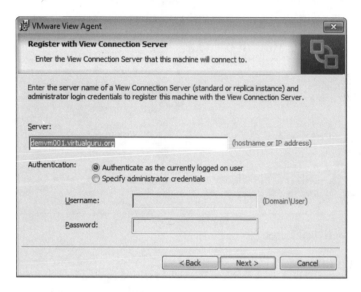

Figure 5.7 Specify the View Connection Server information.

6. Click **Install** and watch the install process on the progress bar.

When everything is installed, you will notice a new service running called the VMware View Agent.

Installing Windows 7 Through VMware Workstation

In an environment where vSphere is deployed, very often you will find an IT administrator with VMware Workstation installed to do common tasks such as image building. With version 8 of VMware Workstation, you can directly connect to a vCenter or vSphere environment. If you combine the automated image build process Workstation 8 with the direct connection to vCenter, you have a very efficient and simple way of building desktop golden images for your environment.

We explain here how easy it is to build and deploy an image to the vCenter from VMware Workstation 8, as shown in Figure 5.8.

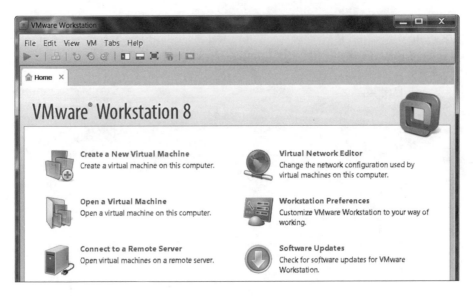

Figure 5.8 VMware Workstation 8.

You start by choosing the Create a New Virtual Machine option in the main screen of Workstation. You then choose the **Custom (Advanced)** installation. Be aware, however, that there are a few parameters you need to adjust for preparation of a gold image for View.

Make sure you choose **Workstation 8.0** for hardware compatibility (see Figure 5.9); this is a requirement for ESXi 5.x, which we suggest you use for the deployment of a View 5.x environment.

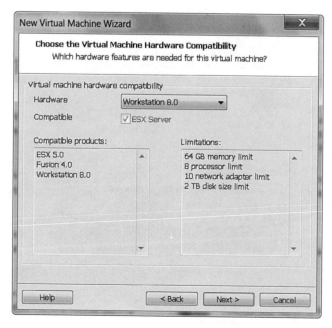

Figure 5.9 Hardware compatibility choices.

The next few steps are familiar and most IT administrators will recognize them. In the Guest Operating System Installation screen, browse to your installation media, which should be either a Windows 7 x32-bit or 64-bit ISO file. Because you are using Workstation 8, if the software properly detects the ISO, it tells you that it can use the Easy Install process, which basically installs the new OS automatically without user interaction, as shown in Figure 5.10.

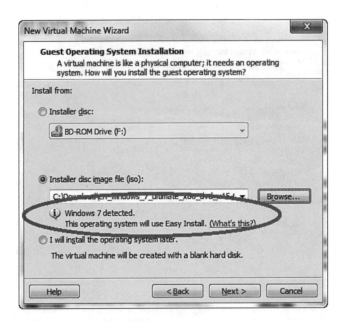

Figure 5.10 Easy Install process selection.

You should configure the next few screens as follows:

1. Enter the product key (remember to use an MAK key or KMS Server).

2. Specify a local administrator account with a complex password. (It is important to note that because you're using the Easy Install process, you should not use Administrator as the username. VMware Workstation is already using that name. Just choose something different.)

3. Put in the virtual machine name. This is the name used locally in VMware Workstation because you are not linked to vCenter yet.

4. Choose the number of processors and number of cores per processor. To make the right choice, you have to go back to your requirements and make sure that the choice you make here will meet your specifications. If uncertain, choose one core and one processor. Windows 7 is peculiar when you are removing a vCPU; it supports moving from single to multiple, but not the other way around.

5. Choose the memory for this virtual machine. It should match your requirements. For a Windows 7 image, it generally should be between 1 and 4 GB, although you may have specific memory requirements.

6. Select the network type. The type is important because it enables you to make any additional changes to the virtual image after the install. You can leave the default setting using Network Address Translation (NAT).

7. Change the controller type to LSI Logic. As an optional step, you can even update the driver from the manufacturer website after the Easy Install is complete. Look for LSI_U320_W2003_IT_MID1011438.zip from www.lsi.com.

8. Create a new virtual hard disk according to your application installation requirements with some additional space for growth. The Windows 7 base image is anywhere from 8 to 10 GB, so make sure you choose a disk size big enough for your users to be able to use applications and their documents, but not too big to overprovision. The default is 60 GB, which might be a little too big. Even though we're talking about linked clones, resizing closer to 30–40 GB is more reasonable. One important point to note: Because you are migrating this virtual machine to a vCenter environment, it is recommended you keep all information from the VM in one file (see Figure 5.11).

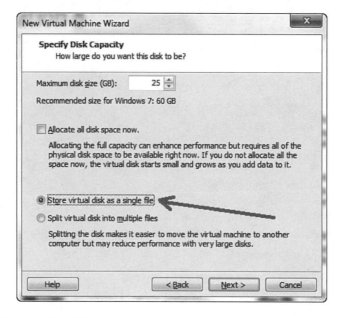

Figure 5.11 Virtual machine disk size.

9. Specify the virtual machine location in this last step before the automated process starts. Use the local drive for now; you upload to vCenter later in this chapter.

10. If all the information was installed properly, you see VMware Workstation install the OS, reboot the VM, and install the VMware tools. If, for any reason, a step does not

work according to plan, you can always pick up where the automated install stopped and complete the installation. This process is straightforward and fast and it works!

When the Easy Install process is complete, you can log in to the virtual machine to check that everything is installed properly and that no outstanding messages need action. When you are satisfied with the results, shut down the virtual machine.

You have two choices regarding how to move this virtual machine to the vCenter. The traditional way is to open the vSphere client, create a new virtual machine, and point the VDMK to the new VM you created.

The second option, now available in VMware Workstation 8, is to export the VM you created in an OVF format. After you choose your virtual machine from the File menu, choose **Export to OVF** (see Figure 5.12).

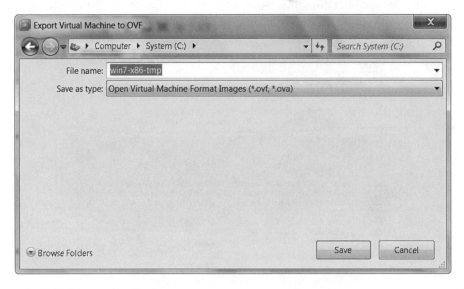

Figure 5.12 OVF export for vCenter.

Then all you need to do is to go into your vSphere client and choose **Deploy OVF Template** from the File menu.

Installing an Image Through vCenter

When you're ready to install an image through vCenter, it's a best practice to have a repository for your gold master images, a place where you keep all your references and corporately approved templates from which all your desktop images are spun off.

1. Start the vSphere client and connect to the vCenter.

2. In Home, Inventory, choose **VMs and Templates**.

3. Create a folder called **Templates**.

4. Create two subfolders underneath Templates and name them **Servers** and **Desktops**, as shown in Figure 5.13.

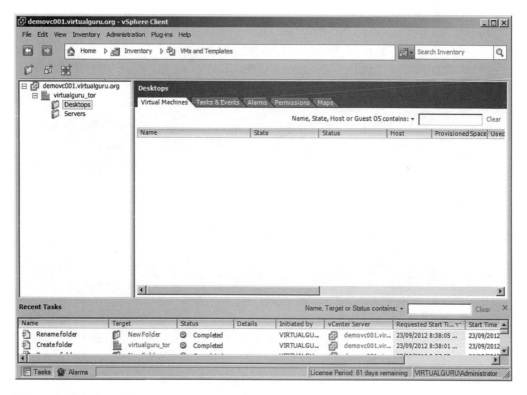

Figure 5.13 VMs and Templates view.

You need to complete a couple more preparation steps before you start the automated build process. You should create a hidden network share from which you will retrieve the ThinApp packages during or after the build process. It is also possible to combine ThinApp applications into your build if you have packaged them as MSIs. Keep in mind that if you do this, the applications will be deployed into the image versus "streamed."

You should upload the master ISO files to your vCenter environment, into the datastore of your choice, one that will be accessible during the build process.

The steps to create your first Windows image are similar for the automated and manual processes. Rather than repeat the steps here, refer to the previous section "Manually Installing Windows 7" or "Installing Windows 7 Through VMware Workstation" for the steps for the initial image creation.

When the image is built, put it in the Templates\Desktops folder.

The goal of creating that initial image is to be able to convert it to a template. In the vCenter client, choose the image you just created and right-click it. Then choose **Template** and **Convert to Template** (see Figure 5.14).

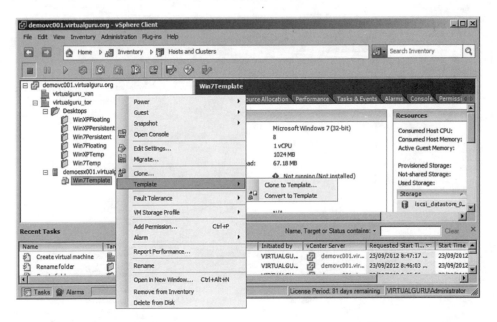

Figure 5.14 Template conversion.

Choosing this option launches the conversion process. This step is actually pretty fast, and the final result is that the Virtual Image icon changes to a Template icon and is ready for you to use for the automated image deployment (see Figure 5.15).

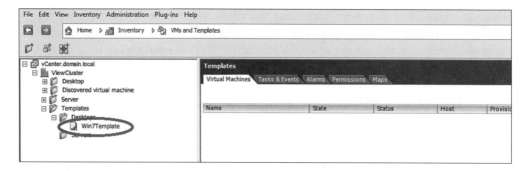

Figure 5.15 Template icon change.

Put this image aside for now. The other part of this process is to create a new customization specs in vCenter. From the Management section of the home screen, choose **Customizations Specification Manager**. Then choose **New** to start the wizard you use to build an answer file for your image and specify any customization for the image, as shown in Figure 5.16.

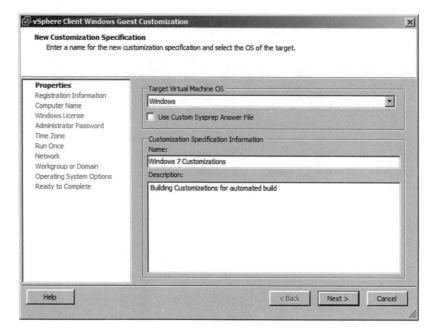

Figure 5.16 Registration information.

The next screen asks you to enter your name and organization name. Then the following screen, shown in Figure 5.17, asks you to enter the computer name; this is a different name from what is used for the linked clones in VMware View. It is a good idea to enter a name that has meaning in the View build process; the OS and pool names are usually good choices.

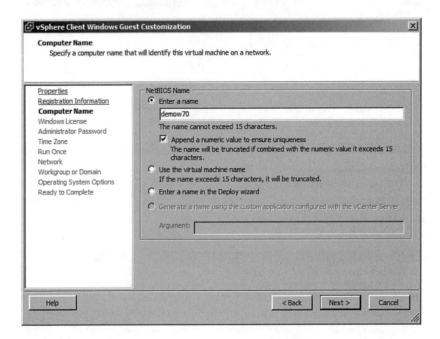

Figure 5.17 Computer name.

The next screen, shown in Figure 5.18, asks you to enter a valid license key. Similar to the build process used earlier, it's a good practice to enter a Multiple Activation Key. This MAK can be the same one used in the earlier process, but it does not have to be.

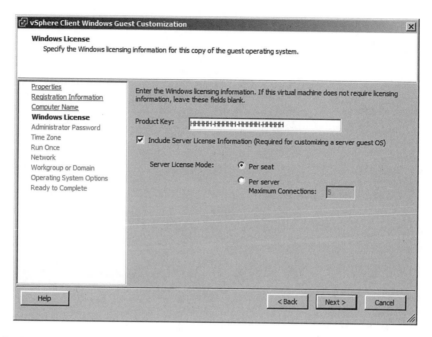

Figure 5.18 Windows product key.

The next screen, shown in Figure 5.19, asks you to enter the credentials for the local administrator account that will be used during the automated image build. Because you will join this machine to the domain when it's being created, it's a good practice to enable the automated logon so that Windows is able to complete its build process and reboot a few times to make sure all steps are completed.

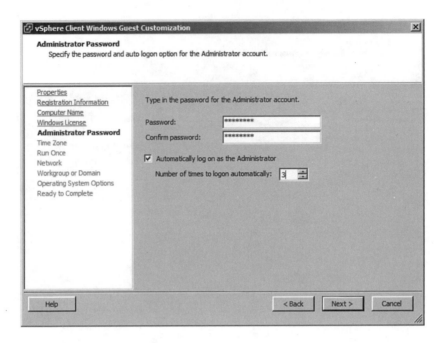

Figure 5.19 Local administrator password.

You are then asked for your time zone. You also can choose the Run Once option (for now, leave these settings at the defaults). On the following screen, enter the right network information. Choose a valid network and make sure to leave DHCP as your choice for IP address.

The following screen, shown in Figure 5.20, asks you to place the virtual image in the domain or leave it in a workgroup. This choice is totally up to you, but the important point to remember, in VMware View version 5 and forward, is that the gold master image does not have to be joined to the domain to be used as the reference image; you can leave it in a workgroup if you prefer. Remember that if you have Group Policy Objects (GPOs) applied to your image, it might be a better idea to place that image into a domain when it's being built.

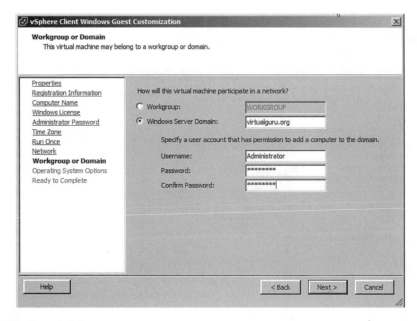

Figure 5.20 Domain join.

Make sure you leave the **Generate New Security ID (SID)** option checked, as shown in Figure 5.21.

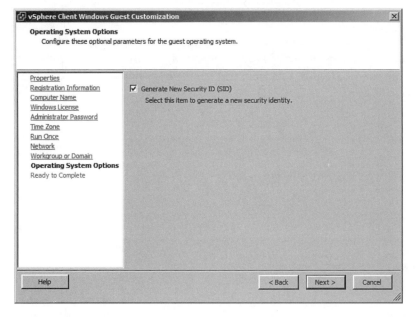

Figure 5.21 SID generation.

Finally, you can review the choices you just made, and if everything is acceptable, click **Finish,** as shown in Figure 5.22.

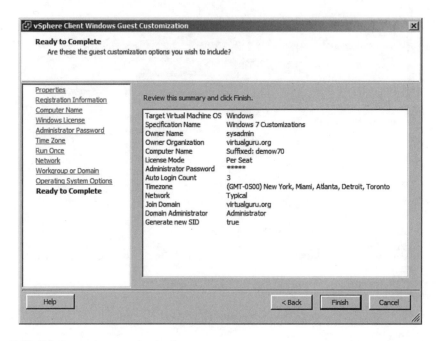

Figure 5.22 Windows guest customization summary.

Now that you have completed your guest customization, you can apply this to your template created earlier. In the VMs and Templates view in vCenter, right-click your template and choose **Deploy VM** from this template (see Figure 5.23) to launch the Deployment Wizard.

Figure 5.23 Deploy Virtual Machine from this Template.

After the wizard starts, give the virtual machine a name (see Figure 5.24). Again, make sure you use something that will be significant in preparation for your VMware View environment. Then you configure the usual information (host/cluster, resource pool, storage).

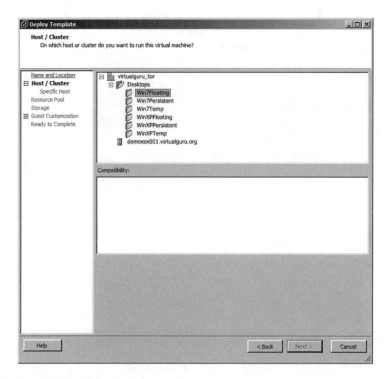

Figure 5.24 Provide Virtual Machine name.

The important part is when you reach the Guest Customization screen, shown in Figure 5.25. Here, you choose one of the many guest customizations you have created and link it back to this virtual machine.

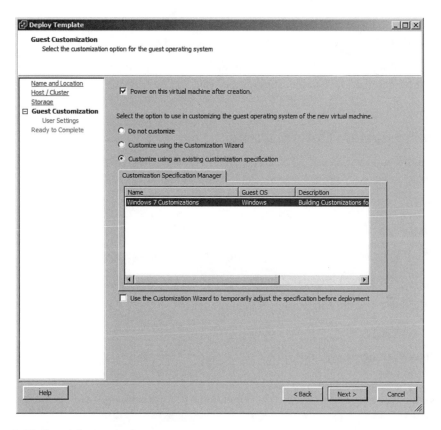

Figure 5.25 Guest Customization screen.

In the final screen, you are able to see all the options you chose, and if these choices are okay, click **Finish**. vCenter launches the creation process and uses the parameters you chose in the Guest Customization script. Repeat the process as many times as needed to prepare your gold master images for your VMware View environment.

General Optimizations

To optimize your virtual machine, you can tweak a number of areas from the virtual machine hardware configuration, the operating system, and general networking and application considerations and settings. For the virtual machine hardware optimizations, make sure the following are completed:

- Install VMware Tools.
- Disable any hardware not required in the virtual machine, such as floppy devices.

- Ensure media devices are all set to Disconnected so that you do not have devices connected and autodiscovered in the Windows 7 OS.

- Turn off logging of the virtual machine. Under the Settings\Options and General option, deselect the Enable Logging option.

Operating System Optimizations

Within the Windows 7 image, you should make the following changes to reduce the number of unnecessary processes running in the virtual machine:

- Disable System Sounds (set the Sound scheme to None).

- Disable serial and parallel ports in Device Manager (if they exist).

- Install Windows Patches; then turn off automatic updates.

- Set Screensaver to None or Blank.

- (Windows 7) Uninstall Tablet PC components.

- Disable Windows Error Reporting.

- Remove unnecessary boot applications (QuickTime, Real, Adobe Acrobat Updater, and so on).

- Remove unneeded Windows components (Outlook Express, Messenger, Games, and so on).

- Disable unnecessary services.

As with any OS image, you should install all common applications but make sure that you have turned off automatic updates and autostarting applications that are not required. Following are some of the more common applications:

- Install Adobe Flash Player (turning off automatic updates).

- Install Adobe Reader and set to Do Not Download or Install Updates Automatically.

- Turn off Java Updater.

- Remove the MS OneNote tray service (if installed).

You should also look at the default network settings for network optimizations. For example, you should disable, configure, and verify the following settings:

- Disable NetBIOS over TCP/IP.

- Disable IPv6.

- Join Master Image to Domain (if using View Composer).

- Add any necessary DNS suffixes.

- Add any necessary HOSTS entries for "custom" applications.

You can also find a number of additional options in the attached commands file in the VMware View Optimization Guide for Windows 7 whitepaper.[2]

These commands can be applied through a single batch file to further tune the operating system.

Manually Installing Windows 2008 RDS Server

To install a Windows 2008 RDS Server within Server Manager, follow these steps:

1. Open Server Manager from the Windows 2008 R2 Server.

2. In the left pane, highlight **Roles**; then on the right under Role Services, select **Add Role Services**.

3. Check **Remote Desktop Connection Broker** and then click **Next**.

4. Click **Install** at the confirmation and then click **Close** after the install is complete.

5. To make the Windows 2008 RDS Server look like a Windows 7 desktop, see the following section.

Making a Terminal Server Look Like a Desktop

The Desktop Experience feature turns on themes on the Windows 2008 R2 operating system. After you install it, you see a new service that supports the themes feature. Using it, you can customize the look and feel of the server desktop.

Of course, you can go further and merge the Windows 7 themes included in the Windows 2008 operating system so that the look is seamless. You need a clean Windows 7 x64-bit operating system and a target Windows 2008 R2 Server operating system. Turning on the desktop experience creates the same folders on the Windows 2008 R2 Server that are included by default on the Windows 7 x64 operating system.

Background images are stored in the following directories on both Windows 7 x64 and Windows 2008 R2:

%SystemRoot%\Web\Wallpaper\

%SystemRoot%\Resources\Themes\

---

[2]http://www.vmware.com/files/pdf/VMware-View-OptimizationGuideWindows7-EN.pdf

Because the default permissions deny access to administrators, you must reset the permissions on the default IMG file. You can do this from the command line using the following commands:

```
takeown /f "%SystemRoot%\Web\Wallpaper\Windows\img0.jpg">nul
icacls "%SystemRoot%\Web\Wallpaper\Windows\img0.jpg" /grant
administrators:F>nul
rename "%SystemRoot%\Web\Wallpaper\Windows\img0.jpg" "img1.jpg">nul
```

You can then copy the img0.jpg file from the Windows 7 x64 desktop's %SystemRoot%\Web\Wallpaper\Windows folder to the same folder on the Windows 2008 R2 Server. You also need to copy the %SystemRoot%\Resources\Themes folder to the same location on the Windows 2008 R2 Server. Copying these folders produces the effect shown in Figure 5.26 on your Terminal Server.

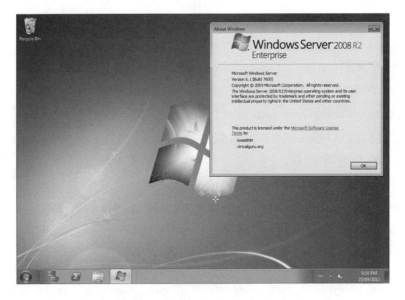

Figure 5.26 Your server now looks like a desktop.

In addition to making the default background, you also can update the login screen to make everything look and feel like a desktop operating system. Of course, in reality, you will most likely brand this "themes and defaults" with corporate logos, but you can easily do this by turning on the OEM background feature and using the default login background from a Windows 7 x64 desktop. To turn on the OEM background feature, you need to enable it in the registry of the Windows 2008 R2 Server. The keys are identical to a Windows 7 desktop. You can complete this part of the process as follows:

1. Click the **Windows** button and type **regedit.exe** in the search field.

2. Browse to HKEY_LOCAL_MACHINE\Software\Microsoft\Windows\ CurrentVersion\Authentication\LogonUI\Background.

3. Change the OEMBackground DWORD value to a Hex value of 1 to enable the feature.

4. Create a subdirectory called **info** in c:\windows\system32\oobe.

5. Under the info subdirectory, create an additional subdirectory called **backgrounds.**

6. From your Windows 7 x64 desktop, browse to c:\windows\system32\oobe.

7. Open the background.bmp file with Microsoft Paint.

8. Save the file as **backgrounddefault** in JPEG format and save it somewhere you can easily copy it to your Windows 2008 R2 Server.

9. Copy backgrounddefault.jpg to c:\windows\system32\oobe\info\backgrounds on the Windows 2008 R2 Server.

10. Reboot the server.

The changes produce the Windows 7 color scheme on the Windows 2008 R2 Server, as shown in Figure 5.27.

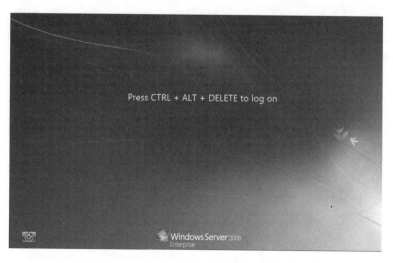

Figure 5.27 Windows 7 color scheme on Windows Server 2008 R2.

View Persona Management

View Persona is an enhancement to using traditional Windows roaming profiles, designed to reduce login times. Unlike a traditional roaming profile that copies the entire profile down during the login, View Persona downloads only what is required for the login. Additional files are downloaded when a user or application requests them. During the user session, synchronization occurs at periodic intervals (10 minutes is the default) to ensure the amount of data required to synchronize at logoff is minimal. During logoff, only the deltas are synced back to the central repository. View Persona is fully compatible with ThinApp and allows sandbox data to be stored in the user persona. This allows application configuration data to roam with the user without a performance penalty. View Persona is not dependent on Windows profiles and can be used instead or in combination with an existing Windows profile management strategy. You can use both by selectively identifying which files or folders should be managed by Windows profiles versus Persona in the synchronize folder policy of View Persona.

View Persona can be used in combination with persistent disks so that a persistent local cache of the user data or persona is available and also that a persona is stored centrally. This capability ensures the user configurations are available locally and can be recovered centrally if a problem occurs with the virtual desktop. View Persona is installed when the VMware View Agent is installed, provided the platform is supported. View Persona is supported only on virtual desktops not using local mode. It is not supported on Terminal Servers, but is supported on physical desktops with VMware View 5.1. It is added to the virtual desktop when you install the VMware View Agent. It is fairly easy to set up but requires some tuning of the default settings to get working properly. At a high level, the steps to implement View Persona are as follows:

1. Set up the file share or remote repository.

2. Install View Agent and ensure the View Persona Management is selected.

3. Add the View Persona Management Administrative Template to the organizational unit (OU) in which the virtual desktops will be deployed.

4. Configure the group policy settings for Persona Management.

5. Deploy virtual desktops with the persona management service running.

6. Verify that the user directories are created on the remote file share.

The exact steps to enable persona management are as follows. You need to create a centralized file share with the same permissions required to set up Windows profiles. If the environment will span multiple sites, you need to have some mechanism to replicate the file repository to ensure it is readily available. You can choose from many methods to do this depending on what you are using for file services. The supported Microsoft method is to use Distributed File Services (DFS). In Chapter 11, "High Availability Considerations," we go through the steps to set up DFS to ensure you have a site-to-site high availability solution. If you do not require this level of availability, simply create a file share with the appropriate permissions applied. The steps to do this follow.

Create a Windows file share and ensure the permissions on the parent folder are as shown in Table 5.2.

Table 5.2 Parent Folder

User Account	Permissions Required
Administrator	Full
Security group permissions	List Folder/Read Data, Create Folders/Append Data (This Folder Only)
Everyone	No Permissions
Local System	Full Control, This Folder, Subfolders and files

Referenced from the Microsoft Technet library at http://technet.microsoft.com/en-us/library/.

On the Share for the View Persona, ensure the permissions are as shown in Table 5.3.

Table 5.3 Share Level (SMB) Permissions for VMware View Persona Share

User Account	Default Permissions	Minimum Permissions Required
Everyone	Read only	No permissions
Security group of users needing to put date on share	N/A	Full control

The NTFS permissions on each user persona folder are shown in Table 5.4.

Table 5.4 User Persona Folder Permissions

User Account	Default Permissions	Minimum Permissions Required
%username%	Full Control, Owner of Folder	Full Control, Owner of Folder
Local System	Full Control	Full Control
Administrators	No Permissions	No Permissions
Everyone	No Permissions	No Permissions

After creating the Share, you need to ensure that View Persona is loaded when the agent is installed on the virtual desktop (see Figure 5.28). Because we covered the installation of the View Agent in the section "Manually Installing the VMware View Agent," we do not cover the installation again here. Ensure the View Persona Management is installed (it is by default).

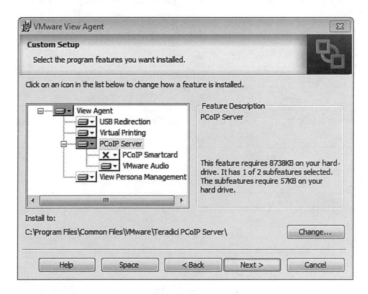

Figure 5.28 Ensure that View Persona is loaded.

To enable View Persona management, you import the policy template and set the policy to Enable. By default, the View Persona administrator templates are located on the VMware View Server at install_directory\VMware\VMware View\Server\extras\ GroupPolicyFiles. There are many additional settings that you can fine tune. Let's go through the steps to turn on View Persona management and then look at the more common configurations.

1. Run the Group Policy Management Utility and select the OU that will contain your VMware View desktops (see Figure 5.29).

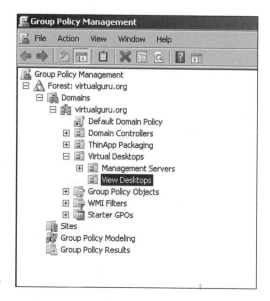

Figure 5.29 Select your View desktop OU.

2. Create a new GPO and provide a descriptive name, as shown in Figure 5.30; then click **OK**.

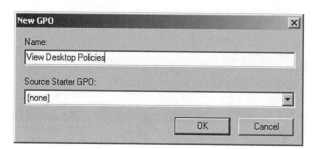

Figure 5.30 Name the new GPO.

3. Right-click the newly created GPO, as shown in Figure 5.31, and click **Edit**.

Figure 5.31 Edit the Policy.

4. Under Group Policy Object, expand Computer Configuration and select Administrative Template. Right-click and select **Add/Remove Templates**; then click **Add**, as shown in Figure 5.32.

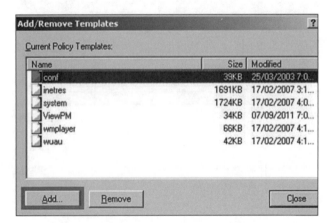

Figure 5.32 Add an administrator template.

5. By default, the View Persona administrator template is located on the VMware View Server at install_directory\VMware\VMware View\Server\extras\GroupPolicyFiles. Browse to this location (see Figure 5.33), select the **ViewPM.adm** file, and click **Open** and then **Close**.

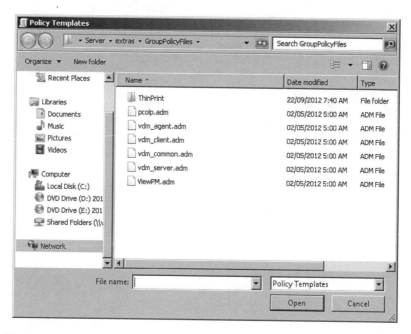

Figure 5.33 Select ViewPM.adm.

6. If you browse under Computer Configuration\VMware View Agent Configuration\Roaming & Synchronization and enable the Manage User Persona setting, by default, the internal synchronization takes place every 10 minutes (see Figure 5.34), but you can adjust it to reduce the amount of data that has to be synced. Shorter intervals require less data to be synchronized; extending the interval means more data has to be synchronized.

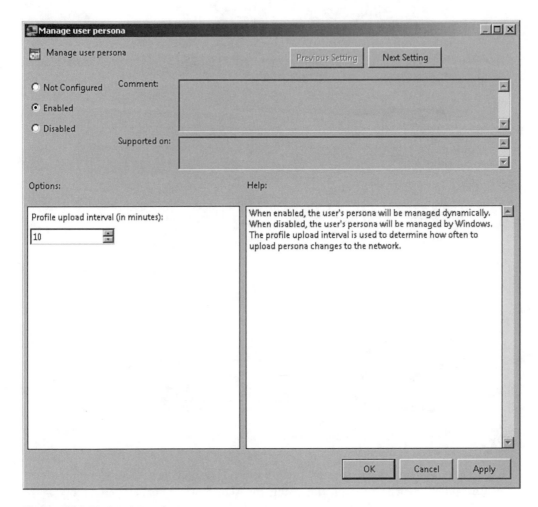

Figure 5.34 Update Interval.

Perhaps the most common configuration is integrating Persona Management into an existing roaming profile environment or transitioning to Persona from roaming. In this case, you can selectively separate which folders are managed by Windows profiles and View. To do this, you simply set the Windows roaming profiles synchronization properties (see Figure 5.35) and define the paths of the folders you would like to remain under Windows roaming profile management functionality. You can find this policy under Computer Configuration\VMware View Agent Configuration\Roaming & Synchronization.

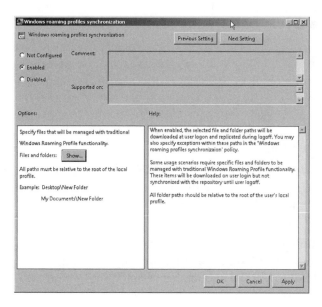

Figure 5.35 Windows roaming profile synchronization.

For a deep dive into Persona Management, you might want to check out some good additional reading at http://www.vmware.com/files/pdf/view/VMware-View-Persona-Management-Deployment-Guide.pdf.

View Persona Management: A New Approach

In a perfect world, everybody would be doing a stateless deployment, or what a lot of people in the industry call it now, a *dynamic desktop*. To achieve this, as you might know from reading previous chapters, you need to manage the data and the applications outside the base image. One of the unspoken use cases that we are seeing more and more often to be able to support a true stateless or dynamic desktop is to put the ThinApp packages in the user data repositories. Doing this, although different, gives you two main benefits. The first is the fact that the OS image will be smaller, will be easier to manage, and should have less "clutter" in the base OS. The second one is that a pool operation like a recompose operation will not lose any user-specific applications that are traditionally installed in the base operating system, by putting these applications in a user partition managed outside that base OS.

You have to balance the size of the application with the size of the user data disk, but it can be done, and more and more customers with very remote sites to manage are leaning toward this configuration.

Completing the Cycle of Persona Management

One of the new features in VMware View 5.1 is Persona Management being able to manage physical desktops. In most VDI projects, you start from an existing state, which means that you have a lot of physical desktops with user data on them. Some of these environments are not able to survive a migration to the virtual world. Users have a habit of storing huge and unreasonable amounts of data under My Documents. However, if processes are in place to educate users around the purpose of VDI, the migration is possible and should be fairly smooth.

You can now use a command-line tool to do a one-time conversion of user profiles from either a physical or virtual Windows XP to a virtual Windows 7. If migration to Windows 7 is not possible yet, you could also use this command to get your users off their physical desktop into their XP View environment.

The last use case, although seldom used, is to use Persona Management to sync user profiles between a physical desktop and a virtual desktop. You might have a few users who need to go back and forth, for valid reasons, between the virtual world and physical world. In that instance, you could synchronize by putting Persona Management on the physical PC. Again, this is a very rare use case but important to note because you have an additional tool in your belt to use during your VDI implementation to shorten the transition.

For a good blog post specifically on the new features of Persona Management in VMware View 5.1, check out http://blogs.vmware.com/euc/2012/05/vmware-view-persona-management-features-new-5-1.html.

Summary

In this chapter, we looked at many of the ways to build a virtual desktop for use in a View environment. In addition, we looked at ways to tune that desktop. Part of that tuning includes making sure that user data persists between logins by integrating View Persona. We also looked at a less common way of integrating Windows 2008 R2 Servers into a View environment to reduce costs while making it appear as a native Windows 7 desktop. You should now have an understanding of the View Management components, ThinApp, and how to build the View desktop.

The next chapter, "View Operations and Management," looks at some of the things you need to know to properly maintain the components in your environment. You also learn how to take groups of desktops or pools and tailor the feature set to match the requirements of the users. The chapter reviews how to control the behavior of the desktop when it is deployed and when the user is logged in and what happens when the user logs off. The information in this chapter is by no means all inclusive, as there is new information published all the time on additional ways to tune your View desktop. I recommend that you also check the VMware website for updates to optimizing your virtual desktops in a way that delivers a great end-user experience.

Chapter 6

View Operations and Management

Managing a VMware View Environment

In the previous few chapters, you have built the functional components of a VMware View environment. You have everything in place to start building virtual or Server-Based Computing (SBC) desktops. You can integrate ThinApp applications and redirect user profiles using Persona Manager, but what should you do with all this new found power? You now need to apply it to the appropriate use case by building up a profile of the types of users in your organization, a process more commonly called *user segmentation*.

As important as allocating the proper capacity in a virtualization environment, applying the right type of View desktop and features ensures the proper use of capacity in your environment. To provide an example, you may have a certain percentage of your users who have a set number of lightly loaded applications that they use. These users may not require high video resolution because the things that they do on the computer are very task orientated and perhaps repetitive. They might be using shared desktop terminals on a manufacturing floor or inventory search terminals in a library or bookstore. It might be better to run these users off a Shared Server desktop by integrating Microsoft Windows 2008 R2 RDS instead of consuming individual View desktops.

To understand how you allocate the resources you have in a VMware View environment, you need to start logically grouping users. These users may be organized by department if the department uses desktop resources in the same general manner or may be by user function—for example, IT or sales. The best way to group users is to start with some high-level generic categories and then to further break them down. For example, you might start with knowledge base, task, and roaming users.

For roaming users, you can deploy View desktops using local mode. This allows you to check out the virtual desktop and run it offline from the VMware View environment on the local client device. Within those three large categories, you may further refine groups to dedicated desktops and floating desktops.

To review, a *dedicated* desktop is assigned to an individual, and a *floating* desktop is assigned only temporarily until logoff. In addition, within the roaming users group, you may have an offline desktop group. When you have your organization logically separated by group, you are ready to start creating Active Directory groups to enable the assignment of desktop objects in VMware View. For a very small organization, you might have only a few categories, but for a large organization, creating these groups may be a time-consuming process. Do not overlook it because it allows you to organize your approach and will save time down the road.

It is also important to introduce a standard naming convention to the Active Directory groups that you use to assign your pools of desktops. Each category should have a desktop description that defines the type of desktop that will be deployed and the functional and application requirements of the desktop instance. For example:

- **Category:** Task-based workers
- **Subcategory:** Manufacturing floor
- **Functional requirements:** Printing, no audio or video enhancements
- **Applications:** Office, Manufacturing Inventory Application

After categorizing, you can start mapping these requirements to actual desktop pools within VMware View.

Using View Folders

Before you start creating pools, take advantage of the ability to create folders to organize your environment and also to enable delegation of roles and responsibilities. If you have followed the steps listed, you likely have some broad categories such as task-based workers, knowledge workers, mobile workers, and power users, for example.

Let's consider the example of task-based workers and assume that they will use Windows Terminal Server pools. We are generalizing here, but you would use your categories based on your own analysis of your environment. You can then create a folder called Task-Based Users and use it to further segregate the Windows Terminal Server pools within the VMware View Administrator Console. You can then use the folder structure to delegate roles and responsibilities. Because it is likely that the team that manages your Terminal

Servers is not the same team that manages your desktops, this is a good use case for creating folders. If you work in a fairly small organization, I still recommend using folders but just restricting their number. This way, you can delegate easily in the future. In this example, use the category Task-Based Users targeted for the manufacturing floor. You use the following steps to create the folder structure:

1. Log in to the VMware View Administrator Console.

2. Browse to Inventory and Pools.

3. On the right pane, select **Folder** and **New Folder** from the drop-down, as shown in Figure 6.1.

Figure 6.1 Create folders.

4. Create the folders that you need to organize your VMware View environment. It is ideal if you take the category details that you have created and paste them into the Description field, as shown in Figure 6.2.

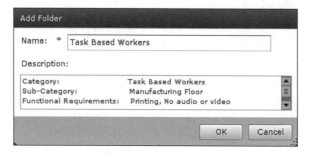

Figure 6.2 Provide verbose descriptions.

5. After you create your pool, under Pool Identification, you now see the folder you created to help categorize your environment properly, as shown in Figure 6.3. This feature also allows you to delegate roles and responsibilities from the category.

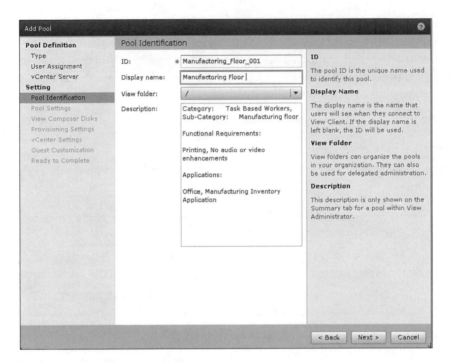

Figure 6.3 Folders logically segregate your environment.

Types of Desktop Pools

Within VMware View, there are several types of desktop pools. Pools are used to describe clusters of desktop types that are assigned to users or groups of users. They are also used as objects in the View Management Console for the same purpose—to define desktop types, associate users, and entitle virtual applications. One type of desktop we have not covered is physical. It is possible to proxy physical desktops by installing the VMware Agent on the desktop and adding it to a pool for assignment. In addition, with View 5.1, you can use View Persona on physical desktops. The process is the same in terms of installing the agent, but the creation of the pool varies slightly. We examine this topic further within this chapter.

Although the integration of physical desktops is no longer common due to the improvements in multimedia support in virtual desktops, it can still be used to transition from a PC blade environment to VMware View. For example, you can proxy PC blade users through the VMware View environment while you migrate from physical desktops to virtual ones and use View Persona to migrate the user settings.

Automated Desktop Pools

Automatic desktop pools are desktops that are provisioned and customized by VMware View automatically. They can be deployed either persistently or floating. You can also set properties of the pools to allow for a dynamic and reactive creation of virtual desktops as they are assigned. For example, you can create minimum number of virtual desktops to be created when the pool first comes online. Desktops are created until the minimum number is reached. This capability ensures that an adequate number of desktops exist to service users.

You also can adjust the maximum setting for the number of virtual desktops that can exist in a pool. You can use this setting to make sure you do not overtask supporting resources to the virtual desktop environment, such as the volume or logical unit number (LUN) on which the desktops are deployed.

Another setting that you can configure in a pool is the available number. The available number ensures that a constant number of virtual desktops exists to deal with demand. As the available number goes down, new virtual desktops are deployed to ensure the available number is consistent.

Within automated desktop pools, you can deploy full desktops or View Composer desktops. View Composer desktops are made up of linked clones. We discuss Composer later in this chapter.

Manual Desktop Pools

Manual desktop pools are created from existing machines or physical desktops. Machines may be managed by vCenter or unmanaged, as in the case of a physical device. If the users are allowed and the desktops are VMs managed by vCenter, manual desktop pools can also be used for offline virtual desktops. As with automated desktop pools, these manual pools can be persistent or floating. The source of either persistent or floating manual pools can be vCenter virtual machines or physical machines.

Microsoft Terminal Services Desktop Pool

Terminal Server sessions can be managed by VMware View using the Microsoft Terminal Services desktop type of pool. As explained in the preceding chapter, with recent releases of Windows, you can add many desktop attributes such as themes to give users the feeling they are using a dedicated and customizable desktop. In this case, the display protocol is restricted to Remote Desktop Protocol (RDP) because PC over IP (PCoIP) is currently not supported on Windows Terminal Servers.

As mentioned, automated and manual pools support two types of desktops: persistent and floating. Persistent pools are assigned to individual users and stay assigned until a View administrator changes the configuration. Persistent pools can be used when the application load is tailored to an individual user or if there is a requirement to store some local data.

Nonpersistent, or floating, pools are assigned for the duration of the session. After a user logs off, the View desktop is available for other users. The desktop typically stores no local data and often reverts to a clean state after the user logs off. Floating desktops are ideal when the environment is tightly controlled, without a lot of customizations allowed by the user.

Creating Desktop Pools

You can create a desktop pool within the VMware View Administrator Console under Inventory and Pools. From the right pane, click **Add**.

You have three types of pools to choose from: automated, manual, or Terminal Services. In the example in Figure 6.4, we selected Automated Pool. In the bottom-right corner, you see a list of supported features. This list varies, especially in the case of a Terminal Services pool.

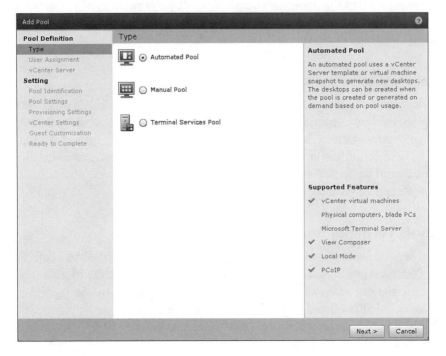

Figure 6.4 Types of pools.

Within the type, desktops can be dedicated or floating. The setting really describes whether or not the relationship between the user and virtual desktop persists when the user logs off. Again in the bottom right of this screen, you see how the features change depending on what options are selected as you build out the pool. In the example shown in Figure 6.5, we selected Floating. After the type is selected, click **Next**.

Figure 6.5 Dedicated or floating pool?

You can create full virtual machines or linked clones using View Composer. If you select View Composer, one of the features is storage savings, as shown in Figure 6.6. Choose either full virtual machines or View Composer linked clones and click **Next**.

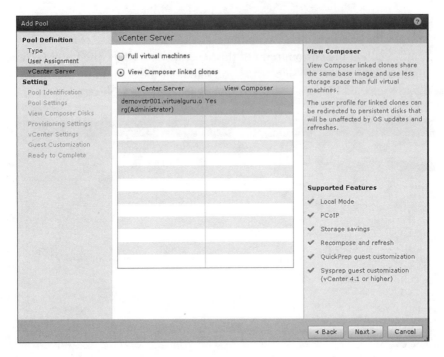

Figure 6.6 View Composer linked clones.

Provide an ID (no spaces allowed), display name, view folder, and description; be verbose, as shown in Figure 6.7. Configure the Pool identification and click **Next**.

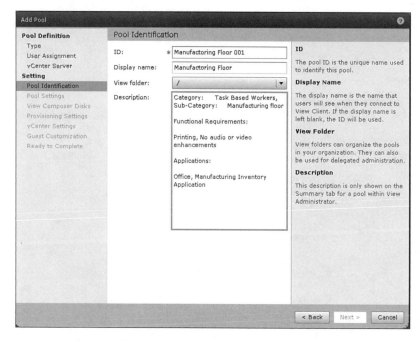

Figure 6.7 Pool Identification.

You can select numerous settings to control the pool, from power to display to Adobe Flash acceleration, as you can see in Figure 6.8. We review these settings after this example. Select the Pool settings and click **Next**.

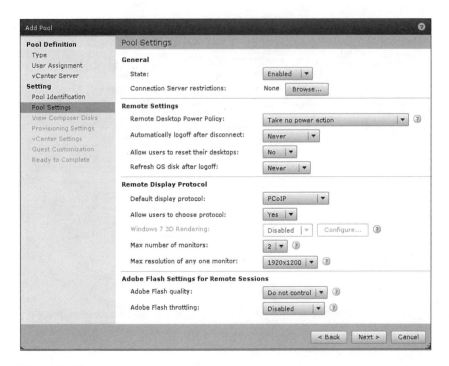

Figure 6.8 Pool settings.

If you select View Composer, you have an opportunity to tailor both the disposable file and the user data disk or persistent disk, as shown in Figure 6.9. We discuss these settings in the "Pool Settings" section later in this chapter.

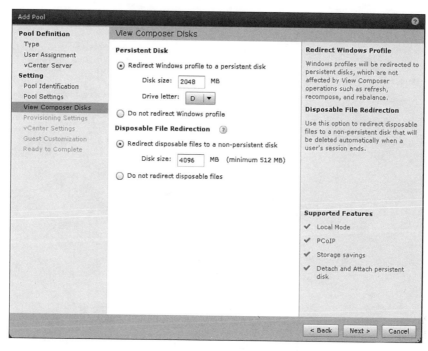

Figure 6.9 View Composer settings.

You can adjust the provisioning of the View desktops under the Provisioning Settings. For example, you can stop the provisioning when an error occurs or allow it to continue by deselecting the option because the default is to stop, as shown in Figure 6.10. You can define a standard naming pattern to keep the names of the View desktops standard and consistent. You also can set a maximum number of desktops allowed in the pool or a spare number. Setting a spare forces desktops to be deployed in the event that all View desktops in the pool are in use. Plus, you can provision desktops as requested or demanded, which allows you to set a minimum number of available desktops to ensure users are not waiting on View Composer to finish provisioning. Alternatively, you can provision them all up front. Select the Provisioning settings and click **Next**.

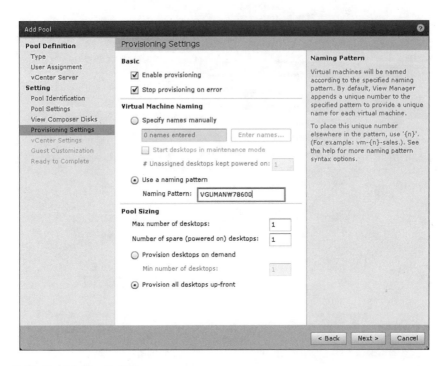

Figure 6.10 Provisioning Settings.

Under vCenter Settings (see Figure 6.11), you select the default image and the VM folder in vCenter under which you would like the virtual machines created, the host or cluster, resource pool, and datastore. View has added some additional options under the Datastore button, which we discuss in the next section when examining the settings. Select a datastore here and click **Next**.

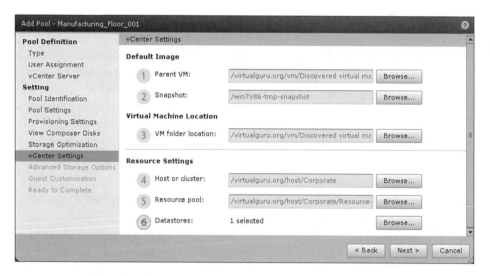

Figure 6.11 vCenter Settings.

SysPrep or QuickPrep?

You can use QuickPrep or select a customization file within virtual center, which provides a full SysPrep to the VM, as shown in Figure 6.12. After selecting the method, click **Next**.

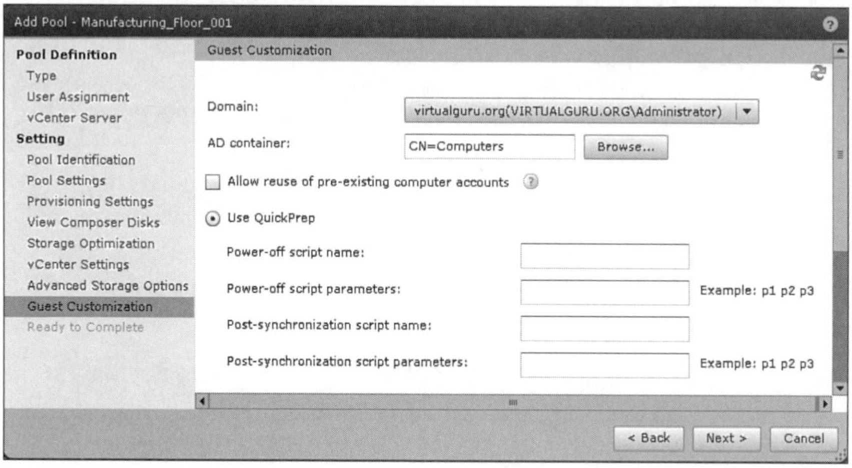

Figure 6.12 Use QuickPrep.

SysPrep, supplied by Microsoft, is designed to change the attributes of the computer to ensure the computer is unique within the environment. This includes the Security ID (SID) of the computer. Each computer should have its own local unique SID number that gets updated when the computer joins a domain. The Security ID is a unique number that is used to identify the system to Windows. SysPrep goes through all files and registry keys on the computer and replaces the current local SID number of the computer with a new local SID. When you use VMware clones, it is possible for two computers to have the same SID. This is why it is necessary to apply a SysPrep or QuickPrep to a virtual machine to ensure it has a unique SID.

SysPrep runs through all the files on the computer and replaces any SID references on the computer with new SIDs and therefore can take longer than QuickPrep. QuickPrep, provided by VMware, is used with View Composer–created virtual machines—in other words, linked clones. It updates the SID only for the newly created computer account in the Active Directory versus the local SID on the computer, taking much less time than SysPrep.

Due to the time difference between using SysPrep and QuickPrep, you should use QuickPrep unless the applications that you are installing require a unique local SID. For example, some antivirus software requires a locally unique SID on each desktop to run properly.

Clicking **Finish**, as shown in Figure 6.13, begins the creation process.

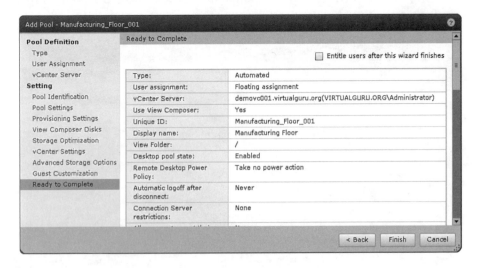

Figure 6.13 Click Finish to begin the creation process.

Power Options

You can make a number of customizations to each pool that allow tighter control over the behavior of a virtual machine, such as what happens when the user logs off. For example, it is possible to power off virtual machines to free up resources so that they are available for use by other virtual desktops in the environment. Some settings should be used in conjunction with other settings. For example, powering off the VM makes sense provided that the available setting is set on the pool to avoid delays in users' waiting for virtual desktops to boot. The other options within the pool are

- **Take No Power Action**—VMware View does not adjust the power option if the user powers down the VM.

- **Always Powered On**—VMware View does not power down the machine, and if it is powered down, the VM is automatically restarted.

- **Suspend When Not in Use**—When a user logs off, the virtual desktop is suspended. This option is also applied to floating desktops when the number of virtual desktops exceeds the setting in the available desktops counter.

- **Power Off When Not in Use**—If a virtual desktop is not in use, it is powered off. When this setting is used, View does not boot the desktop even when a user asks for a connection to the pool. For example, if you deploy 10 desktops and 9 users shut down their desktop, you have only one virtual desktop left to connect to. I recommend that you combine this option with an available desktop number so that you avoid a situation in which you have users waiting for a VM to boot up when connecting. Having a large number of virtual machines start at the same time can cause significant I/O to the storage system and is generally referred to as a boot storm. By using proper care in setting and tuning the power state options, you can avoid this situation in normal operations.

It is also recommended that because you are specifically defining what happens when a user logs off, you disable the user's ability to change the power state of the virtual machine. You can do this through the Group Policy Object associated with the organizational units (OUs) in which the virtual desktops are deployed. Simply run the Group Policy Management tool and browse to the OU in which your View desktops are deployed, as shown in Figure 6.14.

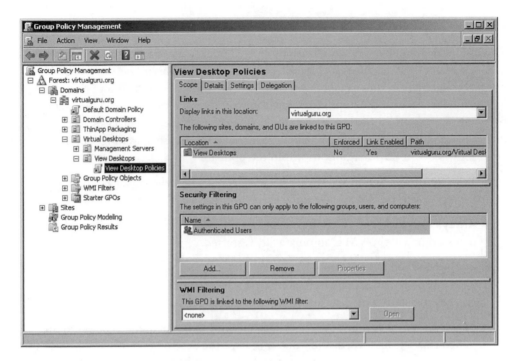

Figure 6.14 Browse to your virtual desktop OU.

You should already have a Group Policy Object defined, but if you do not, create one by using the following procedure:

1. Selecting the OU (View Desktops in Figure 6.14), right-click, select **Create a GPO in This Domain**, and then select **Link it Here**.

2. Provide a name for the Group Policy Object and click **OK**.

3. Select the Group Policy Object (in this example it is named VMware Group Policy Object), right-click, and select **Edit**.

4. Browse to the **User Configuration, Administrative Templates: Policy Definitions** and select the folder **Start Menu and Taskbar**, as shown in Figure 6.15.

5. Select the **Remove and Prevent Access to the Shut Down, Restart, Sleep and Hibernate Commands.**

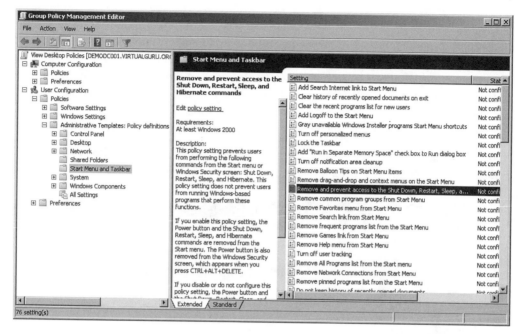

Figure 6.15 Select Start Menu and Taskbar.

Click **Enabled**, as shown in Figure 6.16, and then click **OK**.

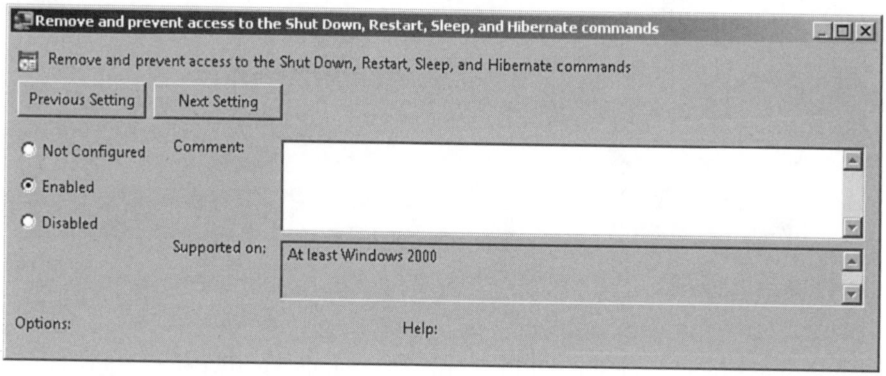

Figure 6.16 Enable the policy.

Pool Settings

It is important to understand all the settings that you can apply when configuring a pool and where they would likely apply. Not all settings are available for each type of desktop. For example, for Windows Terminal Server pools, many of the settings are not available because they are not supported. We step through each setting possible and provide a short description and then give you some idea when they might apply. Because we have covered the types of pools, let's review the settings under the Pool Settings configuration page.

Pool Settings are broken down into General, Remote Settings, Remote Display Protocol and Adobe Flash Settings for Remote Sessions, as shown in Figure 6.17.

Figure 6.17 Pool Settings.

The first setting, which is the state of the pool, determines whether the pool is active or inactive. To activate a pool, set the state to **Enabled**, as shown in Figure 6.18. You can disable the pool if you need to perform maintenance, such as the refreshing of images.

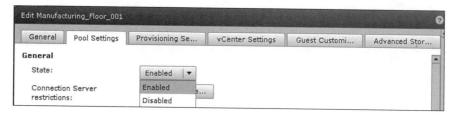

Figure 6.18 Set the state to Enabled to activate the pool.

The next general setting is the capability to restrict the pool to only certain Connection Servers. The general use case is to separate Connection Servers that provide desktops to remote users from Connection Servers providing desktops to users internally. This setting is also handy if you are a hosting provider and need to separate desktops by company, for example. To see the tags, you must first set them using this procedure:

1. In View Administrator, select **View Configuration, Servers**.

2. In View Connection Servers, select the **View Connection Server** instance and click **Edit**.

3. In the Tag text box shown in Figure 6.19, enter a tag. Separate multiple tags.

4. Click **OK** to save your changes.

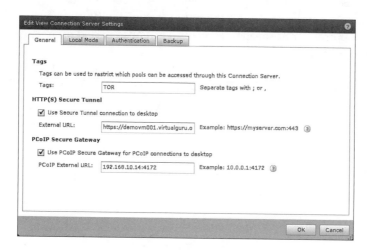

Figure 6.19 Use tags to restrict pools to certain Connection Servers.

The next group of options is in the Remote Settings pane, and the first is the Power Policy. You have the option of not adjusting what happens when the user logs off, always ensuring desktops are on, suspending them, or powering them off. These options are available from the drop-down menu, as shown in Figure 6.20.

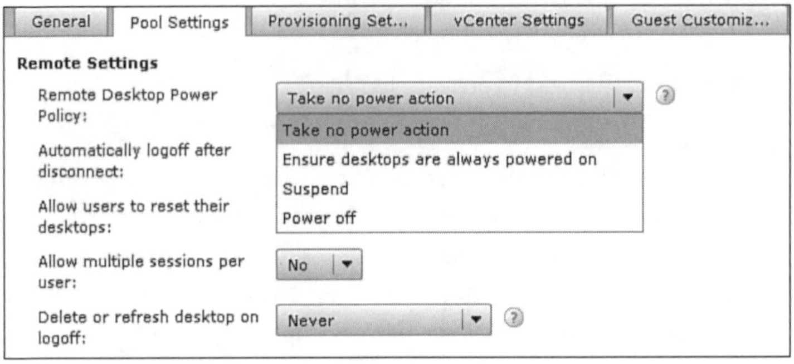

Figure 6.20 Remote Desktop Power Policy.

The next setting controls what happens to the desktop when users disconnect. The options, as shown in Figure 6.21, are Immediately, Never, or After a Set Number of Minutes. Immediate is appropriate in a floating desktop pool in which it does not matter which desktop users log in to. If a pool provides remote access to users, you should allow for a certain number of minutes to compensate for some intermittent connectivity. If the users run batch processes that need to run for an extended period of time, Never might be the more appropriate selection.

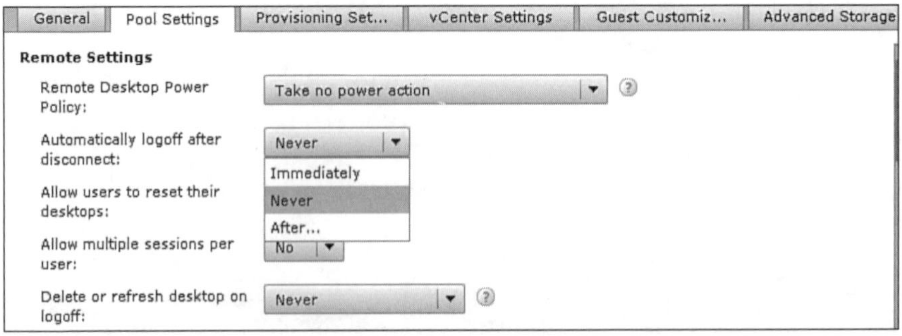

Figure 6.21 The Automatically Log Off After Disconnect option.

The next available option is allowing users to reboot their desktops (see Figure 6.22). If you are controlling the options, you might want to disallow this setting. If users are installing software because their role is development and testing, they may have a functional requirement to reboot desktops after software installations.

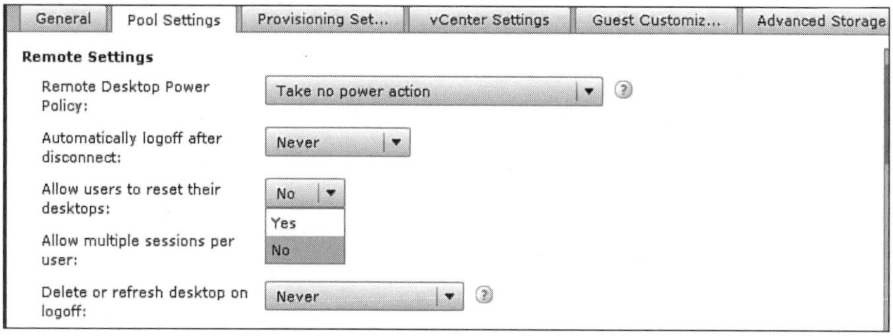

Figure 6.22 The Allow Users to Reset Their Desktops option.

The next category of pool settings adjusts the display. In View 5, you can force either PCoIP or allow users to select which one they would like; the options are shown in the drop-down in Figure 6.23. We discuss testing latency when we look at this topic in depth in Chapter 8, "A Rich End-User Experience."

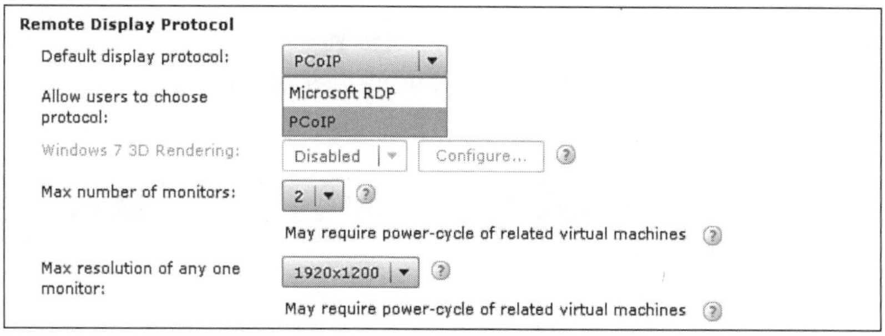

Figure 6.23 Set the default display to PCoIP.

As mentioned, you can let the users determine which display protocol they use (see Figure 6.24). For most users, you should generally control the display protocol. If you do not segregate desktops specifically for remote access, you may provide the option, but it requires some education so that the users understand when to use which protocol.

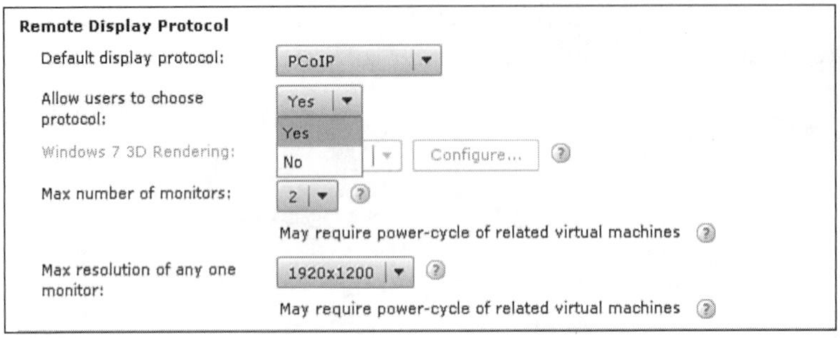

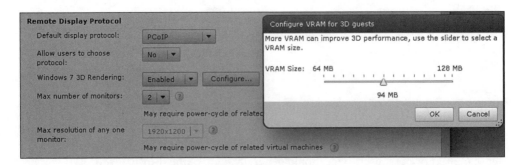

Figure 6.24 The Allow Users to Choose Protocol option.

You can turn on Windows 7 3D Rendering provided you have forced the PCoIP as the display protocol and you are using Windows 7 desktops, of course. Enabling this option restricts the number of monitors to two and the resolution maximum to 1920 × 1200 pixels. Enabling it also provides support for the Aero desktop. Enabling 3D Rendering and allowing a higher maximum resolution increases the number of pixels required to deliver the View Desktop. This, in turn, has an impact on the overall network utilization of the PCoIP session. Take care that you thoroughly test these settings to ensure there is a balance between the quality of the user experience and the overall network utilization. We discuss tuning PCoIP in Chapter 8, "A Rich End-User Experience."

Enabling the Aero desktop allows you to set the vRAM setting within View, as shown in Figure 6.25, which overrides the setting in the properties of the virtual machine within vCenter.

Figure 6.25 Adjust vRAM settings.

Specifically when you are adjusting the vRAM, you are adjusting the Video Card settings under the properties of the virtual machine, as shown in Figure 6.25.

PCoIP supports a maximum of four monitors. (Note: VMware has support for six monitors on its Roadmap.) You can select a maximum number between 1 and 4 for the desktop pool, as shown in Figure 6.26. If you force the RDP protocol, you do not have the option of adjusting the number of monitors or the resolution settings. Max monitors and Max resolutions are designed to allow tuning of PCoIP, which we review in Chapter 8. RDP settings can be tuned through Active Directory policy.

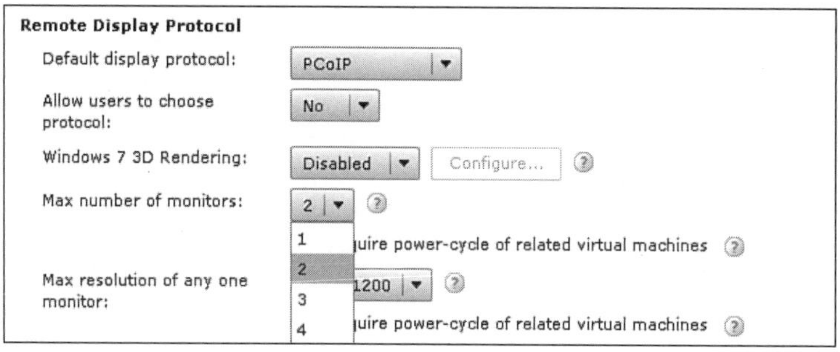

Figure 6.26 Number of monitors.

You can limit the resolution of display (see Figure 6.27) to one of the following:

1680 × 1050

1920 × 1200

2560 × 1600

Lowering the resolution reduces the number of pixel changes required, reducing the bandwidth compared to higher resolution settings. You might want to restrict the Max resolution and the number of monitors to control general bandwidth utilization.

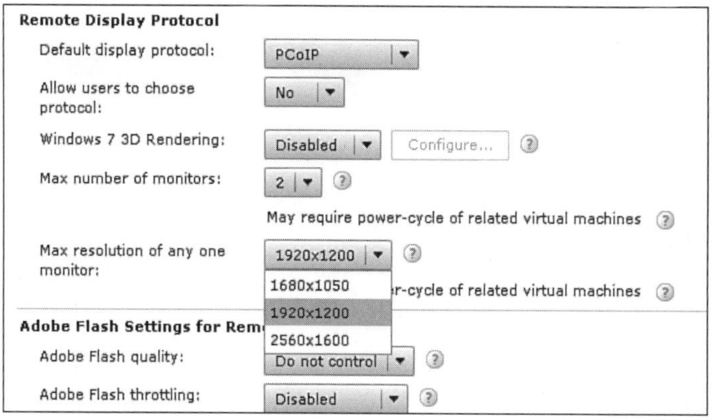

Figure 6.27 Resolution setting.

The last setting, which we discuss in greater detail in Chapter 8, essentially adjusts image quality and frame rate of flash (see Figure 6.28).

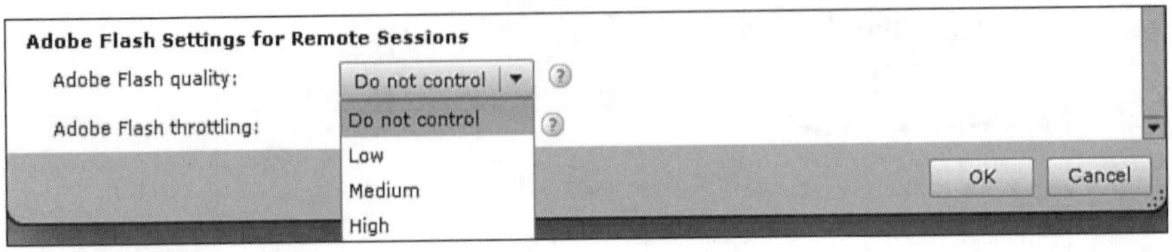

Figure 6.28 Adobe Flash Settings.

View Composer Settings

We look at what types of Virtual Machine Disks (VMDKs) make up a View Composer–created virtual machine later in this chapter to better understand the value of persistent and nonpersistent or disposable drives. You can separate user settings onto a second drive to allow them to persist. This capability is important because virtual machines created by Composer need to be refreshed and rebalanced and can be recomposed. By not separating user data, you run the risk of user data loss when these activities are initiated. The redirection of user data involves changing the default location of the user profile to a persistent disk. In the case of a disposable disk, the default location of Windows temporary files, for example, is redirected. Persistent and disposable drives are thinly provisioned, so they consume space only as they are written to.

You have the option of setting the size of both the persistent and disposable disk and the drive letter in the case of the persistent disk, as shown in Figure 6.29. These settings create two additional VMDKs per VM to store data.

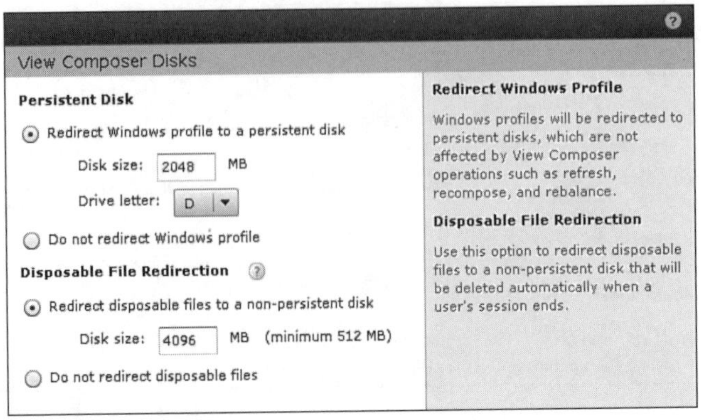

Figure 6.29 Size persistent and disposable disks

View Composer Disks

The virtual machine sees these View Composer drives as additional local drives that are marked as persistent and disposable, as shown in Figure 6.30. If you look at the persistent disk, you see the Users folder containing the profiles and a personality folder if you have integrated Persona. In addition, My Documents is redirected to the persistent disk so that the redirection is transparent to the users. If you look at the disposable disk, you see the Windows TEMP folder. Both the persistent disk and Persona Management are complementary, so it is recommended that you integrate both. The localization of the profile speeds up login, and the View Persona ensures that a central repository exists where all user data is stored.

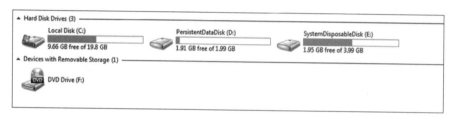

Figure 6.30 View Composer Disks.

vCenter Settings

When we talked about design, we reviewed the notion of using local solid-state drives (SSDs) to store replicas. Under the vCenter settings, you can specifically direct certain components of Composer and the virtual machines' VMDKs; you can separate the location of the replica and the Composer datastore. The default location is to store it on the datastore in which the Composer desktops are created. Let's look at how to do this.

To create the virtual machine, you have to specify the image. You can also specify in which folder the virtual machines are deployed in Virtual Center. These fields are shown in Figure 6.31.

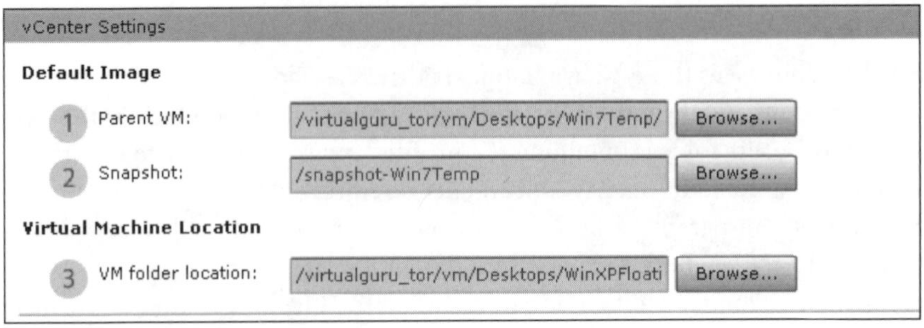

Figure 6.31 Virtual Machine Settings.

Under Resource Settings, you specify the ESX host or cluster and the resource pool to which you are deploying the VMs, as shown in Figure 6.32.

Figure 6.32 Cluster and resource pool settings.

When you click the **Datastore** button, you have greater flexibility in the placement of the replicas and linked clones, and you have the option of separating the OS and persistent disks. Because you have fine control on where certain components of View Composer are located, you can take advantage of all the innovations in SSD storage. New companies and technologies are allowing you to even more effectively manage I/O. Examples of these companies are Nexenta, PureStorage, and Fusion-I/O. You also can combine both local and shared datastores for this purpose. If you have included localized SSDs in your ESXi hosts, you can also store a replica there.

In VMware View 5.1, you can also take advantage of storage features supported in vSphere 5. One of these enhancements is a Content-Based Read Cache (CBRC) or Host-Based Cache. This cache is local to the vSphere ESXi host and stores frequently used blocks of virtual machine disk data. CBRC improves performance by offloading some of the I/O read requests to the local ESXi host versus sending them to the storage system or SAN. Using CBRC, you can significantly reduce your peak input/output per second (IOPS) or read requests in your VMware View environment. You must enable support of CBRC through the View Administrator Console by enabling it under the properties of your vCenter Server and enabling it under the properties of the desktop pool. To enable this support under the properties of the vCenter Server, follow these steps:

1. Open the View Administrator Console and expand Server Configuration.

2. Select your vCenter Server and click the Details button.

3. Select the **Host Caching** tab and select **Enable Host Caching for View**.

After enabling host caching under the vCenter properties, you can selectively enable it under the pool settings. It provides the biggest benefit for shared disks that are read frequently, such as View Composer OS disks. The nature of a read cache is that it can grow stale over time, so you can set the refresh or regenerate cache cycle based on a number of days. You can also set a period of time in which it is not used. This capability comes in handy if you have a maintenance schedule and want to ensure that it is not in use during those times. This schedule is set based on a day and time and referred to as a *blackout schedule*, as displayed in Figure 6.33.

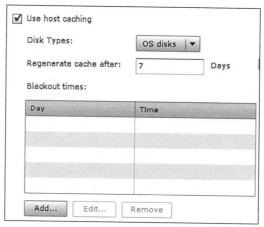

Figure 6.33 Advanced Storage Settings options.

You can edit the Advanced Storage Settings options during the deployment of a desktop pool or afterward by following these steps:

1. Open the View Administrator Console and expand **Inventory**.

2. Select the pool from the right pane and click the **Edit** button.

3. Select the **Pool Settings** tab and **Advanced Storage Options**, which will display the window that allows you to select specific datastores, as shown in Figure 6.34.

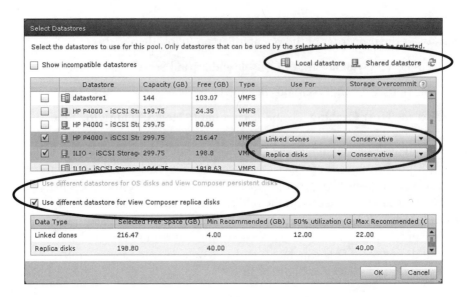

Figure 6.34 Select specific datastores.

VMware View also attempts to calculate the size required for the VMDKs created on the datastore selected; you can override the sizing calculation by changing the storage overcommit.

Storage overcommit adjusts how much capacity VMware View reserves for the dynamic growth of the files. It can be set to Conservative, Moderate, or Aggressive. Setting it to Aggressive, for example, increases the amount of overcapacity View factors into the deployment of virtual machines. Some storage systems do inline deduplication with very little impact to performance. If you have this underlying capability, you can get aggressive, but you should also be aware that depending on how your storage subsystem is designed, you could also be consolidating a larger number of I/Os.

- **None**—Storage is not overcommitted.
- **Conservative**—Four times the size of the datastore. This is the default level.
- **Moderate**—Seven times the size of the datastore.
- **Aggressive**—Fifteen times the size of the datastore.

At the bottom of this screen, you see the sizing estimated provided by VMware View, as shown in Figure 6.35. It is important to understand just how View sets the sizing so that you can understand how much is allocated by default. Additional information is available from VMware at http://www.vmware.com/files/pdf/view_storage_considerations.pdf.

Data Type	Selected Free Space (GB)	Min Recommended (GB)	50% utilization (G	Max Recommended ((
Linked clones	240.82	4.00	12.00	22.00
Replica disks	80.03	40.00		40.00

Figure 6.35 View sizing estimates.

- **Selected Free Space (GB)**—This column shows how much free space is available in the selected datastores. This is just a sum of the real free space with no calculation applied.

- **Min Recommended (GB)**—Based on the Max Number of Desktops, View Administrator calculates the minimum you should have available on your storage and allows

  - Space for two replicas

  - Two times the memory of VM times the number of desktops

  - 20% of the size for persistent desktops times the number of desktops

- **50% Utilization (GB)**—The calculation incorporates 50% OS disk growth compared to the parent virtual machine disk for each desktop and allows

  - Space for two replicas

  - 50% of replica disk times the number of desktops

  - Memory of VM times the number of desktops

  - 50% of the size for the persistent desktops times the number of desktops

- **Max Recommended (GB)**—This calculation determines that each desktop consumes the maximum disk space and allows

  - Space for two replicas

  - 100% of replica disk times the number of desktops

  - Memory of VM times the number of desktops

  - 100% of the size for persistent desktops times the number of desktops

Provisioning Settings

You can adjust how the virtual machines are provisioned using the provisioning settings. You are able to adjust the naming convention and provision all at once or provision on demand, for example. Why would you provision on demand? If you have a group of users who require access to computers periodically throughout the day but are not sitting in front of a computer, as a primary function, provisioning on demand ensures virtual desktops are available upon request but conserves resources until needed. Let's look at these settings a little more closely.

The first part of the provisioning settings allow you to enable and stop provisioning on error (see Figure 6.36). Enabling the Stop on Provisioning option is a good idea while you are testing all the functionality of an environment.

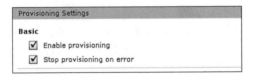

Figure 6.36 Provisioning Settings.

The second part of the provisioning settings allows you to specify a general naming pattern or get very specific and specify virtual machine names manually, as shown in Figure 6.37. If you select a manual naming convention, you can start a desktop in maintenance mode, which denies a login until the desktop is taken out of maintenance mode. You can also associate specific users and start desktops in maintenance mode to allow additional applications to be loaded before users log in.

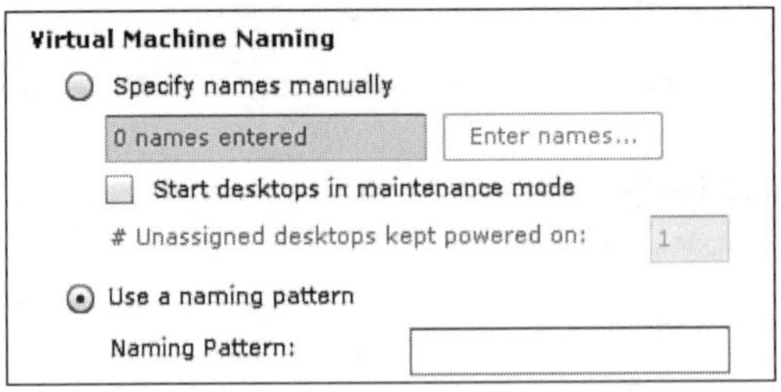

Figure 6.37 Virtual Machine Naming.

If this is a dedicated desktop pool, you can enter a list of names and associated users so that you can selectively control which user is assigned to which desktop, as shown in Figure 6.38. If this is a floating pool, user IDs are ignored. When you click **Next**, a lookup is performed in the Active Directory to ensure the users have associated accounts.

Figure 6.38 Associate users to desktops.

Entitlement

After creating your desktop pools, you need to assign them to users. Within VMware View, this process is called *entitlement*. Entitlements associate a desktop pool with a selected group of users using Active Directory groups. The procedure for entitling users is as follows:

1. Log in to the VMware View Administrator Console.

2. Browse to Inventory and Pools.

3. Select a pool of desktops from the right pane.

4. Select **Entitlements**.

5. You have the option of searching by user or group. Simply deselect the User or Group check box and click **Add**. Generally, you should associate pools of desktops to Active Directory groups and not individual users.

6. Enter a name or description and select **Find** to search for the AD group or user.

7. Select the group and click **OK** and **OK** again to entitle the desktops.

View Composer

If you are using View Composer, you can edit several settings to fine-tune the operation of the linked clones (see http://kb.vmware.com/selfservice/microsites/search.do?language= en_US&cmd=displayKC&externalId=1021506). Before you do, however, it is important to understand how you can treat data when using Composer. View Composer allows you to separate persistent and nonpersistent data into separate virtual machine drives. Rather than have a single drive, you can split them into three: the OS drive, the persistent drive, and the nonpersistent drive. If you actually browse the directory store of the VM's folder, you see five VMDKs per View Composer virtual machine, as shown in Figure 6.39.

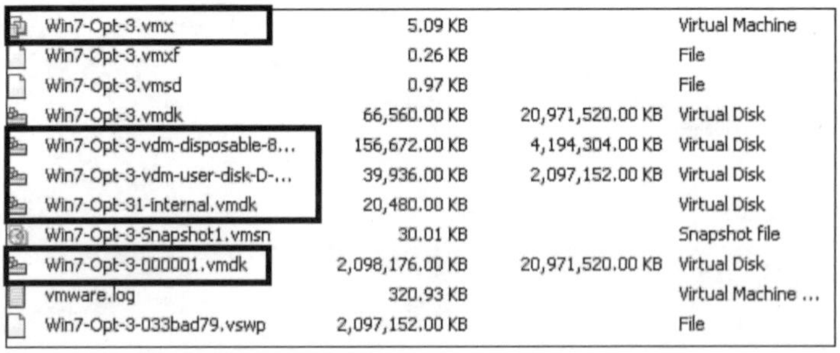

Win7-Opt-3.vmx	5.09 KB		Virtual Machine
Win7-Opt-3.vmxf	0.26 KB		File
Win7-Opt-3.vmsd	0.97 KB		File
Win7-Opt-3.vmdk	66,560.00 KB	20,971,520.00 KB	Virtual Disk
Win7-Opt-3-vdm-disposable-8...	156,672.00 KB	4,194,304.00 KB	Virtual Disk
Win7-Opt-3-vdm-user-disk-D-...	39,936.00 KB	2,097,152.00 KB	Virtual Disk
Win7-Opt-31-internal.vmdk	20,480.00 KB		Virtual Disk
Win7-Opt-3-Snapshot1.vmsn	30.01 KB		Snapshot file
Win7-Opt-3-000001.vmdk	2,098,176.00 KB	20,971,520.00 KB	Virtual Disk
vmware.log	320.93 KB		Virtual Machine ...
Win7-Opt-3-033bad79.vswp	2,097,152.00 KB		File

Figure 6.39 View Composer VMDKs.

In this case, we have win7-opt-3.vmdk, which is this virtual machine's virtual hard drive. We also have Win7-Opt-3-Snapshot1.vmdk, which is the snapshot log file. This file is created automatically when a snapshot is taken of the virtual machine. A snapshot preserves the state of a virtual machine at a specific point in time. Why would a View Composer virtual machine have a snapshot? There are several operational tasks that you can do to a View desktop, such as a *refresh*. If you use a snapshot file, the changes to the operating system can be rolled back, or "refreshed," without redeploying the virtual machine and imposing a substantial performance impact on the virtual desktop environment.

If you look under the snapshot manager, you will see a snapshot called vdm-initial-check-point, as shown in Figure 6.40.

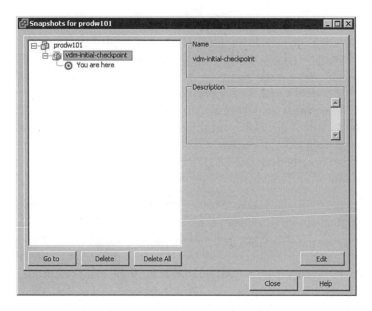

Figure 6.40 The vdm-initial-checkpoint snapshot.

Replicas

A *replica* is a clone of the parent VM plus the snapshot file that locks in the original configuration. View Composer uses the replica to create the linked clone View desktops. The replica is used to rightsize the virtual machine by moving from the parent VM format to a thin provisioned virtual machine. From VMware View 4.5 and on, you can store replicas in separate datastores. This allows you to store the replica on local SSDs because it is from the replica that the linked clone tree is built. Keep in mind, though, that if you use a local disk, the linked clone tree also resides on the local disk. The integration of local SSDs should be reserved for stateless View desktops. The point of using a local SSD is to take advantage of the extremely high I/O capabilities of the technology, but doing so comes at the cost of some of the features available when deploying a View desktop on shared storage.

Creating a large number of View Composer desktops in a short period of time can generate a large number of I/Os that can affect your storage platform. Localizing some of this activity on an SSD contains the storage I/O, making the creation of a large number of desktops less of a performance consideration. When you use View Composer, desktops are created from a replica, a linked clone is created for each virtual machine, and a snapshot is taken to create the redo log.

The other VMDKs that are introduced to a View Composer virtual machine are the disposable disk and the persistent disk, which used to be called the user data disk. The disposable VMDK stores things that are automatically deleted when the virtual machine is powered off, such as Windows Temp files. The persistent disk provides storage for things that should persist between reboots, such as the user's profile and any application configuration changes. The persistent disk can be used to complement Persona Management by creating a local persistent cache for the profile while ensuring it is also stored centrally on a file share. When a user requires a Persona profile, the majority of the data is locally available on the persistent disk. Only the differences between the unsynchronized data need to be downloaded from the central file share. If you are going to use them together, you need to ensure that the Remove Local Persona at Log Off policy is not enabled so that the Persona profile is not removed from the persistent disk.

Logically, the separation of VMDKs makes sense. The master VMDK and snapshots enable you to refresh the environment, the persistent disk allows you to keep user configuration activities so that they are not lost, and the nonpersistent disk flushes temporary files on reboot. What, then, is the internal disk for? The internal disk separates the unique machine information in a separate VMDK so that it can be managed properly. This disk is created when the machine is sysprepped or quickprepped. In addition, the disk stores the machine trust account that is used to authenticate a client machine to a domain controller. It is more generally referred to as the *computer account*. A computer account is changed every 30 days (it is the same for all Windows versions from 2000 on up) and is set by default in the local policy of the operating system.

Within a View Composer–created virtual machine, an additional service called the VMware View Composer Guest Agent Server runs, as shown in Figure 6.41.

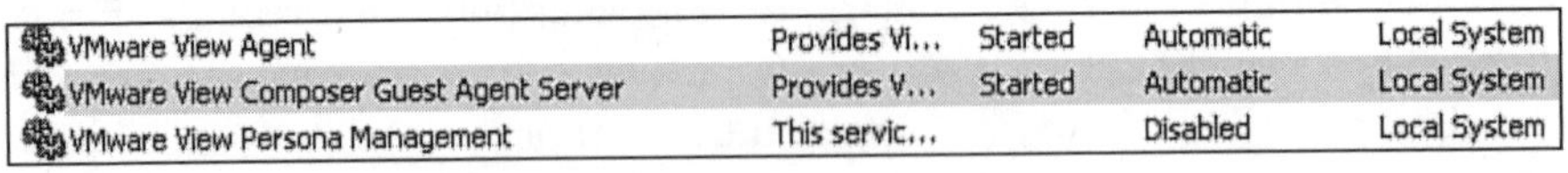

VMware View Agent	Provides Vi...	Started	Automatic	Local System
VMware View Composer Guest Agent Server	Provides V...	Started	Automatic	Local System
VMware View Persona Management	This servic...		Disabled	Local System

Figure 6.41 VMware View Composer Guest Agent Server.

One of the things this service does is monitor changes to the computer account and ensure that any changes are updated to the internal VMDK. This ensures that if you run a recompose, for example, the computer account and its unique identity persist and are not corrupted in the Active Directory.

If you look at this feature logically and break it down by functionality, the design of each virtual machine looks like that in Figure 6.42.

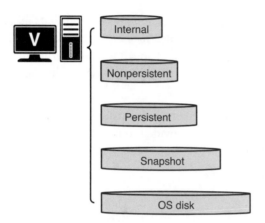

Figure 6.42 VMDKs for View Composer.

Now that you have a basic understanding of the makeup of the Composer VMs, you can look a little more in depth at the operational management. In View Composer, there are several activities you can do to manage the desktops.

Refresh

As the VM grows, the size and storage requirements of the linked clones increase. To reclaim this space and reduce the size of the virtual desktops, you can innitiate a *refresh*. A refresh essentially reverts the machine to the snapshot that was created when the virtual machine was deployed.

Let's look at how this process impacts the files that make up the virtual machine. When you do a refresh, you see that the Revert Snapshot job is run to revert the machine back to the vdm-initial-checkpoint snapshot. If you are looking at the virtual machine folder, prior to the refresh, the OS disk looks like that in Figure 6.43.

| | 3,170,560 KB | demow7001-000002 | | VMware virtual disk file |

Figure 6.43 Observe the size of the redo log.

Post refresh, the redo log looks like that in Figure 6.44.

| | 23,808 KB | demow7001-000002 | | VMware virtual disk file |

Figure 6.44 Post refresh size.

The OS disk is reduced in size as the machine is reverted to its initial creation size, reclaiming the space. Because the virtual machine's machine-specific information is stored in the internal VMDK, this change can happen without having to re-create the computer account in the Active Directory because the trust relationship between the View desktop and the Active Directory is maintained.

You can control how the refresh is initiated. By default, it happens right away, but you can delay it and adjust the notification provided to users. Let's go through the steps to apply a refresh to the desktop pool.

1. Within the VMware View Administrator Console, browse to Inventory and then Pools.

2. Double-click the pool you want to refresh on the right.

3. Select the **Inventory** tab to refresh individual desktops or the **Settings** tab to do the entire pool (see Figure 6.45).

Figure 6.45 Use Inventory to select individual desktops.

You can select individual desktops from the Inventory tab if you like. From the Inventory tab, under the View Composer drop-down menu, you can select operational tasks such as Refresh, Recompose, Rebalance or Publish, as shown in Figure 6.46.

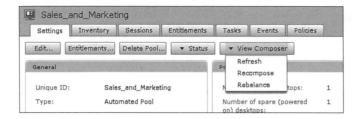

Figure 6.46 Operational tasks in VMware View.

You can reschedule the day and time in which the activity takes place (the default is current day and current time) and force or wait for users to log off (see Figure 6.47). You cannot change the grace period for logoff here, but you can see it and update it in the global settings if it needs to be adjusted. Click **Next**.

Refresh

Scheduling

Specify when you want this task to start

Start at: 02/04/2012 ▦   5 : 12 pm ▲▼

⦿ Force users to log off

  Users will be forced to log off when the system is ready to operate on their virtual machines. Before being forcibly logged off, users may have a grace period in which to save their work (Global Settings).

◯ Wait for users to log off

  Wait for all connected users to disconnect before the task starts. For users without remote sessions, the task will start immediately.

☑ Stop at first error

The warning and grace period can be edited in global settings:

☑ Display warning before forced logoff:

Log off time: 5   minutes

Log off message: Your desktop is
                   scheduled for an ▲▼

                                              Next >   Cancel

Figure 6.47 Scheduling.

Review your settings and click **Finish** when ready (see Figure 6.48).

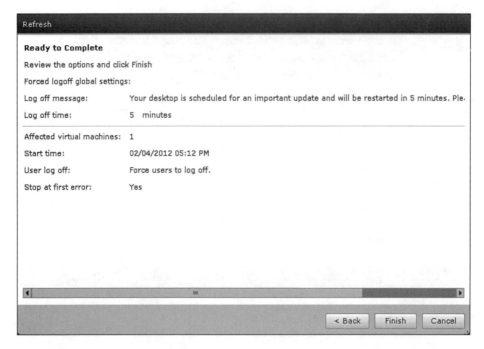

Figure 6.48 Review task and select Finish.

Recompose

A *recompose* is designed to replace the OS disk of the virtual machine, but it has limitations. You cannot recompose to a different operating system. For example, if your linked clones are using a Windows 7 OS, you cannot recompose to a Windows XP OS. Before you can recompose, you must either change the existing parent virtual machine or create a new one to introduce the linked clones. After the parent has been updated or created, View goes through a similar process to the creation of a new pool. A replica is created first, and then the linked clones are built from the replica. A recompose operation generally follows your image refresh or rebuild cycles, which typically happen every six months to a year.

Because a new OS disk is used, a new vdm-initial-checkpoint snapshot is created for use in future refresh operations. The persistent disk with all the user configurations is not replaced as a part of the recompose, allowing the OS to change but perserving the users' settings. Because it is a new OS, the SysPrep or QuickPrep process is rerun, and a new internal disk is created. A recompose can use a lot of resources in the virtual desktop environment, so it is generally recommended that you initiate a recompose after work hours. The process is similar to a refresh, except that you select Recompose from the View Composer drop-down. The exact process to initiate a recompose is as follows:

1. In View Administrator, browse to Inventory and then Pools.

2. Select the pool to recompose by double-clicking the pool ID in the left column.

3. Choose whether to recompose the whole pool or selected desktops.

4. On the selected pool's page, click the **Settings** tab and select **View Composer and Recompose**. To recompose specific desktops, select individual desktops from the pool by clicking the **Inventory** tab. Select the desktops to recompose and select **View Composer and Recompose**.

5. Click **Finish**.

A logical depiction of what happens is shown in Figure 6.49.

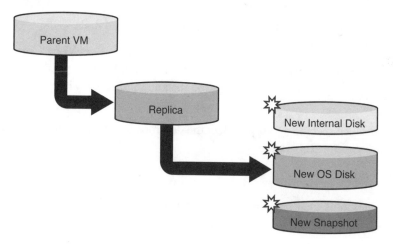

Figure 6.49 Recompose

Rebalance

A *rebalance* of View desktops redistributes linked clones among available datastores based on the amount of free space available (see http://kb.vmware.com/selfservice/microsites /search.do?language=en_US&cmd=displayKC&externalId=1021506). This is the only way to move linked clone trees. The redistribution takes place only if there is an unequal amount of space across datastores. When you rebalance a pool of desktops, the first thing View does is put the virtual machine in maintenance mode so that no one can log in. View then determines what to move based on the amount of space in the datacenters. View separates the OS and persistent disks from the Composer desktop. It then removes the OS and persistent disks and creates a new replica and tree in the datastore. If a replica does not exist in the datastore, it is created first, unless a specific datastore has been identified for replica storage. View deletes the OS disk and creates a new OS linked to the replica. Because this is a new OS disk, SysPrep or QuickPrep is run and a new machine is created. When this process is complete, a new initial-vdm-checkpoint snapshot is created, and the virtual machine's status is updated from provisioned to available. Be aware that the activity you are starting may involve copying a number of full virtual machines to many datastores plus snapshots and delta files to create the replicas and View desktops. The impact of this process can be very heavy in a large environment, so it should be performed within a maintenance window. The persistent disks have moved from the original virtual desktop, so the user configuration information is maintained through the process.

1. In View Administrator, browse to Inventory and then Pools.

2. Select the pool to rebalance by double-clicking the pool ID in the left column.

3. Choose whether to rebalance the whole pool or selected desktops.

4. On the selected pool's page, click the **Settings** tab and select **View Composer and Rebalance**. To rebalance selected desktops. click the **Inventory** tab. To rebalance specific desktops, select the desktops to rebalance and select **View Composer and Rebalance**.

5. To rebalance specific desktops, select the desktops to rebalance and select **View Composer and Rebalance**.

6. Click **Finish**.

A logical dipiction of what happens is shown in Figure 6.50.

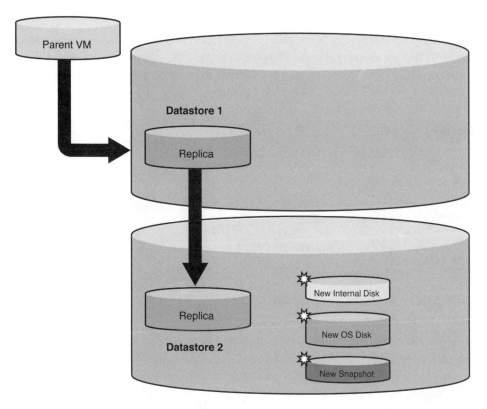

Figure 6.50 Rebalance.

Managing Persistent Disks

It is possible to manage persistent disks on an individual basis. From an operations perspective, you might need to do this if you want to preserve settings from a virtual desktop that has had a problem to be able to copy them to a new one you have re-created. You need to detach and reattach the persistent disk to preserve the settings.

If you have integrated Persona Management, the user configurations and profile are available centrally from the file repository, so there is less need to reattach persistent disks. This capability can come in handy, however, from time to time. For example, if a user is having issues with a persistent desktop, Helpdesk can ask that user to log off and reassign the user to another desktop to which you have reattached the user's persistent disk. Because View Persona ensures the user's settings transfer to the new View desktop, there is minimal impact to the user. While the user is working, troubleshooting can be performed on the problematic virtual desktop.

All persistent disks are organized into a single view under the Inventory and Persistent Disks section in the VMware View Administrator Console. If you look in the right pane, you see all your persistent disks and what state they are in—attached or detached. You also see what desktop, pool, datastore, and the current capacity of the persistent disk, as shown in Figure 6.51.

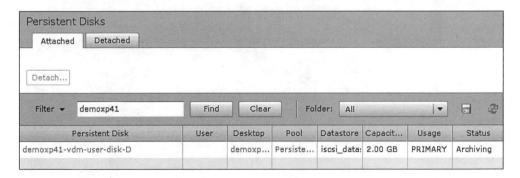

Figure 6.51 Display desktops with persistent disks.

You can select any disk from the Attached tab and detach its persistent disk. When you do, the associated VM is deleted and removed from inventory. When you detach, you are prompted to keep the disk on the current datastore or move it to another. If you move it to another datastore, you are asked to select a virtual machine folder that the persistent disk should be moved to. From the Detached tab, you can view the detached persistent disks, refresh the inventory, and create new virtual machines to be reattached to the persistent disks. This capability is a substantial improvement over older releases of View, which required scripts to be run to reassociate user data disks.

The operational procedures to detach and attach persistent disks are as follows:

1. In View Administrator, click **Inventory** and **Persistent Disks**.

2. Select the persistent disk to detach.

3. Click **Detach.**

4. Choose where to store the persistent disk.

5. Use the current datastore. Store the persistent disk on the datastore where it is currently located.

6. Move to the following datastore. Select a new datastore on which to store the persistent disk. Click **Browse**.

7. Click the down arrow and select a new datastore from the Choose a Datastore menu.

8. The View Composer persistent disk is saved on the datastore. The associated linked clone desktop is deleted and removed from inventory.

Provided the desktop you want to reattach it to is the same OS, you can reattach it using the following procedure:

1. In View Administrator, click **Inventory** and **Persistent Disks**.

2. Click the **Detached** tab.

3. Select the persistent disk.

4. Click **Attach**.

5. Select a linked clone desktop on which to attach the persistent disk.

6. Select **Attach as a Secondary Disk**.

7. Click **Finish**.

IMPORTANT

You should double-check the permissions on the persistent disk to ensure System and Administrators have full access. You should also ensure that the local user group has Read & Execute, List folder contents and Read and the special permission Create Folder and Write Data.

After the desktop is joined to the domain, the domain users group is added to the local users group, ensuring the user has the appropriate access to download or create a profile. From the same Detached tab, you can select a detached disk and re-create a desktop OS by selecting the persistent disk and clicking the **Recreate Desktop** button shown in Figure 6.52.

Figure 6.52 Recreate Desktop button.

Managing Applications

Now that you understand how to manage View desktops, it is important to look at some of the activities required to manage your virtual applications. One of the challenges with managing desktops is that the images and applications required by the users are rarely static. New application requests and updates to existing applications occur all the time. In a VMware View environment, you need to understand how to manage your ThinApp packages. In the following sections, we look at some of the methods you can use to ensure your applications are properly updated and easy to maintain in your View environment.

Updating ThinApp Packages

Updating ThinApp packages can happen at several different levels and can actually refer to several different operational activities. If you started from an evaluation license of ThinApp, after you move to production you might need to update or "relink" your ThinApp packages to a licensed version. To move from an evaluation license to a production license, you first need to update the license in the VMware Setup Capture tool and then run the Relink tool on your ThinApp packages to swap the evaluation license with the production license.

About Relink

The Relink utility was released with ThinApp version 4.5. It allows you not only to relicense but also update the formats of previous packages so that they are upgraded for the new release of ThinApp—for example, from version 4.5 to version 4.6. As part of the process, the Relink utility creates a backup of the package before the updates are applied. Because of this, you should make sure you have adequate space set aside for both the original and upgraded package. Using Relink, you can avoid repackaging when doing version upgrades of ThinApp.

Let's use an example of updating the license of the VMware Setup Capture tool to illustrate the point. Updating the license is actually quite easy to do, so let's take a quick look at this before getting into some of the more sophisticated methods of updating ThinApp packages. When you have your license, simply go to the desktop on which you installed the ThinApp Capture utility.

When the Setup Capture utility launches, update the license key by clicking the **License** button and entering the new license number and a description, as shown in Figure 6.53.

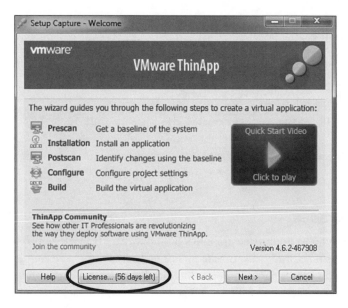

Figure 6.53 Apply licensing.

The Relink utility is used to upgrade virtual packages or relink evaluation packages back to a valid license. It can be found in the install directory of the ThinApp Packaging Utility. The format is to run the following command

```
relink.exe  -Recursive
```

The –Recursive switch allows you to link multiple applications located in a directory, as shown in Figure 6.54

```
C:\Program Files\VMware\VMware ThinApp>relink
Usage: relink [-Recursive] ExistingPackage [ExistingPackage...]
  relink can be used to upgrade an existing virtual package to
  the current ThinApp version.
  ExistingPackage can contain wildcards (*.exe)
  and can also be a .msi package (VirtualPackage.msi)
```

Figure 6.54 Relink utility.

When you run the utility, you see the utility extract the files, update them, and recompress them. If you look at the directory in which the ThinApp package was stored, you should see a *.bak backup file, as shown in Figure 6.55.

```
C:\Program Files\VMware\VMware ThinApp>relink "z:\Install\vm - vmware\vm - thina
pp\thin-notepad++\bin\Notepad++.msi"
VMware ThinApp Runtime Linker Version 4.7.0-519532, Built Nov  2 2011
Copyright 2006-2011, VMware, Inc. All rights reserved.
Enterprise Edition, licensed to virtualguru.org
z:\Install\vm - vmware\vm - thinapp\thin-notepad++\bin\Notepad++.msi:
  Notepad++.exe:
    SUCCESS: Notepad++.exe, size=11008k.
  Populating MSI tables
    SUCCESS: z:\Install\vm - vmware\vm - thinapp\thin-notepad++\bin\Notepad++.msi
WARNING: The package you just created will expire on 2012-12-14
```

Figure 6.55 Relink makes a backup before extracting the package.

Inplace Upgrades

ThinApp allows you to do inplace upgrades by supporting package versioning. They are also referred to as *integer upgrades* or *side-by-side updates*. To see an example of how this works, let's say you have a package in production that users are currently running from \\ThinApp\Prod\Notepad++ called notepad++.exe. If you repackage a newer version of Notepad++ and call the package notepad++.exe.1 and store it in the same directory, the next time the user launches the package, it would automatically select version .1. Even if the user launches notepad++.exe, ThinApp launches the package with the highest integer appended. For a dramatic example of how this works, let's look at two packages that are completely different and give them the same name but append a .1 to the second package. After they are copied to the same directory, you should be able to launch the original EXE and have the "new" version execute.

For example, let's say you package a version of Notepad++.exe and a complete version of Micrsoft Office Professional 2010. You copied both into the same directory and renamed the Microsoft Excel 2010.exe to Notepad++.exe.1. Now when you launch Notepad++.exe, you see the new version of Excel 2010 launch, as shown in Figure 6.56.

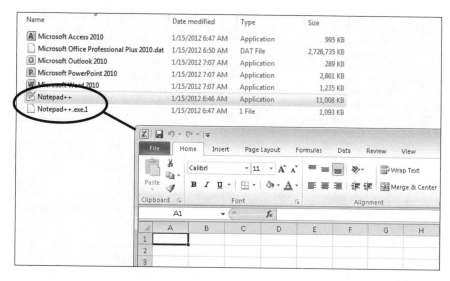

Figure 6.56 The original package is replaced with the "new" version.

Keep in mind that what triggers the side-by-side feature is the appended integer number on the ThinApp package. Because of this, it is very easy to roll backward and forward through application updates or to revert to older versions.

Inplace upgrades are best used when ThinApp packages are stored centrally and streamed to your virtual desktops. You are also able to use the simplicity of the process to revert to older versions. Simply append a higher version to the older application.

SandBox Merge

When we looked at capturing applications using ThinApp, the ThinApp Capture utility created an application-specific build directory, as shown in Figure 6.57.

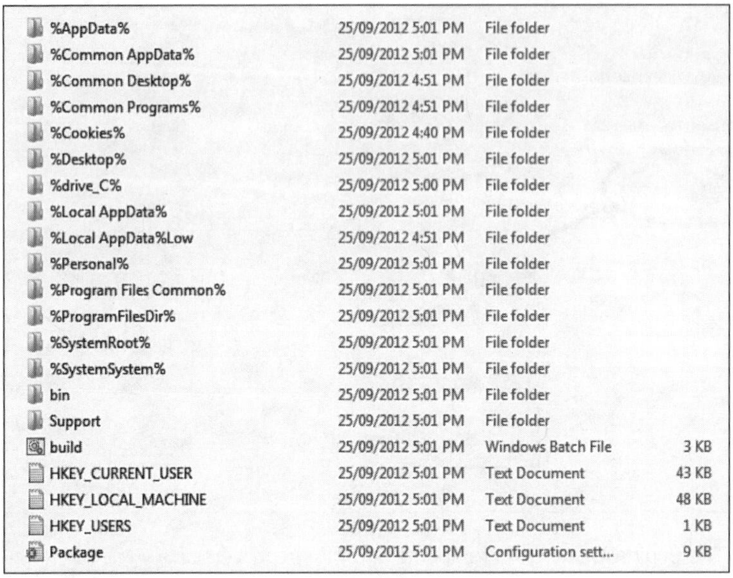

%AppData%	25/09/2012 5:01 PM	File folder	
%Common AppData%	25/09/2012 5:01 PM	File folder	
%Common Desktop%	25/09/2012 4:51 PM	File folder	
%Common Programs%	25/09/2012 4:51 PM	File folder	
%Cookies%	25/09/2012 4:40 PM	File folder	
%Desktop%	25/09/2012 5:01 PM	File folder	
%drive_C%	25/09/2012 5:00 PM	File folder	
%Local AppData%	25/09/2012 5:01 PM	File folder	
%Local AppData%Low	25/09/2012 4:51 PM	File folder	
%Personal%	25/09/2012 5:01 PM	File folder	
%Program Files Common%	25/09/2012 5:01 PM	File folder	
%ProgramFilesDir%	25/09/2012 5:01 PM	File folder	
%SystemRoot%	25/09/2012 5:01 PM	File folder	
%SystemSystem%	25/09/2012 5:01 PM	File folder	
bin	25/09/2012 5:01 PM	File folder	
Support	25/09/2012 5:01 PM	File folder	
build	25/09/2012 5:01 PM	Windows Batch File	3 KB
HKEY_CURRENT_USER	25/09/2012 5:01 PM	Text Document	43 KB
HKEY_LOCAL_MACHINE	25/09/2012 5:01 PM	Text Document	48 KB
HKEY_USERS	25/09/2012 5:01 PM	Text Document	1 KB
Package	25/09/2012 5:01 PM	Configuration sett...	9 KB

Figure 6.57 The build directory.

It is from this build directory that the final ThinApp application *.exe or *.MSI is compiled or created. It is possible to make changes to the ThinApp package and update it in the process. You do this using the SandBox Merge utility, or sbmerge.exe. The sbmerge utility has a few different options. If you launch and make the changes to the application and run a sbmerge print command, you see the exact change that will be applied to the application sandbox. It is a good idea to run this before executing the utility. The sbmerge apply command applies these changes to the application sandbox. This does not re-create or recompile the application into a ThinApp EXE or MSI, however. To do that, you must complete the final step, which is to run the build.bat command.

Let's look at an example to clarify the process.

In this example, you are running a ThinApp version of the Opera web browser application, which, by default, can be found in the bin directory of the project folder, as shown in Figure 6.58.

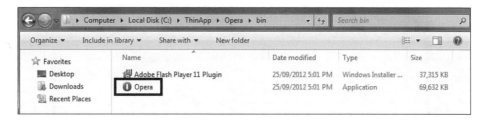

Figure 6.58 Run the Opera ThinApp package.

Make whatever updates or changes you would like to the virtual application. The example in Figure 6.59 shows how to update the startup page.

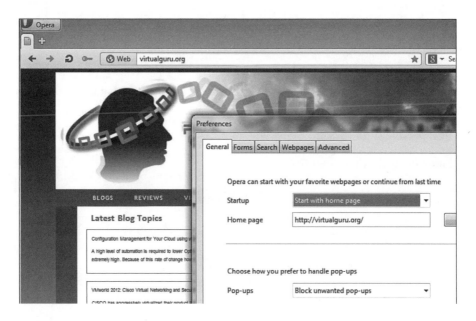

Figure 6.59 Make a change to the ThinApp package.

You can see what changes will be applied by running sbmerge from the VMware ThinApp install directory. Run the following command to bring about the changes:

```
sbmerge print –projectdir [source directory]
```

Note that even though the syntax says you need to use =[source directory], you do not, as you can see in Figure 6.60.

Figure 6.60 The sbmerge print command shows you the changes that will be made.

To apply these changes, you need to switch the print command with apply. For example, you use

```
sbmerge.xe apply -projectdir [path]
```

This command is shown in Figure 6.61.

Figure 6.61 The sbmerge utility applies the changes.

Now switch to the project directory and run the build.bat command to recompile the ThinApp Package, as shown in Figure 6.62.

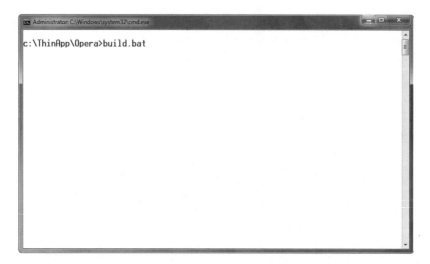

Figure 6.62 The build.bat command compiles the application.

Verify your changes by running the updated ThinApp package, as shown in Figure 6.63.

Figure 6.63 The changes are applied.

You now have an updated version of your original source package with the changes. You can distribute this new version of the package using any of the methods already discussed, or using AppSync, which is discussed in the following section.

Using AppSync

AppSync allows you to use a web server or URL as a source for an updated ThinApp package. Essentially, you store the ThinApp packages in a central location and use

AppSync to keep track of any changes. If you need to update the package, you simply add it to the central location. How do you get the package to check the site for updates? Well, all you need to do is update the settings in the package.ini before the package is built so that the package knows where and when to check for updates. You can do this manually or from the VMware ThinApp capture utility right before the build phase by clicking on the **Edit Package.ini** button, as shown in Figure 6.64.

Figure 6.64 Edit Package.ini.

If you decide to not use the Capture utility and update it manually, simply run the build.bat script within the project directory of the ThinApp application.

If you look at the settings in the package.ini that control AppSync, you see the following settings that can be configured:

```
;-------- AppSync Parameters ----------
;AppSyncURL=https://example.com/some/path/PackageName.exe
;AppSyncUpdateFrequency=1d
;AppSyncExpirePeriod=30d
;AppSyncWarningPeriod=5d
;AppSyncWarningFrequency=1d
;AppSyncWarningMessage=This application will become unavailable for use in
%remaining_days% day(s) if it cannot contact its update server. Check your
network connection to ensure uninterrupted service.
```

```
;AppSyncExpireMessage=This application has been unable to contact its
update server for %expire_days% day(s), so it is unavailable for use. Check
your network connection and try again.
;AppSyncUpdatedMessage=
;AppSyncClearSandboxOnUpdate=0
```

The most important of these is the AppSyncURL and the update frequency, which tells the package where to look for updates and when. To enable AppSync, you must configure both. The source can be a website that is unsecured (http), one that is secured using a certificate (https), or a file share specified by a UNC path or hard drive. An example of each of these is included here for reference:

AppSync Website Example:

```
;-------- AppSync Parameters ----------
AppSyncURL=https://virtualguru.org/ThinApp/notepad++.exe
```

> **NOTE**
>
> The source can be either http or https. It is also possible to use alternate ports by including the port in the path statement. For example,
>
> ```
> AppSyncURL=https://virtualguru.org:448/ThinApp/notepad++.exe
> ```
>
> In addition, it is possible to add a user account and password that is visible in the package.ini but is not after the ThinApp package is compiled.
>
> ```
> AppSyncURL=https://user:password@virtualguru.org:448/ThinApp/notepad++.exe
> ```

AppSync File Share Example (UNC):

```
;-------- AppSync Parameters ----------
AppSyncURL=file://demosrv001/Source/ThinApp/notepad++.exe
```

AppSync File Share Example (Local Drive):

```
;-------- AppSync Parameters ----------
AppSyncURL=file:///v:/ThinApp/notepad++.exe
```

You can also configure how frequently the package should check the source for updates using the AppSyncUpdateFrequency option (that is, AppSyncUpdateFrequency=1d). For test purposes, it is possible to have the application check at launch time by setting the Frequency to 0 (AppSyncUpdateFrequency=0d).

Along with the frequency, you can set an expiry period if no connection request is received. This type of upgrade process is ideal when you deploy ThinApp packages in a distributed mode on machines that are unmanaged although it is possible to use in other scenarios. A good example of using the expiry period is when deploying applications to temporary consultants because you can expire them at the end of the engagement.

You do need to consider where you are going to place your web servers or URL application source repositories. In a large environment that consists of a centrally located datacenter and many branch offices, you may need to repoint updates to a local source. Of course, having to create site-specific package.ini files may not be the way to go.

If you use a simple web server as a source, many technologies designed to cache websites can be used in the AppSync environment. By building in proxy caching to ensure that the package is cached locally to the branch for performance, you avoid having to customize the package.ini, simplifying the distribution but adding additional cost. Another technology that might provide similar value to a large environment is WAN optimization. WAN optimization provides branch-side caching features but generally does not accelerate UDP-based traffic. This helps ThinApp, but it unfortunately cannot help with accelerating of PCoIP traffic. We cover using replication technology when we discuss high availability in Chapter 11, "High Availability Considerations."

Let's look at a sample to illustrate how to do this. In this case, to make it clear how this technology works, you actually use a ThinApp version of Opera and notepad++. You set the AppSync settings to point from within Opera to the ThinApp version of notepad++. In actual production, you would, of course, point the ThinApp package from the original package to the location of the updated package.

You start with the ThinApp version of Opera and launch it normally. At this point, you have not adjusted the AppSync settings, as shown in Figure 6.65.

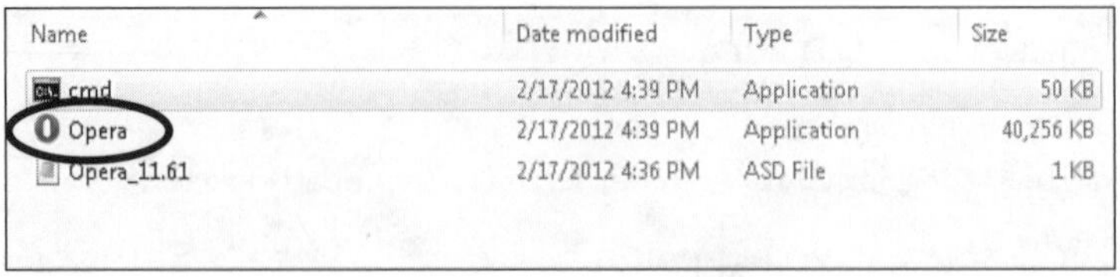

Name		Date modified	Type	Size
cmd		2/17/2012 4:39 PM	Application	50 KB
Opera		2/17/2012 4:39 PM	Application	40,256 KB
Opera_11.61		2/17/2012 4:36 PM	ASD File	1 KB

Figure 6.65 Launch Opera.

After verifying that it launches, you should close it and edit the package.ini file to include the AppSync settings you need. The package.ini is in the project directory of the ThinApp application. You set the AppSync settings under the [BuildOptions] in the AppSync Parameters section.

For purposes of demonstration, set the location to a local directory and a second ThinApp application. Set the Update Frequency to 0 so that the application checks for updates on launch, as shown in Figure 6.66.

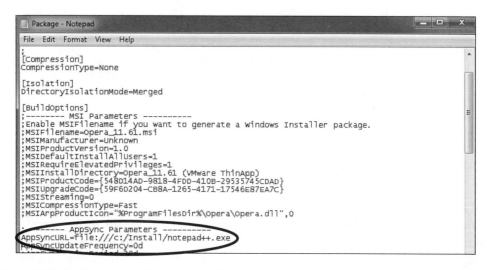

Figure 6.66 AppSync properties are located in Package.ini.

When you launch the application, notice that the original Opera.exe gets updated to the "updated" notepad++ package, as shown in Figure 6.67. AppSync does not do any name comparison; it simply updates the package with whatever file it pointed to in the package. ini in the AppSync parameters.

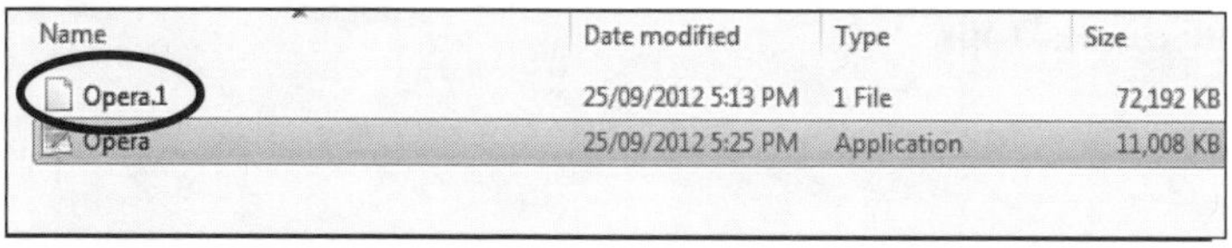

Name	Date modified	Type	Size
Opera.1	25/09/2012 5:13 PM	1 File	72,192 KB
Opera	25/09/2012 5:25 PM	Application	11,008 KB

Figure 6.67 The original package is updated.

It is a good idea to put the ThinReg.exe utility in the update location, along with the updated package. If the ThinReg utility is available in the source, it is automatically applied to ensure the application is registered properly within the desktop.

Summary

This chapter examined the operational steps in creating, configuring, and managing VMware pools. You looked at what it takes to maintain and manage ThinApp packages. Although the steps here are important, they are no substitute for having a good operational process. This involves ensuring you have predetermined operational windows, for example, so that you can do pool refreshes or rebalances and not impact end-user activity in the environment. It also ensures that along with updating and maintaining ThinApp packages you have good operational lifecycle management to allow you to update, replace, and decommision applications as required.

VMware View provides a set of tools that add a lot of capabilities, but it is up to you to integrate them in a way that minimizes disruptions. As with any hosted environment, disruptions to service are amplified in a large VMware View environment. A well-managed change management process for effecting change in your View environment goes a long way to ensuring that users have confidence in the solution and that it remains stable and provides good performance.

In the next chapter, we integrate vShield Endpoint into our VMware View environment. vShield Endpoint helps ensure that we can secure our View desktops from malware or virus attacks. Although we can use the same method of installing anti-virus scanning software on all our virtual desktops, this can affect performance if you are not careful. In addition, the updating of virus definition files can be problematic if you have a large number of stateless desktops.

Chapter 7

VMware vShield EndPoint

VMware vShield EndPoint

Two common problems occur when running antivirus (AV) software on a Windows virtual desktop environment. AV software needs constant updates to the antivirus definition files to ensure the software has the latest profiles of known viruses. In an environment where you have stateless desktops that are constantly being powered on and off, it can be difficult to maintain a consistent level of definition files across all the virtual desktops. The second problem has to do with the I/O load generated on a consolidated virtual desktop platform by antivirus scanning and updating. This load can be quite significant and is generally referred to as an *AV storm*. Before vShield EndPoint was available, administrators were forced to stagger updates and scans to prevent AV storms in virtual desktop environments.

VMware vShield EndPoint allows you to offload the overhead of AV software from within the virtual desktop instances. It works in combination with third-party antivirus software companies. There is a vShield management component and a vShield EndPoint appliance provided by the third party and also a vShield driver that is installed on the protected virtual machines. The driver is part of VMware Tools but is not installed by default.

The framework takes advantage of the VMSafe API built into the platform some time ago. Even though it has been widely available, the integration of third-party AV solutions has been slow, with only a few vendors having products available on the market. Trend Micro was one of the initial adopters. With the increased interest in VMware View, this situation has changed so that most of the major vendors now have products coming to market.

The use of the driver on the VM and vShield EndPoint allows the third-party to collectively view and scan what is active in memory on the virtual machines. This allows you to reduce the need to put AV software on each individual virtual machine. In the early releases of the solution, third-party vendors' solutions did not offer feature parity with the full distributed AV agents. In practice, this required offloading some AV operational activity through EndPoint and doing some using a local agent. Now that the products have matured, there is less need for a combined EndPoint distributed agent approach, but there are a few caveats to be aware of. We discuss them a little later on when we look at a real-world example integrating Trend Micro.

NOTE

Trend Micro was selected because it was one of the first to integrate vShield EndPoint but not to single out Trend Micro as the only solution for your View environment. You should always review each of the options on the market and select the one that both meets your requirements and aligns best with your internal security strategy.

When you are deploying stateless or floating desktops in View leveraging an EndPoint model (which essentially adds a third-party virtual appliance proxy), you can make sure that the definition files are up to date because they are stored on the virtual appliance. You can also consolidate much of the I/O on the appliance versus distributing it across all the virtual machines.

Deploying vShield EndPoint in your VMware View environment allows you to achieve higher virtual desktop consolidations by reducing the overhead required to run the virtual machines. The one challenge that has come up in the past is the lack of support from third parties. This lack of support created a problem if you happened to have standardized on one of the vendors not providing support for vShield EndPoint.

Does it make sense to have a separate AV vendor just for virtual desktop instances? Thankfully, due to the popularity of VMware View Trend Micro, McAfee, BitDefender, and Kapersky will have support within their products for vShield. In the meantime, you may have to consider a two-vendor solution that provides enough value. Keep in mind that although EndPoint is targeted for Virtual Desktop Infrastructure (VDI) environments, it works for both virtual server and desktop environments. If your organization is largely virtualized, you may be able to introduce EndPoint as an advantage to both your server and desktop virtualization infrastructure.

High-Level Architecture

The architecture for vShield EndPoint includes the vShield Manager, where you control all aspects of the vShield product line, not just EndPoint. vShield EndPoint is licensed per virtual machine. The licenses are applied from the vCenter Management Server to enable

EndPoint on a set number of virtual machines. vShield EndPoint licenses enable third-party backdoor access to see what is running in active memory of the virtual machine. By itself, however, EndPoint does not provide any active scanning or malware protection. This is where you need the third-party support. At a high level, the environment looks like that in Figure 7.1.

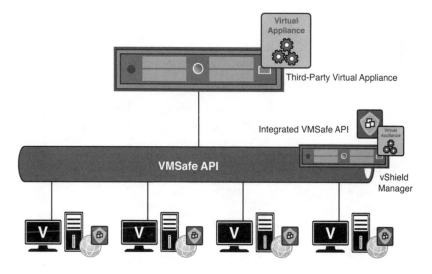

Figure 7.1 VMSafe API and vShield integration.

If you look at an environment in which vShield EndPoint is deployed, you will notice a private switch in which the third-party AV and malware scanning virtual appliance is connected. A third-party appliance is required on each ESX host so that visibility can be turned on for each VM in the environment. This private switch enables the backdoor visibility to the virtual machines, as shown in Figure 7.2.

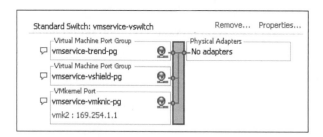

Figure 7.2 Private vSwitch with vShield port group.

When deploying this solution, you prepare the ESX Servers first by installing the vShield Manager and adding the licenses to vCenter and deploying an EndPoint module to each ESXi host server. After completing this task, you need to deploy the third-party virtual appliance and add the vShield endpoint driver to each virtual machine.

The EndPoint module that is deployed to each ESXi host essentially provides the proxy between the module that reads data from the VM and sends it to the private switch and third-party virtual appliance. The communication between the module and the private third-party appliance is enabled through a firewall rule that requires port 48651 to be open from the module to port 48666 on the third-party virtual appliance. This port has to be manually opened for this communication to work properly.

Logically, on each ESXi host, you have an environment that looks like Figure 7.3. The backdoor access is provided by the third-party appliance, as shown logically in Figure 7.3.

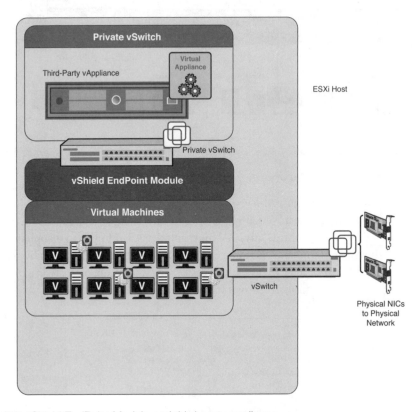

Figure 7.3 vShield EndPoint Module and third-party appliance.

Because vShield has not been around for as long as vCenter and ESXi, the driver was only included starting with VMware Tools 8.6.1, which is included in ESXi 5.0 Patch 1. Because we have not covered it already, we go through the simplest method of upgrading your vSphere environment by using Update Manager.

vSphere Update Manager

To install your vShield, you must upgrade the environment and keep a few issues in mind, such as installing the vShield driver in the parent image if you are using View Composer. You should also update the standard View templates to ensure the virtual machines are deployed "EndPoint ready" when created. To enable the current vSphere 5 environment for vShield, you should start first with a general upgrade across the environment to ensure you are running ESXi 5.0 Patch 1. The best way to upgrade a virtual infrastructure environment is, of course, through Update Manager, which is part of the vCenter Suite. Update Manager allows you to patch a number of features in the virtual environment, including the hosts and tools. (You can find additional information on VMware's site at http://www.vmware.com/products/update-manager/overview.html.)

When deploying Update Manager, you should follow a few general rules to ensure you don't run into problems. You can install Update Manager on the same server as vCenter. Doing so is appropriate for small- to mid-size environments. When your VMware View environment grows to 500 virtual desktops and 50 host servers, you should separate the Update Manager and vCenter database servers. If your View environment will grow larger than the 1,000 virtual desktops and 100 hosts, not only should your database servers be separate, but the VMware Update Manager and vCenter should also be installed separately. If you would like one VMware Update Manager for both your VMware View and VMware Server environments, you can register a single VMware Update Manager to service multiple vCenter Servers. If you are using a dedicated server, you should configure it with separate drives or volumes where you can store the downloads. This way, you ensure that the system or OS partition does not run out of space because of downloads.

Update Manager is not installed by default but can be easily added through the VMware vCenter Installer (see Figure 7.4).

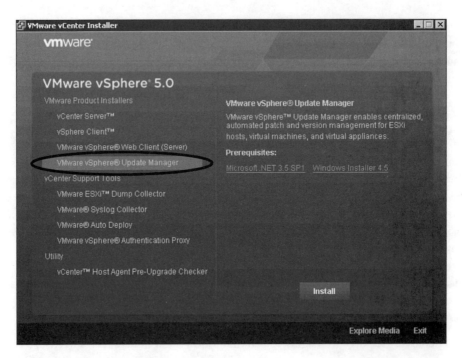

Figure 7.4 Installing vSphere Update Manager.

To install Update Manager, you need to do some preparation. Update Manager requires a database to store the metadata and some space to download the updates. Unlike other components of the vCenter product line, Update Manager requires a 32-bit ODBC connection. The installer detects the 32-bit ODBC connection if it exists and allows the installation to continue.

You do not set up a 32-bit ODBC connection the same way that you install a 64-bit connection on Windows 2008 R2. You can create 64-bit connections with the standard ODBC connection utility. To create a 32-bit connection, you must run the 32-bit version from

    %systemdrive%\Windows\SysWow64\Odbcad32.exe

Before you create the ODBC connector, you need to set up a separate database on your SQL Server. Update Manager also supports using an Oracle database. For additional details on installing on an Oracle database, refer to VMware's online documentation. (You can find additional information on Oracle integration in the administrator guide from VMware at http://pubs.vmware.com/vsphere-50/topic/com.vmware.ICbase/PDF/vsphere-update-manager-50-install-administration-guide.pdf.)

To set up a database on a SQL Server, complete the following steps:

1. Connect to the SQL database instance on the SQL Server.

2. Right-click the Database Module and select new database.

3. Ensure your database names are indicative of what they will be used for, such as vUpdate.

4. Expand the Security Module and add a new login. Ensure the login ID has db_owner access to the Update Manager's database. You should install Update Manager using this account, so double-check that you also have the appropriate rights to install on the vCenter Server if you are planning to install Update Manager on the same server.

Creating the 32-Bit ODBC Connection

Let's run through the steps to integrate Update Manager:

1. Launch odbc32.exe, as shown in Figure 7.5.

ocsetup	7/13/2009 9:14 PM	Application	193 KB
odbc32.dll	10/16/2010 12:34 ...	Application extens...	560 KB
odbc32gt.dll	7/13/2009 9:16 PM	Application extens...	24 KB
odbcad32	7/13/2009 9:14 PM	Application	84 KB
odbcbcp.dll	7/13/2009 9:16 PM	Application extens...	48 KB
odbcconf.dll	7/13/2009 9:16 PM	Application extens...	40 KB

Figure 7.5 Use the 32-bit ODBC connector named odbcad32.exe.

2. Add a system DSN by clicking the **Add** button (see Figure 7.6).

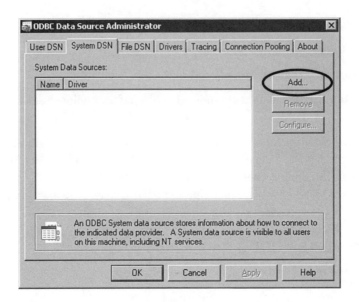

Figure 7.6 Add an ODBC connection.

3. Add the SQL Server client and click **Finish** (see Figure 7.7).

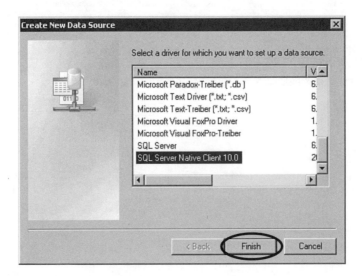

Figure 7.7 Select the SQL Server driver.

4. Specify a name for the data source and enter the SQL Server where vCenter is installed that it should connect to, as shown in Figure 7.8. and click Next.

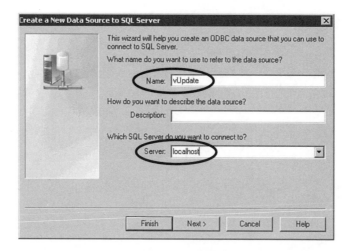

Figure 7.8 Specify a name and the SQL Server where the vCenter database is installed.

5. Leave the defaults and click **Next** (see Figure 7.9).

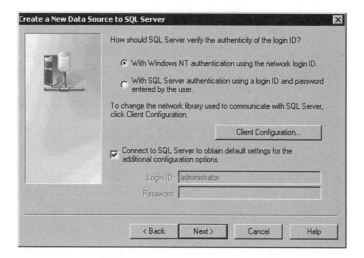

Figure 7.9 Select Windows Authentication.

6. Change the default database to point at the Update Manager database and click **Next** (see Figure 7.10).

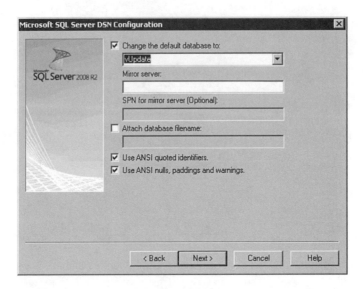

Figure 7.10 Select the Update Manager database; in this example, it is called in vUpdate.

7. Click **Finish** (see Figure 7.11).

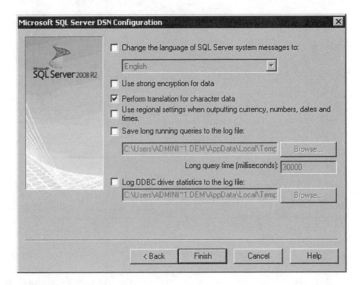

Figure 7.11 Select Finish.

8. Test the data source and click **OK** and **OK** again to close the utility.

With this 32-bit ODBC connection created, you can go ahead and install Update Manager. To install Update Manager, you first need to install the VMware vSphere Update Manager add-in component to vCenter and enable the plug-in in the vSphere Client so that you can manage the service. You also need to specify a location for the updates to be stored or the Patch repository.

Installing Update Manager

VMware Update Manager is a service that manages the installation of updates in vSphere environments. Update Manager tracks vulnerabilities for vSphere and can automatically apply patches based on defined parameters.

VMware Update Manager works like other patch utilities in which patch data is updated at set intervals controlled by the administrator. The service checks VMware's site as well as some third-party locations. One unique feature is that you can perform a rollback snapshot first on a virtual machine to have a fallback point in case you have problems with the applied patch or update. VMware provides several guidelines for configuring your Update Manager Server:

- The Update Manager Server requires a minimum of 2 GB of memory to cache patches in memory.

- Separate physical disks are needed for the Update Manager patch store and Update Manager database. Although this issue is not mentioned by VMware, you should separate the partitions in the VM from the patch store and database and make sure they are two separate VMDKs. Both of these partitions or volumes should be separate from the OS partition. This ensures that if you fill the volume, you can still access the Windows Server to truncate the database and delete files from the repository.

Next, we look at the steps required to install the Update Manager:

1. To install VMware Update Manager, you need to install the service on the vCenter Server and enable the plug-in from the vSphere Infrastructure Client. It can be installed using the VMware vCenter Installer.

2. Accept the end-user patent agreement and click **Next**.

3. Accept the license terms and click **Next**.

4. Deselect Download Updates From Default Sources Immediately After Installation and click **Next** (see Figure 7.12).

    You should deselect the default behavior, which is to automatically kick off the download of the default selections. The default sources include a variety of patches and patch versions that may or may not apply in your environment. It is better to be selective and finely control the types and quantity of downloads in your environment. VMware provided a sizing estimator for Update Manager 4, which is still a good tool to estimate how large the repository will grow. You can download the utility from www.vmware.com/support/vsphere4/doc/ vsp_vum_40_sizing_estimator.xls. The tool estimates the database size and how you should implement Update Manager; all you have to do is fill in details about the host, VMs, and patching activities. Also, note that the VM patching that was included in older versions of Update Manager has not been carried forward in Update Manager 5.0.

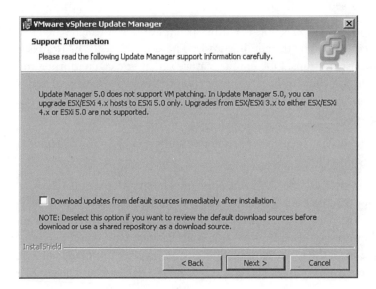

Figure 7.12 Do not automatically start downloading.

5. Provide the information required to connect to the vCenter Server and the user ID used to connect. By default, Update Manager connects over port 80. If you have changed the default vCenter ports during your installation, update the http port used. In addition, provide the administrator account that you will use to connect to vCenter Server (see Figure 7.13) and click **Next**.

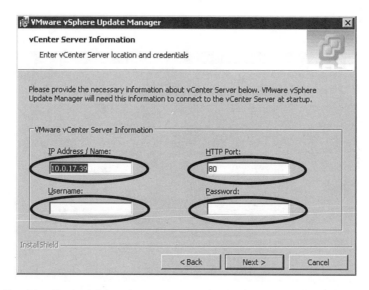

Figure 7.13 Provide vCenter information.

6. If you have pre-created the 32-bit ODBC connection, the installer detects it and presents it to you to continue the installation, as shown in Figure 7.14. If you have not, you need to follow the procedure described in the section "Creating the 32-bit ODBC Connection."

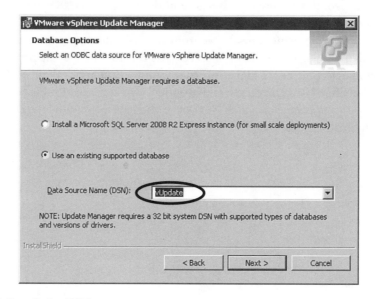

Figure 7.14 Specify the DSN.

7. Confirm the database and ODBC information and click **Next** (see Figure 7.15).

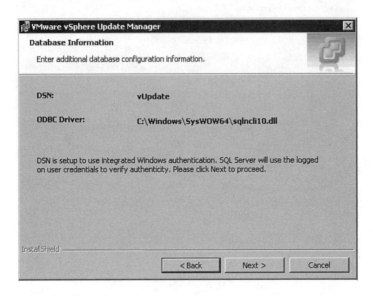

Figure 7.15 Confirm the DSN information.

8. The VMware vSphere Update Manager autodetects the IP of the host it is running on as part of the installation if it has a single network interface card (NIC), as shown in Figure 7.16. If it has multiple NICs, consider using the DNS name. If you are using a dedicated Update Manager Server shared by multiple vCenter Servers, make sure that the DNS name is resolvable from each vCenter Server. If your Internet connectivity is managed by a proxy server, you can add the specific proxy information by selecting **Yes, I Have Internet Connection and I Want to Configure Proxy Settings Now.** If you select this option, you are asked for the proxy server information and port used. Click **Next** once you have configured the correct settings for your environment.

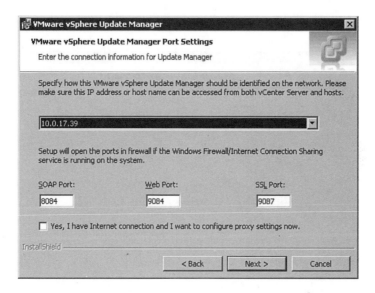

Figure 7.16 Specify ports.

9. By default, the Update Manager services and patch location run off the system drive. I recommend that you change the downloading location to a separate drive and location due to the space it will consume based on update selections (see Figure 7.17). Once configured click **Next**.

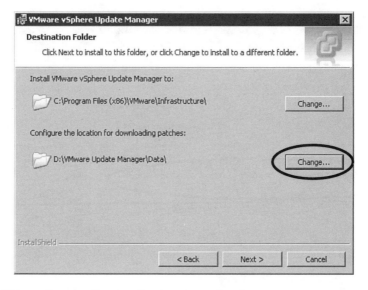

Figure 7.17 Change the repository location to a separate volume.

10. Click **Finish** to complete the installation (see Figure 7.18).

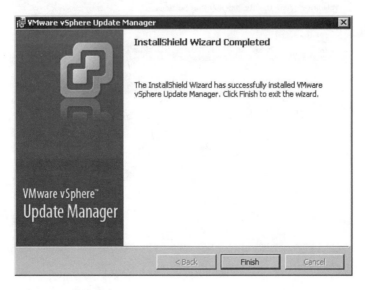

Figure 7.18 Finalize the installation.

At this point, your VMware Update Server is installed, but to administer it, you need to install and enable the plug-in. You can access the executable by launching your virtual infrastructure client and downloading the installer (see Figure 7.19).

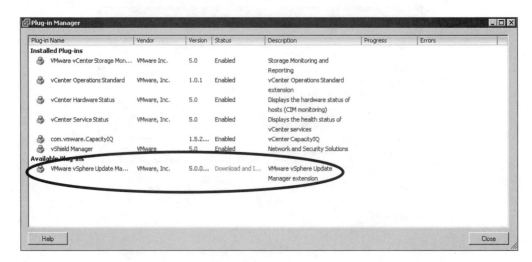

Figure 7.19 You need to install the plug-in.

To install the plug-in, simply download it to the desktop where you are running the virtual infrastructure client and follow these steps:

1. Select the language and click **OK** and **Next**.

2. On the welcome screen, click **Next**.

3. Accept the terms in the license agreement and click **Next**.

4. Click **Install**.

5. Click **Finish**.

When the plug-in is installed, you can go back to the plug-in manager and enable VMware vSphere Update Manager. After it is installed and enabled, a new icon appears under Home for Update Manager, as shown in Figure 7.20.

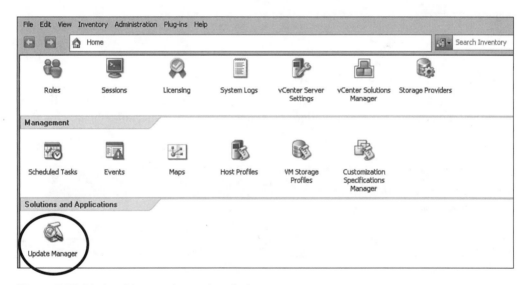

Figure 7.20 Update Manager is now installed.

You also see an additional tab called Update Manager when viewing Hosts and Clusters in the management console (see Figure 7.21).

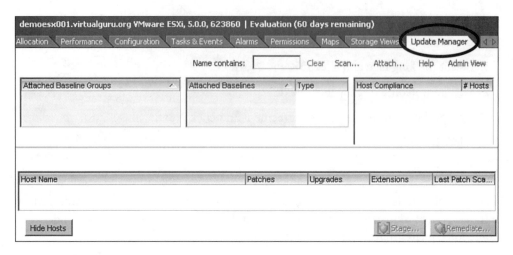

Figure 7.21 Update Manager can be accessed from the Update Manager tab.

Configuring Update Manager

You must configure several things before you can effectively use Update Manager. If you click the Update Manager icon in Home, you are taken to the management pane shown in Figure 7.22.

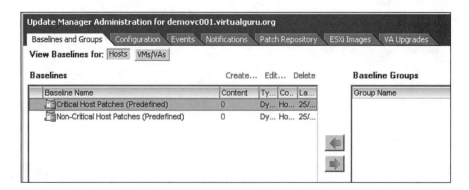

Figure 7.22 Update Manager's management pane.

Select the Configuration tab and ensure you have the configuration set up properly before you start to apply patches in the environment. The first setting is Network Connectivity. This tab provides the communication ports to and from the update management service.

When Update Manager and vCenter are installed in the same location, all incoming connections to Update Manager are connected through a reverse proxy on vCenter. ESXi hosts connect to port 80, and vCenter Server forwards the requests to the Update Manager's web server on port 9084 for host patch downloads. vCenter Server connects to Update Manager on port 8084 because they are on the same machine.

When Update Manager runs on a dedicated server, Update Manager runs the reverse proxy and listens for connections on port 80 and 443. ESXi connects to the dedicated Update Manager on port 80, and the reverse proxy forwards requests to the web server to 9084. vCenter Server connects to Update Manager through port 443, and the reverse proxy forwards requests to port 8084. If you are running firewalls in between, make sure that you have opened the correct ports, as shown in Figure 7.23.

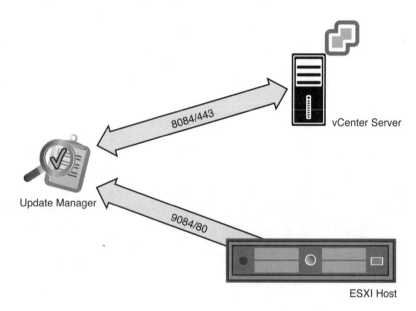

Figure 7.23 Required firewall ports.

You can adjust these ports from the defaults under Network Connectivity settings on the Configuration tab, as shown in Figure 7.24.

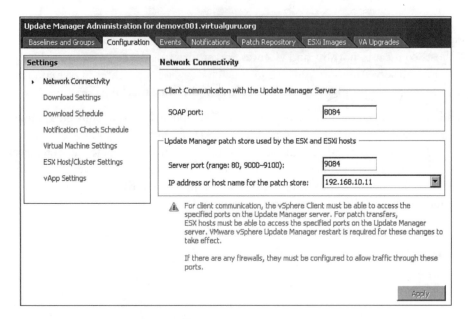

Figure 7.24 Update Manager's Network Connectivity settings.

You can add additional download locations beyond the default provided by VMware on installation. You can also specify a centrally located repository if you have a standardized location for all downloads. If you are running a large VMware environment, you may have multiple vCenter Servers and sufficient scale to warrant a dedicated Update Manager Server and separate database server. Building a centralized environment allows you to maintain consistency and manage multiple vSphere environments from a single Update Manager service. If you are using a web proxy for connection to the Internet, this can be specified here, as shown in Figure 7.25.

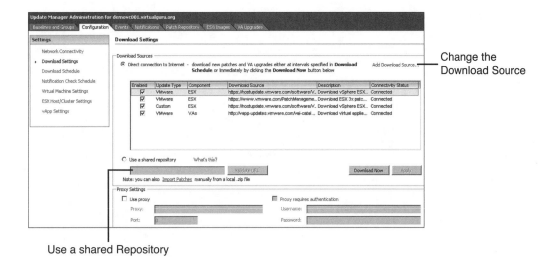

Change the
Download Source

Use a shared Repository

Figure 7.25 Download Settings.

It is possible to change the schedule to have the downloads occur at certain times and on certain days. In a large organization, it is likely that a maintenance window already exists, so it is simply matter of aligning the existing schedule in Update Manager. Simply select the download schedule and click the **Edit Download Schedule** link. You can adjust the time frame from Once, Hourly, Daily, Weekly, or Monthly and have it run a certain number of times during that interval, as shown in Figure 7.26. For example, you could configure it to run twice monthly.

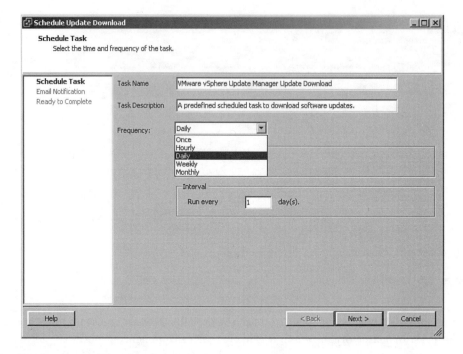

Figure 7.26 You can adjust the schedule.

After configuring the schedule, you can specify e-mail addresses for notification of downloads. Multiple e-mails can be specified by separating them with a semicolon. For example,

> compliance_group@virtualguru.org; security_team@virtualguru.org

The e-mail notifications are dependent on SMTP settings being configured on the vCenter Server. You can find these settings under Home, Administrator, vCenter Server Settings under the Mail configuration (see Figure 7.27).

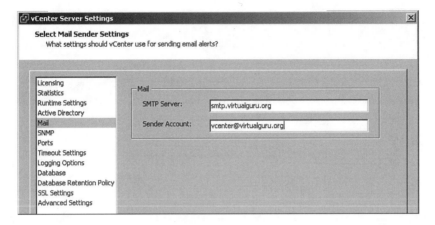

Figure 7.27 SMTP Server for notification.

Under Virtual Machine Settings, you have the option of using a snapshot to set a recovery point in the event that the updates you apply cause problems. It is highly recommended that you do this to ensure you can recover from a patch that causes more harm than good. You can also control when the snapshot is deleted by configuring the hours before the snapshot is deleted, as shown in Figure 7.28. You simply enable the Take a Snapshot option. You should also adjust the Keep For setting to ensure the snapshot is removed. The default is to keep the snapshot indefinitely, which can consume a lot of additional storage space. When OS patches were included, this feature was quite handy. Now that you can upgrade only the hardware and tools, it can still be important but is not quite as critical.

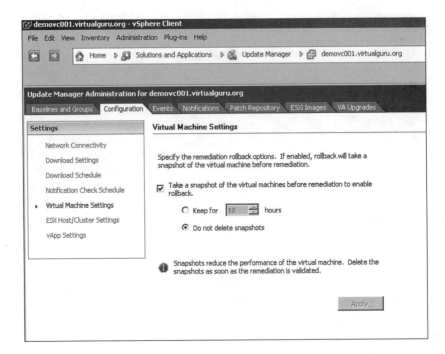

Figure 7.28 Enable snapshots and adjust the retention setting.

To apply host-level patches, the ESXi host must go into maintenance mode. Update Manager provides a finite level of control over what happens when a host goes into maintenance mode. This control can be configured at the host or cluster level. If you are using Auto Deploy, you can also control whether these settings get applied to autodeployed ESXi hosts.

The Host Settings allow you to set what happens to the power state of the VMs; the options are unchanged, power-off, or suspend the VMs. You can also configure how often Update Manager attempts to move the ESXi host into maintenance mode. One handy setting is to temporarily disable any removable media devices that might prevent virtual machine VMotions and prevent the host from going into maintenance mode.

The configurations of specific settings are influenced by your current patch management operational procedures. For example, if you tend to apply patches during the day but delay any reboots till after hours, you might not want to affect the power state of the VMs. If you have prearranged outage windows for patching activities, you may want to ensure everything is completed within the window, so powering off the VMs may be important. You can adjust these settings under the Configuration and Host/Cluster Settings, as shown in Figure 7.29.

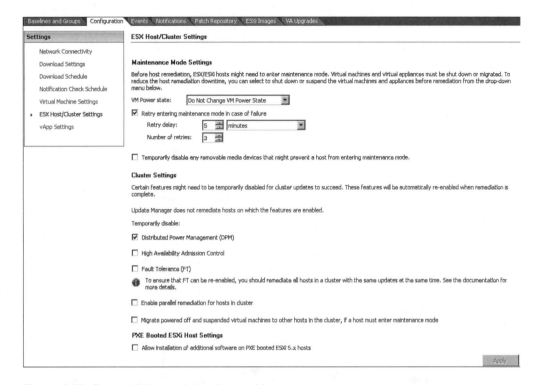

Figure 7.29 Control VM state during the patching process.

At the cluster level, you can disable certain features that may interfere with a clean reboot of the host or virtual machines. You can temporarily disable high availability (HA), Fault Tolerance (FT), and Distributed Power Management (DPM), for example. HA enables cluster heartbeats between hosts or VMs that monitor availability and, in the invent a host or VM fails, allows the VMs to be restarted elsewhere. FT is the application of the vLockStep technology that allows a virtual machine to be completely mirrored to a second virtual machine. In the event the primary fails, the secondary simply takes over without a restart being necessary. DPM allows you to power off underutilized hosts after the VMs have been migrated off (through VMotion) to turn off unused resources in your virtual infrastructure, as shown in Figure 7.30. You can also force VMotions from hosts going into maintenance mode and allow more than one host to be patched at the same time by enabling parallel remediation for hosts in a cluster (the default is to handle updates sequentially).

Cluster Settings

Certain features might need to be temporarily disabled for cluster updates to succeed. These features will be automatically re-enabled when remediation is complete.

Update Manager does not remediate hosts on which the features are enabled.

Temporarily disable:

☑ Distributed Power Management (DPM)

☐ High Availability Admission Control

☐ Fault Tolerance (FT)

ⓘ To ensure that FT can be re-enabled, you should remediate all hosts in a cluster with the same updates at the same time. See the documentation for more details.

☐ Enable parallel remediation for hosts in cluster

☐ Migrate powered off and suspended virtual machines to other hosts in the cluster, if a host must enter maintenance mode

Figure 7.30 Adjust DPM.

The vApp Settings control how Update Manager reboots vApps. A vApp is a logical container that incorporates a number of virtual machines that together create a multitiered application. By incorporating them in a vApp, you can predetermine the start order of the VMs, for example. If you want the vApp boot order to be respected by Update Manager, you need to select **Enable Smart Reboot After Remediation**, as shown in Figure 7.31.

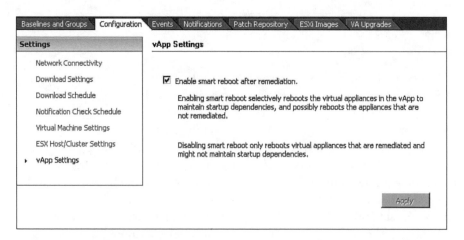

| Baselines and Groups | Configuration | Events | Notifications | Patch Repository | ESXi Images | VA Upgrades |

Settings

Network Connectivity
Download Settings
Download Schedule
Notification Check Schedule
Virtual Machine Settings
ESX Host/Cluster Settings
▸ vApp Settings

vApp Settings

☑ Enable smart reboot after remediation.

Enabling smart reboot selectively reboots the virtual appliances in the vApp to maintain startup dependencies, and possibly reboots the appliances that are not remediated.

Disabling smart reboot only reboots virtual appliances that are remediated and might not maintain startup dependencies.

Apply

Figure 7.31 You can adjust vApp Settings.

When these settings are properly configured, you are ready to configure baselines and test for compliance.

Patching Your Environment

Update Manager downloads available patches to a central location in your environment. It also provides a series of default baselines so that you can check for patch compliance on objects such as the ESXi host. Baselines allow you to bundle patches together for installation. Hosts can be scanned to determine which patches are installed or have yet to be installed. Baselines can be either fixed or dynamic. Use fixed baselines when you want to manually specify patches. Fixed baselines do not change when new patches are downloaded to the repository, unless the administrator adds them to the baseline. Dynamic baselines are created from specific criteria such as text or date range matches. Dynamic baselines are updated if newly downloaded patches match the criteria specified. The default baseline templates can be extended, or new ones can be created, as shown in Figure 7.32.

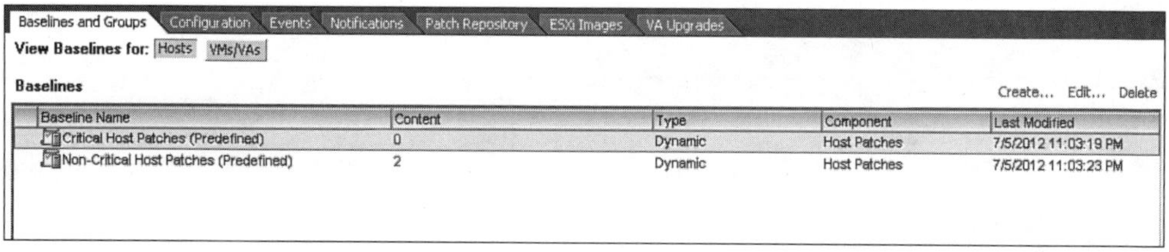

Baseline Name	Content	Type	Component	Last Modified
Critical Host Patches (Predefined)	0	Dynamic	Host Patches	7/5/2012 11:03:19 PM
Non-Critical Host Patches (Predefined)	2	Dynamic	Host Patches	7/5/2012 11:03:23 PM

Figure 7.32 Baselines.

Several defaults are provided for patching hosts, VMs, and virtual appliances. Because you are configuring Update Manager to ensure the tools are up to date, you can either ensure the VMware Tools are part of the default critical or noncritical patch baselines or create a specific baseline that applies exactly what you need. The download to update the VMware Tools is called Updates tools-light. You can edit any of the baselines and select the Additional Patches option. You can specifically add this patch to ensure the upgraded tools are applied in any of the baselines, as shown in Figure 7.33.

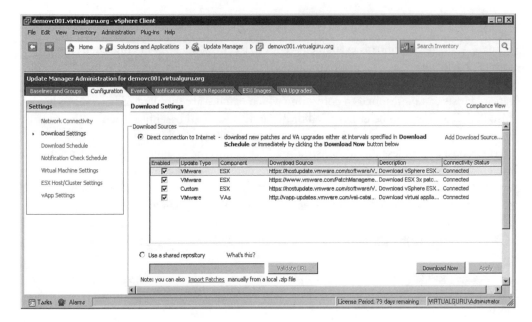

Figure 7.33 Adding patches.

After making sure that the updated tools are part of the baseline, you can attach this baseline to a cluster or individual ESXi host and then scan for compliance. If the objects are noncompliant, you can apply the patches to ensure they meet the baseline. To attach a baseline, simply select the object from Hosts and Clusters, select the **Update Manager** tab, and click the **Attach** link. After you do this, you are asked to select the patch baselines to apply. In this example, we selected an ESXi host and selected the critical and noncritical host patches (see Figure 7.34). We specifically added the VMware Tools to the critical baseline because we want to ensure that we can enable all the VMs for vShield. After you select your baselines, simply click **Attach**.

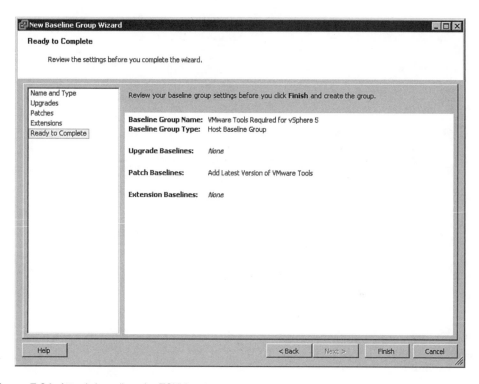

Figure 7.34 Attach baselines to ESXi hosts.

After attaching a baseline to the host, you can scan to determine whether the host is compliant. Clicking the Scan tab kicks off a Scan entity task in the vCenter Server. Assuming that the host is not up to date because it does not have the latest release of the tools, you have an option to remediate—or apply—the patches, as shown in Figure 7.35.

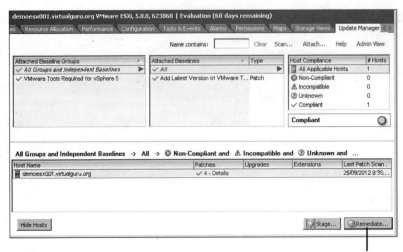

Click the Remediate... button

Figure 7.35 Remediate to apply patches.

You have the option of applying only some of the baseline or patch bundles when you select the Remediate tab (see Figure 7.36).

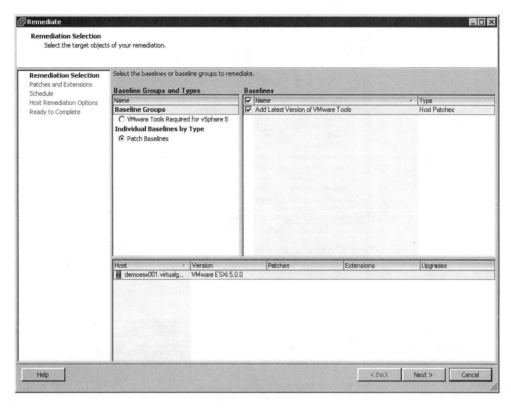

Figure 7.36 You have the option of selectively applying certain baselines.

On the next screen, you can deselect any of the specific patches if you want only some of the patches to be applied in the baseline. By default, all are selected, as shown in Figure 7.37.

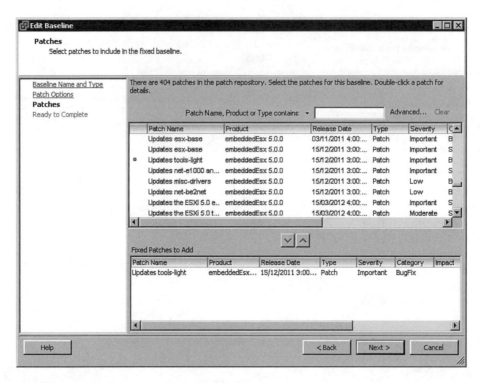

Figure 7.37 You can also selectively apply patches.

On the next screen, you adjust the behavior of some of the advanced cluster and virtual machine features that might prevent an upgrade or reboot from taking place, as shown in Figure 7.38.

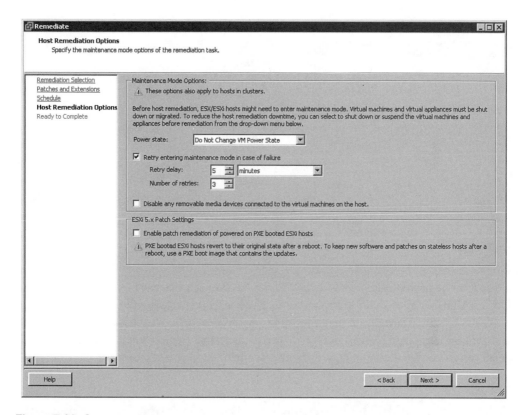

Figure 7.38 Generate reports.

On the next screen, select **Finish** to confirm the changes in the remediation task. The server is put into maintenance mode, the patches are applied, and the host is rebooted if necessary. After the changes are made, you can see that the patches have been applied correctly and the environment is now compliant, as shown in Figure 7.39.

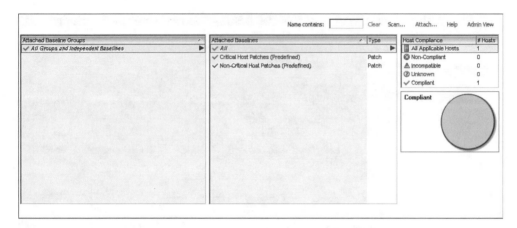

Figure 7.39 The host is now compliant.

To ensure the prerequisites are installed on the ESXi hosts, you use Update Manager. Update Manager allows you to apply the 5.0 Patch 1 to ensure that vShield will function properly. Update Manager ensures that all hosts in the environment have the patch applied and are now compliant. At this point, you are ready to install the vShield Manager. The details on the installation and configuration are included in the next section.

Adding the vShield Manager to the vSphere Environment

All the vShield technologies are controlled through the vShield Manager. It installs as a virtual appliance into your vSphere environment. You should ensure that vShield Manager is installed on a host that will not be managed under vShield. This way, you make sure that any misconfigurations do not lead to a problem accessing the vShield Manager and potentially administrating the environment. In large environments, this host should be a dedicated management cluster. Because this is also recommended for other components such as Auto Deploy, vShield provides one more good reason for a dedicated management cluster. After it is installed, you license it within vCenter and install the necessary plug-ins for vShield. In the case of EndPoint, you also need to prepare the ESXi hosts using the vShield Manager. To deploy vShield Manager, you simply import the Open Virtual Format (OVF) template that creates the virtual appliance in the vSphere environment, as shown in Figure 7.40.

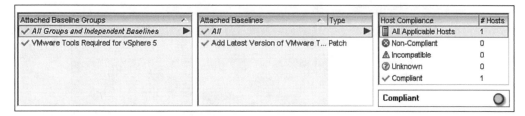

Figure 7.40 Deploy the OVF template.

To deploy the vShield Manager, follow these steps:

1. Open the vSphere Client and browse to Hosts and Clusters.

2. From the File menu, select **Deploy OVF Template**.

3. Select the location of the OVF files and click **Next**.

4. After the Deploy Wizard validates the OVF files, click **Next**.

5. Accept the end-user license agreement and click **Next**.

6. Provide a name for the virtual appliance, that is, vShield Manager, and select an Inventory location. Then click **Next**.

7. To ensure good performance, make sure the disk format is Thick Provisioned Eager Zeroed and click **Next.** A Thick Provisioned Eager Zeroed disk is different from a Thick Provisioned disk, in which all the blocks are allocated when it is provisioned, or Thin, in which they are not. A Thick Provisioned Eager Zeroed disk goes a step further and fully allocates the space on the array by zeroing or writing zeros to the unused space. A Thick Provisioned disk does this post deployment, requiring a short pause as the data expands to the reserved blocks. What this translates to is slightly better performance for Thick Provisioned Eager Zeroed versus Thick or Thin.

8. Make sure **Power On After Deployment** is selected and click **Finish**.

9. **After vShield boots,** log in as the Admin account.

10. Go to enable mode by typing **enable** and launch Setup by typing **setup**, as shown in Figure 7.41.

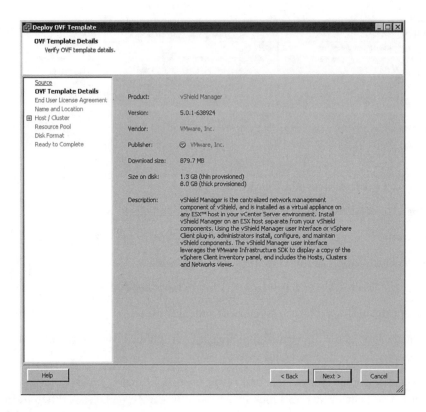

Figure 7.41 Type enable and then setup.

The appliance is set to use 3 GB of RAM. If you are running in a small environment (25 or fewer VMs), you can reduce the memory allocation to 1 or 2 GBs of memory. After the virtual appliance boots, you need to login and then start the Configuration Wizard by typing "enable" and then "setup" to configure the network, subnet mask, and default gateway, as shown in Figure 7.41. It also allows you to configure name resolution by configuring the DNS Servers and domain search list as shown in Figure 7.42. After applying your configuration, simply save the settings. You can also allow DHCP to supply the majority of these values and configure everything from the Configure tab of the VMware vShield Manager.

Figure 7.42 Configure vShield Manager network settings.

At this point, you need to log in to the vShield Manager (see Figure 7.43) and configure it to talk to the vCenter Server. To do this, simply open a web browser and type the IP address of the vShield Manager—in our example it is, **http:192.168.9.220**.

Figure 7.43 Log in to vShield Manager.

The default login for the vShield Manager is userid Admin and the password is default. On the Configuration tab, you need to configure a few things to ensure everything is working properly.

Under vCenter Server Information, provide the connection information required for your vCenter Server and make sure to assign the vShield Enterprise Administrator to the role of the user. Supply the information and click **Save**, as shown in Figure 7.44.

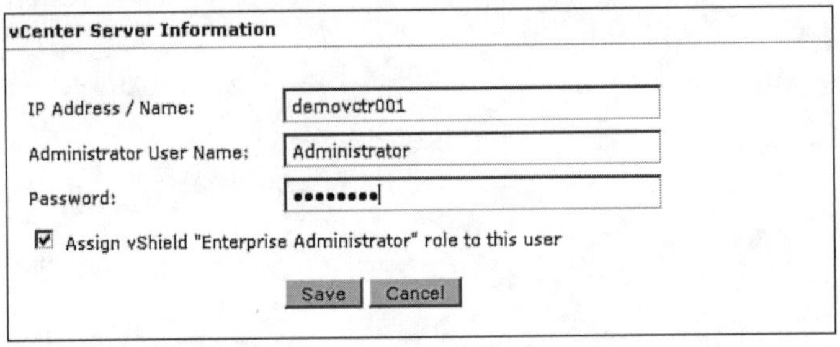

vCenter Server Information

IP Address / Name: demovctr001

Administrator User Name: Administrator

Password: ••••••••

☑ Assign vShield "Enterprise Administrator" role to this user

Save   Cancel

Figure 7.44 Specify vCenter Server Information.

If you are using self-signed certificates for your vCenter environment, you are prompted to accept the vCenter Server's certificate as the vShield Manager attempts to connect to the vCenter Server. To ensure the connection can be established, click **OK** when prompted to trust the host.

When you first install the vShield Manager, the plug-ins are not registered with vCenter Server. To register them, click the **Register** button (see Figure 7.45) under the vSphere Plug-in section on the Configuration tab.

vSphere Plug-in

This vShield Manager is currently not registered as an extension to vSphere server

For NAT environments, you may need to modify the plug-in script download location. By default, the vShield Manager address will be used as "192.169.9.220:443".   Modify Location

Register

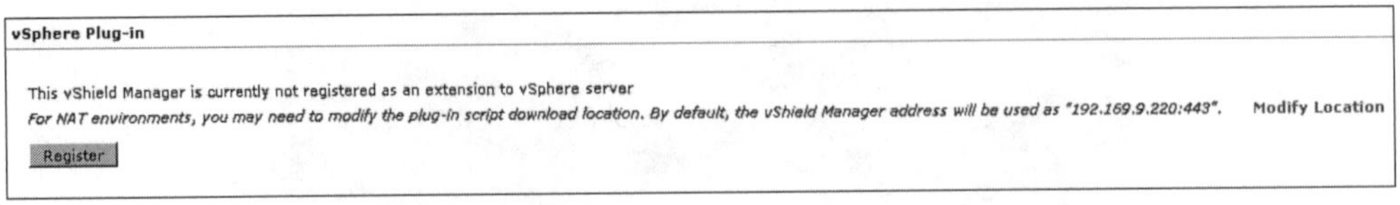

Figure 7.45 Register the vShield plug-in.

If you did not supply the DNS Server information under the console configuration, you can do it under the DNS Servers section on the Configuration tab. Make sure that the time and date are set correctly under Configuration and then click the **Date/Time** link. There are a number of other tabs under Configuration where you can update the appliance, add additional users, check System Events, and also review the logs of the various enabled vShield modules. At this point, however, you should ensure that you have applied for a license to vShield EndPoint so that vShield Manager can be used to prepare the ESXi hosts.

Licensing can be managed from the vCenter and can be found under Home, Administrations, and then Licensing. The licenses are imported into vCenter Server and then applied to the vShield EndPoint. To configure vShield licenses, click the **Manage License Link** under Licensing on the Management tab.

Enter your vShield EndPoint licenses and a description (see Figure 7.46); then click **Next**.

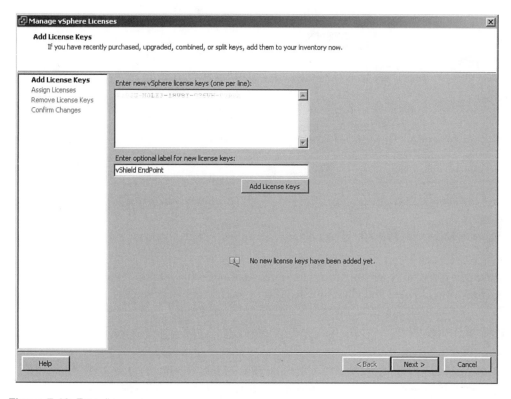

Figure 7.46 Enter licenses.

Under Assign Licenses, click the **Solutions** tab, select **vShield-EndPoint** from the asset pane, and select the license to apply to the EndPoint asset. Finally, click **Next**, as indicated in Figure 7.47.

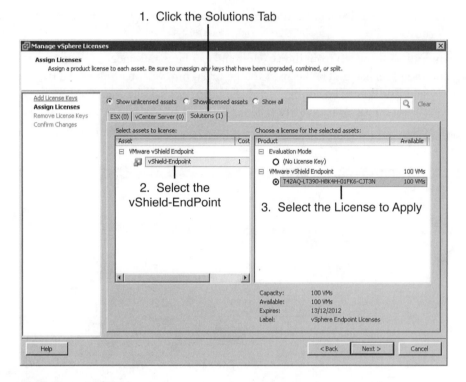

Figure 7.47 License vShield.

On the next screen, you can remove any licenses if necessary. If not, click **Next** and then confirm your changes and click **Finish**. At this point, you have vShield installed, but you have not prepared the ESXi hosts. To do this, you need to ensure the vShield Manager plug-in is enabled in your vSphere client so that the vShield tab appears in your vCenter console.

After enabling the plug-in, you should see a vShield tab when you select an ESXi host from the Hosts and Clusters view in your vSphere client. Simply install the necessary vShield EndPoint component from this tab (see Figure 7.48).

Figure 7.48 Click Install to deploy the vShield EndPoint to an ESXi host.

Adding the vShield Driver to Your VMs

In a VMware View environment, you need to ensure the driver is applied to all the source templates and View Composer Parent images. By doing so, you ensure that the desktops are deployed "vShield ready." Because the driver is not installed by default, you need to go through a manual installation of the VMware Tools and select the vShield driver that was added when the Hosts were patched with the latest VMware Tools (the minimum required is VMware Tools 8.6.0). To install the driver, you need to complete the following steps:

1. Power on the virtual machine.

2. Open the console of the virtual machine.

3. From the menu, select **VM**, **Guest**, **Install/Upgrade VMware Tools**.

4. Change the default from **Automatic Tools Upgrade** to **Interactive Tools Upgrade**.

5. Click **Next** on the welcome screen.

6. Click **Custom** and click **Next**.

7. Expand the VMCI Driver, select **vShield Drivers** for installation, and click **Next**, as shown in Figure 7.49.

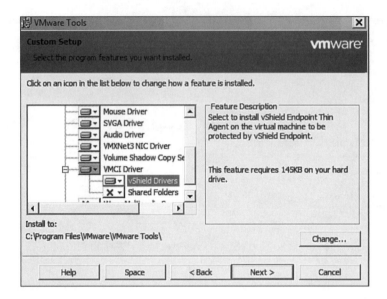

Figure 7.49 Add the vShield driver.

Plugging In Your Third-Party Solution

The third-party support for vShield EndPoint that is shipping to customers is limited to BitDefender and Trend Micro although many more vendors have announced that they will ship products in 2012. We selected Trend Micro to provide an end-to-end example of vShield in operation, but you should do your own evaluation to determine what solution aligns best with your internal security practices. Kapersky and Symantec AV solutions are now compatible with vShield. Ideally, rather than your having to look at separate AV vendors for virtual and physical computers in your environments, all major vendors would include a support option for vShield.

Trend Micro's product is called Deep Security, and as of the time of writing, version 8 was the current product release. Trend Micro's Deep Security product is managed with Deep Security Manager. You can find additional information at http://www.trendmicro.com/cloud-content/us/pdfs/business/datasheets/ds_deep-security.pdf. From this management tool, you can deploy the virtual appliances to integrate with VMware's vShield product.

Because the focus of this chapter is on enabling vShield versus endorsing Trend Micro, refer to the vendor's documents for a complete list of features and capabilities. The Deep Security Architecture consists of Deep Security Agents, which are the agents traditionally deployed to physical desktops and servers. The Deep Security Virtual Appliance is the integration point for vShield and gets installed on each ESXi Server. You also have a Deep Security Relay Server; it can be colocated on the servers running the Deep Security Manager or separate to have a dedicated server or servers downloading updates from Trend Micro's Security Center, which is the company's online service to your distributed Deep Security Agents.

A properly planned environment likely has several relays distributed at primary locations to ensure that a robust distribution model is available to ensure timely updates and good service. A logical diagram of the components is shown in Figure 7.50.

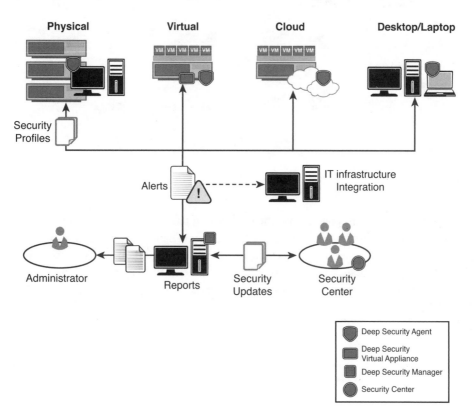

Figure 7.50 Deep Security components.

The Deep Security Manager can be installed on Windows 2003 and Windows 2008 (32-bit and 64-bit) operating systems as well as some versions of Linux but does require a database that can be either SQL or Oracle.

To begin the installation follow the following steps:

1. Launch the installer and click **Next** on the welcome screen.

2. Accept the license agreement and click **Next**.

3. Confirm the Destination directory and click **Next** (see Figure 7.51).

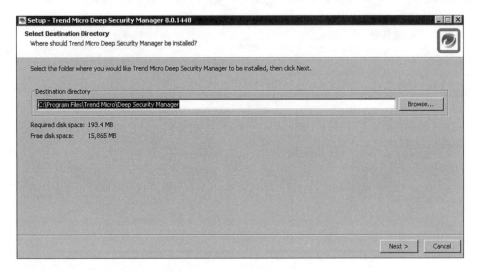

Figure 7.51 Select the Destination directory.

For a smaller installation, you can use the **embedded** database type, which installs a version of SQL Express on the Windows Server, or you can create a database on the existing vCenter SQL instance. For larger installations, you should select a separate Microsoft SQL or Oracle Server. This can be the same SQL Server that is running the VMware database instances. Configure the correct database type and click **Next** (see Figure 7.52).

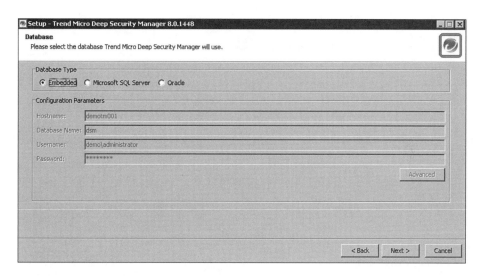

Figure 7.52 Specify a SQL or Oracle Database.

1. The Trend Micro components can all be licensed separately or with one single activation code. If you are evaluating, the product evaluation keys are available on a time-trial basis. Enter your license keys and click **Next** (see Figure 7.53).

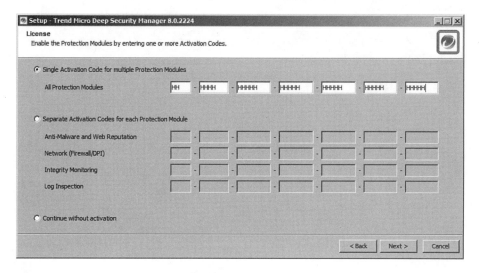

Figure 7.53 Apply the license for Deep Security.

2. Enter the IP address of the host where the Deep Security Manager is installed and click **Next** (see Figure 7.54).

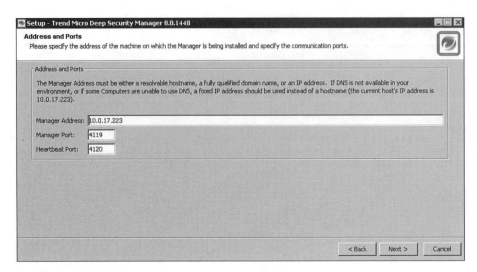

Figure 7.54 Provide IP of the server.

3. The Administrator account for the Deep Security Manager is the MasterAdmin account. Update the password and click **Next** (see Figure 7.55).

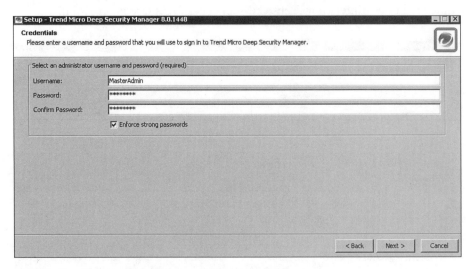

Figure 7.55 Specify a password for the MasterAdmin account.

4. You can manually configure update tasks or have the installer automatically create them. Because updates are critical, I recommend you have the installer create them and manually edit them if you want to adjust them after the fact (see Figure 7.56). Click **Next**.

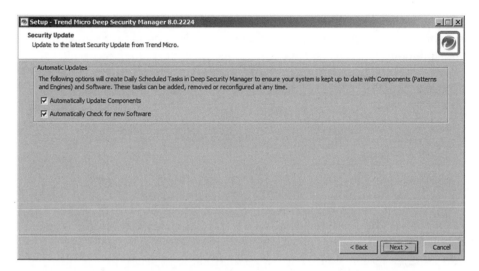

Figure 7.56 You can automatically check for component and software updates.

5. As mentioned, you can and should have dedicated relays for large environments. If this solution is dedicated to the VMware View environment, you can install the Manager and relay on the same server (see Figure 7.57). Click **Next**.

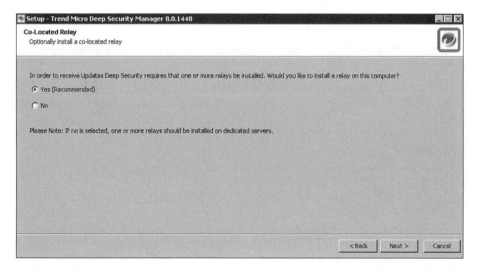

Figure 7.57 Install a relay server.

6. With Trend Micro, you can contribute anonymously to the Trend Micro Security Center (online service). The more customers who contribute, the more proactive

Trend can be in responding to security and malware threats. You also have the option of specifying your industry (see Figure 7.58). Determine whether it is in your organization's best interest to contribute and click **Next** after you decide.

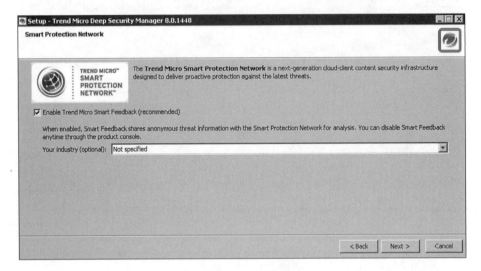

Figure 7.58 Smart feedback allows Trend Micro to pool threat information.

7. On the next screen (see Figure 7.59), click **Finish**.

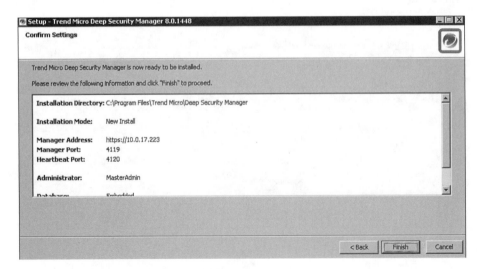

Figure 7.59 Finalize the installation.

8. On the next screen, ensure **Launch the Deep Security Manager Management Console Now** is selected (see Figure 7.60) and click **Finish**.

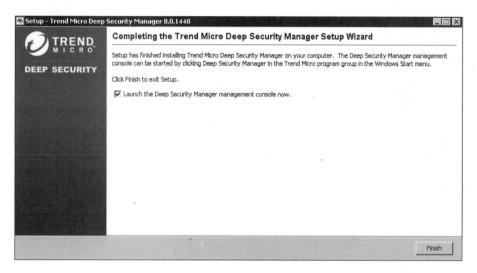

Figure 7.60 Launch the Deep Security Manager Console.

At this point, the Deep Security Manager is installed, but the integration components have not been deployed. The integration components involve deploying the Deep Security virtual appliance on all the ESXi hosts.

Integrating vShield and Trend Micro Deep Security

To integrate vShield and Deep Security, you need to deploy the Deep Security virtual appliance on each ESXi host and enable the VMs for protection. The resource requirements for the Deep Security virtual appliance are as follows:

- Memory: 1 GB

- Disk Space: 20 GB

- vSphere Compatibility: VMware vCenter 5.0 and ESX/ESXi 5.0

To manage the Deep Security environment, you need to log in to the Deep Security Manager. To do this, open a web browser and go to your Deep Security Manager Server on the specified port (see Figure 7.61)—for example, http://10.0.17.223:4119. Log in with the MasterAdmin account using the password you specified during the installation.

Figure 7.61 Log in with the MasterAdmin account.

After you log in from the Dashboard, select the Computers category and then **Add VMware vCenter** (see Figure 7.62). You need to connect the Trend Micro Deep Security Manager to the virtualization environment.

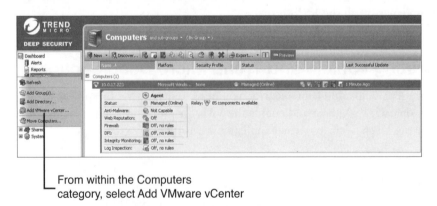

From within the Computers category, select Add VMware vCenter

Figure 7.62 Add the vCenter Server.

Enter your vCenter Server information (see Figure 7.63) and click **Next**.

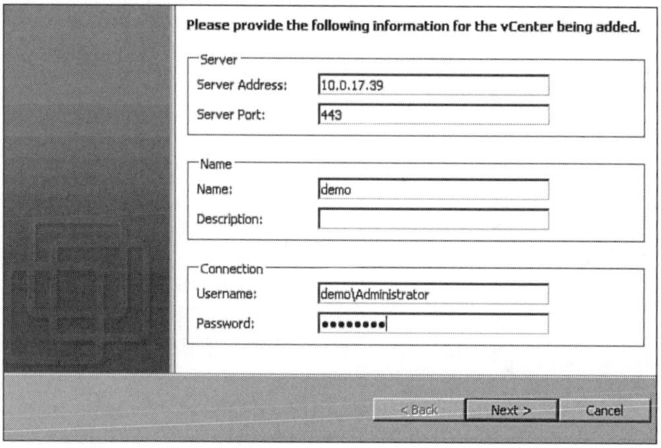

Figure 7.63 Specify vCenter information.

You also need to provide the information for the vShield Manager virtual appliance. Provide the IP or hostname and the admin password (see Figure 7.64) and click **Next**.

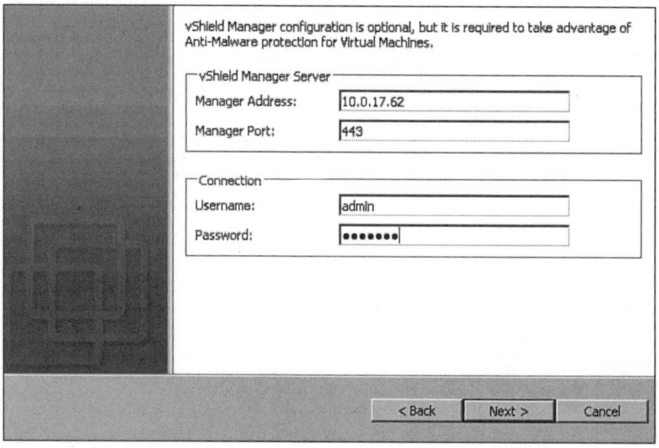

Figure 7.64 Add vShield Manager information.

When the Deep Security Manager is aware of the vCenter Server, you are prompted to accept the certificate from the vShield Manager. Accept the certificate to confirm the connection (see Figure 7.65).

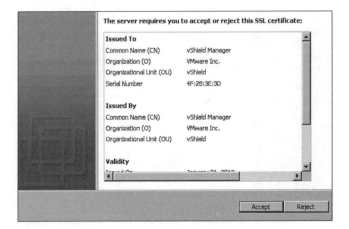

Figure 7.65 Accept the vShield Manager certificate.

When the connection is made, you are asked to confirm the inventory of the vCenter Server to complete the integration of the two components. Click **Finish** (see Figure 7.66).

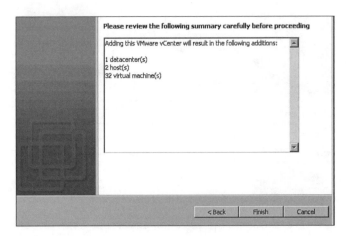

Figure 7.66 Finalize vCenter and vShield Manager configuration.

After integrating the Deep Security Manager and vCenter and vShield Manager, as shown in Figure 7.67, you are prompted to prepare the ESXi hosts with the virtual appliances. Close the Integration Wizard and deploy the Deep Security Virtual Appliances.

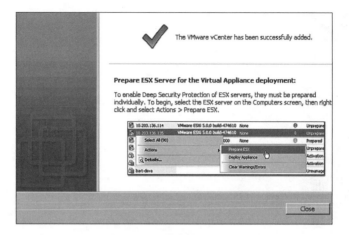

Figure 7.67 Ensure integration of vCenter completes successfully.

When the vCenter connection is made, you are able to browse through to the ESXi hosts under the Computers category in the Deep Security Manager. Select your ESXi host and select **Actions** and **Prepare ESX** (see Figure 7.68).

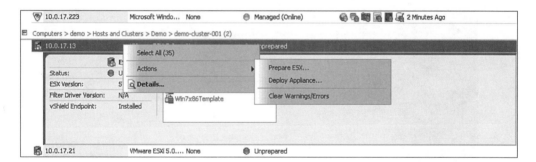

Figure 7.68 Prepare ESX hosts.

The prepare ESX action loads the filter driver onto the ESXi host. The filter driver is provided by Trend Micro, but it is not imported to the Deep Security Manager by default. Because Deep Security Manager recognizes that the filter driver is not installed, it prompts for the location of the filter driver. Select the location of the filter driver (see Figure 7.69) and click **Next**.

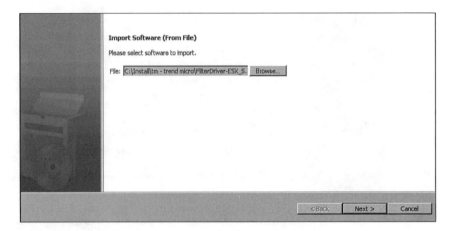

Figure 7.69 Specify the location of the filter driver.

The Import Wizard asks you to confirm the properties of the Filter driver for the ESXi host to finish importing the file. Ensure that the filter driver is the one you specified (see Figure 7.70) and click **Finish**.

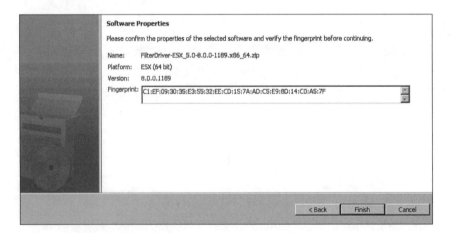

Figure 7.70 Confirm the filter properties.

After the filter driver is imported, the wizard continues the process of preparing the ESXi Server to install the Trend Micro virtual appliance. The Filter driver is installed on the ESXi Server as part of this process. Click **Next** to continue (see Figure 7.71).

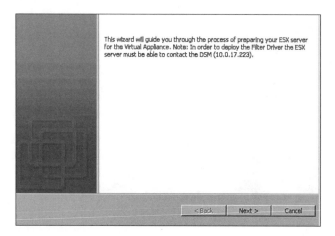

Figure 7.71 Proceed to the filter installation.

To install the filter, the ESXi host needs to enter maintenance mode and requires a reboot. You are prompted to do this automatically through the wizard or manually and then run the wizard. Click **Finish** to have the tool complete the steps or **No** to manually put the ESXi Server in maintenance mode yourself (see Figure 7.72).

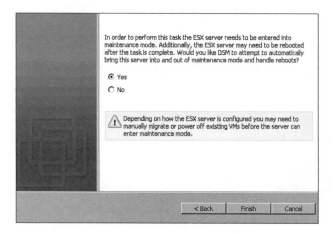

Figure 7.72 Finish the installation.

When the installation of the filter driver completes successfully, you are ready to deploy the Deep Security Virtual Appliance. Click **Next** to continue with the deployment (see Figure 7.73).

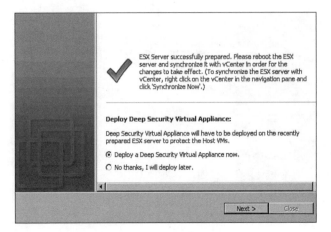

Figure 7.73 Deploy the Deep Security Virtual Appliance.

As with the filter driver, the Deep Security Virtual Appliance is not imported by default. The wizard prompts for the location of the virtual appliance source files. Trend Micro provides these files, so simply point the wizard to the location where you downloaded the files (see Figure 7.74) and click **Next**.

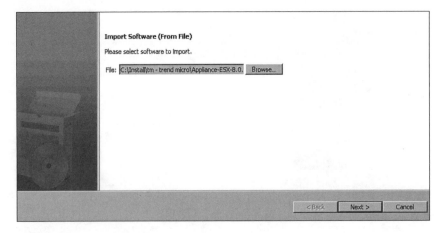

Figure 7.74 Select the appliance.

The Import Wizard prompts you to confirm the virtualization appliance files are the correct source (see Figure 7.75). Then click **Finish**.

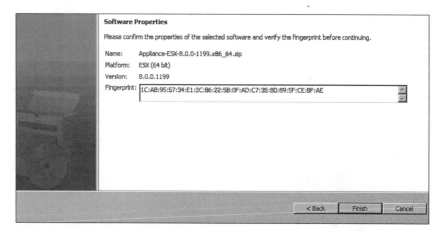

Figure 7.75 Confirm the information for the virtual appliance.

The wizard continues with the deployment of the Deep Security Virtual Appliance. To confirm deployment, click **Next** (see Figure 7.76).

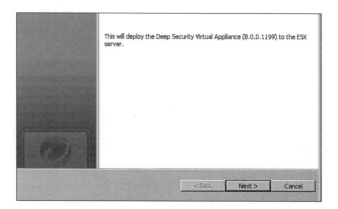

Figure 7.76 Deploy the Deep Security Virtual Appliance.

Provide a name for the virtual appliance, location, folder within vCenter, and the network that the appliance should attach to (see Figure 7.77). Keep in mind that you have to deploy one virtual appliance per ESXi host and that they are dedicated to the host, so local storage (if available) is ideal. You also need to keep in mind that there is no FT or HA possible in this configuration, so you should ensure the Trend Micro Database is backed up properly. It is also a good idea to have a second copy of the Deep Security Manager VM as a cold standby in the event you lose the primary. You should also logically associate the name of this virtual appliance with the ESXi host; these settings apply to vCenter. The next screen allows you to set the hostname and IP of the virtual appliance.

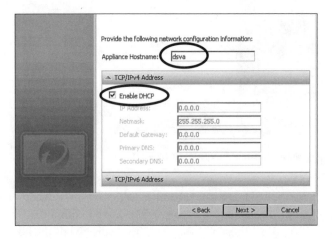

Please provide the following information about the Virtual Appliance being deployed.

Appliance Name: dsva001
Datastore: local01:dmoesx-03
Folder: Demo
Management Network: VM - Development

< Back   Next >   Cancel

Figure 7.77 Configure the appliance properties.

Provide the hostname for the appliance, deselect Enabled DHCP, and enter a static IP, as shown in Figure 7.78. If you are currently running IPv6, you can also enable it and provide the appropriate IP information. After completing the settings for the appliance, click **Next**.

Provide the following network configuration information:

Appliance Hostname: dsva

▲ TCP/IPv4 Address

☑ Enable DHCP
IP Address: 0.0.0.0
Netmask: 255.255.255.0
Default Gateway: 0.0.0.0
Primary DNS: 0.0.0.0
Secondary DNS: 0.0.0.0

▼ TCP/IPv6 Address

< Back   Next >   Cancel

Figure 7.78 Configure the IP of the appliance.

You have the option of thin provisioning the virtual appliance, but for performance, you should select **Thick Provisioned Format** and click **Finish** (see Figure 7.79). The appliance requires 20 GB of space.

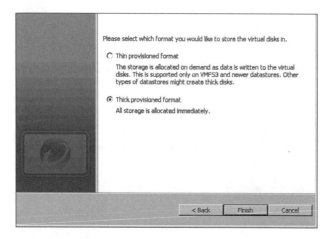

Figure 7.79 The Thick Provisioned Format setting is recommend for performance.

You are prompted to accept the certificate from the vCenter Servers (see Figure 7.80). Accept it, and then the deployment of the virtual appliance begins.

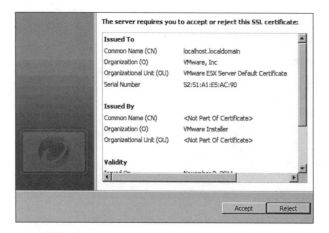

Figure 7.80 Confirm vCenter certificate information.

After the virtual appliance is deployed, you are prompted to activate it (see Figure 7.81). When the activation is applied to the virtual appliance, it is ready to begin monitoring VMs.

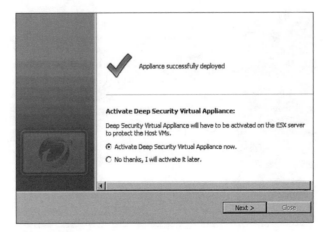

Figure 7.81 Activate the Deep Security Virtual Appliance.

Click **Next** to begin the activation process (see Figure 7.82).

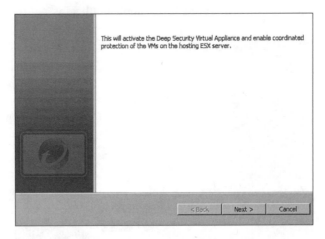

Figure 7.82 Confirm the activation.

The Deep Security Virtual Appliance is selected by default; it is the security profile that you should use (see Figure 7.83). Click **Next** to continue the process.

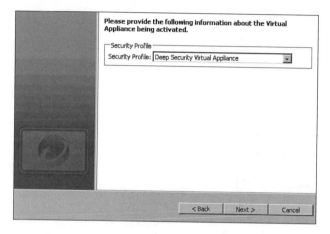

Figure 7.83 Ensure you are activating the Deep Security Virtual Appliance.

You have the option of enabling virtual machine protection at this point or later (see Figure 7.84). Click **Finish**.

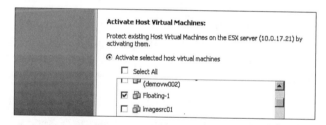

Figure 7.84 Enable VM now or from the console.

The integration of vShield and Trend Micro's Deep Security support is not complete. Click **Close** (see Figure 7.85).

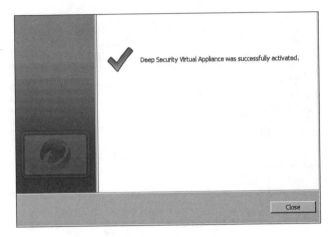

Figure 7.85 Confirm the activation was successful.

If you enabled the virtual machines as part of the wizard process, you have completed the steps required to turn on settings for this particular ESXi host. You must complete the configuration for each ESXi host that is part of your VMware View environment.

If you did not enable the VMs as part of the installation, you can manually enable them by browsing within the Deep Security Manager Console from Computers, vCenter Server virtual machines to the VM in question. From the Actions pane, just select the **Activate** option, as shown in Figure 7.86.

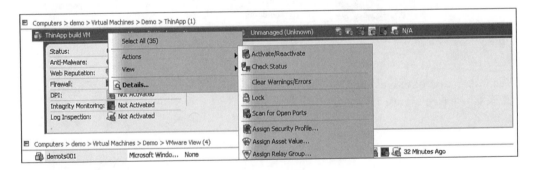

Figure 7.86 Activate a VM.

If you look at your ESXi host, you can see the private switch and Trend Micro port group (vmservice-trend-pg) enabled by the filter communicating with the vShield port group (vmservice-vshield-pg), as shown in Figure 7.87.

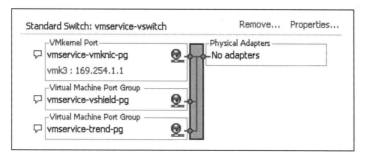

Figure 7.87 Private switch and required port groups.

Summary

This chapter looked at how to maintain software and patch consistency across a View environment through Update Manager. This allows you to bring the environment up to ESXi 5.0 Patch 1.0 to add the additional drivers required to support vShield EndPoint. vShield EndPoint integrated with third-party support allows you to eliminate the performance overhead that comes with deploying antivirus agents to virtual machines. This allows higher consolidation ratios, lowering the overall costs of View desktops. It also improves the operational management of scanning and patching virtual machines in a VMware environment. By integrating an antivirus scanning and patching technology, you improve security and reduce the likelihood of attacks in a View desktop environment. By running these tools, you can ensure you conform to audit and compliance requirements and can provide logs to demonstrate this conformance.

Now that you have properly secured the environment, you are ready to look at ensuring the user is provided a rich desktop experience. In Chapter 8, you see how to quantify this in a way that allows you to make adjustments to measure performance improvements.

Chapter 8

A Rich End-User Experience

To deliver a successful VMware View environment, you must have a strong focus on the end-user experience. Although a virtual desktop environment is largely a datacenter-delivered service, you must be very conscious of how this service is consumed by the end user. The reason that this issue is so crucial is that you are making a change to something that most users consider a personal device: their desktop. Is it a big change? A View desktop presents itself as a physical desktop, so it should be more of a form factor change from physical to virtual versus an end-user change. To carry out this change successfully, you need to understand how the desktop performs from the users' perspective in addition to an IT or infrastructure perspective. If you have implemented changes similar to virtual desktop technology such as Server-Based Computing (Citrix or Terminal services) technologies, you will understand the risks of not getting the experience piece right. As with any new technology, there are some general issues that you can avoid if you investigate them properly upfront. These intangible issues have less to do with technology and more to do with the users' perception of change. They are

- When a change is made to end users' desktops, users blame any and all problems with performance on the virtual desktop platform.

- As the instrument of change, you are likely guilty until you can prove that the issue is unrelated to the desktop.

- When you make the change, any prior issues in the physical desktop environment quickly become your problem even if they have existed for some period of time.

- Due to the highly variable and intermittent nature of issues in a virtual desktop environment, it is important to look at end-user experience up front and to have a set of tools to measure these issues on an ongoing basis. We discuss ongoing monitoring in Chapter 12, "Performance and Monitoring." In this chapter, we look at how to quantify the end-user experience.

How Do You Deliver a Rich End-User Experience?

Today information is delivered in a variety of ways, including audio, video, and rich text and graphics. Rich video and graphical experiences have become the norm for users' viewing, understanding, and developing data. For your VMware View environment to be successful, you must appreciate and deliver a desktop that provides a rich end-user experience.

To provide this experience, you must first understand it. When you understand it, you can determine how it should be optimized to deliver good performance. The primary method for delivering visual information in a VMware View environment is PC over IP (PCoIP), so we spend much of the focus in this chapter addressing how it has been enhanced in VMware View 5 and what you can do to ensure it performs well under a variety of different scenarios. Display, however is not the only aspect of providing a rich end-user experience. It can also entail bidirectional audio communication such as VoIP and ensuring that general performance and functionality are all available within the virtual desktop.

What is new in VMware View 5.1 is many additional methods to control the PCoIP protocol and the bandwidth it uses. You are able to more finely tune the PCoIP protocol to ensure a great user experience under a wider range of environmental conditions. Throttling PCoIP is not a new capability, but the settings are more visible and more granular than any other release prior to View 5.1. To tune your environment you need a controlled environment where you can adjust settings, simulate poor network conditions, and ensure the changes you are making are properly set. This goes for any tuning you are going to do of the VMware View environment.

To provide enhanced graphics, VMware View takes advantage of vSphere 5's support for non-hardware-accelerated 3D graphics. Support is provided for DirectX9 and OpenGl 2.1. This feature in ESXi enables View to run applications requiring OpenGL or DirectX without a video offload card or physical graphical processing unit (GPU).

In addition to software options, you have hardware options for improving the rendering and performance of PCoIP. Teradici released a set of adapter cards that can be installed in a vSphere ESXi host; these cards allow you to offload the PCoIP image encoding tasks, reducing the load on the servers CPUs.

The Teradici APEX 2800 Server Offload Card allows you to ensure a greater consistency in graphics performance of your View desktop. The card dynamically offloads the most active 64 View desktop displays. In so doing, it enables an even greater consolidation ratio. The card ships as a PCI Express card that is inserted into the ESXi Server. After it is physically installed, you install the drivers on the ESXi host and then enable the hardware acceleration in VMware View Administrator. You enable the hardware acceleration under the VMware View Administrator's Policies and Global Policies by selecting **Edit**. Ensure that the **PCoIP Hardware Acceleration** is set to **Allow** (the default), as shown in Figure 8.1. The final step is to install the drivers for the Teradici APEX 2800 card within the View desktops. You can find additional details on Teradici's website at http://www. teradici.com/pcoip/pcoip-products/teradici-apex-2800.php. The cards are fully supported on ESXi 4.1 or greater and VMware View 4.6 or later.

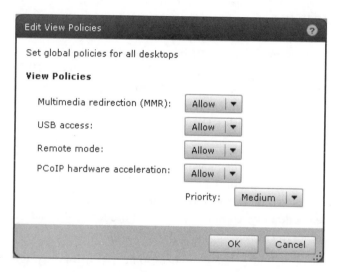

Figure 8.1 Check PCoIP hardware acceleration.

To improve the end-user experience, View 5 provides continuity services. If the user is suddenly disconnected from the session, the PCoIP protocol tries for up to 30 seconds to reconnect or restore the connection without having the user relaunch the connection.

Your desktops and settings should be tuned to deal with the conditions you are going to see in your production environment before the final production version is delivered. We run through a few ways you can do that in this chapter. The goal is to build a contained environment in which you can inject latency and packet-loss, for example, to change settings and quantify the benefit before you put the virtual desktop in front of users. A number of tools are readily available to do this, in addition to the ones mentioned here, such as Lakeside Software SysTrack VMP and LiquidWare Labs Stratusphere. In a large-scale environment, using third-party tools designed for this purpose is recommended, but because each environment has its own approach, we wanted to combine some freely available tools to create a test environment.

This approach allows you to test and verify any number of settings from audio and video to graphics and multimedia performance. It also ensures that the results are reproducible in a way that is much more difficult when you are dealing with a live environment.

Enhancements in PCoIP

In the initial release of the View Virtual Desktop Manager (VDM), the display protocol options were limited to Microsoft's Remote Desktop Protocol (RDP) and HP's Remote Graphics Software (RGS). Because both were developed by the original equipment manufacturer (OEM), VMware decided to develop a third option designed to deliver a graphic rich desktop experience over a TCP network. The leader at the time in digital television graphics chips was Teradici. VMware signed an agreement to develop the physical graphic card technology as a software solution, and the PCoIP protocol was born. Unlike other remote graphics protocols, PCoIP transfers pixels versus caching bitmaps. This makes it more similar to high-definition TV (HDTV) technologies than to its predecessors, Citrix's ICA or Microsoft's RDP.

When you look at the quality of graphics in a display and speed of rendering the display, you are essentially compressing the image and then restoring it to the display. Although lossless compression is superior for many kinds of images, it is only critical in certain situations. For example, you would not want to use lossy compression for an X-ray program for radiology; because the details are critical, you would use lossless. Basically, lossless image compression means all the data from the original file is preserved.

Lossy compression, on the other hand, removes some data from the original file and saves the image with a reduced file size. To provide a high-quality screen, PCoIP monitors the type of data, such as text or image, and applies the correct compression algorithm. For example, you would not want to apply a lossy compression algorithm to text because you may deliver blurred or unfocused text to the screen.

The lossless compression has been significantly improved in the PCoIP protocol in View 5. This improved algorithm can deliver a 75% reduction in bandwidth requirements from prior releases, as shown in Figure 8.2. You can also more fully control the build to lossless algorithm to deliver a good user experience even when less bandwidth is available.

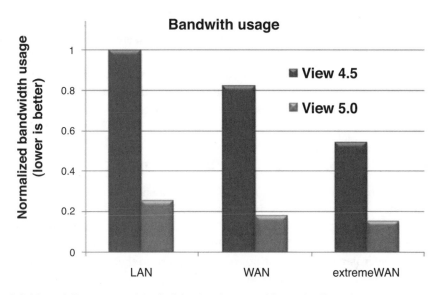

Figure 8.2 Your ability to control the build to lossless provides a significant improvement over prior versions of View.

In addition to compressing pixels, PCoIP uses spacial filtering to ensure only the portions of the screen that change are sent rather than the entire screen. These portions are sent in 8 × 8 pixel blocks. In addition, PCoIP caches image blocks on the client device and uses temporal analysis to reuse this cached data to avoid resending the same information. For example, imagine a user is paging forward and backward through a PDF file within a VMware View session. Much of the screen refresh information could be more efficiently reused from cache rather than reset across the network. The inclusion of the client-side cache saves bandwidth over previous versions of View and the PCoIP protocol.

VMware View provides a series of image quality controls that allow you to adjust the clarity of the image to trade off between less bandwidth and rendering of the screen. These controls impact the lossless nature of PCoIP. Recall that lossless builds a screen by sending all the data so that there is no loss of image pixels, translating to higher quality. If you are deploying VMware View at a hospital, for example, this quality can be critical if the data involves medical images that are being used by doctors to form a prognosis.

If the user is using general office and business applications, this build to lossless is often overkill. The capability to tune lossless behavior is provided in VMware View 5. The options are whether to build to lossless or *perceptually* lossless. In many cases, perceptually lossless is not discernible to the end user. To see the effects of these settings, however, you need to be able to simulate poor network conditions so that the effect is measurable.

From a delivery perspective, it is a great to understand how these adjustments work in a controlled scenario so that you can have confidence that you are tuning the right settings for the right use-cases. This is to say, what is optimal in one use case may not be optimal in another. For example, if you have high latency, you tune and optimize the desktop session much differentially than if it is being delivered on a high-speed corporate network. You tune per use case, and different use cases have different optimization settings.

Building a Performance Test Environment

You need to be able to do two things in a controlled test environment. You need to inject real-world delays and simulate "real" end-user activity. There is not a single tool set that gives you everything, but you can take utilities that have been accepted by the community and use them to build your controlled environment. These tools can be deployed in your virtualization environment at little or no cost. One question that comes to mind is why take the added effort to build out this controlled testing environment? Why not just deploy and tweak in the live VMware View environment?

In Chapter 1, "Virtual Desktop Infrastructure Overview," we talked about the double-edged sword for virtual desktop environments; it can be a huge benefit to the management of desktops, but if poorly implemented, it may not be accepted by the end users. Building a performance test environment is about doing your homework to ensure you have done everything possible to ensure the success of the technology. You might be able to crunch the exam and pass the test, but if you fail, you may not get another opportunity to take it.

In the performance test environment in this chapter, we are going to use the VMware environment, WANem View Planner WireShark, and for detailed analysis, PCoIP Log Viewer.

- WANem is software running on a Linux distribution called Knoppix. WANem can be used to emulate network link qualities (bandwidth size, packet loss, jitter, and latency) to test how a technology performs under simulated real-world scenarios. WANem is launched through a LiveCD or bootable ISO or media file. (You can download WANem from http://wanem.sourceforge.net/.)

- View Planner is a VMware benchmarking tool that allows you to automate and simulate user workload in a VMware View environment. This tool is useful for assessing load versus session tuning. (View Planner is currently available only through either VMware PSO or VMware partners.)

- WireShark is a third-party packet sniffer that allows you to profile your network to ensure you are getting accurate information on what the real conditions are on the network. (You can download WireShark from http://www.wireshark.org/download.html.)

- PCoIP Log Viewer is a tool developed by a member of the user community for parsing and reading PCoIP log files. (You can download PCoIP Log Viewer from http://mindfluxinc.net/?p=195.)

You do not need to be a network expert to use WANem, but you do need to understand the basics of what you will be adjusting:

- *Jitter* is the one-way packet delay variation (PDV) . It is a measure of the variation between one-way packet latency. For example, if within a transaction one packet takes 9 ms and the second takes 11 ms to reach its destination, the jitter is the variation between the first packet and second packet. The less jitter there is on a network, the more predictable the one-way network latency is.

- *Latency* is the time taken for a packet stream to travel between source and destination. When you are injecting latency, it is important to take into account the round-trip nature of network packets. If you are trying to emulate 30 ms of latency because your ping test on the network shows a delay of 30 ms of latency, you configure your emulation device for 15 ms to provide a round-trip time of 30 ms.

- *Bandwidth* is the amount of data that can be carried from one point to another within a time period (typically one second). It is usually expressed in bits or bytes (8 bits/byte).

- *Packet loss* occurs when one or more packets fail to reach their destination.

It is the combination of these four measurements that determines how the transmission is affected. To simulate how the virtual desktop will perform, you need to understand how to identify what your current network is experiencing so that you can configure your simulated network in the controlled environment to fine-tune your VMware View environment.

The environment you are going to build involves creating a path to the View environment that forces the connection to go through the WANem virtual appliance. It, of course, does not have to be a completely isolated View environment because you are testing for session improvements to ensure you have a rich user experience versus capacity of load testing. A single VMware View desktop allows you to create the environment needed.

The environment requires a physical desktop where you run the View client and the metrics and monitoring tools. To configure this environment, you should create a networking facing vSwitch and an Internal vSwitch and a virtual desktop running internally from the perspective of the WANem virtual appliance. Logically, the environment should look like that shown in Figure 8.3.

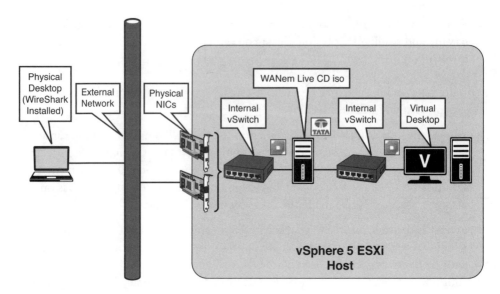

Figure 8.3 End-user performance testing environment.

From the physical desktop to the internal virtual desktop should be a layer two network, or it should be essentially flat. This ensures that nothing will introduce a delay over your network path other than what you introduce yourself through WANem. WANem can be downloaded as a virtual appliance or boot ISO running Knoppix. The virtual appliance is based on VMware Server or workstation and essentially is the bare minimum required to boot from the Knoppix live Linux CD.

The WANem ISO downloads in tarball format (this format allows you to combine multiple files in a single "tarball"), so you might need to have a compression tool such as WinZip, 7-Zip, or WinRAR handy to extract the ISO. You can also download the virtual appliance, which also contains the ISO file, so either or is okay. You create a WANem virtual appliance that boots from the ISO, and when done, you need to configure it in bridge mode. Bridge mode keeps everything at a layer two level and essentially creates a tunnel to the View desktop on the internal vSwitch. This is the most straightforward approach because essentially you do not have to redirect any traffic; it just flows to and from the View desktop.

For example, add IP addresses to the environment and clarify the internal virtual desktop requirement, as shown in Figure 8.4.

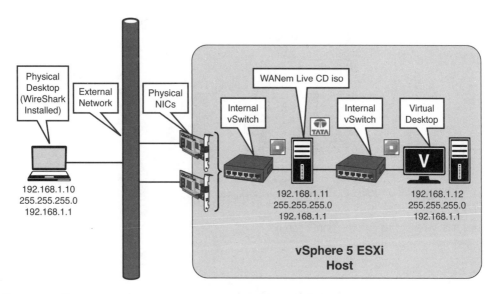

Figure 8.4 End-user performance testing environment with IPs.

In the case of the WANem appliance, it has two interfaces that will be bridged. The bridge is configured with an IP, but the individual interfaces are not. This configuration from the perspective of the ESXi hosts is shown in Figure 8.5.

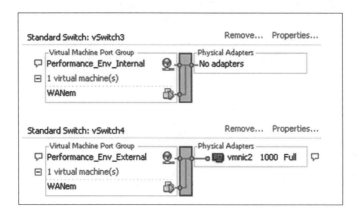

Figure 8.5 Internal and external switches.

You can see that one of WANem's interfaces is connected to the internal switch, and the second interface is connected to the external switch exactly as you intended, as shown in Figure 8.6.

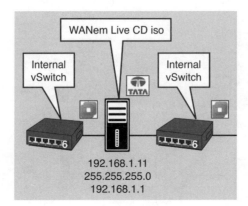

Figure 8.6 WANem-to-switch connection.

Installing and Configuring WANem

The resources for the WANem appliance should be exclusively reserved to ensure you can manage the virtual appliance even when you are introducing a high degree of overhead to the network. This means ensuring that the memory reservations are set on the WANem appliance to ensure the emulator has adequate resources. WANem requires a minimum of 512 MB of memory, which should be reserved to ensure the appliance has sufficient resources for your testing. To create the WANem virtual appliance, create a virtual machine with the following properties:

- Linux operating system based on Ubuntu
- 1 vCPU
- 512 MB of memory
- Two virtual network adapters

Assuming you are not using the virtual appliance, configure the VM to boot from the Knoppix ISO. You will likely want to copy the ISO file locally to the host.

After configuring the VM, follow these steps to configure WANem to operate in bridging mode:

1. Boot the virtual machine from the Knoppix ISO file. Press **Enter** to start the boot process from DVD.

2. You want to hardcode the IP addresses, so when prompted to configure the system using DHCP, type **n** for no (see Figure 8.7).

```
Autoconfiguring devices...  ████████████████ Done.
Mouse is ImPS/2 Generic Wheel Mouse at /dev/input/mice
Accelerated MKXORGCONFIG . (Backgrounding)
Video is VMware Inc Abstract SVGA II Adapter, using Xorg(vmware) Server
Monitor is Generic Monitor, H:28.0-96.0kHz, V:50.0-76.0Hz
Using Modes   "1024x768" "800x600" "640x480" Modes
Scanning for Harddisk partitions and creating /etc/fstab... Done.
Network device eth0 detected, DHCP broadcasting for IP. (Backgrounding)
Network device eth1 detected, DHCP broadcasting for IP. (Backgrounding)
run commands are started : setup_dialog,setup_ja,Done.
INIT: Entering runlevel: 3
Do you want to configure all interfaces via DHCP(y/n): n_
```

Figure 8.7 Configure interfaces by IP.

3. Because you do not want to associate IP addresses to the individual interfaces but configure them as a bridge, you also need to escape the wizard configuration of the individual interfaces. Simply press **Esc** to go back to the command prompt (see Figure 8.8).

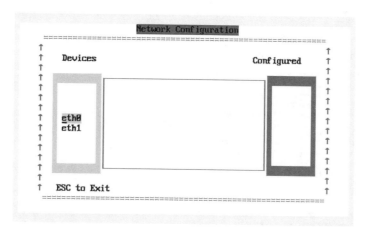

Figure 8.8 Press Esc to exit.

4. Before you configure the interfaces, you need to supply a password for the root account. Supply and confirm the password you would like to use (see Figure 8.9).

```
Network settings ...... ok
 MTU=1500 settings ...... ok
Apache Start........ok
SSH start ...........ok
Adding  user perc...  for remote logins via SSH.....ok
Added user perc.... Password for perc
Enter new UNIX password:
Retype new UNIX password:
passwd: password updated successfully
= = = = = = = = = = = = = = = = = = = = = = = =
Initialization Successful
A shell will be given for WANem Administration.
Check the status of Wanem.
Type help to get the list of commands
Access the WANem from any machine by http://<IP of this machine>/WANem
= = = = = = = = = = = = = = = = = = = = = = = =
```

Figure 8.9 Supply a password for root.

5. You need to exit to the underlying Linux shell to configure the interfaces. This step is quite simple to do; you simply type **exit2shell** at the prompt, as shown in Figure 8.10.

```
Network settings ...... ok
 MTU=1500 settings ...... ok
Apache Start........ok
SSH start ...........ok
Adding  user perc...  for remote logins via SSH.....ok
Added user perc.... Password for perc
Enter new UNIX password:
Retype new UNIX password:
passwd: password updated successfully
= = = = = = = = = = = = = = = = = = = = = = = =
Initialization Successful
A shell will be given for WANem Administration.
Check the status of Wanem.
Type help to get the list of commands
Access the WANem from any machine by http://<IP of this machine>/WANem
= = = = = = = = = = = = = = = = = = = = = = = =


WANemControl@PERC>exit2shell
Type 'wanem' to return to WANem console
root!tty1:/# _
```

Figure 8.10 Exit to the shell.

6. It is important to bring up both interfaces so that you configure and add them to the bridge. You bring up each interface in turn by typing **ifconfig eth0 0.0.0.0 up** and the same for the second interface, **ifconfig eth1 0.0.0.0 up**, as shown in Figure 8.11.

```
WANemControl@PERC>exit2shell
Type 'wanem' to return to WANem console
root!tty1:/# ifconfig eth0 0.0.0.0 up
root!tty1:/# ifconfig eth1 0.0.0.0 up
```

Figure 8.11 Bring up the interfaces.

You are ready to configure the bridge so that traffic can flow through the interfaces.

7. You must first use the bridge control utility to add a new bridge br0 by typing **brctl addbr br0**, as shown in Figure 8.12.

```
WANemControl@PERC>exit2shell
Type 'wanem' to return to WANem console
root!tty1:/# ifconfig eth0 0.0.0.0 up
root!tty1:/# ifconfig eth1 0.0.0.0 up
root!tty1:/# brctl addbr br0_
```

Figure 8.12 Add the bridge interface br0.

8. Now that you have created the bridge, you can add the two interfaces to it to establish the working configuration. Again, you use the bridge configuration utility and add the devices by typing **brctl addif br0 eth0** and **brctl addif br0 eth1**, as shown in Figure 8.13.

```
WANemControl@PERC>exit2shell
Type 'wanem' to return to WANem console
root!tty1:/# ifconfig eth0 0.0.0.0 up
root!tty1:/# ifconfig eth1 0.0.0.0 up
root!tty1:/# brctl addbr br0
Bridge firewalling registered
br0: Dropping NETIF_F_UFO since no NETIF_F_HW_CSUM feature.
root!tty1:/# _
```

Figure 8.13 Add both interfaces to the bridge interface.

9. You need a management interface to adjust the network emulation to simulate the latency. You apply the IP address using the ifconfig utility to the bridge by entering the command **ifconfig br0 10.0.1.4 netmask 255.255.255.0** (see Figure 8.14).

```
WANemControl@PERC>exit2shell
Type 'wanem' to return to WANem console
root!tty1:/# ifconfig eth0 0.0.0.0 up
root!tty1:/# ifconfig eth1 0.0.0.0 up
root!tty1:/# brctl addbr br0
Bridge firewalling registered
br0: Dropping NETIF_F_UFO since no NETIF_F_HW_CSUM feature.
root!tty1:/# brctl addif br0 eth0
audit(1332034268.596:2): dev=eth0 prom=256 old_prom=0 auid=4294967295
root!tty1:/# brctl addif br0 eth1
audit(1332034272.263:3): dev=eth1 prom=256 old_prom=0 auid=4294967295
root!tty1:/# _
```

Figure 8.14 Configure the bridge interface with an IP.

10. To go back to the WANem module, simply type **wanem**.

```
WANemControl@PERC>exit2shell
Type 'wanem' to return to WANem console
root!tty1:/# ifconfig eth0 0.0.0.0 up
root!tty1:/# ifconfig eth1 0.0.0.0 up
root!tty1:/# brctl addbr br0
Bridge firewalling registered
br0: Dropping NETIF_F_UFO since no NETIF_F_HW_CSUM feature.
root!tty1:/# brctl addif br0 eth0
audit(1332034268.596:2): dev=eth0 prom=256 old_prom=0 auid=4294967295
root!tty1:/# brctl addif br0 eth1
audit(1332034272.263:3): dev=eth1 prom=256 old_prom=0 auid=4294967295

root!tty1:/# ifconfig br0 10.0.1.4 netmask 255.255.255.0
```

Figure 8.15 Type wanem to return to the WANem module.

11. To verify everything is reachable and good, simply open an Internet browser and browse to the IP addresses configured on the bridge. If everything is working, you should get the message shown in Figure 8.16.

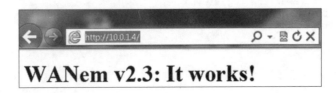

Figure 8.16 Verify WANem.

To adjust the settings, simply browse to the WANem IP /WANem (http://[IP Address] /WANem). To adjust latency only, select **Basic Mode**. Ensure you have the bridge selected and choose a bandwidth type to emulate on each interface. You can add delay or latency by specifying it in the Delay column for each interface and apply the settings (see Figure 8.17).

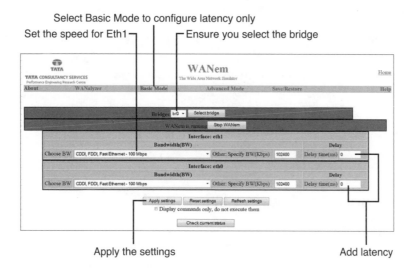

Figure 8.17 Configure WANem.

To add qualities such as jitter or packet loss, you need to go to the Advanced mode screen and select a specific interface. You can add delay and loss settings under the Delay and Loss columns (see Figure 8.18). Don't forget to apply your settings to have them take effect. You can verify the latency by running a ping test from the physical desktop where you are launching the View client to the virtual desktop. You should see a fairly consistent pattern of latency. It varies a little due to the interjection of WANem on the network stream and the time it takes the appliance to process the packets.

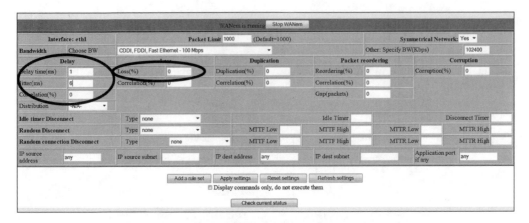

Figure 8.18 You can configure network delay and packet loss.

Installing and Configuring WireShark

Although you now have a method to simulate distance and see how a virtual machine performs, you will want a better level of visibility on the traffic you are impacting. One of my favorite tools for viewing packet streams is WireShark. WireShark is a packet sniffer that allows you to zero in on certain traffic streams. In this case, you should look at PCoIP traffic between the virtual and physical desktops. When you install WireShark, it installs WinPcap, which allows your network device to run in promiscuous mode. Promiscuous mode allows you to see the network traffic through the WireShark interface. To install WireShark, you can download it from wireshark.org and follow these steps:

1. Launch the installer, and on the welcome screen, click **Next**.

2. On the next screen, you can choose what components you want. Because the defaults are good, just click **Next**.

3. On the additional task screen, you can create additional shortcuts to launch WireShark and associate the trace extensions; this setting is checked by default. Click **Next**.

4. Select the destination and click **Next**.

5. On the next screen, you are prompted to install WinPcap, which is necessary, so click **Next**.

6. Click **Next** on the WinPcap Installer screen and **Next** on the welcome screen.

7. Agree to the license terms and click **Install** on the next screen. You have the option of automatically starting WinPcap at boot time, but this is not necessary.

8. Click **Finish** on the WinPcap installation screen, which takes you back to the WireShark Installer. Click **Next** to proceed with the installation.

9. On the Completing Installation screen, select the option **Run WireShark** and click **Finish**.

When you launch WireShark, you are prompted to start a capture on an interface. Simply select the appropriate interface, and you are taken to the capture window (see Figure 8.19).

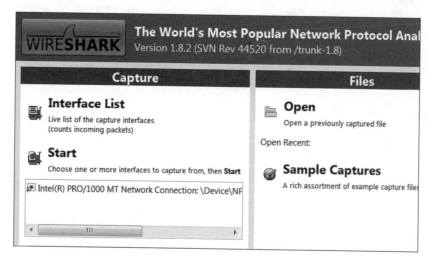

Figure 8.19 Select the interface.

Because you want to look at PCoIP traffic in a graphical way, you should drill down and use filters to target just the traffic that you want to see. From the capture window, select **Statistics** and then **IO Graphs**, as shown in Figure 8.20.

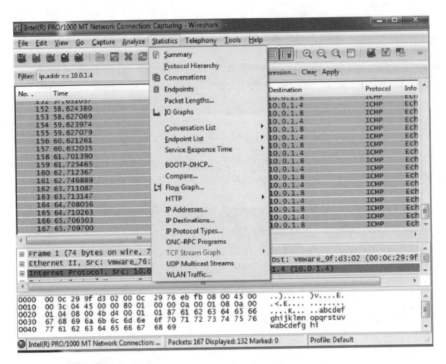

Figure 8.20 Display the IO graphs.

Now you have a graphical representation of the network flow, but you should adjust the Unit setting from Packets/Tick to Bytes/Tick (see Figure 8.21).

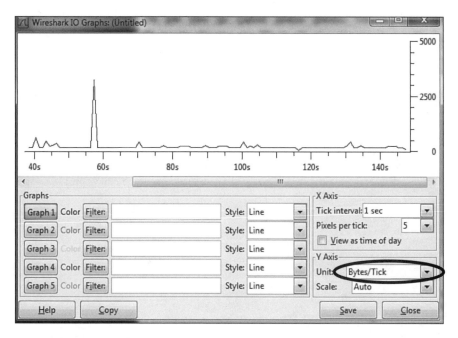

Figure 8.21 Adjust to Bytes/Tick.

The final task is to apply filters so that you are capturing only the PCoIP stream. Specifically, you want to capture traffic to and from the client and virtual desktop. To add an IP filter for a specific address, you simply enter

ip.addr == [IP ADDRESS]

For example, if your IP address is 10.0.1.3, you enter

ip.addr == 10.0.1.3 (Note: there is no space between the double equal signs).

Of course, you want the traffic to and from both machines, so you need to add a second IP address. To concatenate or add the second IP address, you specify && and the second IP. If your virtual machine address is 10.0.1.8, your final notation is

ip.addr == 10.0.1.3 && ip.addr == 10.0.1.8

This gets you the traffic only between these two points, but you should be specific to the PCoIP protocol. The PCoIP protocol is UDP based and uses only UDP port 50002 on the virtual machine and UDP port 4172 on the client side. To filter only the UDP traffic on those two ports, you simply append the UDP port filters to the statement

&& udp.port == 50002 && udp.port == 4172

In the example (see Figure 8.22), the complete statement is

    ip.addr == 10.0.1.3 && ip.addr == 10.0.1.8 && udp.port == 50002 && udp.port
    == 4172

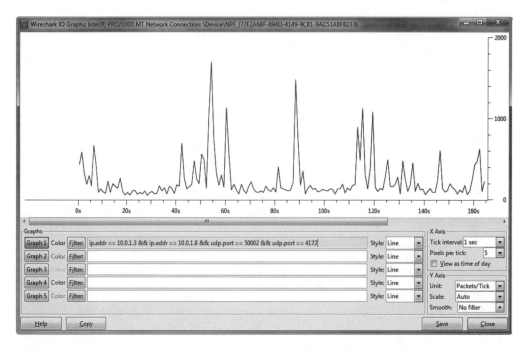

Figure 8.22 Real-time PCoIP information.

You are now looking only at the PCoIP traffic between your client and virtual machine. Now you can tune the environment and see the relative impact you are having on traffic and how it impacts your overall user experience. With WireShark, you get a general sense of the live traffic flow while you make adjustments. It is also useful to go back and analyze your PCoIP stream if you are troubleshooting or want a detailed breakdown of the changes you are making.

Tuning PCoIP

Perhaps before we go into the *how* to tune, we should cover *when* to tune. PCoIP is a real-time protocol that adapts based on existing network conditions. Before you start adjusting the settings, you should make sure you have already followed best practices, such as wrapping quality of service (QoS) around the PCoIP data stream and ensuring that your desktop image is properly tuned. Network QoS allows a network to handle application traffic in a way that meets the service requirements of the stream. Within QoS, you can set up a series of queues that allow you to prioritize real-time traffic over other network traffic.

Altering parameters can have unexpected results if you cannot measure the change. This is why we started creating a tuning environment. Keep in mind that as you tune, you are trading off on performance versus impact to the end-user experience. You may have certain virtual desktops that require tuning and others that do not. Keep this in mind when you are setting up your OUs for the View desktops because most of the tuning parameters are applied through Active Directory policy.

As mentioned, you tune PCoIP through the Active Directory using templates provided with VMware View. It is similar to the process of enabling Persona Management. The PCoIP templates can be found in the following location:

> <install_directory>\VMware\VMwareView\Server\extras\GroupPolicyFiles\ pcoip.adm

To import them into the AD, follow these steps:

1. Open your Group Policy Management Console.

2. Right-click your View Desktop OU and create or link a GPO policy.

3. Enter a name such as **View PCoIP Tuning Policy**.

4. Right-click the new policy and select **Edit**.

5. Browse to Administrative Templates and select **Add/Remove Templates**.

6. Click **Add** again, browse to the location on the View Server, and select the **pcoip. adm** template. (Note: In Windows 2003, a template has an *.adm extension; for Windows 2008, the extension has been changed to *.admx.)

7. Expand the Administrative Templates and PCoIP Session Variables.

Tuning Parameters

As you adjust the tuning parameters, review how they affect the controlled performance tuning environment. For it to be clear, I recommend you adjust each individually and then run a gpupdate /force command on the virtual machine so that the policy is applied to the session. In some cases, you may have to restart the user session to see any differences.

Enabling the Build-to-Lossless feature actually disables the build to lossless and requires that you acknowledge this when you enable it (see Figure 8.23). You should enable this feature when the quality of the image is not critical. Keep in mind that you will likely have a percentage of desktops on which graphic quality is not critical and a portion on which it is. In general, enabling this feature is not noticeable to most users who are not modeling or reviewing medical information.

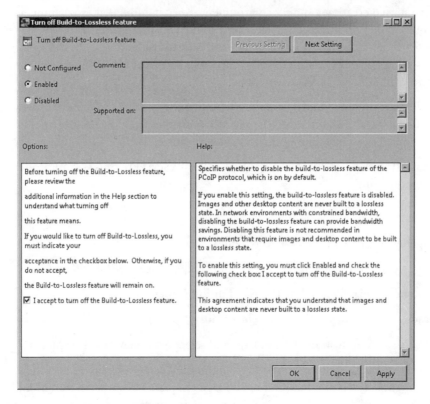

Figure 8.23 Enabling Build-to-Lossless.

Setting the session bandwidth limit can be helpful in low bandwidth situations or on highly utilized LAN connections. VMware recommends that you set it to 10% lower than the maximum bandwidth rate. For example, on a Fast Ethernet connection of 100 Mbps, the kilobits per second is equal to 102,204. The default setting is 90,000 kbps, which is roughly 10% below the maximum throughput for Fast Ethernet (see Figure 8.24).

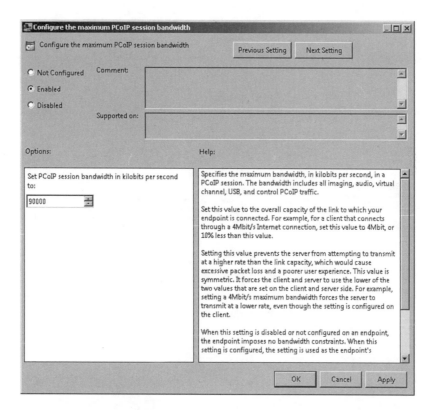

Figure 8.24 Session bandwidth limits.

Setting the PCoIP session bandwidth is like setting a minimum reservation for the display traffic. It can be helpful if there is a large amount of packet loss on the network, such as wireless or 3G or 4G networks.

When you get into detailed configuration of the PCoIP protocol, that is where the PCoIP Log Viewer can be an invaluable asset because it breaks down the PCoIP traffic so that you know how to adjust the bandwidth floor setting in the policy, as shown in Figure 8.25.

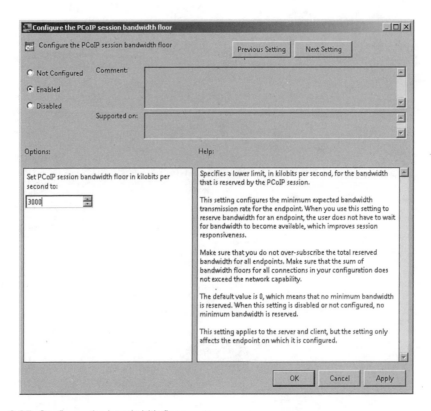

Figure 8.25 Configure the bandwidth floor.

Configuring image quality can be important to ensure a good user experience. The default maximum value for image quality is 90%. The maximum value limits the image quality of the changed regions of the display. Over a WAN, VMware recommends you adjust this number down to 50%–60% to reduce the bandwidth requirement of the session. On a LAN, a minor adjustment may improve the user experience without a noticeable difference to the user. The minimum value of the display sets the minimum quality of the images. This can be used in limited bandwidth environments when you want to ensure a certain quality of image. For example, if you are using medical imaging or a healthcare application, you might want to ensure that the image is a certain quality before displaying. The minimum value cannot exceed the maximum value.

The other image quality setting is the frame rate, which determines the maximum frames per second (FPS). The default setting of 30 frames is ideal for good network conditions. You should adjust the frame rate from 30 to 10–15 frames in WAN network conditions (see Figure 8.26). You can also adjust this setting up as high as 120 frames per second, but you must be careful to ensure your network conditions can support a higher frame rate.

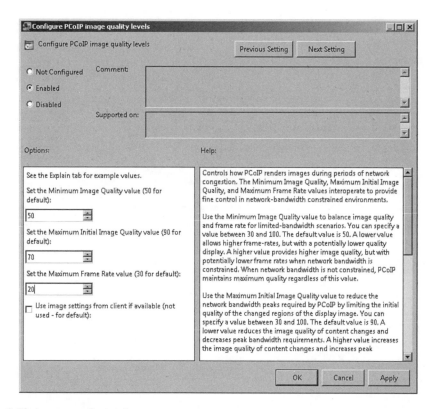

Figure 8.26 Image quality levels.

Audio quality can be adjusted to set a predefined limit on the amount of bandwidth that the audio stream can use in kilobits per second (kbps). You can adjust audio between 50 and 450 kbps, but it requires fine-tuning and testing to determine what the trade-off is between audio quality and bandwidth savings (see Figure 8.27). If audio is not required, it can be turned off.

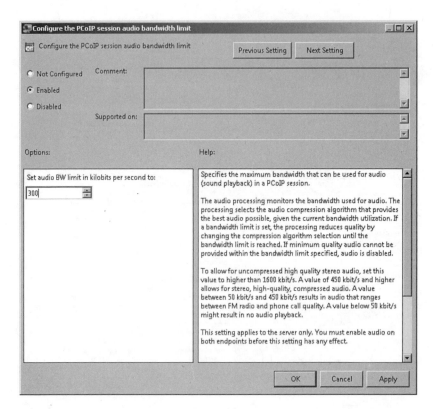

Figure 8.27 Audio bandwidth.

One of the new features of PCoIP is a client-side image cache. The size of this cache can be adjusted from the default of 250 MB. If you are using thin clients that have a restricted cache setting, you should adjust this value to match what is available in the thin clients. Attempting to use a larger cache than what is supported could lead to disconnects and timeouts (see Figure 8.28).

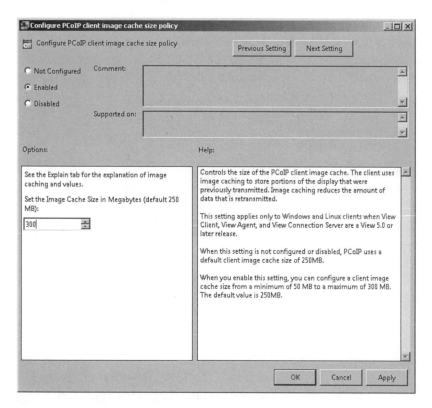

Figure 8.28 Adjust image cache.

You also can adjust more settings, but these are some of the major ones that impact both user experience and performance. Use your performance tuning environment to test and adjust so that you find the best combination of performance and utilization. In all cases, I have found that it is a good idea to adjust the settings from the defaults to either provide bandwidth savings or improve the overall user experience.

Further Analysis

If you need to break down the PCoIP protocol further, a number of good third-party tools are available. One of the best that is freely available is the PCoIP Log Viewer. PCoIP creates log files that are stored in c:\ProgramData\VMware\VDM\Logs by default. There are agent and server log files. The server logs are the ones that contain a wealth of information on how PCoIP is performing on the network. The PCoIP Log Viewer provides a parser and a viewer for looking at these log files. The parser converts the server log files into XML format so that they can be loaded into the viewer. The viewer is based on Java and requires you to have Java installed on the machine you want to run it from. The tool was developed by Chuck Hirstius and can be downloaded at http://mindfluxinc.net/. It downloads as the parser and the Java file for the GUI. The first thing you must do is run the parser on the server log files. For example, run

```
pcoip_parse.exe [path to pcoip_server log files]
```

The output is shown in Figure 8.29.

Figure 8.29 Run the parser on the log files.

After parsing the log files, you can then click on **PCoIPLogViewer.jnlp** to begin the installation. The first time you run the file, it downloads the remaining files from mindfluxin.net (see Figure 8.30). After you open it a second time, it checks to see if any updates are available. If a connection to the Internet is not available, it takes much longer to launch but does launch after a period of time.

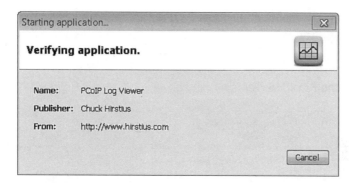

Figure 8.30 PCoIP Log Viewer updates.

After the PCoIP Log Viewer is installed, you simply open the file that was converted to XML by the parser utility to display the interface, as shown in Figure 8.31.

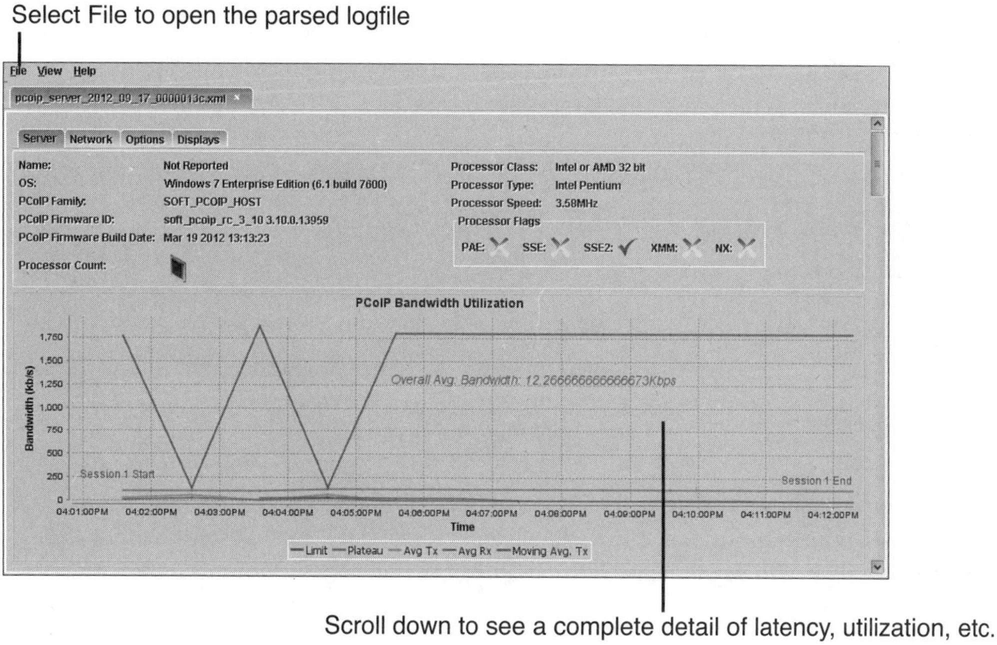

Select File to open the parsed logfile

Figure 8.31 PCoIP Log Viewer.

With the Log Viewer, you have access to specific information on bandwidth, PCoIP connection quality, packet count, latency, client-side performance, and so on. It is important, however, to understand how to interpret the information to make the necessary adjustments. Under the menu of the items, you see a series of tabs: Server, Network, Options, and Displays (see Figure 8.32). The Server tab provides information on where the PCoIP Server service is running, such as the OS and CPU information.

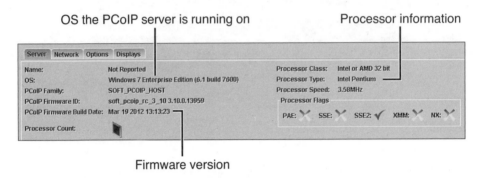

OS the PCoIP server is running on   Processor information

Firmware version

Figure 8.32 Server tab.

The Network tab (shown in Figure 8.33) provides the IP address of the virtual machine running the PCoIP Server services, the link speed, and maximum transmission unit (MTU) size, which is the size of the largest packet the network can transmit.

pcoip_server_2012_03_18_00000474.xml		
Server **Network** **Options** **Displays**		
Network Adapter: Not Reported	**Link Speed**	**MTU**
Server Address: 10.0.1.8	Server: 1000000	Server: 1300
Server Port: 4172	Client: 1000000	Client: 1300
Server MAC: N/A	Negotiated: 1000000	Negotiated: 1300

Figure 8.33 Network tab.

The Options tab shows you what options have been configured for the PCoIP session (see Figure 8.34). These options are either the defaults if you have not adjusted them or the adjusted values. In this example, we have disabled the build to lossless and set the cache size from 250 to 300 MB.

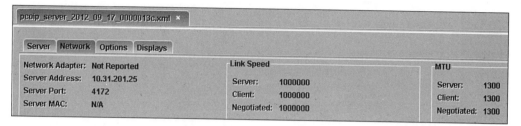

Figure 8.34 Options tab.

The Displays tab shows you information on the display, such as how many are in use, the number that are allowed, and the image quality settings, as shown in Figure 8.35.

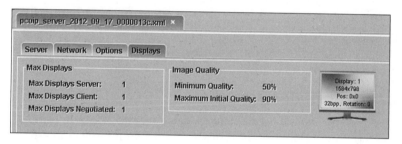

Figure 8.35 Displays tab.

PCoIP Bandwidth Utilization

The details of the PCoIP Log Viewer are displayed in a graph that identifies key aspects of how the PCoIP protocol is functioning. These details allow you to troubleshoot certain issues and tune specific values. The first graph (see Figure 8.36) is the PCoIP Bandwidth Utilization graph. This graph displays any limit. In this example, we set a limit of 90,000 kbps or 10% less than the total. You also see the plateau or ideal utilization of the session when all the virtual channels are considered. You can also break down traffic from the VM and to the VM as well as the overage.

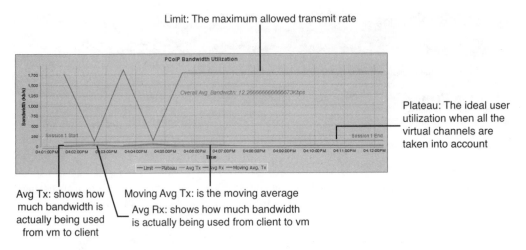

Figure 8.36 Bandwidth Utilization graph.

PCoIP Bandwidth Rate Limiting

PCoIP adjusts both the flow of packets and the minimum reserved bandwidth if it detects packet loss or a lack of responsiveness from the client. This information is displayed on the PCoIP Bandwidth Rate Limiting graph. It displays the old and adjusted bandwidth rates using the Loss Old and Loss New graph lines. It displays the overflow or graphs how much the PCoIP Server is exceeding the client's capability to receive packets. The Overrun Old and Overrun New graph lines show the preadjusted rate and post. The minimum reserved bandwidth values are represented by the Floor Old and Floor New graph lines (see Figure 8.37).

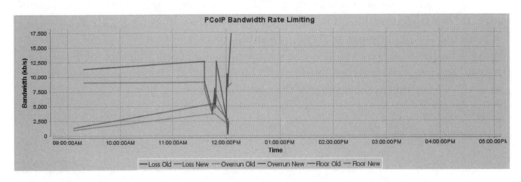

Figure 8.37 Bandwidth Rate Limiting graph.

PCoIP Connection Quality

The PCoIP Connection Quality graph tells you about packet loss from the PCoIP Server running on the virtual machine and also from the client to the PCoIP Server service. A large number of transmit losses occur when PCoIP is doing some rate limiting, as depicted in the Connection Quality Graph (see Figure 8.38).

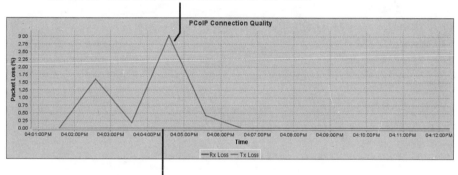

Figure 8.38 Connection Quality graph.

PCoIP Packet Counts

The PCoIP Packet Counts graph provides a better breakdown between image, audio, and other packets (see Figure 8.39). It allows you to see the changes when you are adjusting the PCoIP tuning options that affect image and audio in relation to the other channels.

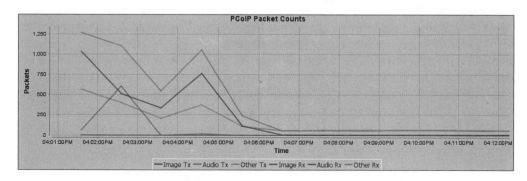

Figure 8.39 Packet Counts graph.

PCoIP Connection Latency

Latency is the round-trip time from PCoIP Server service to the client, and the variance between each measured round trip. It is shown in the Connection Latency graph (see Figure 8.40).

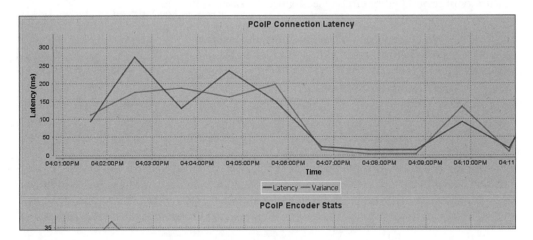

Figure 8.40 Connection Latency graph.

Encoding Graphs

The architecture of PCoIP is based on a server that encodes the pixels using algorithms and a client that decodes the information to translate it to the screen. The encoder is the PCoIP Server service that is installed on the View virtual desktop when the agent is installed. The decoder is the View client that is installed on the access point. The next series of graphs deals with the performance of the Encoder and Decoder running in the virtual machine and client, respectively.

The PCoIP Encoder stats measure the performance of the Encoder in encoding packets to send to the View client for decoding. The encoding is measured in UDP packets in frames per second (FPS) and video sample rate of Flips (see Figure 8.41). The Quality Table measures the level of quality for the build to Lossless. Generally a lower Quality Table number is considered better. A lower number translates to fewer dropped packets and lower rate limiting activity. A high quality number usually corresponds to a poorer user experience. You can use this graph to lower the frames per second for better bandwidth while keeping an eye on the Quality Table.

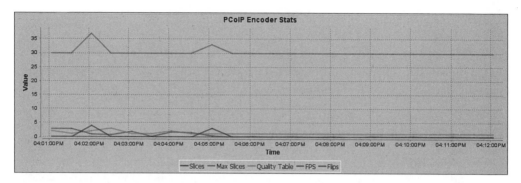

Figure 8.41 Encoder Stats graph.

The PCoIP Encoder Stats graph tells you how many pixels have changed in the last 30 seconds. The PCoIP Encoder Stats—Delta Bits tells you how many lossless packets (Delta Build Bits) you have in relation to general data packets (Delta Bits). A high number of lossless data packets generally translates to a good overall user experience. The PCoIP Encoder Stats—Encoder Performance tells you how much compression is happening in the Bits Per Pixel line graph. The lower bits per pixel value, the higher the compression ratio is. The final graph tells you about Client Performance. If the Client Decode Rate is less than the Average Transfer Rate found in the PCoIP Bandwidth Utilization graph, that may indicate a client processing problem.

Although the PCoIP Log Viewer can be used for real-time data, I prefer to use WireShark to get a sense of the traffic rate and then the viewer to better understand how PCoIP is reacting to the network. The Log Viewer requires a number of changes to support real-time data; these changes are fine in the controlled performance-tuning environment built previously, but more of a security risk to measure in production. The steps to enable real-time monitoring are included here but are not recommended for use in a production environment:

1. You must allow DCOM traffic through all Windows Firewalls (View desktop to the PC running the PCoIP Log Viewer).

2. The Remote Registry Service must be started and set to automatic startup.

3. You need to change permissions on the following registry so that Administrators have Full Control:

   *HKEY*_CLASSES_ROOT\CLSID\{76A64158-CB41-11d1-8B02-00600806D9B6}

Configuring these settings in production makes the desktop vulnerable to a security exploit.

You can use a combination of these tools to tune measure and apply your configurations to maximize the user experience while still getting the most out of your bandwidth. One issue you need to also review is overall performance. So far, this chapter has focused on session tuning, but you must also understand the overall performance of the environment to ensure the user experience is optimal.

The Impact of Load or IOPS

To ensure a rich end-user experience, you must have accounted for load properly in your design and architecture. Load is generally measured in terms of input/output per second (IOPS) in a View environment, which refers to the number of reads and writes on the storage system. Load is a difficult thing to quantify until you have deployed virtual desktops into production. You should have a benchmark of relative performance of the environment ahead of that time to ensure the virtual desktops will perform well for users in production.

VMware released the View Planner, which allows you to benchmark an environment under a simulated workload. Although the result is not identical to what you will experience in production, it is reasonably close. The value of benchmarking is that it further reduces your risk that users will not get a good user experience and ensures the environment has adequate resource capacity.

View Planner consists of a VDI controller virtual appliance, client and desktop virtual machines, and your virtual infrastructure, as shown in Figure 8.42. You can leverage AD and View Server or choose not to, depending on the type of test you are running.

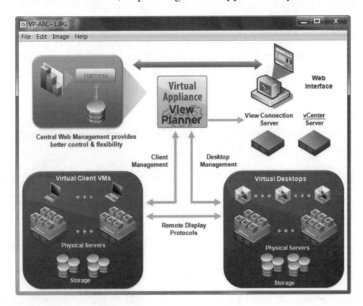

Figure 8.42 View Planner architecture.

VMware View Planner allows you to conduct three types of tests, depending on the amount of infrastructure you are willing to commit and what you are most interested in stressing. The three modes are

■ *Remote Mode* requires one client per virtual machine and is closest to a real-world simulation. It requires the most amount of infrastructure for load testing.

■ *Passive Client Mode* allows multiple virtual machines per client. This requires less infrastructure for your load testing but still incorporates a client component.

■ *Local Mode* requires no client virtual machines but still allows you to simulate a "real" workload for benchmark testing. It requires the least commitment to infrastructure.

For a complete list of hardware and software requirements, refer to VMware's documentation.

Setting Up VMware ViewPlanner

View Planner comes as an OVF file you simply download and import into your virtualization environment, as shown in Figure 8.43. After the installation, you need to run a series of commands from the console to prepare the appliance.

Figure 8.43 Import the virtual appliance.

After importing the appliance, you need to prepare it. You prepare the appliance by running the following commands:

1. Boot the appliance and, if prompted, type **yes** to accept the license agreement.

2. Log in to the appliance using the root and password **vmware**.

3. Change to the /root/ViewPlanner directory by running **cd /root/ViewPlanner**.

4. Set the path for Python by running **source setup.sh**.

5. Hardcode an IP address using the Python script and the following syntax (as shown in Figure 4.44):

python ./harness_setup.pyc –i [IP ADDRESS] –m [NETMASK] =g [GATEWAY] –d {DOMAIN NAME] –n [DNS SERVER]

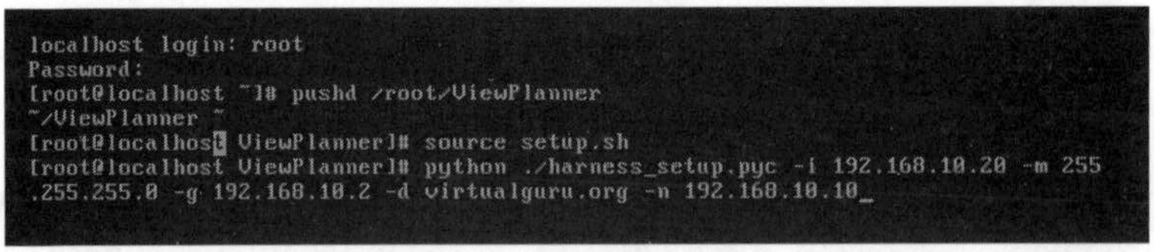

Figure 8.44 Hardcode an IP address.

After configuring the appliance, you can browse to the web page and log in using root and the default password **abc123** (see Figure 8.45).

Figure 8.45 Log in to View Planner.

After you log in, you need to configure connections to the vCenter, View, and AD Servers, as shown in Figure 8.46. What connections you need to configure are determined by whether you are running a remote, passive, or local mode test. For example, for a local mode test, you do not need an AD Server, but you still need to put a dummy entry in the AD portion—for example, 127.0.0.1. After you put entries in the configuration section, simply click **Save** to have them saved and stored.

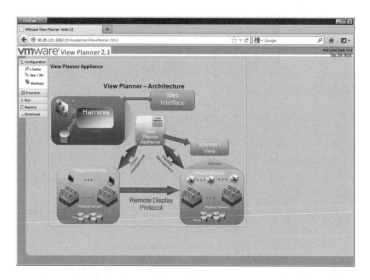

Figure 8.46 Configure vCenter, View, and AD Servers.

To have the View Planner automate the workload and deployment, you need to install several bundles on your AD, View, client, and virtual workstations. These bundles install Python and the various default scripts to run the components. These bundles are available as downloadable packages from the View Planner virtual appliance under the Download section (see Figure 8.47).

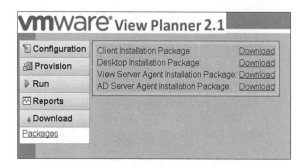

Figure 8.47 Download View Planner components.

You also need to make some configuration adjustments to the virtual machines and View Servers. For an extensive list, refer to the documentation. At a high level, you need to configure the following:

- VMware View Server

    - Install the View Server Agent Installation Package.

    - Set PowerShell execution to unrestricted using the following command from the PowerShell window:

    Set-ExecutionPolicy unrestricted

    - Configure an external URL for the VMware View Server by logging in to the View Administrator Console, View Configuration, Servers. Select View Server and click **Edit** and enter an external URL in the format **https://[View Server IP]:443**.

- Golden Master Image

    - Install Windows 7 or Windows XP image. (Note: You need to ensure either Microsoft Key Management Services exists in the environment or that the image has a Multiple Activation Key [MAK].)

    - Ensure you have a second E: drive labeled datadisk for user data.

    - Install all the applications required for the simulation. You can see the complete list under the profile creation tab on the View Planner (see Figure 8.48). In addition to the defaults, you can add additional custom applications if required, including ThinApp applications.

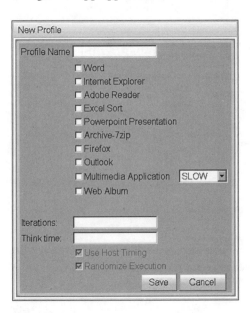

Figure 8.48 Run ThinApp packages.

- You need to install the Desktop bundle python package.

Many more optimizations that you can tweak are suggested in the deployment guide.

- Active Directory

- Install the AD Server Agent Install Package

Setting Up the Client Desktop

To test the client desktop, you need to create a separate client template. The reason is that both the client machines and virtual machines are virtualized in the load testing done by View Planner. In addition to a client desktop, you need to install the Client Installation Package on the client machine.

When everything is prepped, you are ready to configure the provisioning settings. You have the option of using vCenter or View Composer. Simply enter the vCenter information or View or both (see Figure 8.49).

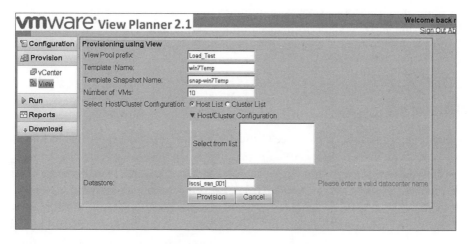

Figure 8.49 Incorporate View Composer.

After you have everything properly staged, you can create a profile that defines which applications to run, how many iterations, and the pauses (think time) between iterations. You simply specify a profile name, click which applications you want to instantiate, specify the iterations and think time, and save the profile (see Figure 8.50).

When you have a profile, you can specify the number of virtual machines to run, which workload profile, and what percentage of the total number of VMs should run this specific profile. You can build a variety of different types of profiles to simulate light, medium, and heavy users to ensure you have properly stressed the environment.

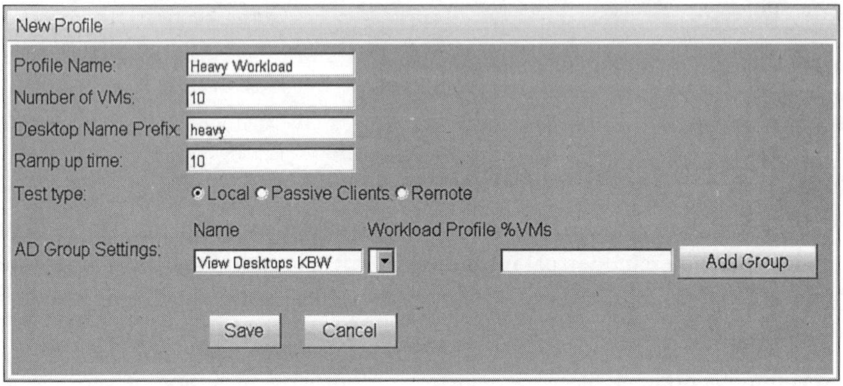

Figure 8.50 Simulating workload.

At this point, you have looked at session tuning and load testing to ensure you have validated session and overall performance of the environment. Proper testing and tuning ensures your environment can deliver a rich end-user experience.

Summary

This chapter discussed the importance of measuring the end-user experience to fine-tune each use case. You looked at tools to help quantify this by simulating distance through the use of WANem to apply latency, packet loss, and jitter to your PCoIP stream. You should now understand how to use standard networking tools such as WireShark to look at real-time PCoIP traffic flows. In addition, you looked at the PCoIP Log Viewer utility to break down and analyze each of the components that work to deliver the PCoIP protocol from the View desktop to the client. You also reviewed a tool to simulate IOPs in the View environment so that you can load test your virtual desktop environment. I cannot stress enough the importance of ensuring that you have taken the time to use these tools or tools like these to examine how things like PCoIP perform in different use cases and how your virtual desktop environment will perform under various load stresses.

In Chapter 9, "Offline Desktops," we look at why and how to deliver local mode desktops. Using local mode desktops is another way to distribute load in a VMware View environment. For example, you can run a local mode desktop as the primary user desktop and enforce synchronization so that the centrally stored View desktop is required only if something happens to the local mode one.

Chapter 9

Offline Desktops

Why Deliver an Offline Desktop?

VMware View allows you to enable users to check out their virtual desktops and run them offline. But why would you do this, and what should you consider if you do? Initially, the concept of offline desktops was designed to close the last mile on consolidating desktops in centralized vSphere environments, namely laptops. When VDI first hit the market, it struggled to address users who use a laptop as their primary device. Since the solution was introduced, however, technology has evolved so that mobile devices have proliferated, and the form factor has become a combination of tablets and laptops. Because the tablet is more dependent on online content, it has improved the availability of connectivity everywhere. So the original offline desktop solution becomes more interesting when used for more than just a disconnected laptop. The technology does, of course, have certain prerequisites that must be met to enable functionality that we review in this chapter.

Although many solutions available today allow virtual desktops to run and make use of desktop resources, such as client hypervisors or virtualization software running on an OS, VMware uses the software approach. Generally, these two types are more broadly described as type 1 or type 2 hypervisors. The difference is type 1 hypervisors are their own OSes, such as ESXi, and type 2 run on an underlying operating system such as Windows. Although type 1 hypervisors offer better performance, the challenge is with hardware compatibility. The benefit of a type 2 hypervisor is that the underlying OS looks after hardware compatibility.

It is interesting that the company that invented the bare metal hypervisor would choose to take a different approach when it comes to the desktop, but the rationale makes sense. From a historical perspective, VMware did have a desktop type 1 hypervisor for offline desktops, but it stopped development in beta because of all the negative feedback around hardware dependencies. Most virtual desktop solutions are designed to run Windows desktop operating systems. In this environment, the original target for offline desktops—laptops—would also be Windows based (note: VMware has MAC and Linux offline desktops on its roadmap). Type 1 hypervisors do have natural limitations that become important when you look at mobility.

Let's set virtual desktops aside and just look at how to enable service to a mobile laptop. When you are enabling laptop users to work remotely, they are doing it in one of two modes: either connected or disconnected. If the mode is disconnected, they are running an application that may cache data until it can be connected and synced. If you are running in connected mode, some security is likely wrapped around this connection to enable the users to connect to centralized business content. If you look at the profile you are trying to address in the View environment, it can be summarized as follows:

1. Windows-based users

2. Running laptops

3. Two primary modes: online or offline

4. Software layer to provide secure connection to business data

Although we mentioned tablets, which are not typically Windows devices, they are potentially an easier problem to solve because they are primarily online devices or always connected. You just need a client and a layer of security to enable the content to be viewed over the Internet. VMware makes View clients for most tablet devices.

With the proliferation of tablets, Mobile Device Management has developed into its own industry with companies such as MobileIron, AirWatch, and MaaS360 offering the capability to add policy control to enforce security and ensure manageability within a corporate environment.

Getting back to our target profile, the simplest way to serve a Windows laptop is to use a layer two hypervisor. Notice I did not say the *only* way, because a bare metal hypervisor suffers from both hardware and software compatibility problems that introduce a cost to meet the hardware requirements. Consider, for example, if you have standard VPN software that runs on Windows to enable users to connect remotely. A Type 2 hypervisor allows you to combine the virtual desktop and the secure connection to provide a good user experience.

Now that we have looked at the reasoning, let's look at how VMware has approached the notion of offline desktops. In Chapter 2, "VMware View Architecture," we looked at installing the VMware Transfer Server. Now let's take a closer look at the mechanics of what goes on and then what we should do to properly test and enable these features for our users. In addition, let's look at complementary technologies that can provide even more flexibility on how we make use of offline desktops.

The technology that enables the checkout feature is the View Transfer Server. In VMware View 5, the Transfer Server does more than file copies. The Transfer Server provides the following capabilities:

1. The View Transfer Server authorizes and manages the check-in and check-out process in the VMware View.

2. The Transfer Server synchronizes any changes made in the offline virtual desktop to the one stored on the virtual infrastructure in the datacenter. Replication intervals can be configured and are operator controlled.

3. The View Transfer Server distributes the virtual desktop image from the Transfer Server to the client machine.

The Transfer Server can be a virtual machine, but there are a few limitations around the number of transfers that a single server can handle. In addition, VMware supports only the BusLogic or LSI Logic controller, which is NOT the default, as shown in Figure 9.1.

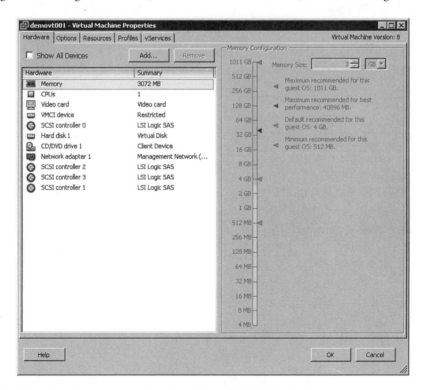

Figure 9.1 The Transfer Server requires the LSI Logic SCSI Controller.

During installation, you need to change the controller from the LSI Logic SAS controller to the appropriate one. You must also ensure you have enough drive space on the Transfer Server to accommodate the images.

The Transfer Server stores the image files locally before they are copied to the client. VMware has tested the Transfer Server using 20 concurrent user check-out sessions over a 1 GB link. Theoretically, the Transfer Server can handle 60 sessions, but it is likely the link would saturate before the Transfer Server becomes the bottleneck. The resource requirements for the Transfer Server are shown in Table 9.1.

Table 9.1 Transfer Server Requirements

Item	Detail
Operating system	64-bit Windows Server 2008 R2
RAM	4GB
Virtual CPU	2
System disk capacity	20 GB
Virtual SCSI adapter type	LSI Logic Parallel (not the default, which is SAS)
Virtual network adapter	E1000 (the default)
1 NIC	1 Gigabit

When you add a Transfer Server to your VMware View environment, the virtual machine is configured with four SCSI controllers and is prevented from doing an automatic VMotion through the application of a manual rule in the DRS cluster. This configuration ensures that any VMotion needs to be started manually.

Although View 5 supported only local mode with VMware Version 7 hardware, this is no longer the case with View 5.1. VMware Version 7 or 8 hardware is supported for local mode desktops (see Figure 9.2).

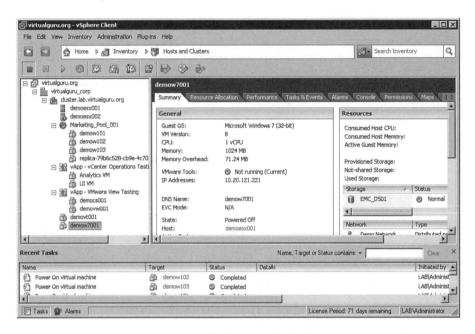

Figure 9.2 Version 7 or 8 is now supported for local mode desktops.

Let's go through the sequence of events that happen under the covers. When you create an image repository (under the View Administrator, View Configuration, Transfer Server Repository), the creation process allows you to specify a local path or file share as shown in Figure 9.3.

Figure 9.3 Transfer Server Repository.

The first folder under the share (in this case demovt001\transfer) is called the ImageRepository. Beneath this folder are two folders called Processing and Published. When you publish a desktop, it kicks off a file copy from the datastore where the linked clone base image is located to the Transfer Server. We covered the steps to add a Transfer Server and storage repository in Chapter 3, "VMware View 5 Implementation." To publish a desktop, follow these steps:

1. Under the View Administrator Console, select **View Configuration**.

2. Select **Servers**, and on the right, select the **Transfer Servers** tab.

3. Under the Section Transfer Server Repository, select the **Contents** tab.

4. Select the View desktop and click **Publish**, as shown in Figure 9.4.

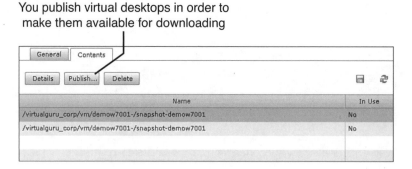

Figure 9.4 Publish desktop.

The Transfer Server does not simply copy the files to the ImageRepository location. It creates a 36-character subdirectory under Processing for the VM and two subfolders called work and transfer. The files are first copied into the subfolder called work under the VM subdirectory beneath Processing (see Figure 9.5).

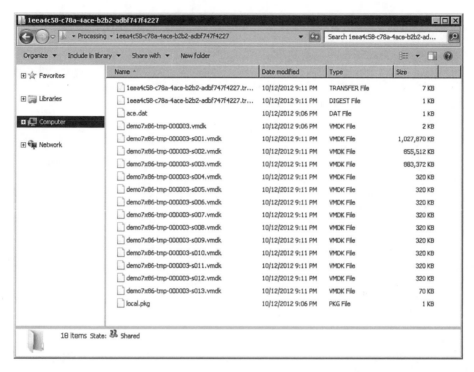

Figure 9.5 The subfolder named work is the place where the files are processed.

Within the work subfolder, the files are processed and transferred to a subfolder called transform, again under Processing and the VM subfolder (see Figure 9.6). Essentially, the files are converted from a single VMDK stored on the datastore to multiple VMDK files, making them easier to transfer.

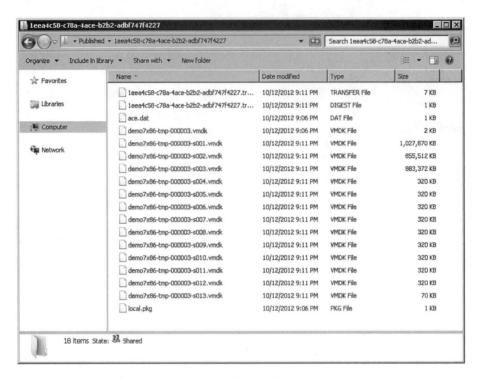

Figure 9.6   After processing, the files are moved to the VM subfolder.

After the files are processed, they are moved to a subfolder of the ImageRepository under Published, and the 36-character VM subfolder and both the work and transform folders are deleted. The VM can now be checked out of the View environment. Processwise, it looks like Figure 9.7.

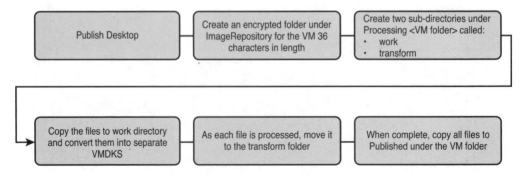

Figure 9.7   Publishing a VM from vCenter.

If you run into problems with the transfer, transform, or anything else related to the process, you can turn to the log files to help you identify what has gone wrong.

On the VMware View Transfer Server, you can select the level of logging that takes place. By default, the Debug and Detailed logging is turned off. You can turn on this additional level of logging using the following steps:

1. Log in to the VMware View Transfer Server.

2. Go to Start, VMware, Set View Connection Server Log Levels.

3. Because Option 3 sets full logging, simply type **3** at the command prompt and press Enter. You see a window like the one in Figure 9.8.

Figure 9.8 Setting the View Connection Server log levels.

All logs are located in c:\ProgramData\VMware\VDM\Logs. The Debug log is particularly useful for determining whether or not you are having trouble with transferring VMs from the datastore to the Transfer Server. If you look at a few sections of the log, you can see the publish progress starting, and much later in the file, you see the transfer process ending and the transform process beginning (see Figure 9.9).

Figure 9.9 Transfer Server debug log.

When the publish process is finished, the desktop is available for users to check out. When a user checks out the desktop, the base disk, the View Composer persistent disk, and the linked clone delta disk are required to ensure the offline desktop matches the one currently running in the VMware View environment.

It is important in planning for local mode desktops to ensure you have allocated sufficient resources (CPU, memory, and local storage) on the laptop or desktop to run the VM. The base disk is copied first from the Transfer Server to the client's local disk. After the base disk is copied from the Transfer Server, the View Composer persistent disk and linked clone delta disk are copied from the datastore. After the files are copied locally, the Composer persistent disk and delta disk are locked from View to ensure no changes can be made while the local mode virtual machine is running on the laptop. The user can now disconnect the laptop and take the virtual machine offline.

The client must be running the local mode client, which installs not just the VMware View client but also a version of VMware Player that allows the virtual machine to run locally. Be aware that the View with Local Mode client takes significantly more space than the View Client without Local Mode, especially when you factor in the virtual machine.

Because the client installs VMware Player, you cannot already be running VMware View Client, VMware Player, VMware Workstation, VMware ACE, or VMware Server. If you are, you need to remove it first. VMware Player gets installed in C:\Program Files\ VMware\VMware View\Client\Local Mode. The virtual desktops that are checked out get downloaded to the user profile under AppData\Local\VMware\VDM\Local Desktops. This behavior is something to keep in mind if, for whatever reason, you are enabling offline mode for users with roaming profiles and considering redirecting the AppData directory within the profile (which is not recommended).

If you begin the download, you see all the files that you would expect to see in a virtual machine, such as the configuration files, snapshot file, and the VMDK files (see Figure 9.10).

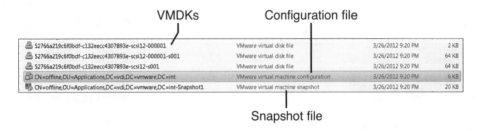

Figure 9.10 Files copied locally.

If you get an error message like that shown in Figure 9.11, don't panic; it just means that you have not published the base image.

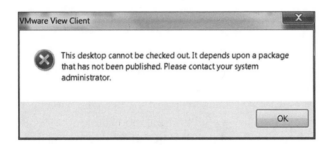

Figure 9.11 This is a common error message.

All you need to do is go back to the VMware View Administrator. Look under View Configuration and Transfer Server Repository; then publish the base template that goes with the offline desktop, as shown in Figure 9.12.

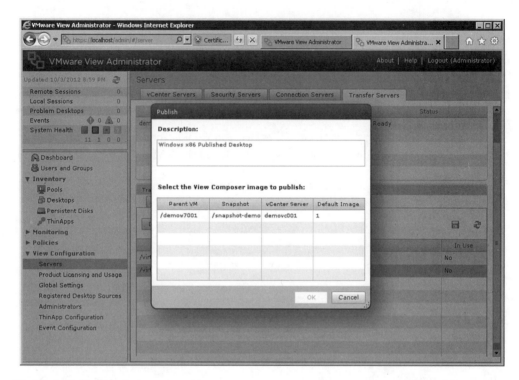

Figure 9.12 Publish the base template.

Best Practices

The three types of user groups to consider when you are planning to implement local mode are users who will primarily run their virtual desktop locally, users who will never run their virtual desktops locally, and a hybrid of the two who will check in and out desktops. It is a good idea to have a pool for local mode desktops because you may need to optimize features such as the size of the VMDK to facilitate an efficient checkout process. The hybrid group is a little trickier to plan for, but because these users are also likely to be the exception and tend to be IT workers who understand technology, you can easily set some operating parameters. An example is ensuring checkouts take place only while a user is onsite. Again, doing so warrants a separate desktop pool because these users likely have very specific requirements.

Two types of pools can be configured for local mode: automated (View Composer) or manual. The primary stipulations are that the desktop is dedicated to a single user, is a virtual desktop and is managed by vCenter. This way, the VM can be locked when taken offline, and any changes can be propagated or synced back to the right desktop within VMware View.

To control who has access to local mode, you need to configure an explicit deny at the global level (the default is to allow). To do this, log in as the VMware View Administrator. Under Policies and Global Policies, set Local Mode Policy to Deny (see Figure 9.13).

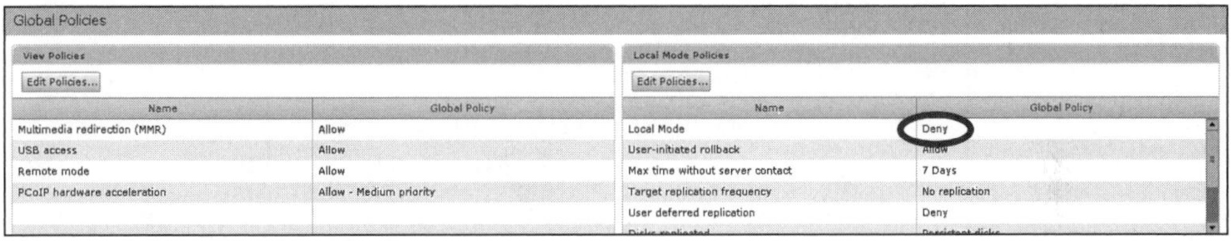

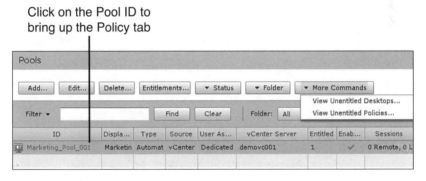

Figure 9.13 Edit the Local Mode Policies.

You can selectively force local mode while denying remote mode and vice versa. To adjust the pool settings to force a local mode, open the VMware View Administrator. Under Inventory, select Pools. Select the ID tab of the Floating desktop pool where you want to adjust the pool policy (see Figure 9.14).

Figure 9.14 Click on the Pool ID.

To set the pool to force local mode access, you simply edit the policy under View Policies and set the Remote Mode to Deny. Under Local Mode Policies, set the Local Mode to Allow (see Figure 9.15). This setting takes precedence over the global setting.

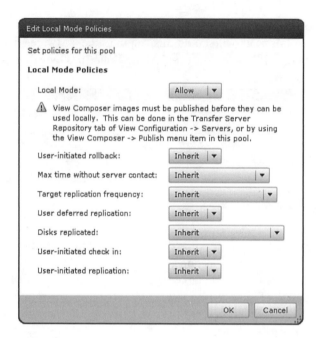

Figure 9.15 Configure the pool policies.

When the user launches the VMware View client, the user is prompted to run the VMware View desktop in local mode, as shown in Figure 9.16.

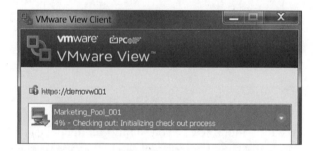

Figure 9.16 The user is prompted to download the virtual desktop.

Of course, if this pool does not use local mode, you set Remote Mode to Allow under View Policies and Local Mode to Deny under Local Mode Policies.

You can set other policies to enable or enforce communication, replication, or rollback of the desktop. They are as follows:

1. **User initiated rollback:** This setting allows the user to delete the local copy, which may have been changed, and download a copy of the original virtual machine. Essentially, this setting rolls back any changes that may have been made locally.

2. **Max time without server contact:** This setting ensures that the local mode desktop communicates with the VMware View Connection Server within a defined number of days (a maximum is specified).

3. **Target replication frequency:** This setting allows you to predefine how often replication occurs, if at all (you can specify no replication). The time can be set in Days, Hours, or Minutes, as shown in Figure 9.17. The benefit to having a short time between synchronization events is to reduce the amount of data that is lost if the physical laptop or desktop fails or has a problem Setting a short amount of time has a larger impact on the network, however, and may not be appropriate in every circumstance. For example, if the user is working remotely, you may want a longer period of time to transpire so that replication is not running constantly; whereas if the user is using a local mode desktop within the office, you may want the updates to occur more frequently because the network connectivity is more predictable. Of course, the longer the time between synchronization events, the larger the amount of data must be transferred.

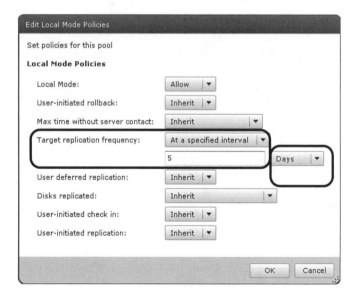

Figure 9.17 Replication frequency can be set in Days, Hours, or Minutes.

4. **User deferred replication:** This setting allows a user to pause a replication that is underway. The default value is Deny. When the value is set to Allow, the deferment period is two hours.

5. **Disks replicated:** This setting affects View Composer–created virtual machines. If you remember, a View Composer virtual desktop is actually made up of a combination of virtual machine hard drives. You can select persistent disks, OS disks, and OS and persistent disks (the default is persistent).

6. **User-initiated check-in:** This setting allows a user to check in the desktop. The default is to allow this activity.

7. **User-initiated replication:** This setting allows the user to selectively replicate the changes made on the local mode desktop to the VMware View stored desktop. The default is Allow.

You need to keep in mind several issues when deploying local mode desktops. Perhaps the most essential issue is that the target desktop needs to have adequate resources to run the virtual machine. You need to ensure the desktop that you enable for local mode can meet the minimum configuration of virtual hardware configured on the virtual machine.

When you deploy the virtual machine, the network connectivity is Nat'd when running locally on the desktop, allowing it to share the network connection. If you are deploying with Virtual Private Network (VPN) software, the host desktop would run the software. If you change the mode to bridge, the VPN software would have to be run within the virtual machine.

The initial check-out that copies the parent image can be quite time consuming, so it is best carried out on the LAN. In addition, the virtual desktop is thick provisioned on the endpoint. This means that if the VM is configured with a 25 GB virtual hard drive it will consume 25 GB on the end-point. It is a good idea to prestage this initial copy to your target desktops because after the initial copy, the synchronization traffic can be quite minimal if tuned properly.

If you are enforcing a policy that requires the virtual desktop to contact the View Server, ensure you have a remote access presence so that the local mode desktop can communicate even when running remotely.

When using Composer desktops, keep your local mode pool separate and do not run operational processes such as a recompose that overwrite the desktops. A recompose requires that the initial download be rerun because you have essentially re-created the desktop.

Several things are not supported in local mode desktops. The following is a list of known limitations:

1. Logging in as the local user is not supported. The user needs to log in to the physical desktop first and then the virtual desktop.

2. A local mode desktop does not have multimonitor support.

3. You cannot entitle ThinApp applications from the VMware View console to local mode desktops.

4. Persona Management is not supported on local mode desktops (requiring you to have separate OUs for offline desktops if you are using Persona).

Summary

Although local mode desktops are typically attributed to an offline mode, they do not have to be. Keep in mind that within your environment, you are likely to use a combination of View desktop configurations and not just a one-size-fits-all approach. Using local mode and pool policies, you can force the View desktop to use resources on the users' physical desktops for normal operations and fall back to your vSphere environment only if they need to. One possible scenario is a user who has a high-end desktop; this user works out of the company's head office but travels occasionally to a second location that provides thin client–equipped hoteling stations. In this case, you may use a local mode desktop while the user is working in the head office location but allow the user to check it in to use a thin client to access the virtual desktop environment in the secondary site.

The flexibility in which View allows you to deliver a virtual desktop makes the user segmentation activity discussed in Chapter 2 all the more important. It is important to really understand the user requirements to be able to configure the appropriate mode of access (either local or delivered over PCoIP) and the right policies, features, and settings. In the next chapter, we discuss how to migrate from older versions of View to ensure you can take advantage of both local mode desktops and many of the new features in VMware View 5.

Chapter 10

Migrating from Older Versions of View

Upgrading to New Versions of View

When you are considering moving between major versions of VMware View, such as 4.6 to 5, it is easier to migrate than it is to upgrade. (Note that major releases are full number releases, such as versions 4–5; whereas minor releases are dot releases, such as 5 to 5.1.) The reason for this is that there are often interdependencies that prevent one version from working with another. For example, because of the changes in the way View Composer deals with persistent and nonpersistent data, you often are not able to carry forward Composer-created VMs from one major version to the next. VMware View 5 is also optimal on a 64-bit operating system (ideally, Windows 2008 R2), although it still runs on Windows 2003 R2 x86, so you might want to reinstall anyway.

If you are in a position to upgrade, you must follow a set process to ensure everything goes smoothly. In addition, VMware publishes migration guides to assist you. You can find the migration guide for VMware View available for download at http://pubs.vmware.com/view-50/topic/com.vmware.ICbase/PDF/view-50-upgrades.pdf.

In this chapter, we look at the prerequisites for upgrading, the process to upgrade, and the potential problems along the way. In addition, if you decide to migrate, this chapter addresses some issues that you must consider.

The prerequisites to upgrading largely depend on vSphere requirements if you are considering "5 on 5," or vSphere 5 on View 5. If you are not, the prerequisites are related to the supported operating system, backward compatibility of the components, and interoperability during the upgrade with your existing version. If you are moving from 4.5 and higher and are running on 64-bit operating systems, you can upgrade in place. If you are moving from an older version such as 4.0.x, you need to reinstall some of the components.

Let's assume you are running VMware View 4.5 and are planning a major upgrade to View 5. If you are upgrading, the sequence of events is as follows:[1]

1. Back up the configuration information on the View Connection Server Instances.

2. On the servers that host vCenter and View Composer, make backups and temporarily disable certain scheduled tasks.

3. Request that users check in any Client with Local Mode desktops.

4. Upgrade View Connection Servers.

5. Upgrade View Transfer Servers.

6. Upgrade your View Composer if you are *not* also migrating to vSphere 5. If you *are* migrating to vSphere, you need to deploy a new vCenter Server and View Composer service.

7. If you have upgraded vSphere versions, upgrade the VM Tools first. After this upgrade is complete, upgrade the View Agent on any of the View desktops' sources (which can be virtual or physical).

8. Re-create the virtual desktop pools using these updated sources.

9. Upgrade the View Composer desktop pools.

10. Upgrade the client-side components.

Be aware that in many cases after the process is initiated, you need to complete it from start to finish. You should therefore run through the process in a nonproduction environment before performing it in a production environment.

If you are upgrading from VMware View 4.0.x, you must complete a few additional steps because many of the features are not yet available in the View 4.0.x platform. The process is as follows:

1. Back up the configuration information on the View Connection Server Instances.

2. On the servers that host vCenter and View Composer, make backups and temporarily disable certain scheduled tasks.

3. Request that users check in any Client with Offline desktops.

4. Install and configure an Event Database.

5. Install View Connection Servers.

---

[1]VMware View Upgrade whitepaper: http://pubs.vmware.com/view-50/topic/com.vmware.ICbase/PDF/view-50-upgrades.pdf

6. Install a View Transfer Server.

7. Deploy a new vCenter Server and View Composer service.

8. If you have upgraded vSphere versions, upgrade the VM Tools first. After this upgrade is complete, upgrade the View Agent on any of the View desktops' sources (which can be virtual or physical).

9. Re-create the virtual desktop pools using these updated sources.

10. Re-create the View Composer desktop pools.

11. Upgrade the client-side components

12. Install Windows 2003 R2 32-bit environment and then install VMware View 4.0.

You can install a Security Server, either physical or virtual, on Windows 2003 server. VMware's best practice is to host a physical Windows Security Server in the DMZ that does not participate in the AD. Having a physical server ensures complete separation, but there is no technical reason it cannot be on an isolated virtual machine. On a Windows 2003 server, however, you can only proxy RDP. If you need to proxy PCoIP securely, the underlying operating system must by Windows Server 2008 R2. Note that this requirement does not extend to the Connection Server, so you can combine a 2008 secure server with a 2003 Connection Server without losing the capability to proxy PCoIP. If you have built in some load balancing between Security Servers to make sure your remote access point is highly available, you need to ensure that all the underlying Security Server operating systems are the same.

The license key between VMware View 4.0 and View 5.0 has changed format so that the license key is now made up of 25 characters.

To install View 5, you need an account that is both an administrator on the Connection Server and an administrator on the vCenter Server.

View 5 must be combined with

- vSphere 4.0 Update 3 or later

- vSphere 4.1 Update 1 or later

- vSphere 5.0 or later (Note: ensure you check vSphere compatibility if you are migrating directly to View 5.1)

Upgrading Example

To make this upgrade process clear, let's use a real-world example, plan it out from start to finish, and take all the necessary steps to complete the upgrade successfully. We do a major upgrade from 4.X to 5.X versus a minor upgrade from 5.0 to 5.1, for example. Let's start with a fictitious company called ABC. ABC has been running VMware View for some time but has not had the opportunity to upgrade until recently. The company is currently running VMware View 4.0.2, which is running on vSphere 4 managed by VMware vCenter 4. ABC has been testing VMware View 5 for some time and is now ready to upgrade from one to the other.

ABC has several decisions to make at this point to be able to deploy VMware View 5. The first is whether it will upgrade the virtual infrastructure as part of the upgrade. Equally as important because this environment services a large population of VDI users is what it can carry over from the current environment to the new environment to avoid reconfiguring their desktop pools.

The folks who manage the desktop environment follow best practices and have a standard build process for both physical and virtual desktops. The fundamental differences between the images are largely tuning related versus maintaining separate images for physical and virtual desktops within the organization.

The standard desktop at the moment is Windows XP, although efforts are underway to deliver a standard Windows 7 image; however, this is happening outside the migration of the VMware View environment. The requirement within VMware View 5 is to run the current image Windows XP and then, after the standard image has been developed, to cut over to Windows 7. All planning should assume that the desktop image will not change over the course of the View migration.

The current environment makes use of View Composer as will the new VMware View 5 environment. The environment is not separated from the current server environment because it was built organically out of spare capacity. This time around, the environment will be separated, but the vSphere version will be consistent between both the VMware View environment and the server virtualization environment. Because the team managing the server virtualization environment is not yet ready to go to vSphere 5, the environment will be built to a standard of vSphere 4.1 update 2.

Currently, the entire environment is managed by a single vCenter Server. Because offline or local mode desktops were experimental in this release 4.02 of VMware View, ABC has a small percentage of test users currently running it but wants to make better use of it in VMware View 5.

The server team is in the process of upgrading to Windows 2008 x64 R2, but for now Windows 2003 is the current standard.

Both the server and virtual desktop environment use the same enterprise SAN environment. When VMware View 5 is deployed, an additional business unit will be added consisting of 300 users; this addition should be factored into the migration planning. You should also review the additional IOPS that the new View desktops will generate and ensure you have made any adjustments to hardware and storage.

You must consider several issues beyond the steps required to implement the upgrade. The first is what factors should be considered in the migration? Often, many of the early VDI environments were built with only a small understanding of how they impact the supporting infrastructure. For example, in this scenario the virtual server environment was extended to also deploy virtual desktops. The decision was made when the initial pilot user group was 50 users. As the environment grew, this original design decision was never reviewed.

The back-end infrastructure for the environment is an enterprise SAN that is used by the entire organization. It is quite typical that performance in the first year of a VMware View environment is robust. Over several years, as the overall utilization and IOPS increase, SAN performance issues start to appear. The point of looking at storage as part of any migration is not to just upgrade the environment but also to address any operational deficiencies that have been noted in the premigration environment. Many will be addressed directly by VMware View 5 because of the inclusion of Persona Management, for example. Others, however, require you to take a critical look at the environment and assumptions that were made when the solution was originally deployed. One good example is how PCoIP is treated on the network. In earlier environments, it was not very common to classify the PCoIP network stream so that it is treated with priority from a networking perspective as is done with VoIP traffic. Today, in any large environment, it is considered a best practice to apply QoS to ensure PCoIP is differentiated from other network traffic streams.

Getting back to the scenario, the team has looked at several options to provide consistent performance, including

- Buying dedicated storage for the new VMware View environment.

- Utilizing virtual storage proxies to provide high I/O assurances on the existing SAN environment. Virtual storage proxies are virtual appliances that essentially allow you to build a storage appliance from physical ESXi host memory (products such as the Atlantic Computing ILIO; http://atlantiscomputing.com/). The virtual appliance allows quick I/O performance because it uses RAM versus controllers and drives. It offloads some of the performance problems by serializing and deduping the writes. VDI environments are quite notorious for high random read/write requests.

- Taking advantage of local SSD drives after the migration to vSphere 5 takes place.

As part of the migration, the team has decided to use new dedicated SAN storage because the environment has historically scaled faster and required a more demanding workload. Team members are also looking to leverage VMware View more aggressively because the company is planning several acquisitions in which View will become strategic in delivering the corporate desktop quickly and securely.

The environment is accessed remotely and includes two Security Servers deployed in the DMZ. They need to be upgraded as part of the migration.

Because the VMware View 5 environment will service an additional 300 users, some additional hardware will be purchased. The team has decided to upgrade what can be upgraded and newly install any component that cannot be safely upgraded

To begin the process and prior to upgrading any of the components, you should take a snapshot of each server in the environment before beginning if they are virtual machines. Doing so ensures that if you run into any problems, you have a fallback point. The first step after you take a snapshot of the servers is to back up the configuration in the View Connection Servers. You should ensure that you have arranged a maintenance window because you need to ensure that no activity is taking place on the server.

To ensure you have this window, you disable provisioning in each pool and disable each desktop pool, as shown in Figure 10.1.

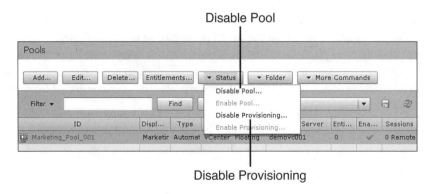

Figure 10.1 Disable a desktop pool.

Each desktop pool should now appear as Disabled, as shown in Figure 10.2.

Figure 10.2 Verify the pool is disabled.

A utility named vdmexport is provided to back up a View Connection Server. You can back up Windows Active Directory Lightweight Directory Service (AD LDS) using a utility included within the VMware View Server. You also can use this backup to restore settings in the new environment as needed. This utility is stored in a variety of locations depending on what version you are running. On View 4 or 5 servers, it is located at C:\ Program Files\VMware\VMware View\Server\tools\bin\vdmexport.exe.

Running the tool dumps all the data, so to save it to a file, simply redirect the output, as shown in Figure 10.3:

```
vdmexport.exe > ldmconfig.ldf
```

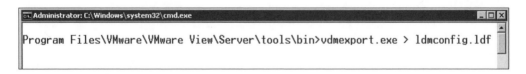

Figure 10.3 Using vdmexport.

If you review this file, you can see that the details of each group you have created are exported to the ldmconfig.ldf file, as shown in Figure 10.4.

```
replace: description
description: GROUP=vdi_Marketing_Users_001
description: DOMAIN=virtualguru.org
description: EMAIL=null
description: DISPLAYNAME=virtualguru.org\vdi_Marketing_Users_001
description: GIVENNAME=null
description: CN=vdi_Marketing_Users_001
description: SN=null
```

Figure 10.4 Contents of ldmconfig.ldf.

If you intend to install VMware View on to the same server, you do not have to reimport this information because it will be retained during the installation. If you are creating a new Connection Server, you need to import the information back to the new Connection Server. After you dump the information, you can keep the pool disabled if you are upgrading the View server, or you can re-enable the pool if you are planning a side-by-side deployment of new View Servers running alongside the existing servers. You should not, however, re-enable the provisioning because View Composer is much more compatibility sensitive than the Connection Servers. If you are using a lot of dynamic provisioning, you should proceed through the entire upgrade so that the View Agent is upgraded to ensure compatibility with View Composer 3.0, which is the version in View 5.1.

The next step is to disable the running Composer service on the vCenter server and then back up the database. One point to note if you are staggering these steps: you require the users to be logged off to complete the AD LDS backup. To stop the Composer service and back up the database, you can allow the users to be logged on (provided you do not have any dynamic provisioning set) if the virtual desktops are already deployed, as shown in Figure 10.5.

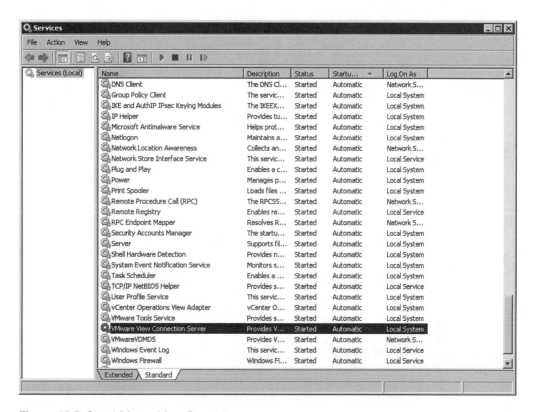

Figure 10.5 Stop VMware View Composer.

The next step in this scenario is to ensure that the entire vSphere infrastructure is running vSphere 4.1 Update 2. Because vSphere Update Manager was covered in Chapter 7, we do not cover it again in this chapter. Update Manager is the utility within vCenter that allows you to upgrade your virtual infrastructure components.

After this upgrade is done, you can start the upgrade process. In this case, we decided to separate the vCenter Server for the View environment, which also should simplify the license compliance. If you recall from earlier chapters, a separate licensing model applies to virtual desktop environments, so keeping separate vCenters ensures a more straight-forward approach when managing license. Again, we will adhere to the company standard and install vCenter 4.1 Update 2 and reinstall the View Composer piece.

The current environment runs the View Composer piece on a local database. Because you will be migrating this piece to the new vCenter Server, you should do a full backup of the database so that you can import it to the new vCenter Server. You can upgrade the database only if the schema does not change. The schema changed from View Composer

1.0 (included in VMware View 3.0), so a direct update is not supported. In this example we are upgrading from View 4.0.x, which requires no schema changes.

It is a good idea to verify the integrity of the database and then back it up before beginning your migration. To verify the integrity of the database, you can run CHECKDB to check the logical and physical integrity of any object specified in the database. To perform an integrity check of the vCenter database, follow these steps:

1. Open Microsoft SQL Server Management Studio and connect to your SQL Server instance.

2. Select the New Query button from the File menu.

3. From the drop-down list, select your vCenter database. In this example, in Figure 10.6, we selected VIM_SQLEXP. (Note that you should execute this tool against all the vSphere and View databases.)

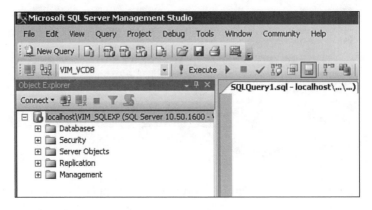

Figure 10.6 Select your vCenter database.

4. In the SQLQuery window on the right, type

   dbcc CHECKDB

5. Click the **Execute** button, and in the Results pane, ensure that the database reports no errors.

We covered backing up the databases in previous chapters, but it is quite easy to do. Just log in to your full or express SQL Management Studio console and right-click the database. Under Tasks, select Back Up, as shown in Figure 10.7.

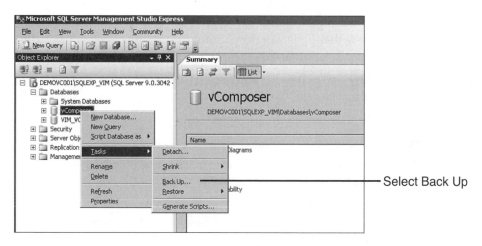

Figure 10.7 Back up your Composer Database.

On the next window, select the drop-down and ensure your Composer database is selected and the backup type is Full (see Figure 10.8). Also note the default location if you have not changed it.

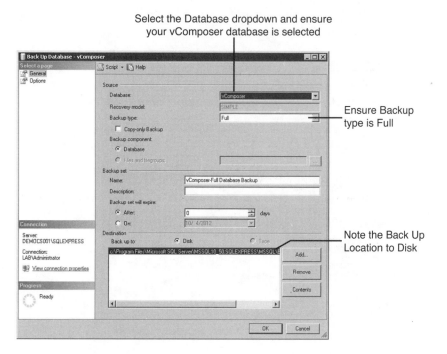

Figure 10.8 Perform a full backup.

Now that you have a backup of the database, you need to install the new vCenter 4.1 environment in keeping with the company's current standard. Because we already covered the installation of vCenter 5, let's touch on the installation of vCenter 4.1 briefly.

1. Launch the vCenter Server Installer and select vCenter Server from the list of VMware Product Installers.

2. Click **Next** on the welcome screen.

3. Agree to the license agreement and click **Next.**

4. On the Customer Information screen, enter a User Name, Organization, and the License Key; then click **Next.**

5. On the Database Options screen, select either **Install a Microsoft SQL Server 2005 Express Instance** or **Use an Existing Supported Database and Create the DSN Information**; then click **Next.**

6. On the vCenter Server Service, select **Use a SYSTEM Account or Domain Account** and click **Next.**

7. Accept the destination folder and click **Next.**

8. Because this is the second vCenter Server on the Linked Mode Options screen, shown in Figure 10.9, select **Join a VMware vCenter Server Group Using Linked Mode to Share Information** versus **Create a Standalone VMware vCenter Server Instance**; then click **Next.**

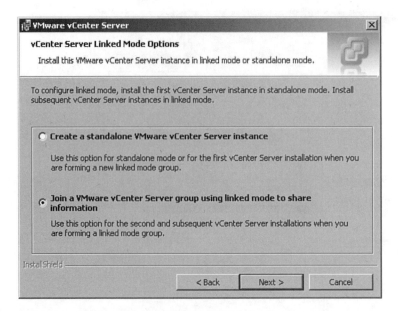

Figure 10.9 Link this vCenter to an existing vCenter Server.

9. On the Connect to a vCenter Server Instance (linked mode), specify the Fully Qualified Domain Name (FQDN), accept the default AD LDS Port 389, and click **Next.**

10. On the Configure Ports options, accept the defaults and click **Next.**

11. Click **Install** on the Ready to Install the Program screen.

12. Click **Finish** when completed.

To install the vSphere Client, launch the VMware vCenter Installer and follow these steps:

1. Select the vSphere Client from the list of VMware Product Installers.

2. Choose the Setup Language and click **OK.**

3. Click **Next** on the welcome screen.

4. Select the radio button **I Agree to the Terms in the License Agreement** and click **Next.**

5. On the Customer Information screen, type your User Name and Organization and click **Next.**

6. Accept the defaults on the Custom Setup screen (Install vSphere Host Update Utility 4.0 is deselected) and click **Next.**

7. Accept the Defaults for the Destination Folder and click **Next.**

8. Click **Install** to begin the installation.

When your new vCenter Server is installed, you should restore the Composer database from the previous vCenter server to this server. To restore a database, you launch the Microsoft SQL Management Studio or Studio Express, right-click the Databases folder, and select **Restore Database,** as shown in Figure 10.10.

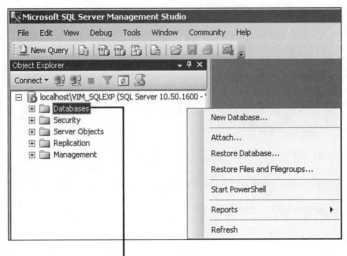

Right Click Databases and
select Restore Database...

Figure 10.10 Restoring the database.

On the next screen under the Source for Restore, select the From Device radio button. Select the Browse (...) button, and on the next screen, add the location where the backup from the original vCenter was stored. Select Restore to restore the database, and then in the To Database field, use the drop-down to specify the right name (in the case of this example, View Composer), as shown in Figure 10.11.

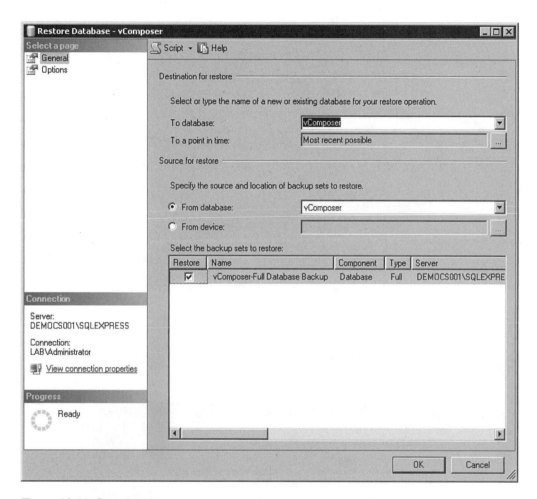

Figure 10.11 Complete the restore.

Ensure the restore completes successfully. Now that the database is restored, you can install the upgraded View Composer service on this vCenter Server. The installation of View Composer is the standard installation method that we covered in Chapter 3. When you create the System Data Sources, you ensure they point to the new location of the recently restored Composer database, as shown in Figure 10.12.

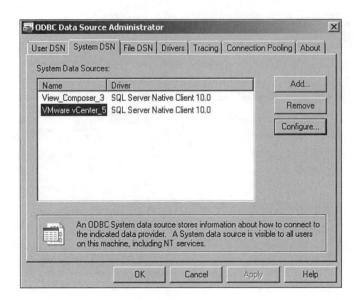

Figure 10.12 Create the data source.

After you create the System Data Source, the installation continues normally, as shown in Figure 10.13.

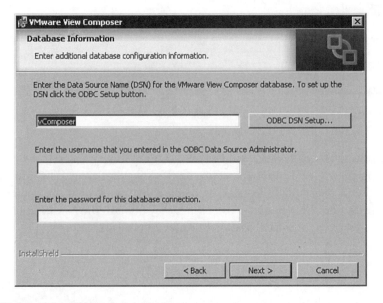

Figure 10.13 Select the DSN and click Next.

After installing vCenter and migrating the Composer service, you are ready to upgrade the VMware View Servers. If you are upgrading the existing VMware View Servers, you can simply install VMware View 5 onto the existing Windows 2003 VMware View 4 servers, and the configuration information is maintained. If you are installing on separate servers, you need to reimport the configuration.

In this case, you have both a Primary and a Replica VMware View 4 Server, which requires a slightly different approach than upgrading a single server. In the case of multiple VMware View Servers, you need to disable the VMware View Connection Service on all View Connection Servers but keep the VMware VDMDS service running to ensure the Connection Servers are not attempting to sync and cause errors (see Figure 10.14).

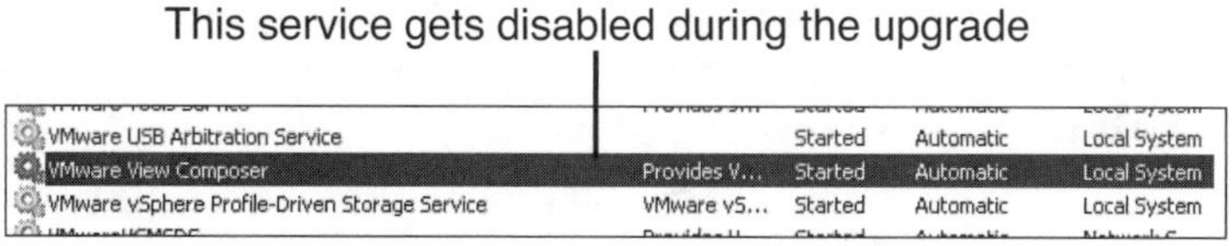

This service gets disabled during the upgrade

Figure 10.14 Disable the VMware View Connection Server service.

The VMware VDMDS service is needed to upgrade the AD LDS database. After the upgrade, the service ensures that the changes are reflected on each VMware View Connection Server in the environment to prevent corruption of the AD LDS database. You can start the upgrade on any server in the VMware View Farm, provided that the service is disabled on all the View servers before you start.

Let's go through the first example because there are some minor differences with the installation:

1. Launch the VMware View 5 Installer.
2. Click **Next** on the welcome screen.
3. On the End User Patent Agreement, click **Next**.
4. Accept the license agreement and click **Next**.
5. Because this server is a Windows 2003 server, you receive the warning shown in Figure 10.15 because this is a Connection Server, not a secure server. Click **OK**.

VMware View Connection Server

⚠ PCoIP Gateway functionality is not supported for this operating system. Please upgrade to Windows Server 2008 R2 to get this functionality.

OK

Figure 10.15 PCoIP is not supported on a Windows 2003 Secure Server.

6. Click **Install** to begin the installation. (Note: You do not have to specify the type of server as part of the upgrade.)

7. Click **Finish** when the installation is completed.

8. Verify that the VMware View Connection service restarts.

Although VMware View 5 will install on Windows 2003, the minimum browser version required to connect to the View Administrator Console is Internet Explorer 7 or higher. In addition, Adobe Flash 10.0 or higher is required. Either connect to the VMware View console remotely from a supported browser, or update the browser on the server and add the required version of Flash.

Start with one server at a time, and as the VMware View 5 installation completes, the VMware View Connection Server service restarts. You need to complete this sequence of events on each VMware View Server.

Because the current version of VMware View did not require an Events database, you need to create one for the VMware View Server, as shown in Figure 10.16. The Events database is very important in assisting in troubleshooting and diagnostics in a VMware View environment.

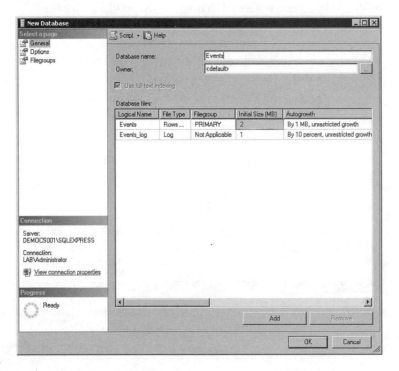

Figure 10.16 Create an Events database.

Because VMware View 5 is installed on the same server, you will notice that all the pool information from the VMware View 4 environment is available under the upgraded VMware View Administrator console (see Figure 10.17).

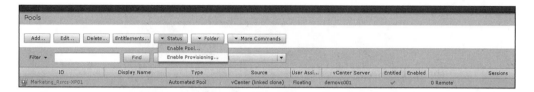

Figure 10.17 Pool information is available.

To ensure a seamless transition from the existing vCenter Server to the new vCenter Server, simply add the new vCenter Server to the configuration of the VMware View 5 Connection Server, as shown in Figure 10.18. Because you have already migrated the View Composer, you also can enable the View Composer on the second vCenter Server, as shown in Figure 10.18.

Edit vCenter Server

View Composer Settings

○ Do not use View Composer

⦿ View Composer co-installed with vCenter Server

    Choose this if View Composer is installed on the same server as vCenter

    Port: 18443

○ Standalone View Composer Server

    Choose this if View Composer is installed on a separate server from vCenter

    Server address:

    User name:

    Password:

    Port: 18443

        OK   Cancel

Figure 10.18 Enable View Composer.

At this point, it is a good idea to verify whether the client connections can still talk to the existing pools that have been migrated using the same client from VMware View 4. When you perform a simple test, you can see that the older versions of the clients can still connect to the pools of desktops, as shown in Figure 10.19. To facilitate the test, you should restart the View Composer service on the original vCenter Server and re-enable the pools from the new VMware View Administrator console. After everything is moved over, you can decommission View Composer on the original vCenter Server in favor of the latest version running on the new vCenter Server.

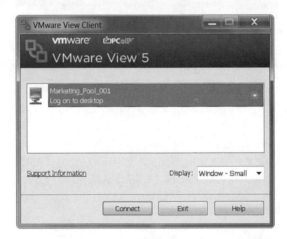

Figure 10.19 Check to see whether you can connect to your View desktops.

You can talk to the pools because the VMware View 5 Connection Server is backward compatible with both the VMware View Client and View Agent from 4.0.x all the way forward to 5. If you look at the pools, you can see that although the desktops are available, the Agent Version is listed as Unknown (see Figure 10.20). You should upgrade the clients and agents on the master templates as part of the cleanup post-migration. Keep in mind that the View Agent is more sensitive to compatibility with View Composer. View Composer 2.7, which is included in VMware View 5, supports compatibility only with View 4.5 and 4.6.

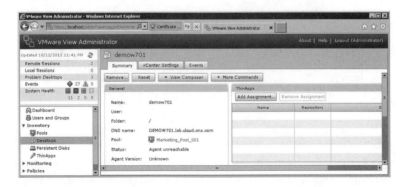

Figure 10.20 Agents are listed as unknown.

In this scenario, we wanted to keep the original templates standard across the vCenter Servers to ensure consistency while the desktop team developed a Windows 7 image. There are a few different ways to get the templates into the new View vCenter Server (keep in mind that a vCenter Server is a logical boundary on moving objects in the virtualization environment). The easiest way is to simply export the original templates and import into the new environment. The process to do so is as follows:

1. Open of the vSphere client and connect to vCenter (if you use the linked mode console, you can do this from one place because you have access to both vCenters).

2. Select the template and then select **File, Export,** and **Export OVF Template.**

3. Provide the name of the OVF template and the directory for the export; then select **Optimized for Physical Media (OVA)**, as shown in Figure 10.21. The process may take some time.

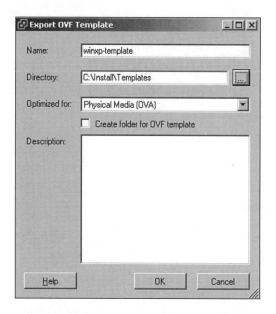

Figure 10.21 Export templates as OVFs.

To import the template, simply reverse the process:

1. Open the vSphere client and connect to vCenter.

2. Select **Deploy OVF Template** and browse to the exported location. Select the template OVA file, as shown in Figure 10.22, and click **Next.**

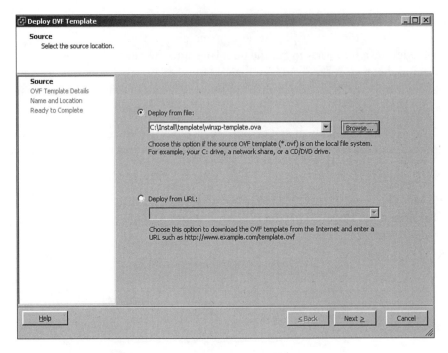

Figure 10.22 Import the OVF.

3. Click **Next.**

4. Specify the name and location within vCenter for the new template.

5. Select the host/cluster.

6. Select the resource pool.

7. Review your settings and click **Finish** to start the import.

Before creating a snapshot, ensure that you have updated the VMware View agent in the template. When you are done, ensure the VM is powered off and take a snapshot so that you can build new VMware View Composer desktops from the template.

At this point, if you have additional VMware View Servers, you also should upgrade them. The upgrade restarts the VMware View Connection Service. After the upgrade, you should log in and ensure that the configuration looks okay in comparison to the first upgraded server.

You have to upgrade the Security Servers next. If you take a look under the server configuration of the VMware View Administrator console, you can see that the View 4.0.x Security Servers come up as version unknown (see Figure 10.23).

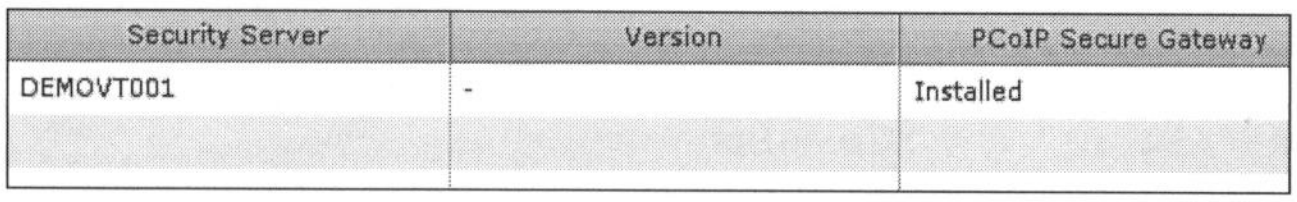

Security Server	Version	PCoIP Secure Gateway
DEMOVT001	-	Installed

Figure 10.23 The Security Server version is not recognized.

Upgrading your Security Servers is similar to upgrading the Connection Servers, except you are prompted to specify the associated Connection Server (Security Servers are linked to a specific Connection Server) and a password to form the connection. The password is referred to as the *pairing password*. In View 4, you do not have to provide a pairing password, but it is mandatory in View 5. You can configure the password ahead of time by opening the View Administrator Console under View Configuration, Servers. Then select the View Connection Server, go to More Commands, and specify the Security Server Pairing Password. In the dialog box that comes up, shown in Figure 10.24, input the pairing password, confirm it, and click **OK**.

Specify Security Server Pairing Password

This password is a one-time password that allows a security server to be paired with this connection server. It is invalidated when any authentication attempt is made for pairing.

This password will also be invalidated based on the password timeout value below.

⚠ This View environment is configured to enable IPsec for communication between the DEMOVW001 View Connection Server and the security server. IPsec requires the Windows Firewall to be turned on for the active profile used for pairing the Connection Server to the Security Server.

Please ensure the Windows Firewall for the active profile on the DEMOVW001 Connection Server is turned on before continuing. You can turn the Windows Firewall on for the active profile from "Windows Firewall with Advanced Security" under "Administrative Tools".

Pairing password: ********

Confirm password: ********

Password timeout: 30   Minutes ▼

OK   Cancel

Figure 10.24 Specify the pairing password.

The complete process to upgrade the Security Servers is as follows:

1. Launch the VMware View 5 Installer.

2. Click **Next** on the welcome screen.

3. On the end user patent agreement, click **Next.**

4. Accept the license agreement and click **Next.**

5. Because this server is a Windows 2003 server, you receive the warning "PCoIP Gateway functionality is not supported for this operating system. Please upgrade to Windows Server 2008 R2 to get this functionality" because this is a Connection Server, not a Security Server. Click **OK.**

6. You are asked to specify the View Connection Server this Security Server will be paired with (see Figure 10.25). Input the Fully Qualified Domain Name and click **Next.**

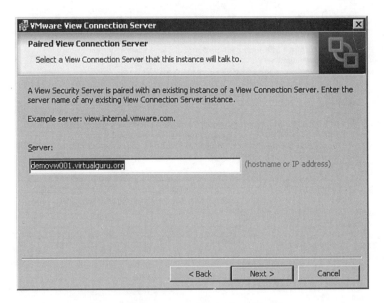

Figure 10.25 Connect the Security Server to the Connection Server.

7. You are asked to enter the pairing password you specified (see Figure 10.26). Input the password and click **Next.**

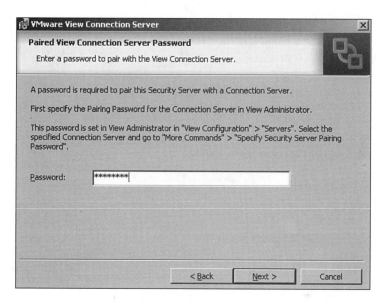

Figure 10.26 Provide the pairing password.

8. Security Servers require an external URL to which they respond to requests. You are prompted to input the external URL information (see Figure 10.27). This external URL is the one that the users connect to when accessing the View environment remotely. Input the URL and click **Next**. Because the Security Servers are Windows 2003 Server, the option to proxy PCoIP is dimmed, as it requires Windows Server 2008.

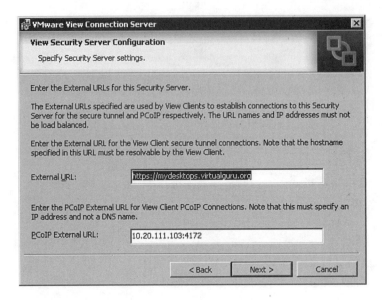

Figure 10.27 Provide the external URL.

9. Click **Install** to begin the installation. (Note: You do not have to specify the type of server as part of the upgrade.)

10. Click **Finish** after the installation is complete.

11. Verify that the Security Server shows up under the Security Server configuration paired with the right server and with the right version of software (see Figure 10.28).

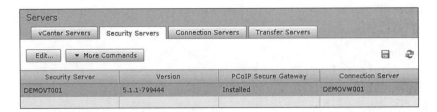

Figure 10.28 Security Server now shows version information.

If you intend to add local mode clients, you should add Transfer Servers. Because Transfer Servers are new in this example, you can follow the same process as you would to initially install them.

In most cases, it is more typical to do a new installation of VMware View 5.1 and then migrate because this approach reduces the likelihood of problems and potential issues down the road. Documentation for migrating to View 5.1 is available from VMware at http://pubs.vmware.com/view-51/index.jsp. It is possible, however, for an in-place upgrade to be part of a larger migration plan. As with this example, if you are going to View 5 and are somewhat limited due to other factors within your organization, it may make sense to upgrade in-place while you build out a new cluster. Additional resources are available on VMware's site regarding upgrades. If you are migrating from older versions, you should definitely review the documentation online.

Summary

In this chapter, we took a long look at doing a major version upgrade from 4 to 5. We went through the steps to ensure that you have a recovery or backout point if a problem should occur. As with any upgrade, it is important to be comfortable with the process before applying it to your production environment. Although it is generally better to build a clean environment, in some situations you might want to upgrade. For example, if you are several major versions behind in your production environment and running on an older version of vSphere, you may upgrade to take advantage of better performance of the PCoIP protocol before implementing all the features. Another reason you may upgrade is that often new capabilities require additional hardware and may require making architecture adjustments that can be more time-consuming than performing a straight upgrade.

Making minor upgrades should be an ongoing operational activity and is typically fairly straightforward. That being said, you should always review the upgrade procedures provided by VMware so that you completely understand the process before moving forward. Often due to the complexity of virtual desktop environments, there is a reluctance to keep up with version upgrades. Because with each new release performance gets better and more issues are resolved, keeping current is an operational requirement.

In a VMware View environment you should ensure you are keeping current with version updates but it is important to await a certain amount of time (i.e., 3 months) to elapse before applying the latest version. This way, VMware can address any minor fixes before you make changes in your environment. In addition, you should always evaluate the new capabilities of major revisions so you understand what value they bring and how they are applied. One benefit in maintaining current versions of View in your environment is that upgrading at regular intervals ensures that the people supporting the environment maintain and grow their expertise. A well-supported environment generally translates to higher end-user satisfaction and more stability, and ensures your company is getting the most out of the technology.

Chapter 11

High Availability Considerations

Making Your View Environment Resilient

You need to consider making a number of points within a VMware View architecture redundant or highly available. High availability (HA) is relevant within a single site or across multiple sites if you are deploying active VMware View environments across multiple datacenters. You can use a number of technologies to ensure HA in addition to native features of vSphere 5. In this chapter, we look at each point in the architecture that you need to consider making highly available, what native features can be used, what are some low-cost alternatives, and when you should consider dedicated appliances or technology.

Architecting an HA solution is typically very customized toward the environment because a great deal depends on the combination of products that have been incorporated into the environment and what native capabilities they have. For example, if a customer is using storage replication between sites, this may change your architecture depending on what capabilities the storage area network (SAN) has. Because it is not possible to cover every combination of changes that can be made, we instead focus on what features are readily available in the virtualization and OS layers, staying away from the hardware.

Keeping this principle in mind, we discuss Microsoft Clustering in detail. I know that the comfort level with Microsoft Clustering varies, and integrating it into an HA solution may be controversial in some environments in which the technology has historically not performed well. With Windows 2008 R2, clustering has improved immensely, and virtualization in general makes clustering more dependable. One of the challenges in clustering has been the difficulty in keeping the nodes in the cluster as close in configuration as possible. Virtualization in providing consistent hardware configurations has simplified this issue dramatically. In many cases, it is not necessarily the cluster technology that is problematic but the difference in configuration among nodes leading to problems with the cluster.

Using Windows servers is not the only way to provide file services. You can provide highly available file services using network-attached storage (NAS) appliances. Either approach is fairly common in the industry. NAS appliances are purpose-built storage appliances, so they offer better performance and have built-in high availability and recovery services through replication and snapshots. If you are using NAS appliances, then you may have no need for Windows Clustering. The configurations in this chapter used to build highly available Windows file servers can also be applied to building Windows SQL clusters in VMware View environments.

It is difficult to provide a one-size-fits-all approach in discussing HA because it tends to be highly customized depending on the collection of technologies available in the environment. To provide an example, we use a scenario that requires several layers of high availability to ensure at least some of the items will be relevant to your design.

Along with clustering, we address replication because both clustering and replication are essential for site and site-to-site failover. Of course, many third-party solutions can be added into an HA design, but because it is unfeasible to cover all of them, we stick to the ones that are readily available.

With HA, there is also a balance between complexity and availability that you need to consider. Many of these technologies introduce a level of complexity that, if not properly implemented, actually provides more instability, not less. In your own environment, you have to judge whether enough familiarity exists to properly implement these solutions to ensure they are stable and not be the source of problems.

In a VMware View environment, there is both dynamic and static data; for example, the folders for ThinApp applications and offline virtual desktops are more static in nature, whereas the directories for View Persona are more dynamic. With dynamic folders and directories, there are limitations in what can be done without causing problems. Of course, like everything else, there are purpose-built products that address making user profiles highly available within and across sites. Because they vary, we talk about them generally but do not cover them in great detail.

In addition to HA as it pertains to the VMware View environments, a number of HA features are built into vSphere 5, from multipathing connectivity to the SAN to VM-specific technologies such as VMware Fault Tolerance (FT) that runs both VMs in lock step so that if a failure occurs, the service is not interrupted.

Let's start with the connectivity from the ESXi host to the storage and then go through the HA features of the vSphere platform. Finally, let's deal with redundancy of the View servers and back-end components.

Why are we starting with ensuring the vSphere environment is configured properly? Well, when you consider high availability, any discussion starts with careful consideration of all your single points of failure. Because the vSphere platform is an intelligent cluster that has the capability to react at many different levels to a failure, you need to construct the cluster properly. When it is constructed properly within a site, you can look at site-to-site to provide both high availability and failover capacity. We discuss disaster recovery briefly, but our primary focus is around site availability.

There is also a point to make about redundant physical switches in connecting your vSphere 5 environments. Essentially, when it comes to the virtual infrastructure on which you are deploying your VDI environment, you should consider the following:

- The configuration of network cards and host bus adapters

- The servers themselves (i.e., the number of power supplies and network cards)

- Redundant physical switches

- The deployment and configuration of your SAN

When you are considering your physical servers, it is a best practice to use identical servers that have redundant power, fault-tolerant or failure-resistant memory, and the proper monitoring solution in place. Again, you are looking to remove any points of failure. Using identical server hardware configuration simplifies deployment (especially if you incorporate features such as Auto Deploy and Configuration Manager). It also ensures that you can handle host failures with minimal disruption to service and performance.

In a virtual desktop environment, you also should avoid rules that segregate or restrict the ability of the virtual machine to move around the environment. For example, setting anti-affinity rules, while appropriate for the VMware View Connection Servers, should not be used on the virtual desktop instances to ensure Distributed Resource Scheduler (DRS) and High Availability can react to resource contention and host failures in the environment.

Also, it is important to consider the capacity of the cluster from an HA design and capacity perspective. For example, if you want to allow for a failure of 50% of your nodes, you should target about 50% utilization in operation. The larger the cluster, the more flexibility you have in reducing your overall costs. Fundamentally, the reason is that the more nodes you have in your cluster, the less likely that you will lose 50% within a single site. If your VMware View environment is essentially a 2-node cluster, you may have each running at 50% utilization, or half of the View desktops, so if a host failure occurs, you can run 100% of the load on a single node (I am not advocating for 2-node clusters, just explaining a point). If you have a 10-node cluster, the failure of 5 nodes would be very unlikely, so you can adjust the design to run at a much higher utilization because a single-node failure can be evenly absorbed across the remaining 9 nodes in the cluster.

Because VMware vCenter Server takes on new importance in a VMware View environment, it is important that you look at ensuring it is highly available as well. VMware has a solution called vCenter Server Heartbeat, which we discuss shortly, but the other possibility is to use vSphere FT if your vCenter is a single vCPU virtual machine.

If your vSphere View environment makes use of Auto Deploy, there are a few rules that you should consider when evaluating failure risk. It is recommended that you ensure that both vCenter and Auto Deploy are highly available because your hosts depend on them to boot properly. In addition, VMware recommends that vCenter does not manage the host on which it is deployed. For example, you can have the vCenter Server that manages your View environment run on your virtual server cluster while the View desktops run in a separate cluster. If your vCenter is a virtual machine, you should set the restart priority so that it is one of the first VMs to boot. This setting is extremely important and should not be overlooked because it is not a default setting. You can configure it using the following process:

1. Connect to vCenter using the vSphere Client.

2. Browse from Home to Inventory to Hosts and Clusters.

3. Select your virtual cluster, right-click, and select **Edit Settings**.

4. Under vSphere HA, select **Virtual Machine Options**.

5. Select your vCenter Server, and from the drop-down, set the VM restart priority to **High** (see Figure 11.1). Then click **OK**.

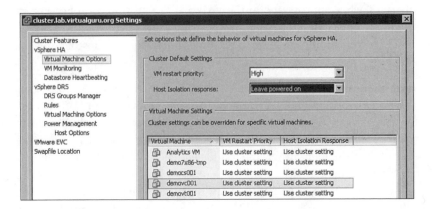

Figure 11.1 Make sure the restart priority is set on your vCenter VM.

In addition, it is also important to run your vCenter Server on at least two hosts that are not using Auto Deploy to ensure the service is always available. When designing the connectivity of your ESXi host, you should make sure that you are using redundant network adapters connected to different physical switches. By doing so, you ensure that in the event a single, physical network interface card (NIC) fails, you do not lose connectivity for either the virtual machines or management services. If you are using the iSCSI software adapter, there is a very specific method for ensuring your configuration is fault tolerant.

Storage Heartbeats

In vSphere 5.0, HA has been redesigned so that it is no longer based on primary and secondary hosts. HA now uses a master/slave relationship between the nodes in the cluster. In normal operations, one host is the master with all others acting as slaves. If the master fails, an election occurs to promote a new master.

A new feature of vSphere 5 is storage heartbeats, which function similarly to a quorum in standard cluster designs. Essentially, storage heartbeats enable the vSphere hosts to use a datastore as a second communication method in the event the management network goes down. They protect against partitioning. Although you can configure this feature manually, you don't need to do so. vCenter automatically selects two datastores to enable the service. To facilitate this feature, make sure that all hosts are connected to all datastores, and if you are using iSCSI, make sure that the management traffic and iSCSI traffic are segregated and that the paths are redundant.

In addition, you should ensure that you have properly configured multiple paths to your storage subsystem. This is more commonly referred to as *multipathing*. In vSphere 5, it is much easier to configure multipathing for the ESXi iSCSI initiator. Essentially, you leverage several VMKernel ports in different port groups to define explicit paths. Multipathing can be configured on a vSphere Distributed Switch (vDS) or a standard vSphere switch, but the process is similar. Let's look at how to do this on a Distributed Switch. A Distributed Switch essentially allows you to centralize the configuration of virtual networking across your vSphere infrastructure and in so doing adds additional functionality. To migrate to a vDS, you need to keep in mind that it is a staged process to ensure you do not lose connectivity during the cutover. Let's look quickly at the setup of a vDS so that you can drill down on the steps to configure a multipath configuration for the software iSCSI initiator bundled with ESXi.

1. Launch your vSphere Client.

2. Browse to Home Inventory Networking.

3. If you have more than one vCenter, select one, right-click, and select the option **New vSphere Distributed Switch**.

4. If you have older ESX Servers in your farm, you are offered different version settings for the vSwitch. If you are running vSphere 5, you can leave the default version, which is vSphere Distributed Switch Version 5.0.0 (see Figure 11.2), and click **Next**.

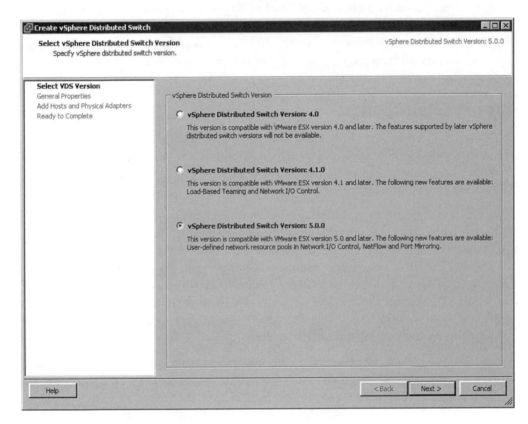

Figure 11.2 Create a new Distributed Switch.

5. You need to specify the number of uplinks. This is the point at which having the same hardware configuration for ESXi hosts makes things simple because the number of uplink ports corresponds with the number of physical NICs on an ESXi host. Keep in mind you are just specifying ports at this time, not associating any physical adapters. You can also change the name of the Distributed Switch so that it is more descriptive than the default. After you revise those fields, click **Next**.

6. The next screen allows you to add hosts and associate physical adapters. Add a host and click **Next**, or select **Add Later** and click **Next**.

7. On the final screen. click **Finish**.

Although the preceding steps install the vDS, it is not configured if you do not have host or physical adapters defined. You define the associations and manage the virtual adapters from the ESXi host. To complete this portion, simply browse to a host under your cluster and under Configuration, Hardware, select Networking. You should now see two tabs, the original vSphere Standard Switch and the new vSphere Distributed Switch, as shown in Figure 11.3.

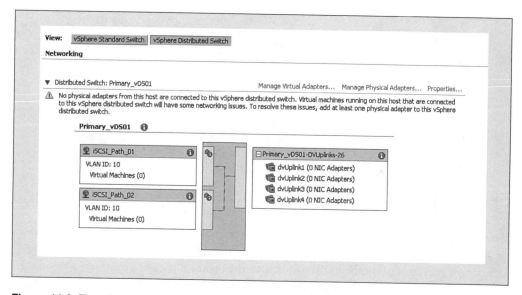

Figure 11.3 The vSphere Standard Switch and vSphere Distributed Switch tabs.

From the vSphere Distributed Switch tab, you can manage your physical and virtual adapters. If you did not associate any NICs during the creation of the vDS, you can do that by selecting the Manage Physical Adapters link, selecting each uplink, and clicking to add a NIC (see Figure 11.4). Doing this is a VMware best practice when you are moving to vDS from a vSphere Standard Switch. You are not actually adding a network card but associating a network card on the host to an Uplink port on the vDS. After you associate your NIC, click **OK**.

CAUTION

Make sure that you do not associate the NIC where your service console is running before you have configured a second VMKernel port for the migration. If you do, you lose connectivity to your host.

Click to associate a physical NIC to Uplink port

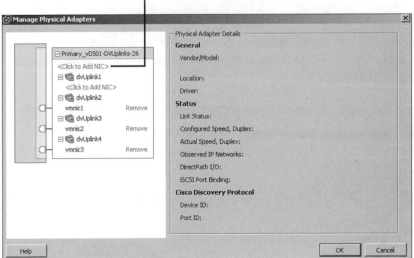

Figure 11.4 Associate physical NICs.

To migrate all your configurations from the host to the vDS, you need to create port groups on the vDS that correspond to the ones configured on your local host. The creation of port groups on the vDS is similar to the creation of port groups on a standard switch, but you have additional options. You can, as on a standard switch, define VLANs and have specific fault-tolerant settings for the uplinks. This is very important in the configuration of your iSCSI multipathing. To migrate all your settings to the vDS, complete the following steps:

1. Browse to your newly created vDS (Home, Inventory and Networking).

2. From the General tab, on the right under the Commands, select **New Port Group**.

3. Provide a name and configure the VLAN type (None, VLAN, Trunking, or Private VLANs). Private VLANs allow further segregation of a general VLAN. Click **Next** and **Finish**. Make sure that your port groups match the ones that are currently configured in your host.

4. Go back to the host (Home, Inventory, Hosts and Clusters and select the host).

5. Right-click and select **Enter Maintenance Mode**.

6. Select the **Configuration** tab and then **Networking** and the **vSphere Distributed Switch**.

7. Select **Manage Virtual Adapters** and select **Add** from the link at the top (it is highlighted in blue).

8. Select **New Virtual Adapters**.

9. Leave VMKernel selected and click **Next**.

10. Select the port group on the vDS this should go into (it should correspond with the one where the current service console is located on the standard switch). Select **Use This Virtual Adapter for Management Traffic** and click **Next**.

11. Apply an IP address, click **Next,** and click **Finish**.

12. Make sure that you can reach this IP address by pinging it on the network.

13. After ensuring you have connectivity, you can migrate the other management connections. You can do this by adding the remaining physical NIC to the vDS and re-creating the VMKernel ports.

Configuring iSCSI Multipathing

To properly configure multipathing, you need to create two separate port groups on your vDS, as depicted in Figure 11.5.

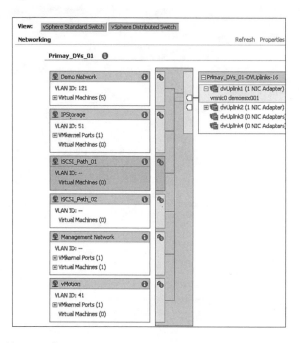

Figure 11.5 Multipathing requires two separate port groups.

To create the two separate port groups, follow these steps:

1. Browse to Home, Inventory and Networking; then select your vDS.

2. From the Summary tab, on the right under Commands, select **New Port Group**.

3. Specify a name and a VLAN type, click **Next**, and then click **Finish** (remember you need two groups).

To make sure that each port group allows a specific path to the storage network, you make sure that only a single uplink is in use for each of the newly created iSCSI port groups. To ensure this, complete the following steps:

1. Browse to Home, Inventory, Networking, your vDS, and one of the newly created iSCSI port groups.

2. On the Summary pane, click **Edit Settings**.

3. Select the **Teaming and Failover** section (see Figure 11.6).

4. Move any active links down by selecting them and clicking **Move Down** until they are in the Unused Uplinks section. (You do this with each of your newly created port groups, ensuring that each one has a different single active uplink.)

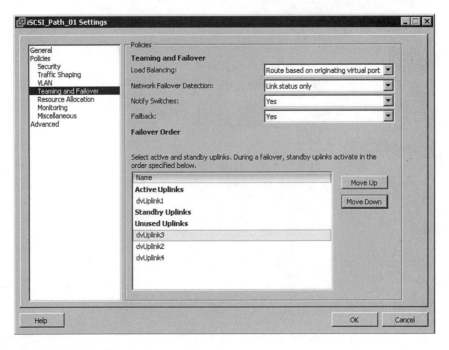

Figure 11.6 Use only a single uplink.

Now you need to add a VMKernel port for the iSCSI traffic to pass through in each port group. You can do this from ESXi host under the vSphere Distributed Switch tab. The exact process is as follows:

1. Go to the host (Home, Inventory, Hosts and Clusters and select the host).

2. Under Configuration, select **Networking** and then select the **vSphere Distributed Switch** tab.

3. Select **Manage Virtual Adapters** and **Add a New Virtual Adapter**.

4. On the next screen, from the drop-down, select the first iSCSI port group (note that you do not need VMotion, Fault Tolerant, or Management traffic) and click **Next**.

5. Provide an IP address and subnet mask. Then click **Next** and **Finish**. (You need to do this again, but this time you select the alternate iSCSI port group and new IP information).

At this point, you have the two VMKernel ports and two separate paths. You can actually verify your configuration by selecting each of the VMKernel ports from the vSphere Distributed Switch. You should see one path through a single uplink adapter, as shown in Figure 11.7. After you verify everything, the last step is to create the iSCSI software initiator and specify each path.

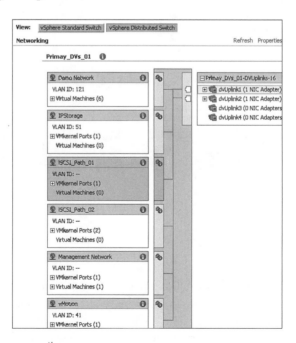

Figure 11.7 Verifying your paths.

To add a new software initiator, you need to select the Storage Adapters section under Configuration, the Hardware Pane, and then Storage Adapters. To add an iSCSI initiator, select **Add** from the right pane. After you click the link, you are notified that one will be created and that you must select the properties of the adapter after it is created. When the iSCSI software adapter is visible, right-click and select the properties. Under the Network Configuration tab, you can add each VMKernel port binding that you have created. When you are finished, the configuration should look similar to Figure 11.8.

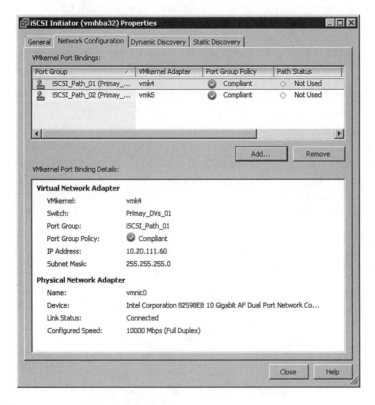

Figure 11.8 Two separate paths are displayed.

VMware FT

VMware Fault Tolerance is the capability to have two VMs running in lock step. Think of it as a constantly running VMotion. If the primary virtual machine fails, the secondary takes over with very minimal interruption. Although you can make extensive use of VMware FT to protect certain aspects of your VMware View environment, it does come with some limitations. Another issue to realize with FT is that it does not protect against problems within the Windows OS. For example, if the Windows OS crashes on the primary VM, the secondary also crashes. The current limitations are set to go away with the next release of vSphere as the number of supported vCPUs increases to four. The current release does have the following limitations:

- Only a single vCPU is supported.

- The virtual machine cannot have more than 64 GB of memory.

- The Virtual Machine Disk (VMDK) should be a thick-eager zeroed disk.

- The virtual machine cannot have any snapshots associated.

vCenter Heartbeat

VMware's recommended approach to ensuring that vCenter is highly available is through vCenter Heartbeat. vCenter Heartbeat is a Windows application designed to make vCenter highly available without any special hardware. It can be applied to either physical or virtual vCenters.

vCenter Heartbeat is a combination of two servers, which are generally described as a vCenter Heartbeat Pair. The Pair operate in an active–passive configuration. Each vCenter Server must have two network interfaces: : one for network connections (the Public IP) and the second for synchronizing data (the Heartbeat Channel). In addition each server must have 2 associated IPs; one for the vCenter Heartbeat channel link and one for the Public IP (Note: ensure that only the Public IP registers in DNS). This second NIC is referred to as the VMware Channel through which synchronization data flows.

Before applying vCenter Heartbeat, make sure that all components of vCenter are installed and configured properly. The way the technology works is that your primary vCenter Server is cloned. You do not touch the computer account or domain membership because VMware Heartbeat uses packet filtering to mask the second identical vCenter Server from the network. While you are making changes to your primary vCenter, the changes are synced to the clone. If the primary is unavailable, the packet filtering is switched off and the clone takes over.

It is a good idea to put both vCenter Servers in a specific OU and to turn off the machine account synchronization to avoid any problems. The technology was developed by a company called NeverFail. The difference between it and something like VMware FT is that it works on both physical and virtual servers and does not have the same vCPU limita-tions. In addition, it also protects locally installed SQL services, including View Composer.

In the OU on which you have installed your vCenter Servers where you intend to deploy vCenter Heartbeat, configure a policy and disable Machine Account synchronization. You can find this policy under Computer Configuration, Security Settings, Local Policies, Security Options. Under Domain Member: Disable Machine Account Password Changes, select **Define This Policy Setting** and then **Enabled;** finally click **OK** (see Figure 11.9). To have the policy go into effect immediately, simply open a command prompt from your vCenter Server and type **gpupdate /force**.

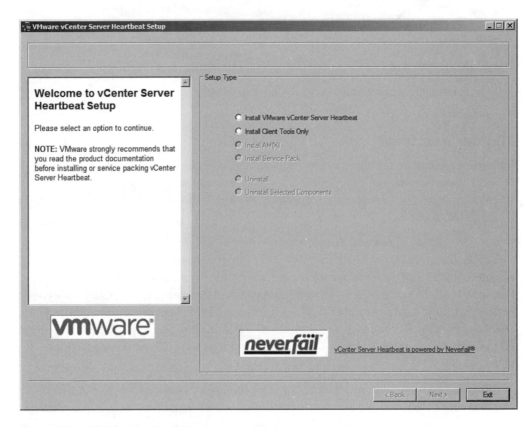

Figure 11.9 Disable machine account password changes.

Installing VMware vCenter Server Heartbeat

Ensure that everything you want installed and enabled is done. Also, configure the vCenter Server so that it has two network interfaces: one for the synchronization traffic and the second for access to vCenter. You should also create a share on the local computer to facilitate the synchronization of data. When that is done, you can go ahead and clone your vCenter Server (Note: vCenter Heartbeat can be installed using Physical or virtual machines. For other configurations please refer to VMware's documentation http://www.vmware.com/support/pubs/heartbeat_pubs.html). Boot the vCenter Server in isolation and update the VMware Channel IP to a new IP address and nothing else (the public IP is masked from the network by the packet filter and remains the same). Remember that you do not change the computer account or domain membership because it is the packet filtering that masks the clone from the network. To install vCenter Heartbeat, follow these steps:

1. When you launch the installer, you are prompted to click **OK** to begin the process.

2. The files come as a WinZip extraction file; click **Setup** to begin the extraction.

3. The install begins, and on the setup page, you have the option of installing the Client Tools or the VMware vCenter Server Heartbeat. Select VMware vCenter Server Heartbeat and click **Next**.

4. If this is the first server, it is the primary and the clone is the secondary, as shown in Figure 11.10. Select **Primary** and click **Next**.

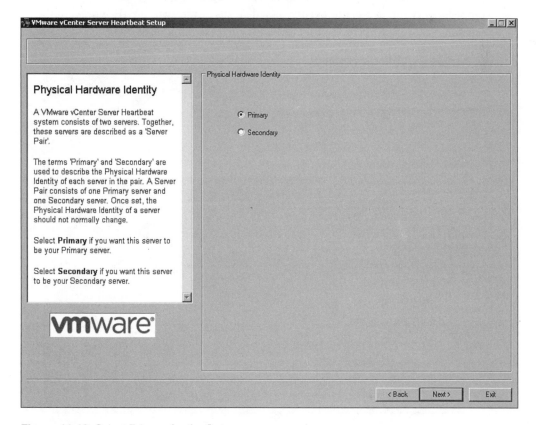

Figure 11.10 Select Primary for the first server.

5. On the end user license agreement, select that you agree and click **Next**.

6. On the next page, you are prompted to provide a license. Click **Add** to type your license key and then click **Next**.

7. One of two options is presented: either LAN or WAN. Determine which scenario fits your situation and click the appropriate topology; then click **Next**.

8. Identify whether your secondary server is virtual or physical. Select the correct option on the Deployment Option page and click **Next**.

9. The next page is Installation Paths; the source is predefined, and by default, Heartbeat is installed in **c:\Program files**. You also have the option of creating desktop icons. In general, the defaults are okay, so click **Next**.

10. Select the network adapter that will be used for synchronization, generally referred to as the VMware Channel, and click **Next**.

11. Define the IP address on the primary and secondary servers. Click **Add** on the IP address. On Primary, select the drop-down and choose the correct IP. Because the secondary server has not been installed at this point, type the IP address of the secondary server, as shown in Figure 11.11, click **OK**, and click **Next**.

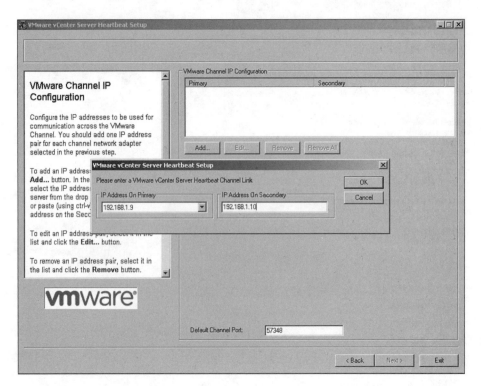

Figure 11.11 Select the IP of the primary and type the IP of the secondary.

12. On the next screen, you select the public or access interface and click **Next**.

13. On the Public IP Address Configuration, you have the option of keeping the address the same as when the service fails over or specifying different IPs. Within a site or campus, it is likely that **Use the Same IP Addresses for Secondary** is the right selection. When you are moving between sites, it is likely that the IPs do not remain the same, so a different address needs to be configured. If it is the same, you can select this option and click **Next**. If it is different, you need to add the IP address on the secondary server and click **Next**.

14. The next screen confirms the Client Connection Port. It is recommended that you do not change this setting, so click **Next**.

15. On the next page, you set the predefined application protections. Note that if you are running local SQL and View Composer, you can protect those services, too. You also need to provide the vCenter login information and click **Next** (see Figure 11.12).

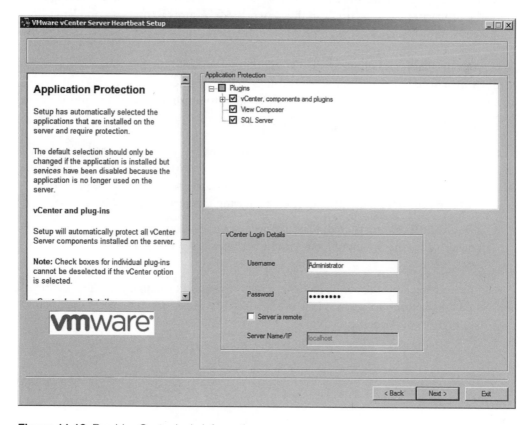

Figure 11.12 Provide vCenter login information.

16. As with many of these synchronization technologies, the data is queued before it is transferred so that in the event the network is interrupted, the data can be recovered and resynced with a minimal amount of disruption. This location must be specified as a UNC path, so you use \\server name\\share name. Deciding on which server you should create the share is a little confusing, but as out example is based on two virtual machines, you should create in on the primary server. Specify the location and click **Next**.

17. Review your installation information and click **Next** to proceed.

18. The installer completes a series of pre-installation checks before proceeding. Review to make sure the checks completed successfully and click **Next**.

19. The next page provides the status of the installation. Make sure it completed successfully and click **Next**.

20. The next page installs the packet filters that enable the masking and unmasking of the primary and secondary from the network. Make sure the process completed successfully and click **Next** and **Finish** on the next page.

When the installation is complete, the Configuration Wizard launches. Some of the settings are a little repetitive, but going through this wizard does give you a second chance to ensure your settings are correct. Follow these steps to finish the Configuration Wizard:

1. Select **Next** on the introduction screen.

2. On the Machine Configuration page, you set how this machine is identified, which is a little confusing because the wizard indicates Physical Machine Hardware Identify. Because this is the first installation, it is, of course, the primary, and the primary is active and the port is the default. After reviewing this page, click **Next**.

3. The Channel routing page displays the primary and secondary IPs for your channel. You also have the option of identifying whether this is a low-bandwidth connection. Click **Next**.

4. The next screen is the public identity, which determines whether the same identity is used for the machine when it fails over. Select **Identical**, which removes the options (see Figure 11.13), and click **Next**.

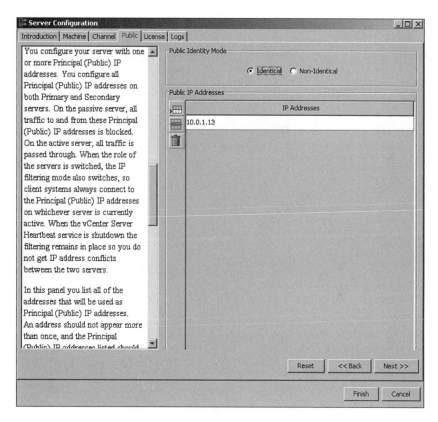

Figure 11.13 Select Identical.

5. The next screen allows you to reset the license, but because you choose to configure the license during installation, click **Next**.

6. On the Logs screen, you see the Queue file location. You should adjust the Maximum Disk Usage depending on the resiliency of the connection. A more indeterminate connection may warrant a larger maximum disk usage size. Click **Finish** when you're done.

You complete the same process on the secondary server, but this time you select Secondary, of course. When the Heartbeat service is installed, you see a packet filter drive bound to the public interface, and the vCenter Servers are set to manual because VMware Heartbeat now completely manages the availability. The process is largely the same except that this service gets installed as the secondary server. While using the Configuration Wizard, you notice that this server is listed as the secondary and the active server is listed as the primary (see Figure 11.14).

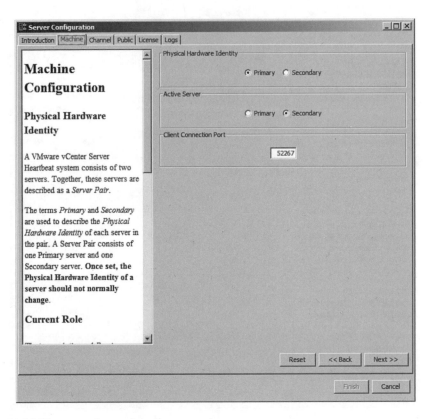

Figure 11.14 The server is now listed as secondary.

Configuring VMware vCenter Server Heartbeat

When everything is installed, you still need to start the service and then start the group. From the primary server, right-click the icon on the system tray and start the service. You should also start the service on the secondary server. The first couple of messages from the system tray icon notify you that the channel is connected and that the primary server is attempting to establish connectivity with the secondary server, as shown in Figure 11.15.

Figure 11.15 The primary server is connecting to a peer server.

After you start the service, you can click the **Manage Server** option. You need to enter the Administrator account and password and click **OK** to connect to the server. Because replication has not yet started, your initial configuration may not quite be synchronized and stable, as shown in Figure 11.16.

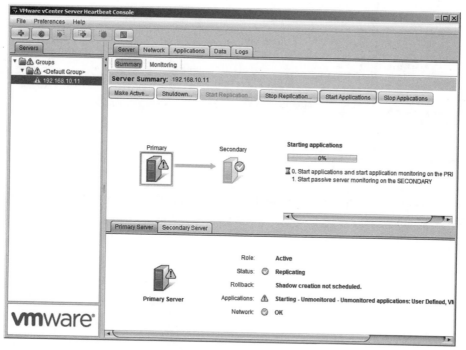

Figure 11.16 Replication has not started.

Start replication now. NeverFail starts to verify each connection and begins the synchro-nization process. The checks include a full registry and file check, so this process may take some time. You can see the status of these checks by selecting the Data tab. After all the checks are completed, you should see the file and registry settings update to synchronized (see Figure 11.17).

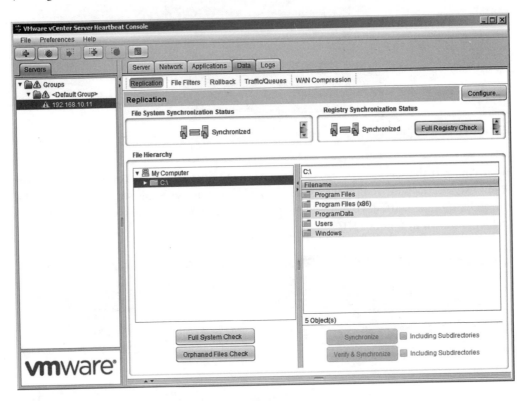

Figure 11.17 Full registry and file checks are done.

When this check is complete, you can select the Server and Summary tabs and see that the servers are replicating and synchronized (see Figure 11.18).

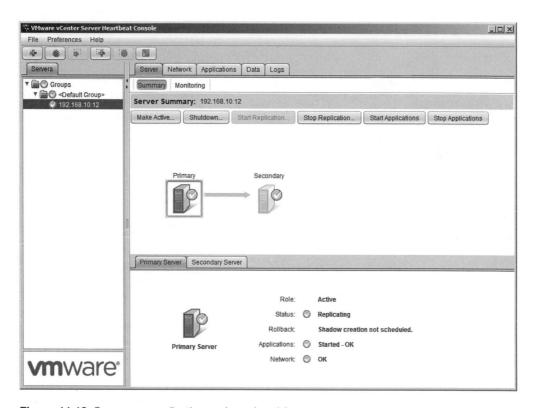

Figure 11.18 Servers are replicating and synchronizing.

Testing VMware vCenter Server Heartbeat

To complete a failover test, simply select the secondary server and click **Make Active**. You are prompted with a message that asks whether you are sure you want to make the secondary active. Click **OK**, and you notice the system goes through the failover process and masks the primary and reveals the secondary on the network (this process may take a little time), as shown in Figure 11.19. Simply reverse the process to reset things back to the correct primary and secondary configuration. In addition to testing using the VMware vCenter Heartbeat Console, you should test a failure of the VM. For example, with two physical vCenter Servers, you can shut down the interface on the switch to allow the failover to occur. After the failover occurs, you should test the failback by bringing the interface back online. Make sure you are comfortable with the way vCenter Heartbeat reacts under various failures, such as hardware component failure, so that you understand exactly what will happen.

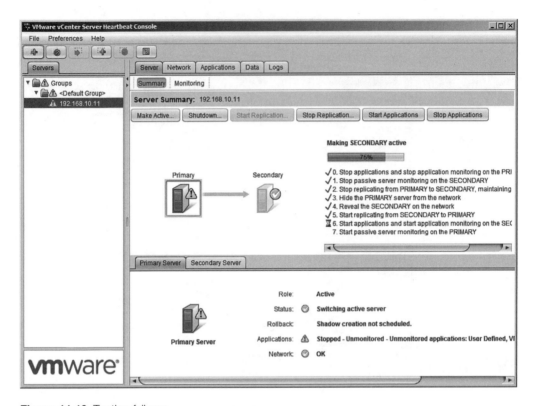

Figure 11.19 Testing failover.

Other Services and Considerations

To provide a real-world example, let's consider a deployment scenario in which you deploy VMware View desktops in an active–active configuration across two distinct datacenters. You want both datacenters to be failover locations for each other in the event that there is a regional failure affecting an entire datacenter.

In developing this solution for the VMware View environment, there are a number of issues that you need to consider. You need to first review what needs to be available in both sites, what data needs to be exchanged between sites, and what technologies you can use to enable the replication of information.

Developing an active–passive configuration would be quite easy because you could rely solely on storage replication to take everything that is running in a single datacenter and move it to a second location. Perhaps the only challenge would be in ensuring that the View clients can be rerouted to the secondary datacenter in the event of a problem. This, however, is not a big technical challenge if you use proper DNS entries to connect clients to the View environment. Unfortunately, this approach may require some manual intervention because the View client does not support a second DNS entry.

Often, when you are developing an active–active architecture, what prevents a truly active–active configuration that is completely fault resistant is the lack of distinct paths to each datacenter which do not include some network interdependency. For example, Figure 11.20 better illustrates this point.

Figure 11.20 shows two datacenters: one located at the organization's head office and the second located some distance away from the head office. If the network traffic is routed through the primary datacenter to access resources in the second datacenter and no backup direct connection exists, as shown in Figure 11.20, although you can still build an active–active VMware View environment across the two sites, you do not have complete redundancy.

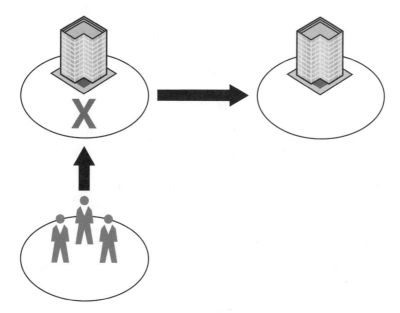

Figure 11.20 If network connectivity flows through a single datacenter, it is difficult to have true redundancy.

A more redundant configuration allows the users a direct connection to the secondary site in the event there is a problem, as shown in Figure 11.21.

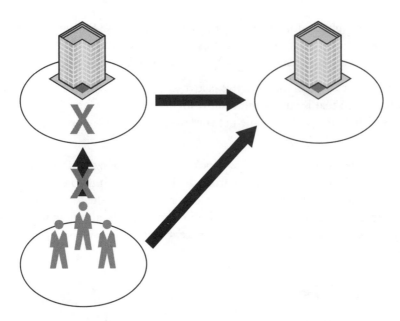

Figure 11.21 An alternate direct connection to the secondary datacenter provides better redundancy.

Configuring complete redundancy can be expensive, so during a major failure it may be more realistic to consider that redundancy is provided through remote access to the VMware View environment. Having everyone use the external/remote access portal for connecting back to the remaining View site might be more cost effective (see Figure 11.22). The obvious benefit in this scenario is that if the outage also impacted user desktop connectivity with the head office, the use of remote access would add value in this situation.

In large environments, hardware load balancers like F5 are used to provide this level of redundancy. Hardware load balancers actively monitor back-end service availability and automatically failover user sessions in the event there is a problem. In a true multisite configuration, hardware load balancers should be used for their advanced capabilities in managing sessions and monitoring services between sites.

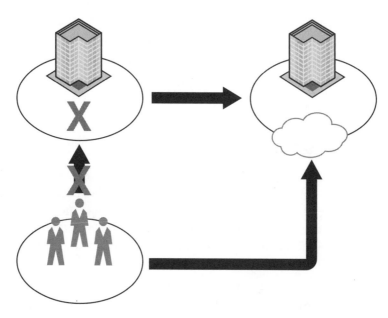

Figure 11.22 Remote access can provide a second method to connect to a View environment if you plan for such situations.

Fundamentally, the point around looking at HA and, by extension, failover and Disaster Recovery is that it is important to consider not just the core features of VMware View, but also all the supporting infrastructure. These factors also need to be weighed against cost and what you actually are achieving in developing this level of resiliency in the environment. Take the scenario in Figure 11.22 and consider the services that the View desktops are accessing; because they are essentially Windows clients, there is an assumption that back-end services are already distributed between datacenters (line of business applications such as Exchange, SAP, or Oracle DBs) to support the remaining virtual desktop environment. If this is not the case, you need to rationalize your design against what can be reasonably provided in each datacenter.

In developing your high availability approach, it is helpful to consider the current company policies toward desktops. Is there a policy to save any configuration information such as user profiles from the desktops? If the answer is no, you are still not off the hook because centralization and virtualization of desktops introduce additional risk. In addition, if you want to reduce the costs, some of the technologies that may not have been applied to the company's physical desktops are necessary in a virtual desktop environment, such as high availability and View Persona.

There is also a question of scale when discussing high availability because scale affects load and therefore adjusts the number of options you have in developing your HA approach.

For example, in a small proof of concept environment, you may have a single VMware View Connection Server configured to use VMware FT. This setup may be perfectly fine when you are testing only a small number of virtual desktops. As this solution grows, however, you will want to introduce technologies such as hardware-based load balancers that are designed to deal with failover in critical environments.

High Availability Scenario

Every case is slightly different, of course, so it is helpful to develop a scenario and then build it out to provide a good example for reference. To provide an example scenario let's take the requirement of deploying VMware View across two datacenters. Each datacenter must have local site redundancy and also serve as a failover site for each other. In normal operations, users are evenly distributed across each datacenter because, although they are separated by 200 km (125 miles), latency is around 2 ms.

Each site is built with local site HA so that multiple Secure Servers and Connection Servers exist in each location. Core network services are available in both locations (AD, DNS, and DHCP), and back-end services are already highly available in both locations. Across both sites in normal operation, each datacenter VMware View environment runs at 50% utilization, or half of the View desktops, so that in the event of a failure, all VMware View desktops can be run from a single location. VMware View has been designed to be accessed both internally and externally from both locations.

The network team has developed smart load balancing in front of the VMware View sites so that the IPs that represent the internal Connection Servers and external security services are managed and monitored. Team members monitor all four IPs (one for the internal Connection Servers in each site and one for the Secure Servers in each site) and service ports to ensure they are online and available. Local load balancing ensures availability within a site. If a site fails to respond, the load balancers update the DNS information so that clients are redirected to the active site. DNS time-to-live (TTL) values are set low to ensure that the DNS updates happen quickly so that from the perspective of the client, the downtime is minimized. As the architect of the VMware View environment, your job is to make sure that the VMware View environment is highly available. You can leverage native Windows or VMware technology for load balancing the View components, but due to costs, no other technology is used.

At a high level, the environment looks like that shown in Figure 11.23.

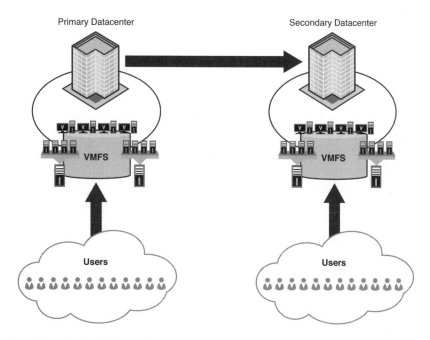

Figure 11.23 You deploy VMware View across two datacenters.

The following combination of technologies will be used to support the design (although other services are required, such as general file services and printing, this example focuses on the pieces directly required by VMware View versus general Windows desktop requirements).

Windows Network Load Balancing (NLB)

- Configured to load balance both VMware View Servers

- Configured to load balance both Security Servers

Windows File Cluster

- To create a site redundant file service for providing availability of

  - View Persona data

  - Application virtualization files

  - Image repositories

Distributed File Services

- Replicate View Persona data

- Replicate application virtualization files
- Replicate image repositories

Although there are other ways of replicating Common Internet File System (CIFS) shares, such as using NAS-based appliances, because each vendor has its own configuration, you run the risk of either having too broad or too narrow an example. Because you generally use Windows services within the desktop environment, you are going to use the Windows-supported method of providing redundancy. In your environment, if you have moved from Windows-based file services to NAS-based appliances, the design principles apply, but your configurations obviously differ.

Your order of configuration is as follows:

- Configure Windows File Server Cluster.
    - Verify Cluster is working.
- Configure Distributed File Servers.
    - Verify Replication.
- Configure NLB.
    - Verify IP failover.

When you have back-end services in place, you can do some failure testing to ensure everything is working as you expect it to. A Windows 2008 R2 cluster can be used as a file server and run Distributed File System (DFS). This ensures a highly available local cluster with both one-way and bidirectional replication. We talk more about DFS in a little bit.

Deploying a Microsoft Cluster on vSphere

The requirements for deploying a Microsoft cluster have changed significantly with vSphere 5. It used to be that you had to deploy your cluster in a certain fashion with cluster nodes deployed on local disk and Raw Device Mapping (RDM) used for both the quorum and cluster storage. The quorum disk is used as an alternate communication method between nodes in addition to the network link. (The quorum disk is also generally referred to as the *cluster gab disk*.) VMware recommends Fibre Channel (FC) and RDM for Microsoft clusters, but if you are using iSCSI, VMware suggests you look to Microsoft for support because it is transparent to the virtual infrastructure. Because iSCSI is supported by Microsoft, many of the conditions that were available in prior releases of vSphere are no longer in effect, providing you flexibility. It is likely that you would still exclude your cluster nodes from DRS or, at a minimum, make sure you have anti-affinity rules to ensure that the VMs do not run on the same hosts. vSphere 5 offers traditional DRS and also storage DRS, so you can also set anti-affinity rules to ensure the VMs' virtual disks do not wind up on the same datastore. In this example, you use two Windows 2008 R2 Servers in the primary datacenter setup with VM anti-affinity and two Windows 2008 R2 Servers in the secondary datacenter setup with VM anti-affinity. To create the rule, complete the following steps:

1. In the vSphere Client, right-click the cluster in the inventory and select **Edit Settings.**

2. In the left pane of the Cluster Settings dialog box, under vSphere DRS, select **Rules** and click **Add.**

3. In the Rule dialog box, type a name for the rule, such as **Primary Cluster Anti-Affinity Rule.**

4. From the Type menu, select **Separate Virtual Machines** and click **Add.**

5. Select at least two virtual machines to which the rule will apply and click **OK** and click **OK** again

Creating a Microsoft Windows 2008 R2 Cluster

Microsoft recommends that you have at least two NICs on a cluster VM, but I recommend you have a minimum of five if you are going to use iSCSI and multipathing or the native Microsoft Multiple Connections per Session (MC/S or simply MCS). They are fairly similar in functionality, but MCS is a single session with multiple connections. To use MCS, you need to ensure your SAN supports it as well; otherwise, you are best to use multipathing with multipath I/O (MPIO). They are mutually exclusive, so if you are going to use one, you do not use the other.

The purpose of requiring five NICs is to provide two separate paths for your iSCSI connectivity to your shared storage: one for the heartbeat network, which I like to call the service network (where clients connect from), and one for management. The service network can be one and the same, but I like to separate management and data traffic. Of course, I may want to maintain a distinct path down to the vSwitch and physical NIC as well, so my networking looks like Figure 11.24 (Note: the diagram is a little simplistic as I could use port groups and specify the primary and failover physical NICs to separate physical paths for the storage). Note that given the redundancy in the vSphere Server and vNICs, the multiple paths are not really required for availability, but this setup does allow the iSCSI traffic to use both paths for performance.

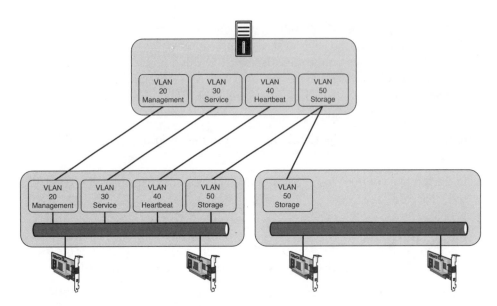

Figure 11.24 Logical breakdown of networking.

Let's look at the installation so that you have a good idea of how to apply the configuration. One of the most important factors in cluster configuration is consistency. You should start with consistency by making sure that everything is labeled so that you can easily tell at a glance what is associated with what. For example, I labeled the NICs in the virtual machines so that they correspond with the planned network configuration (see Figure 11.25).

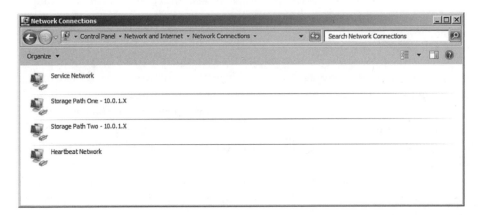

Figure 11.25 Ensure your NICs are labeled properly.

Connecting the Windows Cluster to the SAN

To meet the requirement, you have deployed two Windows 2008 R2 Servers in each environment. You have configured each identically in terms of network. Now you need to assign some SAN storage. You require a quorum disk and a cluster volume for storage. You need to enable access for the iSCSI initiators on each Windows 2008 R2 Server. The iSCSI initiator is the iSCSI client that requests access to storage from the storage target or provider. The target is the SAN appliance, and it waits for requests and provides access to blocks of storage or LUNs. Your SAN solution may provide specific drivers for the initiator, but in most cases, the native Windows 2008 R2 iSCSI software is fine. When you first select the iSCSI configuration utility from the control panel of your Windows server, it starts the service if it is not yet running (see Figure 11.26).

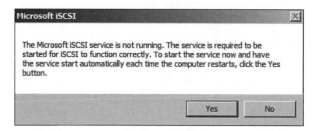

Figure 11.26 Start the iSCSI service.

The iSCSI initiator name is created automatically based on the iSCSI Qualified Name (IQN) format. The IQN has the format iqn.yyyy-mm plus the reverse domain name and the SCSI alias and/or hash. It is this name that is used to assign blocks of storage for use to the server. To enable the Microsoft cluster, you should assign a small amount of block storage for the quorum and a large amount of storage for the clustered file server. Microsoft recommends 500 MB for quorum size; below that, the efficiency of an NTFS runs into problems. The quorum is used to store information only on the current state of the cluster, so 500 MB is sufficient.

You assign LUNs to the initiators using the IQN from the management utility provided by the storage vendor. Because each vendor has its own series of steps, just make sure that a LUN is assigned for the quorum and clustered volume for both nodes in the primary datacenter and that the same is done for both nodes in the secondary datacenter. In most cases (but not all), you have to mark the LUN as clustered to allow it to be shared by two servers. You can find the IQN by launching the iSCSI Initiator configuration utility from the Control Panel and clicking the **Configuration** tab (see Figure 11.27).

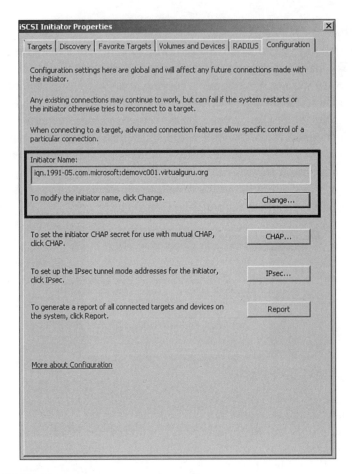

Figure 11.27 iSCSI initiator name.

Using MCS

At this point, you need to determine whether you will be using MCS or multipathing to connect the storage to the Windows servers so that you can create the cluster. MCS is a feature of the iSCSI protocol in which multiple connections are made inside a single session for performance purposes, whereas MPIO uses multiple sessions, leading to better performance.

Let's run through the iSCSI configuration and then look at the different configurations for both MPIO and MCS. To find the targets, you need to configure Discovery. Many SAN solutions support multiple portals, which just means they can listen for connections on multiple IPs. To configure Discovery, complete the following steps:

1. Launch the iSCSI Initiator control panel applet.

2. Select the **Discovery** tab and click **Discover Portal**.

3. If you are not enforcing Challenge Handshake Authentication Protocol (CHAP) or Internet Protocol Security (IPSec) and don't want to specify the explicit path, just type in the IP. The default port used for discovery is 3260. If you are using CHAP or want an explicit path, select **Advanced**, as shown in Figure 11.28.

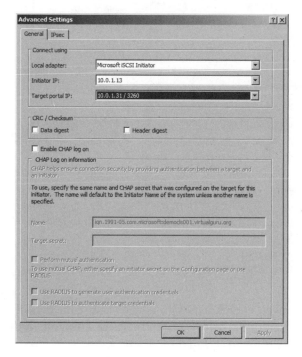

Figure 11.28 Configure the iSCSI Initiator.

4. If the SAN device has multiple portals or is listening on several IPs, add additional Discovery targets.

Configuring MCS

If you chose to use MPIO, at this point the configuration differs from MCS. Let's go through the configuration of MCS first because it is straightforward. To configure MCS, you do not need to install MPIO; you just need to configure a single session with multiple connections. To complete this, open the iSCSI initiator and select one of the newly discovered and inactive targets; then select Properties to set up the connections (see Figure 11.29).

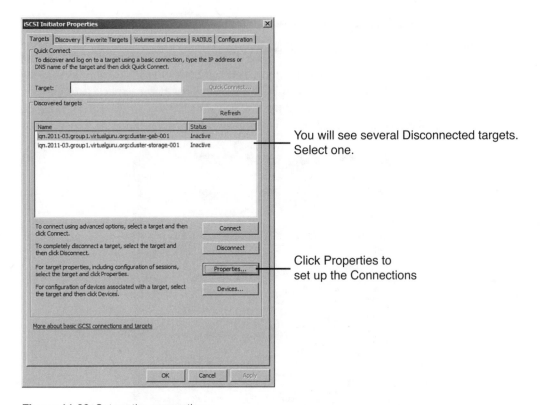

Figure 11.29 Set up the connections.

From the Properties page, click **Add Session**. Then accept the default to **Add This Connection to the List of Favorite Targets**, make sure **Enable multi-path** is deselected, and click **Advanced** (see Figure 11.30).

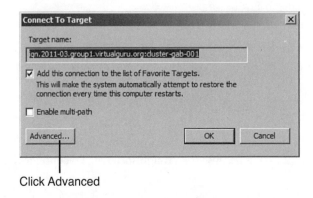

Figure 11.30 Select Advanced to define the properties of the initiator.

Under Connect Using on the General tab, select Microsoft iSCSI Initiator for the Local Adapter, set the Initiator IP and Target Portal IP, enable CHAP logon, and provide the target secret if you are using CHAP (see Figure 11.31). Click **OK** and **OK** again on the Connect to Target screen.

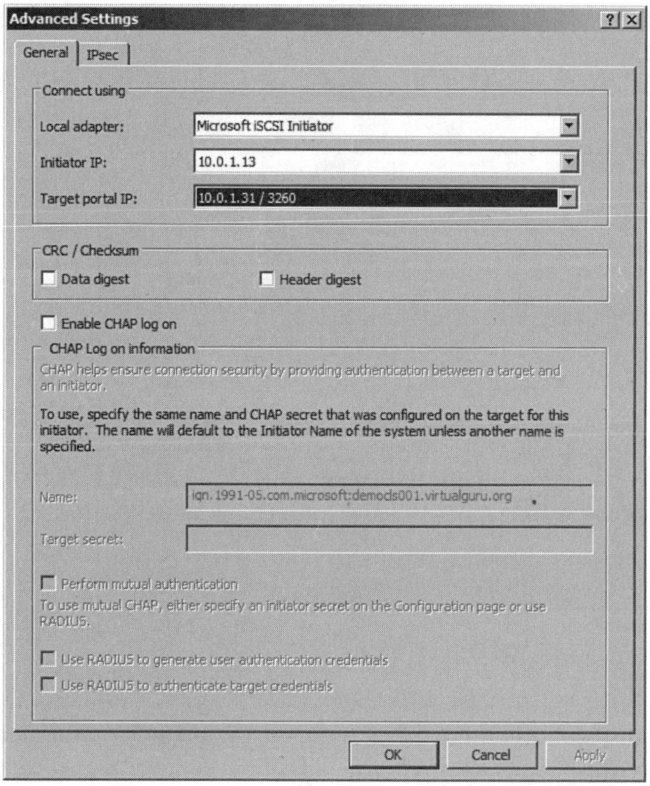

Figure 11.31 Configure the initiator.

Figure 11.32 shows the original session and the default MCS policy, which is Round Robin. With MCS, you add a connection to this session.

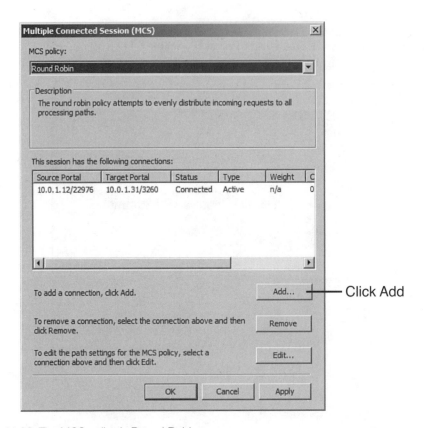

Figure 11.32 The MCS policy is Round Robin.

To add an additional connection to this session, select **Add**, and on the Add Connection screen, you click **Advanced** to specify the details of the connection. As with the first session, you provide the details of the second connection from the other IP address. Again, you can enable CHAP and specify a target secret for connectivity (see Figure 11.33). You click **OK** and then **Connect** on the Connection screen.

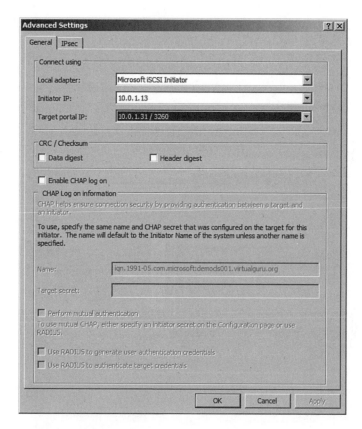

Figure 11.33 Add a second connection.

You now have two connections in a single session. If you are going to use MCS, you configure all the cluster nodes in the same manner. Although you have two connections in the same session, this is different from having two sessions or paths to the SAN target.

Using MPIO

To use multipathing, you must install MPIO and complete some additional configuration steps. MPIO is a *feature* versus a *role* on Windows 2008 R2. You can install it using the following procedure:

1. Within the Windows 2008 R2 Server, right-click **Features** and click **Add Features**.

2. Select **Multipath I/O** and click **Next**.

3. Click **Install**.

By default, support for iSCSI multipath is not installed, so you need to enable it using the MPIO control panel applet after you install Multipath I/O. After the applet launches, select the **Discover Multi-Paths** tab, select **Add Support for iSCSI Devices**, and click **Add** (see Figure 11.34).

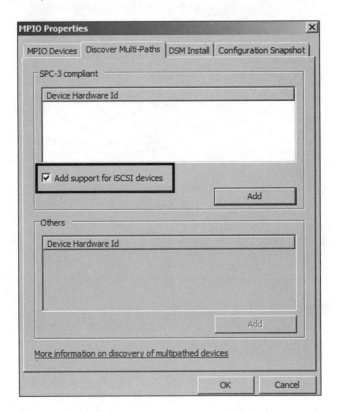

Figure 11.34 Install support for MPIO.

After you add support, you are prompted to reboot your server to complete the installation. At this point, you are ready to configure multipathing on the server. You can set up multipaths and ensure each connection to the SAN target is made of two sessions. The process is similar to the method of configuring MCS and is done within the iSCSI control panel applet. As before, you select a disconnected target from the Target tab to configure connectivity.

Configuring MPIO

If you are reconfiguring a connected target, you can select it and disconnect. If you configured it as an MCS connection, you should select **Properties**, select the **MCS** button, and remove the second session, as shown in Figure 11.35. When the second session is removed, click **OK** because you cannot remove the primary session from this screen. From the Properties page, you can, however.

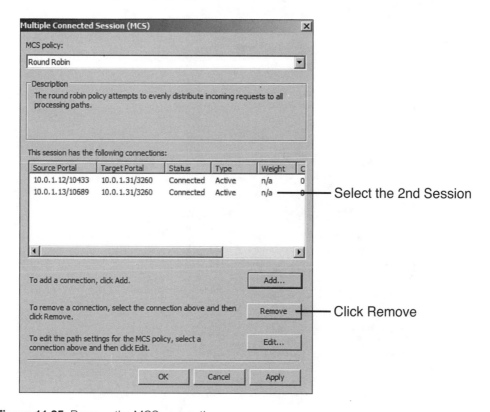

Figure 11.35 Remove the MCS connection.

On the second page, simply select the original session and click **Disconnect**. When it is disconnected, you can click **OK** (see Figure 11.36). After you configure your cluster, you will notice that if the resource is online on the cluster node you are not able to disconnect the connection. This issue is easy to resolve, however, if you ever need to reconfigure settings by either taking the resource offline, or taking it offline on this node and bringing it online on the second node.

Select the first Session

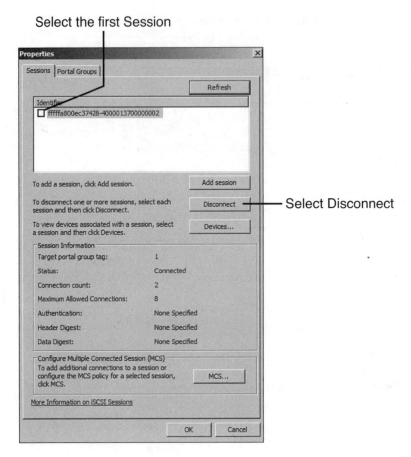

Select Disconnect

Figure 11.36 Disconnect the first session.

You are ready to configure this connection for multipath. As before, select the disconnected target and click **Properties**. In this case, select Enable Multi-path and click **Advanced** (see Figure 11.37) so that you can explicitly select the attributes of the session.

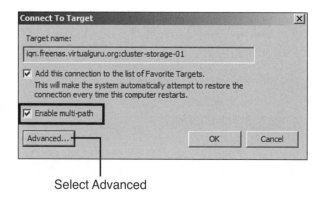

Figure 11.37 Select the Enable Multi-path option.

As before, you define the local adapter as the Microsoft iSCSI Initiator and set the Initiator IP and Target Portal IP (see Figure 11.38). If you are using CHAP, you can enable it, provide the target secret or password, and click **OK**.

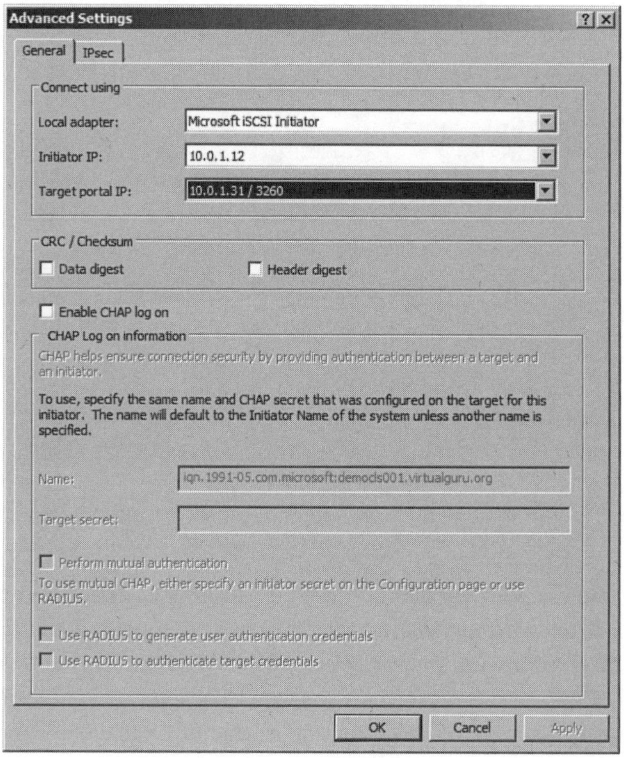

Figure 11.38 Configure the initiator.

You are not finished yet because you need two sessions, each originating from different IPs. To add them, select **Add Session** (see Figure 11.39). On the Add Connection tab, as before, you select Enable Multi-path and Advanced to explicitly define the connection properties. In this case, the Initiator IP is the second IP address that you set up to access the iSCSI storage.

Figure 11.39 Select Add Session.

You should complete the configuration on each of the cluster nodes in the primary datacenter view environment and secondary view environment. It is important to double-check your configuration because mistakes can lead to unstable cluster environments. There are a number of ways you can verify that your configuration is accurate if you are using multipathing. We run through them here so that you can ensure the connections are configured properly before proceeding. (Be aware that some storage vendors provide very specific procedures for connecting Windows hosts. If this is the case, the recommended vendor configuration supersedes the ones provided here for reference.)

One of the ways to check that multipathing is functional in your environment is to look at the properties of the volume under disk configuration. Complete the following steps to check this:

1. From one of your Windows 2008 R2 cluster nodes, launch Server Manager.

2. Expand Storage and Disk Management.

3. Select each of the iSCSI attached disks, right-click, and select **Properties**.

4. Under the MPIO tab, ensure that the MPIO Policy is set. In this case, the default is Round Robin. Also ensure that there are two path IDs (see Figure 11.40).

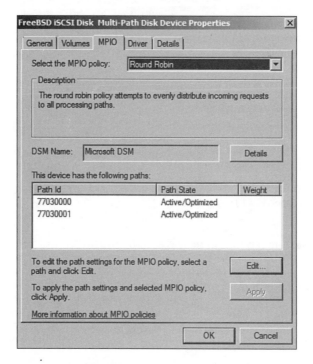

Figure 11.40 The MPIO is set to Round Robin.

You can also run a report from the MPIO control panel applet to verify that you have two paths to the storage system. To verify this, complete the following steps:

1. From one of the Windows 2008 R2 cluster nodes, launch the MPIO applet from the control panel.

2. Select the **Configuration Snapshot** tab, set the filename, select **Open File upon Capture**, and click **Capture** (see Figure 11.41).

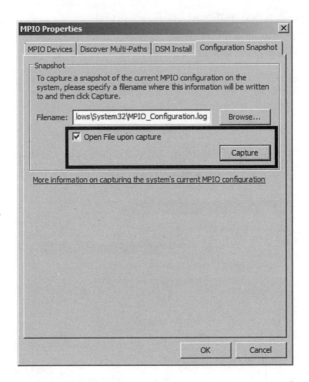

Figure 11.41 Select Open File Upon Capture.

3. Make sure that you have multiple paths in the MPIO section (see Figure 11.42).

```
MPIO Disk0: 02 Paths, Round Robin, ALUA Not Supported
      SN: 30000CD39B4D
      Supported Load Balance Policies: FOO RR RRWS LQD WP LB

Path ID              State            SCSI Address        Weight
------------------------------------------------------------------------
0000000077030000 Active/Optimized   003|000|000|000    0
      Adapter: Microsoft iSCSI Initiator...              (B|D|F: 000|000|000)
      Controller: 46616B65436F6E74726F6C6C6572 (State: Active)

0000000077030001 Active/Optimized   003|000|001|000    0
      Adapter: Microsoft iSCSI Initiator...              (B|D|F: 000|000|000)
      Controller: 46616B65436F6E74726F6C6C6572 (State: Active)
```

Figure 11.42 Ensure you have multiple paths.

Preparing the Volumes

After verifying that your storage is connected, you can go ahead and format the disk so that it is available for use in the cluster. After you connect your storage, the disks appear under Disk Management within the Storage module in Server Manager. The disks show up as Unknown and Offline. If they do not, right-click **Disk Management** and run the Rescan Disks to have Windows look for additional partitions. To make the storage available to the cluster, you need to format the disk. You can do this by running the following process:

1. From one of the Windows 2008 R2 Servers in the cluster, run Server Manager and expand the Storage and Disk Management modules.

2. If the disks do not appear, right-click **Disk Management** and click **Rescan Disks**.

3. Select one of the Unknown and Offline disks (see Figure 11.43) and click **Online**. Ensure you are selecting the disk, not the unpartitioned space.

Figure 11.43 Select the Offline disk.

4. Right-click it again and select **Initialize Disk**. Windows applies a signature to the disk so that the OS recognizes it. When the disk is initialized, it should now show as Unallocated Space.

5. Select **Unallocated Space** this time, right-click, and select **New Simple Volume**.

6. Select the volume when the wizard starts and click **Next** to allocate all the space to the volume.

7. On the next page, assign a drive letter (it is a good idea to keep these letters consistent across all your clusters, such as Q for quorum disk). Make sure you are using letters above the common drive letters (A, C, and D, for example) and click **Next**.

8. The defaults for Format Partition screen are okay. I recommend that you change the volume label so that the intended use is associated with the name, as shown in Figure 11.44. Maintaining naming consistency all through the creation and configuration of the cluster will save you a lot of time if you need to troubleshoot problems. After you update the volume label, click **Next** and **Finish**.

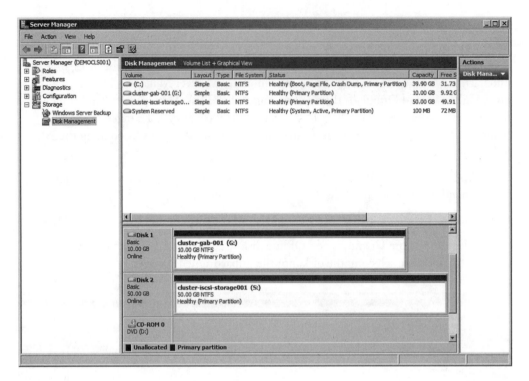

Figure 11.44 Be consistent in naming all your volumes.

9. You should format each of your volumes to ensure they are cluster ready. When this step is complete, you are ready to install the Cluster Service.

Installing the Microsoft Cluster

You should install several services in addition to the Cluster Services. Because you will use File Services and DFS, you should make sure that they are added to each node in the cluster. DFS is a part of File Services. Cluster Service is a feature, and File Services is a role. Complete the following steps to configure and install the Cluster feature:

1. From Server Manager on one of the Windows 2008 R2 Servers, select **Features** and **Add Features** from the right panel. (You need to install the service on both.)

2. Select **Failover Clustering**. Then, on the confirmation page, click **Next** and **Finish** to install the service.

3. Expand the Features module from Server Manager and select the **Failover Cluster Manager** module. You then see a pane on the right under Failover Cluster Manager

with several sections: Overview, Clusters, Management, and More Information, plus an Action Pane (see Figure 11.45). Under Management or the Action Pane, select **Create a Cluster**.

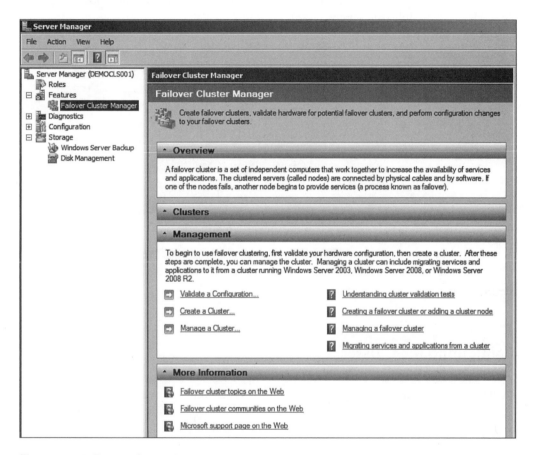

Figure 11.45 Failover Cluster Manager.

4. On the Before you Begin dialog, click **Do Not Show This Page Again** and **Next**.

5. On the Select Servers page, select both servers that should be members of the cluster. (Be aware that you are not restricted to two, but a two-node cluster is a very typical cluster configuration.) Add both your servers. (If you have not installed the feature on the second server, you must do so for it to be allowed to be selected.) After they are added, click **Next**.

6. You have the option of running a validation check; doing so is a good idea to verify that everything is set up properly. Because you have run the validation already, however, click **No** and then **Next**.

7. Provide a name for the cluster that properly identifies it, such as **primary_site_ cluster**, and click **Next** and **Next** to create the cluster.

8. You should now see your cluster configuration underneath the Failover Cluster Manager module (see Figure 11.46).

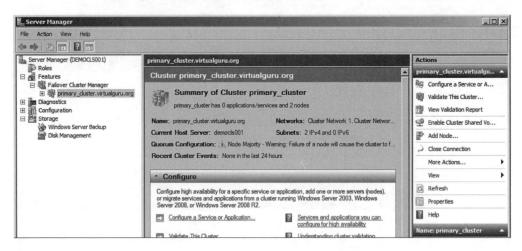

Figure 11.46 The cluster is created.

Configuring the Cluster

When the cluster is created, default names are applied to both storage and networking configurations. Because they are not very intuitive, I recommend renaming these specific things in accordance with what you have named both the volumes and network connections on a cluster node. Although this approach may seem a little picky, it is these simple things that save you time when you run into a problem. If you expand your cluster configuration, you see Services and Applications, Nodes, Storage, and Networks. Under Networks, select Properties and rename the networks to match the renaming you did earlier on the cluster node. Turn off cluster network communication for everything except the Heartbeat Network. Your configuration should look something like that in Figure 11.47.

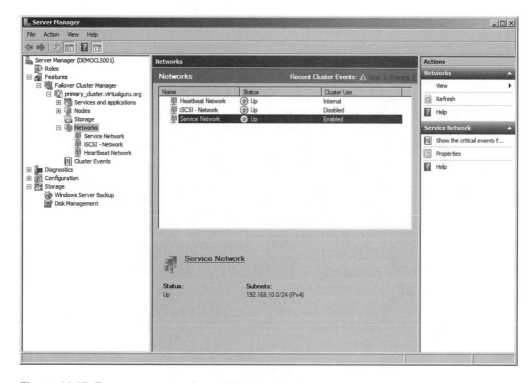

Figure 11.47 Ensure your networks are labeled properly.

Next, make sure that your storage is online on the cluster by selecting the Storage module and your Available Storage and Bring This Resource Online from the right pane if it is not currently online. Now you have created both a quorum and storage clustered partition. Although you have created the quorum, you have not yet enabled it. To do this, complete the following steps:

1. From Server Manager, expand Failover Cluster Manager and select your cluster.

2. On the panel on the far right called Actions, select **More Actions** and **Configure Cluster Quorum Settings**.

3. Select **Next** on the Before you Begin page. Then accept the defaults on the Select Quorum Configuration page (Node and Disk Majority), as shown in Figure 11.48, and click **Next**.

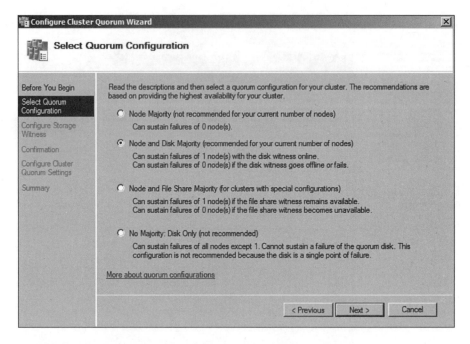

Figure 11.48 Ensure the Node and Disk Majority option is selected.

4. Select the quorum partition that you have verified is online and click **Next**.

5. On the confirmation page, click **Next** and **Finish**.

Adding File Services and the Distributed File System

Because the point to creating this cluster is to store the Persona, ThinApp, and Offline View desktops, you need File Services. Because you want to replicate the folders from one datacenter to the other to meet the HA scenario, you also need to install Distributed File Services. DFS is part of the File Services role. You need to install the role on each node in the cluster. To install these services, complete the following steps:

1. From Server Manager, select **Roles**, and from the right, select **Add Role**.

2. Select **File Services** under the Server Roles page and click **Next**.

3. On the intro page, click **Next**, and on the Role Services page, select **File Server and Distributed File System**, as shown in Figure 11.49.

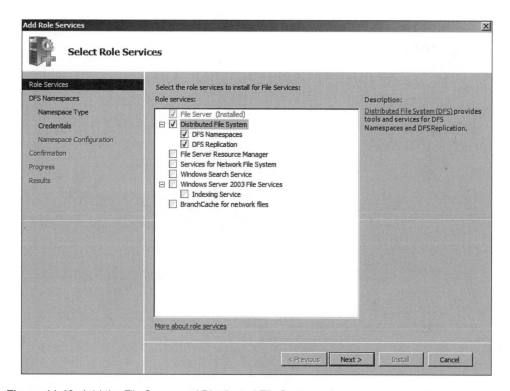

Figure 11.49 Add the File Server and Distributed File System roles.

4. On the confirmation page, click **Install** and then **Finish**.

When all nodes in the cluster are running the File Server role, you are able to create a clustered file server. To create the clustered file server, complete the following steps:

1. Expand Server Manager, Failover Cluster Manager, and your cluster.

2. Select the Services and Applications module.

3. On the Action pane on the far right, select **Configure a Service or Application**.

4. Click **Next** on the Before You Begin Wizard, select **File Server** from the Service or Application page, and click **Next**.

5. Provide the name for the client access point, as shown in Figure 11.50. This is the name by which the clients will recognize the file server. Type a name and click **Next**.

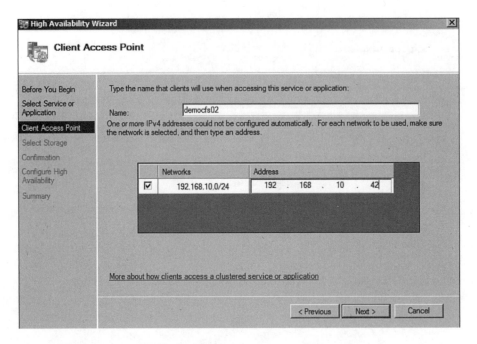

Figure 11.50 Type the name of the Client Access Point.

6. Check the cluster storage you created and click **Next**.

7. On the confirmation page, click **Next** to complete the configuration.

In a clustered file server, the management of the shares and user permissions is done directly through the Failover Cluster Manager tool. To add file shares for the View Persona directories, the ThinApp files, and the Offline View desktop, complete the following steps:

1. Expand Server Manager, Failover Cluster Manager, and your cluster.

2. Select the Services and Applications module.

3. Select your newly created cluster file server and make sure the related services are all online (the client access point or name and the storage).

4. From the Action Pane on the right, select **Add a Shared Folder**.

5. On the Provision a Shared Folder Wizard, select **Browse**. Then select the root of your shared cluster volume, select **Make New Folder**, and type a name. In the example in Figure 11.51, we created the Persona folder on the V:\ drive, which is the shared cluster volume.

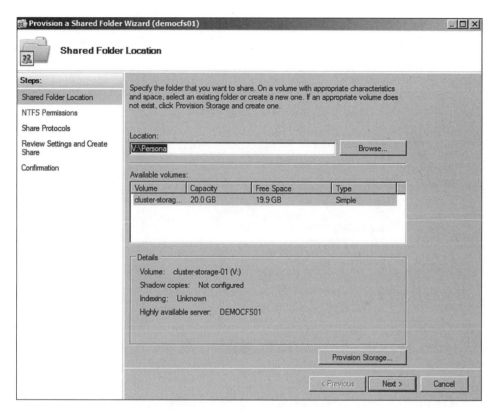

Figure 11.51 Create a folder.

6. Click **Next**. You have the option to change the NTFS permissions (local folder permissions) or accept the default configuration. If you want to change them, select **Yes** and **Edit the Permissions**. Make sure the permissions are set properly and click **Next**.

7. The default for the share type is SMB, which is fine, and the share name is the name of the folder. You can change this name or keep it the same and then select **Next**.

8. On the next screen, you have the option of specifying the number of connections allowed or turning on offline mode by selecting the **Advanced** tab. Because you do not need to adjust these, select **Next**.

9. The next screen allows you to select the share permissions. You have a number of typical default options, or you can customize them by selecting **Users and Groups Have Custom Share Permissions** and selecting **Permissions**. Set the permissions properly and click **Next**.

10. Leave the DFS Namespace Publishing for now; it enables replication from a clustered folder, which is a new feature of Windows 2008 R2. Click **Next**.

11. Review the settings and click **Create** to create the folders and close.

Make sure you create a folder for View Persona, Production ThinApp packages, and local mode desktops, as shown in Figure 11.52.

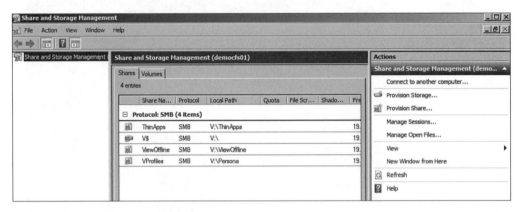

Figure 11.52 Create folders for Production ThinApp packages, local mode desktops, and View Persona.

Going back to the original scenario, you would deploy two clustered file servers in each datacenter to support the View environment. At this point, if you have installed vCenter Heartbeat, you have protected the vCenter Server, View Composer (because it is running on vCenter), and also the local database. You have also set up highly resilient file services in each location. If you want to sync the files in both locations, you can take advantage of the integration of Windows 2008 R2 clustering and DFS.

There are a few limitations with DFS. Microsoft supports data that is largely static, such as the ThinApp and offline virtual desktop data. User profiles are supported only under a very specific configuration. This configuration does require some intervention in the event there is a failover. This is where third-party profile management solutions can add some value such as LiquidwareLabs ProfileUnity (http://www.liquidwarelabs.com/products /profileunity.asp) or AppSense User Virtualization Platform (http://www.appsense.com/ vmware). Because we don't want to recommend one profile solution over another, we review the supported setup from Microsoft and you can weigh the value of the third-party products.

Distributed File System

DFS is a replication technology that uses Remote Differential Compression (RDC) to conserve bandwidth and ensure only the changed data is replicated, not entire files. DFS allows you to maintain folder and file conformity across your environment. Changes made in one location are replicated and synchronized according to your setup.

The second piece of DFS is a namespace, which allows the folder locations to be masked using a single root name to simplify access and, in the case of multiple targets or file folders, to load balance connections. You do not need to use a namespace when replicating either the ThinApp or offline virtual desktops. You can use a namespace to simplify the View Persona folder location. For folder locations storing profiles, such as the View Persona folder, they are supported with only one target. This means that in the HA scenario, you could use a single namespace in each location pointing back to the local Persona folder on the cluster server, but not to both. Because this adds a degree of complexity without a lot of value, a namespace is really not necessary.

Windows 2008 DFS has been improved in Windows 2008 R2, including significant improvements to performance and monitoring. Specifically, Microsoft added the ability to add a failover cluster as a member of a replication group. This allows you to have a file cluster in each location (for local site availability) and then use the failover cluster support to add each cluster to DFS. You can use one-way replication from the cluster in the primary location to the cluster in the secondary location and one-way replication from the cluster in the secondary location to the cluster in the primary.

In normal operations, your View Desktops would run in an active–active configuration in each datacenter. In the scenario presented here, you would use replication only to ensure that a copy of the Persona directory is available in each location so that in the event of a failure, you could update the desktops to use the backup as the new location for their Persona profile. This ensures no user configuration information is lost. This would require the View Desktops in the primary location and secondary location to be in separate OUs. In the event of a failure, additional desktops would be deployed from the secondary location using View Composer and the policy for View Persona would be updated.

Let's run through the DFS replication piece so that you have each file cluster replicating its respective information so that it is available in an outage disaster.

Installing and Configuring DFS

DFS is managed from the DFS Management console, which can be found under Server Manager, under Roles and File Services in DFS Management. There are two options: Namespaces and Replication. You configure each folder to replicate to the cluster in the other datacenter and vice versa. To do this, complete the following steps:

1. Under Server Manager, expand Rolés, File Services, and DFS Management.

2. Select the Replication module, and from the Actions Pane, select **New Replication Group**.

3. On the Replication Group Type page, select **Replication Group for Data Collection** (one-way replication in other words), as shown in Figure 11.53.

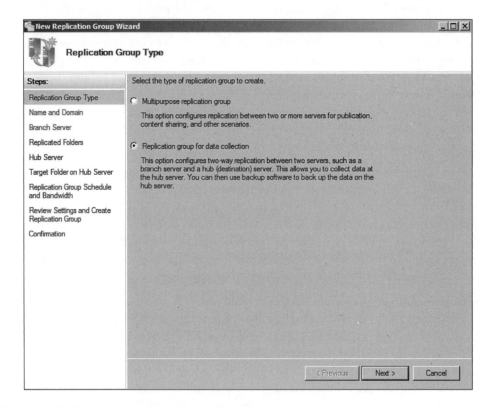

Figure 11.53 Replication group for data collection.

4. On the Name and Domain screen, type the name of the replication group and the domain.

5. The branch server is the source—in this case, the local cluster file server or client access point. Type or browse to the server and click **Next**.

6. On the Add Folder to Replicate page, browse to the folder and click **OK**. Add all the folders (Persona, ThinApp, and offline virtual desktops). In the secondary datacenter, you just select the local Persona folder because you do not need to replicate the ThinApp or offline virtual desktop folders. The hub server is the target, or where

they are going to; if you are in the primary datacenter, it is the cluster in the secondary site and vice versa.

7. On the next screen, you select the target folder on the hub server, as shown in Figure 11.54. For the ThinApp and offline desktops, it can be the same folder names; however, for the View Persona folder, it needs to be different because it is truly a backup. You have the option of setting continuous or scheduled replication.

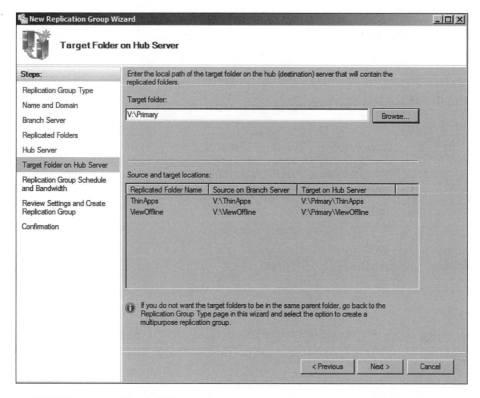

Figure 11.54 Select the Target folder.

8. On the next screen, click **Create** and **Close**.

Setting Up Windows NLB

At this point in the scenario, you should have resilient management and back-end services, but you have done nothing to ensure the local View Servers are highly available. To provide a failover for the View Connection and Secure Servers, you can configure Windows Network Load Balancing. Windows NLB is included with Windows 2008 R2.

If you use multicast mode, each adapter has two MAC addresses: the one on the network interface and the virtual one. Multicast mode requires you to have only a single adapter. You need to be aware that to configure this properly, you need to update the physical networking configuration because most routers reject a response that includes both the unicast packet from the NIC and the virtual multicast MAC address. It requires you to turn on the capability to support static Address Resolution Protocol (ARP) and then assign the multicast MAC to each interface on the ESXi host. It is probably easier to configure NLB than to look at the configuration required on the switch.

On Windows 2008 R2, NLB is a feature. To install and configure NLB, just complete the following steps:

1. Open Server Manager and select the Features module.

2. Select **Network Load Balancing**, click **Next**, and then close it after it finishes installing.

3. Run Start, Administrative Tools, and Network Load Balancing Manager.

4. Select the Network Load Balancing Clusters, right-click, and select **New Cluster**.

5. Type the name of the local host and click **Connect**.

6. Under Interfaces, select the interface to be used and click **Next**.

7. On the next screen, add the IP of the second VMware View Server by clicking **Add** and then typing the IP. Click **Next**.

8. Add the Cluster IP or virtual IP by selecting **Add**, typing the IP address and subnet mask, and clicking **OK** and then **Next**.

9. Type a host name under Full Internet Name and change the cluster operation node to Multicast. Note the network address, which is the multicast MAC that you will need to configure the switches later.

10. You can specify ports by editing what ports are listed, or you can allow all. When you're done, click **Finish**.

Updating Cisco Switches to Support NLB

If you have Cisco switches, you need to update them with the multicast MAC because otherwise they reject the unicast response with the multicast MAC. To complete this, you telnet to the switch and change to configuration mode using the following command:

```
config t
```

You then turn on static ARP resolution and associate the virtual IP to the cluster multicast by using the following command:

```
arp [ip] [cluster multicast mac] ARPA
```

After you do that, you associate all MAC and physical interfaces on the ESXi Servers. You either do this across all interfaces if your View Servers are enabled for VMotion or exclude them from VMotion and separate them on individual ESXi hosts. The command to associate the MAC address to the physical interfaces of the ESXi hosts is as follows:

```
mac-address-table static [cluster multicast mac] [vlan id] [list all the ↩
interfaces connected to the ESXi hosts]
```

Summary

You have now finished the configuration of the HA scenario. You used Microsoft Cluster Services combined with File and Distributed File Services to ensure that the environment is highly available within a site and across sites. You also set up Windows NLB between the two VMware View Connection Servers in each site to ensure they are also highly available. The method described here is not the only way to do this because you could have used hardware load balancers or SAN replication, but this approach provides a lower-cost alternative using native toolsets. As with any environment, make sure you test everything by doing extensive failure testing so that you know what to expect, and also test your configurations before releasing the environment into production.

At the beginning of the chapter, we looked at how to ensure the components of a vSphere infrastructure are highly available by making sure that redundant paths were configured in storage using VMware's best practices. In addition, we integrated VMware vCenter Server Heartbeat. Making sure the environment is highly available is a base requirement for consolidating desktops. It should be integrated into a comprehensive monitoring and alerting framework to make sure that when problems arise, you are aware of them and can respond to minimize the service interruption. In the next chapter, we look closely at monitoring the environment for both performance and failures.

Chapter 12

Performance and Monitoring

Establishing a Performance Baseline

One of the most difficult things to do in any IT infrastructure is to establish what normal operations look like. The extremes are always easy to spot, of course, but the heavy demand that equates to normal business use is much more difficult to understand without good visibility. Establishing normal operations can be more complex in a virtual infrastructure but no less important. If you are not sure what normal is, how can you properly identify what is problematic and needs to be investigated before it impacts your end users? This issue is critical in a virtual desktop environment because often much higher expectations are placed on performance. I had a conversation about this topic with a customer who had a mixture of older and newer physical desktops, and what we concluded is that users often do not report problems with physical desktops that are fixed with a reboot; they simply shut it off and on, and if the problem goes away, they consider it "fixed." Ask yourself how often the computer logs of a desktop are actually inspected for problems. When was the last time a system administrator looked at the application or system log of a Windows desktop?

With virtual desktops, however, these hiccups get a lot of visibility in the early stages of adoption, so you need high visibility on how everything is performing. This visibility must include the View desktops, management components, performance of the PCoIP protocol on the LAN and WAN, and the hosts and storage of the vSphere environment. Monitoring all these pieces with traditional monitoring tools can quickly produce a lot of information that becomes difficult to correlate and understand. Traditional monitoring tools based on static thresholds generate alerts on utilization or monitor the Windows Event Viewer logs but do not provide a complete picture of the how the entire environment is performing.

Although a number of products from a variety of vendors monitor various aspects of the virtual infrastructure, VMware has developed vCenter Operations to bring this capability to VMware vSphere environments. It also has developed custom dashboards for monitoring the performance of a VMware View environment to extend the benefits to your virtual desktops. What is unique about vCenter Operations (vCOPs) is that you get near real-time, capacity, and historical performance and problem-tracking information. The visibility extends to all components of your virtual infrastructure, down to the storage and its dependencies. Many third parties have also used the VMware APIs to extend monitoring and alerting to their products, but vCenter Operations is tightly integrated with VMware View.

vCenter Operations Manager aggregates information that is collected by vCenter. For vCOPs, you need to ensure that you are running VMware vCenter Server 4.0 Update 2 or later at a minimum to be able to view storage system performance. Storage visibility closes a huge operational gap in running large virtual desktop environments. Often you see symptoms of underperforming storage, such as delayed SCSI transactions in the Windows Event Viewer. However, it is difficult to identify what the cause is. Because many storage systems incorporate storage virtualization and distribute all writes across all spindles, it is difficult to pinpoint the source of the problem. It is rare now that a SAN administrator dedicates certain drives to certain LUNs. This can make identifying storage bottlenecks extremely difficult because SAN performance reports average performance over time and across a large portion of the storage system.

vCenter Operations allows you to view specific performance characteristics of your datastores in relation to each other. VMware has extended vCenter Operations to aggregate information from both the View Connection Server and Composer to provide even greater visibility into your virtualization environment.

The benefits of vCenter Operations are many, but rather than go through them all, let's look at each in relationship to the VMware View environment to understand how they deliver value. The first thing you must do is install vCenter Operations and configure the adapter to turn on the performance and monitoring of the VMware View environment.

Installing vCenter Operations

vCenter Operations (vCOPs) Manager ships as a virtual appliance and comes in several different versions; Standard, Advanced, Enterprise, and Enterprise Plus. The fundamental difference between each version is that Standard does not integrate the historical trending, reporting, and capacity planning features. Advanced does but does not allow you to customize the look, or dashboard as it is called. Enterprise does allow you to customize the dashboard but is restricted to virtualization environments only. Enterprise Plus allows you to apply the tool to both physical and virtual environments. For a complete list of differences, refer to the VMware comparison matrix located at http://www.vmware.com/products/datacenter-virtualization/vcenter-operations-management/compare-editions.html.

vCOPs can be extended to input additional metrics through the use of adapters. The visibility into VMware View is facilitated through an adapter and the creation of seven VMware View specific dashboards to display information such as user login times, virtual desktop performance, and overall health of the environment. Because it does install several custom dashboards, you do need Enterprise to turn up these features. For an overview of vCOPS integration, refer to http://www.vmware.com/products/desktop_virtualization/vcenter-operations-manager-view/overview.html.

Historically, the product was developed from both Capacity IQ and vCenter Operations. In vCOPs 5, the two independent products have become one. They are still two distinct virtual appliances—the analytics and user interface (UI) appliances—but they are deployed as a single unit or vApp. A *vApp* is a collection of virtual machines that are grouped to allow common configuration and to provide a complete service. For additional details on vApps, refer to the vSphere 5 documentation available online at http://pubs.vmware.com/vsphere-50/index.jsp.

vApps were introduced as a method of controlling multitier applications. In this case, the vApp allows you to control the network, shares, and boot order as a single entity. In the case of vCenter Operations, it ensures that the Analytics virtual appliance is booted before the UI appliance.

vApps are designed to work with IP pools. IP pools add a DHCP-like service that is associated with certain switch ports. As with DHCP, you configure a range, gateway, and DNS settings. After these settings are configured, you can tell the vApp appliances to use them by editing its properties and changing the IP allocation policy from Fixed to Transient.

The three types of IP allocation policies are Fixed, which is a static IP assignment; DHCP, which tells the vApp that a traditional DHCP service exists on the network; and Transient, which tells the vApp that an IP pool is available to allocate network information (see Figure 12.1).

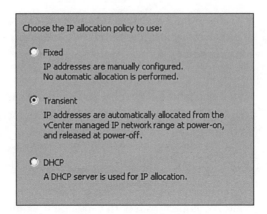

Figure 12.1 IP allocation pool.

Create an IP Pool

The specific steps to install vCenter Operations require the preparation of an IP pool and then the deployment of an Adapter virtual machine. You can then import and configure the vCenter Operations vApp and then configure the adapter. The adapter aggregates information from the View Connection Server, vComposer, and vCenter and feeds it to vCenter Operations. To create an IP pool, follow these steps:

1. Launch the vSphere client.

2. From the Home screen, select **Networking.**

3. From the left pane, ensure you have selected your datacenter, and on the right, select the **IP Pools** tab (see Figure 12.2).

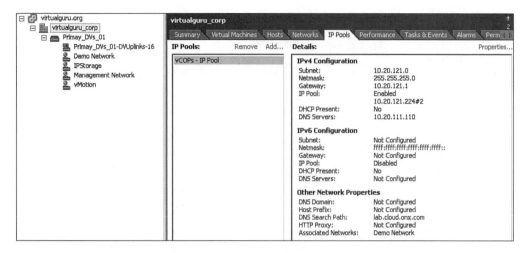

Figure 12.2 Configure an IP pool.

4. Click **Add** to add an IP pool configuration.

5. Provide a name and configure a set of IP addresses. There are various ways to do this; you can use a restrictive subnet mask to provide only the number of IPs required. In the case of vCenter Operations, you need one for Analytics and UI virtual appliances, so you can use /30 to provide two IPs, as shown in Figure 12.3. The interface accepts the mask in Classless Inter Domain Routing (CIDR) format and then translates it to a subnet mask, which requires the slash (/) and prefix number.

The other method of specifying IPs is to use a smaller subnet mask and provide a range of IP addresses. In this case, you may use a 24-bit subnet mask and enter a range such as 10.0.1.20#2, for example. You can configure IPv6 addresses or tell the pool to actually use an existing DHCP service under the DHCP tab. DNS name servers, domains, and search prefixes can be configured under the DNS tab. If you are using an HTTP proxy, you can specify it under the Proxy tab.

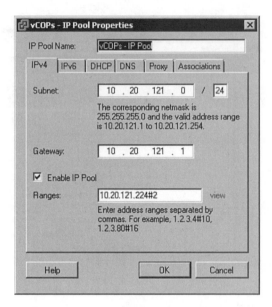

Figure 12.3 Specify the mask in CIDR format (/30).

6. After you configure the details for the networking attributes, you can associate the IP pool to a certain port group to enable the use of the addresses, as shown in Figure 12.4. After making the association, click **OK** to enable the pool.

Figure 12.4 Associate the IP pool to the port group.

Deploy vCenter Operations

When the IP pool is in place, you are ready to import the virtual appliance. To deploy the virtual appliance, complete these steps:

1. From the File menu under the vSphere client, select **Deploy OVF Template** (see Figure 12.5).

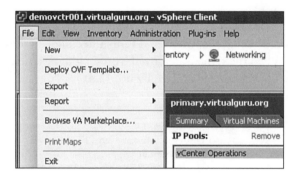

Figure 12.5 Deploy OVF template.

2. Browse to your vCenter OVF template and click **Next**.

3. On the OVF detail page, note that the thick disk requirement for vCenter Operations is 336 GB (for thin, it is 3.6 GB). It is recommended that the appliance is deployed thick. Click **Next**.

4. Accept the End User License Agreement and click **Next**.

5. Provide the name and select the location in the vCenter environment to which you want the vApp deployed.

6. Select the deployment configuration or size of the environment. Size is defined as Small, Medium, or Large. Large is defined as more than 3000 VMs but requires 16 vCPUs and 34 GB of memory. Small is fewer than 1500 VMs but still requires 4 vCPUs and 16 GB of memory. Medium is between 1500 and 3000 VMs and requires 8 vCPUs and 25 GB of memory. If needed, you can actually throttle down the requiremetns and see how the appliance reacts, so these configurations are suggested rather than hard-coded limits. Note: Even though the resource requirements are suggested, you should not adjust the configuration of the VM below the minimum requirements to start the VM. Select the configuration that best suits your environment and click **Next**.

7. Select the host and cluster and click **Next**.

8. Select **Resource Pool** and click **Next**.

9. Select **Storage** and click **Next**.

10. Select **Disk Format** for the VM; recommended is Thick Provisioned Eager Zeroed. Select the format and click **Next**.

11. Map the vApp to a network and click **Next**.

12. Select **Transient** for the IP Policy because you have created an IP pool for this vApp.

13. Select the appropiate time zone and click **Next**.

14. Select **Power on after Deployment** and **Finish** to complete the deployment configuration. When the vApp is deployed, you should see a new vApp with both the Analytics and UI VM powered on (see Figure 12.6).

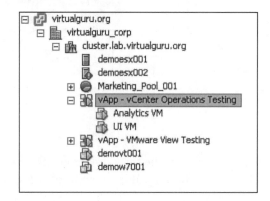

Figure 12.6 The deployed vApp has two virtual appliances.

Configure vCenter Operations

After the vApp is deployed, you must do several things to properly configure vCenter Operations to get everything working. You should complete the configuration before deploying the integration to VMware View.

To configure vCenter Operations Manager, you must log in to the UI virtual appliance. To determine which IP, you should browse to select the UI VM from your Hosts and Clusters view in the vSphere client and note the IP address on the Summary tab under the General section. When you have the IP address, browse to the appliance using a web browser, that is, http://[IP Address]/admin. The default username for the vCenter UI Console is admin, and the password is admin (see Figure 12.7).

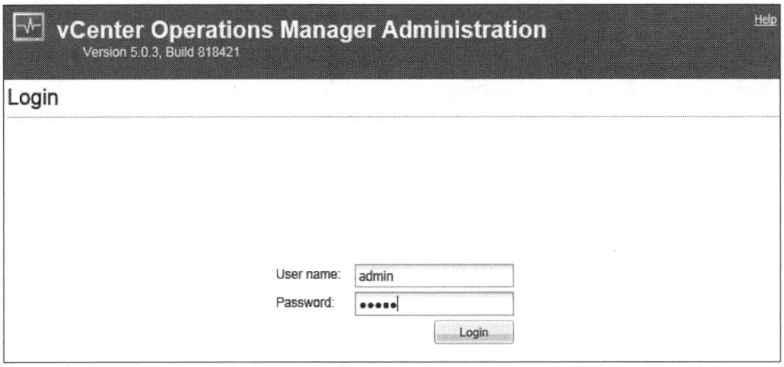

Figure 12.7 Log in to configure vCenter Operations.

After you log in, the registration wizard begins. It prompts you to reset the default password and register your vCenter Operations application with vCenter. You can have vCenter Operations monitor several vCenter Servers, so multiple registrations are allowed. To register a vCenter, provide the IP and an account that has access to everything (typically, the administrator). When you are registered, your vCenter configuration should look similar to Figure 12.8.

Figure 12.8 Register the vCenter Server.

You also need to configure SMTP if you would like to have alerting enabled in the vCenter Operations application. To configure it, click the SMPT/SNMP tab and enable **Enable Report Email Service**; then supply the SMTP Server address and port (typically port 25). Also provide a default sender name and default sender e-mail address that the alerts will come from. To save the configuration, click **Update**.

License vCenter Operations

vCenter Operations Manager looks to vCenter to supply a license. Therefore, the next procedure is to ensure a license key is installed in vCenter so that when you register vCenter Operations to the vCenter Server, it is properly enabled. To add a vCenter Operations License to vCenter, complete the following steps:

1. From the vSphere client, connect to vCenter.

2. From Home, select **Licensing** under the Administration section.

3. Select Manage vSphere Licenses (Note: It is the blue "Manage vSphere Licenses" hyperlink on the right of the screen to the left of the Refresh and Export links), as shown in Figure 12.9.

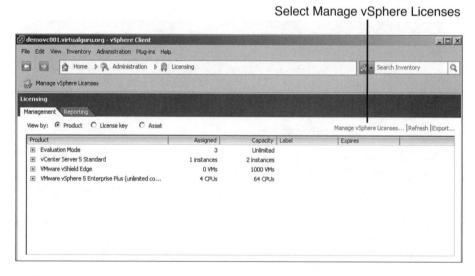

Figure 12.9 Select Manage vSphere Licenses.

4. Enter the license key in the Enter new vSphere License Keys section and provide a label such as vOPs. Click **Next**.

5. Under Assign Licenses, click the Solutions tab and select **Show All** (see Figure 12.10). Select your vCenter Operations, select the license key, and click **Next**.

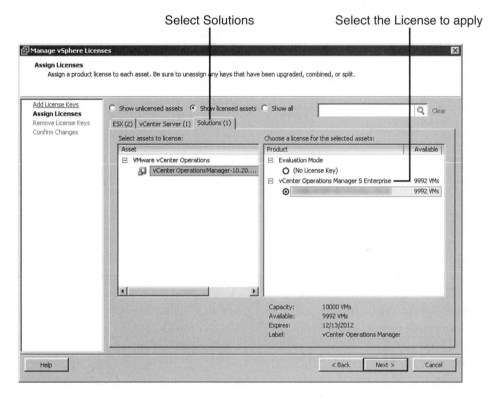

Figure 12.10 Apply Licenses.

6. If you want to remove any license keys, do so; otherwise, click **Next** and **Finish** on the confirmation page to apply your license changes.

After it is installed, configured, and licensed, you can enable the plug-in to view the components of vCenter operations. To do this within your vSphere Client, select **Plug-ins** and **Manage Plug-ins** and enable the vCenter Operations Manager (see Figure 12.11).

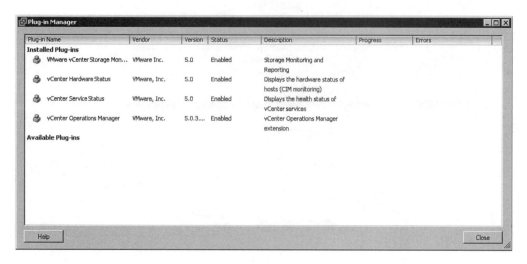

Figure 12.11 Install the plug-in.

To access vCenter Operations Manager, open your vSphere client, and from the Home tab, click **vCenter Operations** under the Solutions and Applications pane. You can also access vCenter Operations by browsing directly to the IP of the UI appliance, which can be quicker. It is important to realize that there is a relationship between the Hosts and Clusters tree view on the left and the display panels on the right. Certain objects in the tree on the left don't display certain properties because they are not relevant to what you have selected. For example, virtual machines that are gray in color are typically not powered on. To get a high-level view of general health, select your datacenter on the left and ensure the dashboard is visible on the right (see Figure 12.12).

Select your datacenter

Figure 12.12 Select your datacenter and view your dashboard on the right.

Notice that the datacenter has three high-level ratings more commonly referred to as *badges* in vCenter Operations. Each of these major badges is made up of a combination of minor badges to help you get a good picture of the environment. In general, Health is largely made up of real-time metrics, Risk looks at capacity and how long over a period of time the VMs may be stressed or struggling for resources, and Efficiency looks at how well you are currently using the environment. Efficiency includes a reference for optimal configurations such as your host-to-VM ratio or CPU-to-VM ratio.

The Health badge is a combination of Workload, Anomalies, and Faults. Workload measures the four pillars of performance in virtual infrastructure: CPU, Memory, Disk I/O, and Network I/O (see Figure 12.13). A high workload number indicates resources that are heavily utilized.

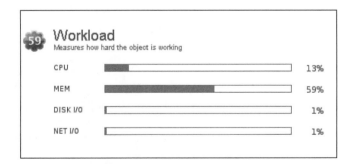

Figure 12.13 The Workload badge.

In addition to Workload, Health also measures the anomalies found in the environment. vCenter Operations tries to understand what is normal and abnormal behavior for an object in your vSphere environment by using dynamic as well as static thresholds (see Figure 12.14). Dynamic thresholds are learned over time to understand whether it is normal for a particular VM to be busier on a Friday, for example, or that heavier utilization normally occurs during a backup window. vCOPS also detects trends in longer cycles, such as monthly and quarterly. It allows you to apply some intelligence to your understanding of what is going on; for example, if you see high workload activity but a low number of anomalies, you know that this high workload is typical and can be expected.

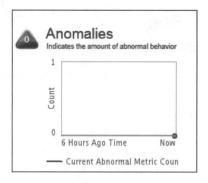

Figure 12.14 Anomalies.

The last minor badge under Health is Faults (see Figure 12.15). Faults are pulled from vCenter Alerts and tell you about component failures. An example of a fault is a loss of redundancy of NICs or HBAs or possibly an HA failure. A high number of faults indicates an unstable environment.

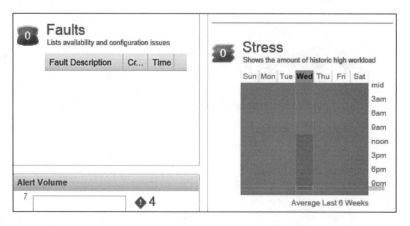

Figure 12.15 Faults.

The combination of Faults, Anomalies, and Workload create an overall picture of Health. From the dashboard, you can drill down to see an additional level of detail on these minor badge categories.

The second major badge is Risk. Risk provides information on the time remaining given the current capacity of the environment and how much stress it is experiencing. The major badge Risk is made up of Time Remaining, Capacity Remaining, and Stress.

Time Remaining answers the question of how much time is available before you need to add additional capacity, such as host servers, storage, and networking (see Figure 12.16). It measures CPU, Memory, Disk, and Networking IOPS. Time Remaining is like an early warning system for the major four resources.

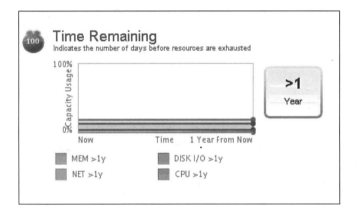

Figure 12.16 Time Remaining.

Capacity Remaining takes the average size of a VM and determines how many can be run before capacity runs out (see Figure 12.17). This badge breaks out this estimate against CPU, Memory, Disk, and Networking IOPs so that you can see what are the limiting resources in your environment.

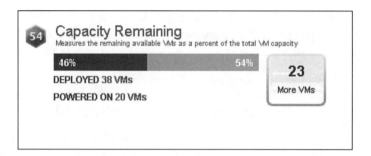

Figure 12.17 Capacity Remaining.

Stress takes the amount of time that the object is running under duress and breaks it out as a percentage from a historical perspective (see Figure 12.18). If an object in your vSphere environment is repeatedly running over the threshold amount on a regular basis, that is likely an indication of stress.

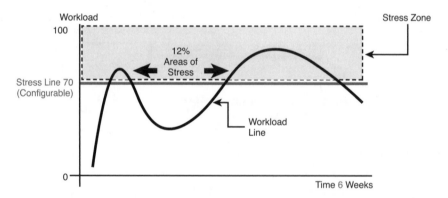

Figure 12.18 Stress.

The combination of Time, Capacity, and Stress identifies the level of risk in the environment. A lower score represents an environment running with less risk.

Efficiency is a combination of reclaimable waste or resources that could be more efficiently utilized and a measure of optimal density. Reclaimable Waste tells you if you are overprovisioning resources (see Figure 12.19). It is broken down by CPU, Disk, and Memory.

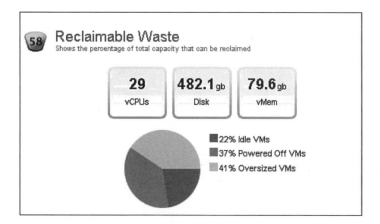

Figure 12.19 Reclaimable Waste.

Density provides a picture of what your current consolidation ratio looks like and what is optimal (see Figure 12.20). It is measured against the VM per host ratio as well as the number of virtual CPUs to physical CPUs and virtual memory to physical memory.

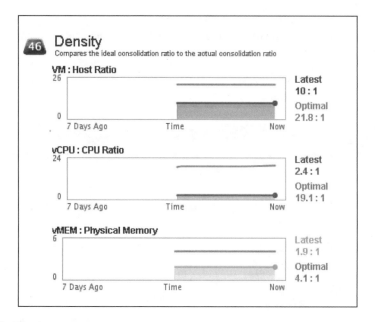

Figure 12.20 Density.

You can drill down from any of the dashboard views to understand the details. You can also see health and performance of objects in your vSphere environment relative to other objects. One great way to do this is to look under the Analysis section through heat maps. Heat maps color-code objects to allow you to focus quickly on problem areas. In virtual desktop environments, storage IO contention can be difficult to isolate. In Figure 12.21, the datastore contention is sized by IO usage grouped by datacenter. You can see that most of the datastores are performing well, but a few are underperforming relative to others.

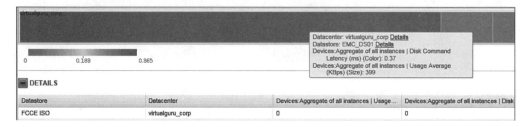

Figure 12.21 Datastore contention sized by IO usage grouped by datacenter.

In addition to a high level of information on overall health of the environment, you can also enable alerting. To do this, you have to enable SMTP reporting on the UI appliance, as you did when installing and configuring vCenter Operations, and complete the following steps.

Open vCenter Operations and select the **Notifications** link on the top right (see Figure 12.22).

Figure 12.22 Notifications.

Click the **Add Rule** icon and specify a descriptive name for the rule and e-mail address it should go to. In the Conditions, select the type of condition. In this example, I specified Health and specifically critical Workload and Faults. In addition, I set the Object level at the cluster and included all children of the cluster. Children of an object are objects that appear at a lower level in the object tree. In this case, rather than all child objects, I specifically selected Host. After configuring the alert (see Figure 12.23), click **OK** and then **OK** again to have the rule go into effect.

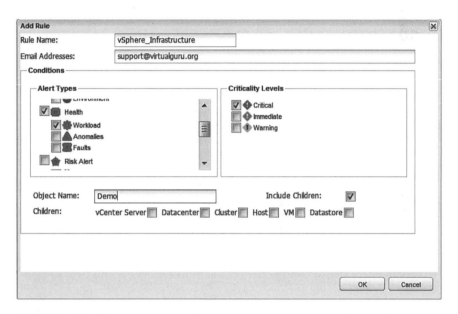

Figure 12.23 Set Conditions.

Here are a few general best practices you should follow when it comes to configuring alerting:

1. Ensure you are using group addresses versus individual e-mail addresses.

2. Be specific in what you are alerting on and where you would like the alerts to go.

3. Ensure that the team members whom you are sending alerts know how to take control of the alert in the console. Taking control of an alert lets everyone know that someone is working on the issue. To take control of an alert, from the right panel, select **Alerts**, the alert you would like to take control of, and click the **Take Control** icon (see Figure 12.24). When prompted to answer Yes or No, select **Yes**.

Criticality	Type	Sub-Type	Resource Kind	Object Name	▾ Metric
◆	▪	▪	Host System	demoesx002	
◆	▪	▪	Host System	demoesx002	
◆	▪	▪	Virtual Machine	demow7001	Badge | Stress
◆	▪	◉	Virtual Machine	demow7001	Badge | Time Remaining - Planning, Cyclical
◆	▪	▪	Virtual Machine	demo7x86-tmp	Badge | Stress

Figure 12.24 Take control of alerts.

Now that you have a general idea of the value vCenter Operations Manager can provide, let's look at the customizations that are available in the adapter for VMware View. To install the adapter for View, you need to complete several steps. The first one is to install the adapter on a server. The vCenter Operations View Adapter supports Windows 2003 or 2008 R2 server.

The vCenter Operations View Adapter requires a PowerShell script to be run on the View Connection Server and .NET framework 3.5 to be installed on the Adapter Server. To install PowerShell on Windows 2008 R2, you simply add it from the feature's options using the following steps:

1. Run Server Manager from a Windows 2008 R2 Server.

2. Right-click the Features module and select **Add Feature** (or run **Add Feature** from the Action Panel).

3. Select **Windows PowerShell Integrated Scripting Environment** and click **Next**.

If this is the Adapter Server, install the .NET Framework using the Add Feature module but select .NET Framework Features 3.5.1 instead of the Windows PowerShell Integrated Scripting Environment. When the necessary requirements are installed, you can install the View Adapter on the Adapter Server using these steps:

1. Launch the vCenter Operations Manager for View installation.

2. Click **Next** on the welcome screen.

3. Click **Next** on the End User Patent Agreement screen.

4. Accept the license terms and click **Next**.

5. You can change the default installation path; otherwise, accept the defaults and click **Next**.

6. Select the box to automatically start the VMware vCenter Operations Manager for View Configuration tool and click **Install**.

After you have installed the software, you need to set up the connections, but you need to run the PowerShell script on the View Connection Server to enable vCenter Operations Manager for View. The PowerShell script is called EnableViewPS and is provided as part of the installation; you can find it in c:\program files\VMware\vCenter Operations\View Adapter. On your View Connection Server, open a PowerShell window, change to the location, and run EnableViewPS.cmd (see Figure 12.25). The script sets up a Windows Remote Management (WinRM) listener to allow the adapter to connect to the server. You run the command and type **y** to tell the script to make the necessary changes. (Note: You may have to run the **Set-ExecutionPolicy unrestricted** command first if the script generates an error.)

```
PS C:\Program Files\VMware\vCenter Operations\View Adapter> .\EnableViewPS.cmd
WinRM already is set up to receive requests on this machine.
WinRM is not set up to allow remote access to this machine for management.
The following changes must be made:

Create a WinRM listener on HTTP://* to accept WS-Man requests to any IP on this machine.
Enable the WinRM firewall exception.

Make these changes [y/n]? y

WinRM has been updated for remote management.

Created a WinRM listener on HTTP://* to accept WS-Man requests to any IP on this machine.
WinRM firewall exception enabled.
Loading VMware View PowerCLI

        Welcome to VMware View PowerCLI


PS C:\Program Files\VMware\vCenter Operations\View Adapter>
```

Figure 12.25 Run EnableViewPS.cmd.

After you have enabled the Windows Remote Management Listener, you can configure the adapter. On the first tab of the adapter configuration, set up the connection to the View Connection Server. You need to specify the server name and account that has access. You can test the connection by clicking **Test**. You can also monitor change events and provisioning errors by configuring a connection to the View Event database. Configure the connection and click **Test**. Configure the settings and click **Apply** (see Figure 12.26).

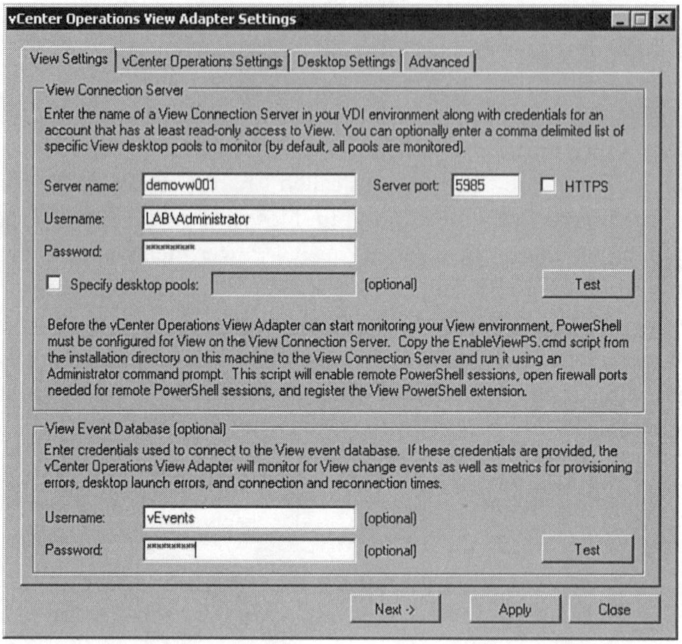

Figure 12.26 Configure connectivity.

On the next tab, you configure connectivity to your vCenter Operations Server, which is actually the UI virtual appliance. This step is very confusing because the username in this section is the vCOPs admin user even though it requests a user with administrative access. It does not work with any other account but the admin user. Configure the settings and click **Apply** (see Figure 12.27).

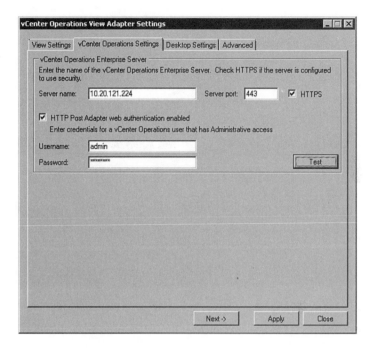

Figure 12.27 Specify vCOPs user.

To view the logs on the virtual desktops, you need to provide a domain account and administrator credentials to the desktop. This way, the adapter can collect performance metrics for PCoIP and disk, memory network, and CPU information. Configure the account and click **Apply** (see Figure 12.28).

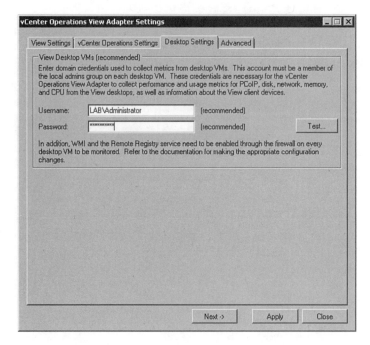

Figure 12.28 User with administrator access to desktops.

On the Advanced tab, you can set the level of logging, the frequency of collection based on the size of the environment, and the number of CPU threads used for collection. In addition, you can start the service. Start the service and click **Apply** (see Figure 12.29).

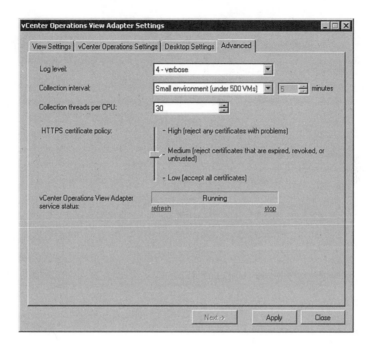

Figure 12.29 Set the logging level.

Now that the adapter is properly configured, you can go ahead and add the custom dashboards designed to display the important information from your VMware View environment. You load the customizations from the UI virtual appliance. To do so, complete the following steps:

1. Browse to the UI virtual appliance at http://[IP address]/admin.

2. Log in using the admin ID and password.

3. Select the Update tab and browse to the location of the **VMware-vcops-viewadapter.pak** file. Click **I Accept the Terms of This Agreement** and click **OK** (see Figure 12.30).

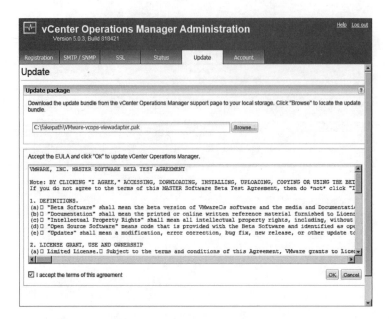

Figure 12.30 Add the View adapter to vCOPs.

You have now completed the integration of vCenter Operations Manager for View. To access the new dashboards, browse to your UI virtual appliance at http://[IP Address]/vcops-custom. There, you see six additional dashboards plus the vSphere one included in the Advanced version. The first dashboard, called View Main, is the main one (see Figure 12.31). It gives a high-level overview of the general health of the environment from end to end. It includes important information such as underlying vSphere health, PCoIP latency, VDI capacity, and bandwidth utilization.

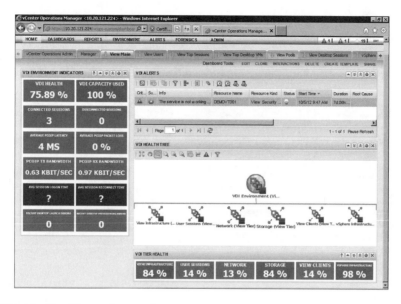

Figure 12.31 Health of the environment.

The next dashboard, View Users (see Figure 12.32), gives detailed information on specific user sessions, such as the current active sessions. You can use it for troubleshooting specific end-user problems such as connection drops and poor performance.

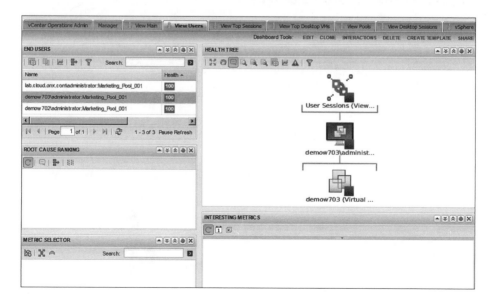

Figure 12.32 View Users.

The next dashboard, View Top Sessions (see Figure 12.33), provides information on the top View Sessions and includes pool capacity, logon times, and the number of connections in a pool. It ranks the pool information in each of these categories. You can use it to compare performance and configuration or problems at the pool level.

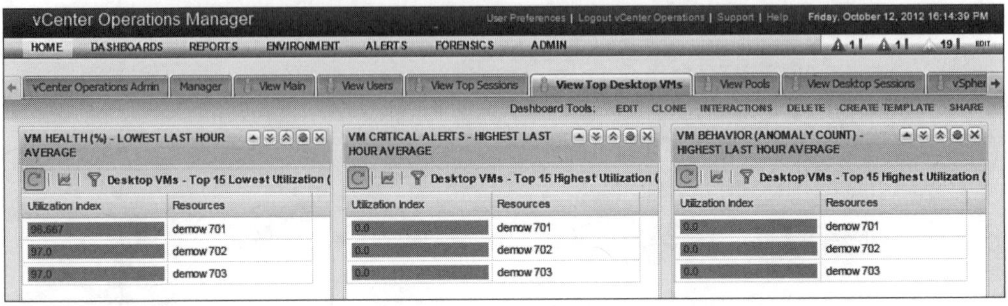

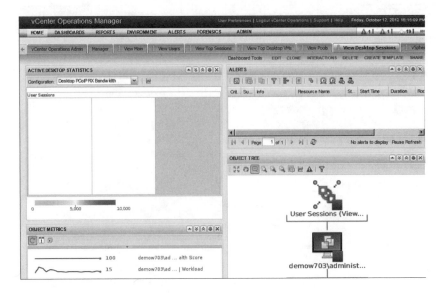

Figure 12.33 Top View Sessions.

In addition, similar information is displayed at the desktop level on the Top Desktop VMs. The information in this screen shows more VM performance metrics and critical alerts. It can provide a quick snapshot to help you determine whether any virtual desktops are experiencing performance problems. You also have a View Pools dashboard (see Figure 12.34), which is a heatmap showing all your virtual desktops. It can quickly show performance issues from the VM to the datastore level.

Figure 12.34 View Pool Performance.

In addition, the vSphere Infrastructure dashboard (see Figure 12.35) provides all the metrics and views previously discussed.

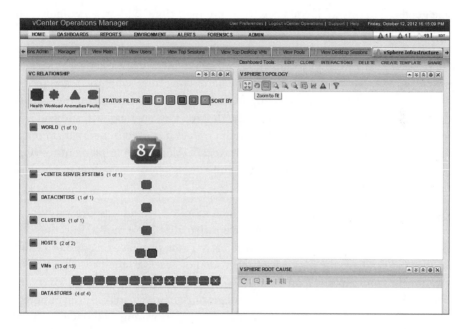

Figure 12.35 Infrastructure dashboard.

With the integration of vCenter Operations and VMware View, you have a comprehensive tool for understanding end-to-end performance and overall health. You have specific information on how key components of the technology are performing, such as PCoIP and the desktop pools. In addition, you can make sure that your environment is optimally configured to ensure you have the highest density without sacrificing performance. Plus, you can plan the scaling out of your environment because you have detailed information on when you are likely to need additional resources in your virtual desktop environment.

Summary

Because a virtual desktop environment separates the relationship between desktops, the Windows operating system, and desktop applications, it is important to have accurate metrics that examine the real end-user experience. Very few monitoring solutions aggregate all the information in a vSphere and View environment in a way that makes it simple to understand, allowing you to react quickly when problems occur. vCenter Operations for View provides a comprehensive look at all the pieces, allowing you not only to see problem spots but also to plan for additional capacity and growth.

To make good use of this tool, you need to ensure that, along with good visibility, you have defined roles and responsibilities within your IT organization for who supports what and at what level they support it. For example, it is quite common for server virtualization teams to be actively involved in architecting and deploying a VMware View environment because they already have a background in the underlying infrastructure. Care needs to be taken, however, to ensure that the desktop support team is also trained on the management tools they will need to continue to support the desktop OS, applications, and end users. Having an end-to-end monitoring tool helps but only if it is used in a way that complements both desktop and infrastructure support teams. Along with implementing vCenter Operations Manager, make sure that you carefully discuss how alerts flow and how issues are escalated when they occur.

I have seen virtual desktop deployments in which monitoring and support were not reviewed and discussed. When the desktops were virtualized and moved into the datacenter, the desktop team was not engaged early in the process. The desktop team felt that they did not have the necessary background or access to the tools to support the environment. The support load then fell to the server support team, who were not equipped to support end users. Along with integrating the tools, make sure you integrate your teams to ensure that not only is the environment performing well but also that the support and service are provided.

Index

T

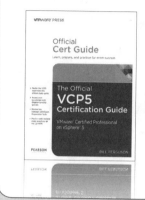

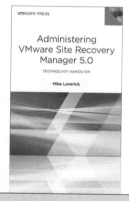
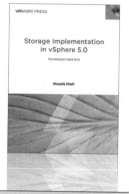

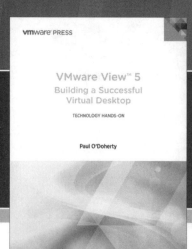

FREE
Online Edition

Your purchase of **VMware View 5** includes access to a free online edition for 45 days through the **Safari Books Online** subscription service. Nearly every VMware Press book is available online through **Safari Books Online**, along with thousands of books and videos from publishers such as Addison-Wesley Professional, Cisco Press, Exam Cram, IBM Press, O'Reilly Media, Prentice Hall, Que, and Sams.

Safari Books Online is a digital library providing searchable, on-demand access to thousands of technology, digital media, and professional development books and videos from leading publishers. With one monthly or yearly subscription price, you get unlimited access to learning tools and information on topics including mobile app and software development, tips and tricks on using your favorite gadgets, networking, project management, graphic design, and much more.

Activate your FREE Online Edition at
informit.com/safarifree

STEP 1:   Enter the coupon code: OHJPYYG.

STEP 2:   New Safari users, complete the brief registration form.
           Safari subscribers, just log in.

If you have difficulty registering on Safari or accessing the online edition,
please e-mail customer-service@safaribooksonline.com